ROYAL TARS

PRAISE FOR BRIAN LAVERY

IN WHICH THEY SERVED: The Royal Navy Officer Experience in the Second World War

'Lavery's intimate knowledge of the navy's history, culture and operations is in evidence as he constructs an endearing and digestible narrative ... informative, well-illustrated and approachable.' BBC History

'Lavery has an impeccable command of the sources, and he is able to bring to vivid life the experiences of the "hostilities-only" naval officers: recruitment; training; life at sea; and, not least, combat ... He writes extremely well and this is an enjoyable book, notwithstanding the frequently grim nature of his subject. A highlight is the skilful use he makes of first-hand material ... This book is ideal for anyone who wants to learn more about the life led by a naval ancestor.' BBC Who Do You Think You Are?

'Brian Lavery is a rare breed among naval historians: he understands ships and sailors (many authors favour one or the other) ... The author has done an excellent job of weaving together a large number of published and unpublished accounts, plus official reports and documents, to paint a comprehensive picture of the gamut of experiences.' Navy News

CHURCHILL'S NAVY: The Ships, Men and Organisation 1939-1945

'Incredibly comprehensive...this really is a tour de force. Fascinating and informative, it is also a delight to read. Highly recommended.' History Today

Churchill's Navy breaks new ground in its comprehensive approach to the subject...and should be in the library of everyone interested in the Royal Navy of World War 2' Navy News

NELSON'S NAVY: The Ships, Men and Organisation 1793-1815

'There is no royal road to a knowledge of the Navy of Nelson's time...but Brian Lavery's book is the most nearly regal that I have come across in many years of reading on the subject...you name it, Nelson's Navy has it.' Patrick O'Brian

'A masterpiece on life in the Senior Service under England's favourite seafaring son.' The Times

ROYAL TARS

The Lower Deck of the ROYAL NAVY, 875–1850

BRIAN LAVERY

NAVAL INSTITUTE PRESS
Annapolis, Maryland

Naval Institute Press

© Brian Lavery, 2010

First published in Great Britain
in 2010 by Conway Publishing, an imprint of Anova Books Company Limited,
10 Southcombe Street, London W14 0RA
www.anovabooks.com

This edition published and distributed in the United States of America
and Canada by the Naval Institute Press, 291 Wood Road,
Annapolis, Maryland 21402-5034
www.nip.org

ISBN 9781591147435

Library of Congress Control Number: 2010932305

Editing and design by DAG Publications Ltd
Printed by T. J. International Ltd., Cornwall

CONTENTS

MAPS AND DIAGRAMS
IN THE TEXT

PREFACE

The story of the lower deck, the ordinary sailors of the Royal Navy, is not one that has been told in detail before. There have been slightly sketchy general histories, and excellent if limited ones for particular periods, mostly the twentieth century. The class has featured strongly in general histories of the Royal Navy, and featured in some collections of documents.[1]

In this volume I have tried to tell the story as a whole, while taking into account the factors that influenced the development of the lower deck – it is impossible to ignore general and naval history, or the role of officers in shaping (or failing to shape) the lives of the men. This story has proved impossible to fit into one single volume, so the next one will tell the story after 1850.

I hope to convey the character of the seaman through the ages, his skills and daily routine, his attitudes to those set over him and the regulations that affect him, and the experience of battle as seen (or not seen) from the gundeck or the engine room. Ideally I would like to tell the story of the Royal Navy through the seaman's eyes, but that is perhaps too difficult, as the ordinary seamen often had little knowledge of the factors that shaped their history. The authentic voice of the lower deck is not always easy to find. Letters are quite rare but valuable in that they were written at the time rather than in hindsight; however they are likely to put a certain gloss on things for the sake of friends and family. Moreover, the writer of such letters often finds it impossible to convey anything like the overpowering sense of lower-deck life, and perhaps he does not really try. Official documents such as muster books are generally devoid of any intimate detail. Courts martial were carefully recorded and can provide an occasional glimpse of ordinary life on board ship, as well as establishing what behaviour was considered unacceptable by the officers.

In most cases the spelling of contemporary documents is modernised, but in the case of letters written by seamen I have usually kept to the original where possible, as it may illuminate the speech patterns and pronunciation of the time. Comparisons in money are difficult after decades of inflation. No factor such as the cost of living index can really show the value of money at the time, but perhaps the reader should start from the fact that in 1760 a 74-gun ship of the line coast around £45,000 to build and fit; and that the annual wage of an able seaman, after some deductions, was £14.12s.6d (£14.62½p) from 1658 to 1797. This raises another issue, of pounds, shillings and pence. It is easy enough to convert to the modern decimal system, remembering that there were 12 pence to the shilling and 20 shillings to the pound, but that tends to make it seem much more banal. Twelve-and-a-half pence has nothing of the ring that '2/6' or 'half a crown' had fifty or sixty years ago.

I would like to acknowledge the help given, often unwittingly, by many friends and colleagues over the years. These include the late David Lyon, David Syrett and Colin White. Museum colleagues include Roger Knight, Simon Stephens, Robert Blyth and Rina Prentice of the National Maritime Museum; Jenny Wraight and Iain Mackenzie, of the Naval Historical Library, and Campbell MacMurray of the Royal Naval Museum. Academics include Eric Grove of Salford, Nicolas Rodger of All Souls, Oxford, Andrew Lambert of Kings College, London, Pat Crimmin of Royal Holloway College and many more.

Former members of the lower deck I have spoken to include Rear-Admiral Roy Clare, Peter Goodwin of HMS *Victory*, David Taylor of the National Maritime Museum and Len Barnett.

Much material is from manuscripts in the National Archives, supplemented by material in the British Library and the National Maritime Museum; thanks are due to the staffs of these institutions. For printed books I have used the British Library and the National Maritime Museum, and especially the London Library, with its huge range of books available for borrowing.

INTRODUCTION

What is the lower deck? It is a group of men (and later women) who perform the essential tasks of any navy with little expectation of promotion to the higher ranks. This does not exclude the possibility of a minority of its members rising to officer status, but it does not include cadets and midshipmen, who are recruited in the belief that they will eventually be commissioned.

The concept of the lower deck demands several preconditions. It requires some kind of permanent navy, even if it does not offer permanent employment to the ordinary sailors. In practice that assumes specialised warships that create the need for the state to build and maintain them rather than hire or requisition them. And it requires a degree of class distinction, in which the officers are segregated from the men. This was not the case in early medieval ships, for example, where the only 'officer' was the steersman, who rose from among the crew and tended to live among them. It is not easy to say exactly when the lower deck emerged as a distinct concept, but Tudor times are as close as one is likely to get. By then, warships were large and purpose-built, they needed large crews, which encouraged the separation of the 'officer class', and they needed a good deal of specialised skills. Perhaps, some time in the future, electronics will take over all the tasks that do not need decision making at officer level, and the lower deck will become obsolete – though as yet developments in electronics have not gone nearly far enough for that. Until that happens, every navy needs its lower deck.

That statement is axiomatic, and seems almost trite until one comes across the sort of naval history that almost ignores its importance, even its existence. One could search such major histories as William James's *Naval History of Great Britain*, Alfred Thayer Mahan's *The Influence of Sea Power upon History*, or S. W. Roskill's *The War at Sea, 1939–45* for some time without learning much about the lower deck. Strangely, two of these classic histories were written by naval officers, who must have been constantly aware of the lower deck and its problems during their own service. Occasionally a hero might appear such as John Crawford, who nailed a flag to the mast at Camperdown in 1797, or Jack Cornwell, who stood by his gun to win a Victoria Cross at Jutland in 1916; but otherwise the lower deck is only noticed when it is a problem. It is rather like the working class in traditional British drama, when it only appears as servants, clowns or miscreants. Seamen are often difficult to recruit, sometimes they mutiny on board ship, they are liable to drunkenness or venereal disease, they tend to desert, or to behave in a feckless manner. Modern naval history has moved on from this approach, although oddly enough it is very difficult to find any analytical literature on the lower deck from 1939 onwards. For earlier periods most modern naval historians have appreciated the full importance of the lower deck in naval history.

More recent naval history has opened up new areas. Administrative history is very valuable and provides many insights into the life of the seaman, but it is seen mostly from the point of view of the central administrators. Dockyard history provides many glimpses into the life of the working classes, but only the shore-based dockyard employees, who are very different from the seafarers and are often disliked by them.

It is not difficult to see why the lower deck should be largely ignored. Unlike the labouring classes ashore, it does not attract much attention from social historians, who are often of a left-wing persuasion and have difficulty dealing with such an essentially conservative institution as the Royal Navy. Naval history was traditionally written by officers such as Mahan and Roskill, and tended to reflect their views. Even early civilian historians, such as William James, tended to interview officers or read their logs and reports as their primary sources. The members of the lower deck wrote far less than the officers, partly because many of them were illiterate, partly because they did not usually have to produce reports as part of their duties – but also because publications by members or ex-members of the lower deck often turned into complaints against the system and were not officially encouraged.

There is a tendency to assume that the lower deck has no real importance in its own right, that it is simply a creation of the officers who recruited and trained the men. This does not bear much examination at any stage of modern British naval history. The lower deck in the age of sail was largely trained in the merchant service before being pressed into the navy, and naval officers can only claim credit for its skill in gunnery, not in seamanship. It also ignores the fact that the lower deck has a life and social history of its own and often struggled hard to maintain a measure of independence from higher authority. Furthermore, it is equally easy to forget that the lower deck, by its own actions, changed the course of British history on several occasions. It chose the Parliamentary side at the beginning of the English Civil War, with profound effects on history. The mutinies of 1797 and 1931 altered government policy. The lower deck's fighting qualities were what made Nelson's great victories possible. And World War II, a 'people's war' in general, was truly a lower-deck war in which individual radar and asdic operators, landing-craft coxswains and anti-aircraft gunners could often turn the scale at a vital moment.

On the face of it, there are few groups and societies that have more restrictions on their freedom of movement and action than the lower deck of the navy. But in practice the seamen found many ways to get around this, to establish small but important pockets of freedom, to assert their independence of authority. As part of this, they established a strong and vivid culture with its own scale of values, language and rituals.

Like its much larger land-based counterpart, the working class, the lower deck is not always easy to define precisely. Like the working class it took some time to emerge in the form that is generally recognised. It is divided in many ways, vertically between different skills and trades, horizontally between different levels of authority, some types of which, like foremen and petty officers, are delegated from the classes above. It has its own 'aristocracy' in the form of highly skilled tradesmen. It usually includes a small but important proportion of people who hoped some day to move into a higher group. If the lower deck as a whole had a single culture of its own, it was largely formed to distinguish it from other groups in society. The lower deck, then, can only exist in distinction from its superiors, known from much of the period as the quarterdeck, or more generally as the officers. That term too is often ambiguous, and can be taken to mean the holder of a particular office, rather than one with a permanent status.

A good naval officer needs many qualities – leadership, technical skill, bravery, determination, loyalty and integrity among others. But these are not enough to define an officer class, and many, if not all of these attributes can be found on the lower deck in almost equal measure. In practice, an officer group in modern times is defined by two factors – class and education, and are not unrelated – it is almost universally true that those in a higher social class have much better access to education.

Of course, lower-deck history cannot be considered in isolation. I do not attempt to write about the Royal Marines in any detail, as they deserve a history of their own. I have dealt with them inasmuch as they affect the story of the lower deck in general, and that should be enough to show how essential they were to the running of a ship, and to the history of the navy and its battles. I have tried to see the lower deck from many different points of view. Historically it is essential to naval and therefore world history – not just as 'haulers on ropes' and 'loaders of guns', but in many cases as a significant political factor. To the statesman or naval administrator, its recruitment, training and morale are constant problems. It is necessary to consider the effects of policies and regulations, and by tradition the experienced seaman, the 'three-badge AB' of the early twentieth century, knew the rules as far as they affected him. In theory, no institution in Britain was more powerful than the Admiralty, but it had to take many factors into account, and lower-deck feeling was not the least of these. This affected pressing and later recruitment policies, uniform, working and living conditions and many other factors. Naval officers regulate the lives on board ship. Even if they were not always obeyed, the very fact of a regulation might throw some light in itself. When eighteenth century rules forbade men from 'easing themselves' in the hold, it seems reasonable to assume that it really happened. All these issues have an effect on the seaman himself, for few people live in such a tightly controlled environment. The perception of the seaman by the outside world also has to be considered – is he a hero or a drunken lout, or both? The general public also has views on the sailor. It pays taxes for the navy and in dockyard towns it provides services for him, ranging from evangelism to prostitution.

But the most important perspective is the lower deck seaman's own – his reasons for joining, his skills, ambitions, friendships, daily life, attitude to dangers and death, relations with family ashore, standard of living and retirement. This can be quite difficult to discover. Lower-deck memoirs are rare before the last twenty years of the eighteenth century and they are usually written by men of above average education and literacy. Perhaps also they put forward a particular point of view. A high proportion of lower deck memoir-writers were Scots, such as John Nicol and Robert Hay, which partly reflects higher standards of literacy in that country. More of them, such as Edward Coxere and Thomas Lurting, became deeply religious, and that too is reflected in their writing. Others, such as William Robinson and Samuel Leech, were disillusioned with naval service, and that also shows.

I have tried to show the experience of battle through lower-deck eyes, and that too has its limitations. Obviously the average seamen knew far less about what was going on than the admiral at the time, or the later historian. According to one man in *Belleisle* at Trafalgar, 'the men were as much in the dark as if they had been blindfolded ...', and senior officers rarely took the trouble to keep them informed. Some lower-deck writers perhaps had a tendency to fill in the detail with what they heard later, so I have tried to confine quotes to those that have a ring of truth and personal observation. Naturally, that is subjective, and I cannot be sure that I have always succeeded.

The EARLY SEAMAN
Before 1642

THE BIRTH OF SEA POWER

Britain's independent maritime history might be said to begin around 6500 BC, when the sea broke through the chalk to create the Strait of Dover. The Britons apparently developed cross-Channel travel, as suggested by the Dover boat that dates from around 1300 BC. The Romans occupied the country from AD 43 and based a large fleet of around 7,000 men, the *Classis Britannica*, at Dover. Though we know very little about it, it was probably Britain's first taste of organised naval power. The Anglo-Saxons and the Scots arrived by sea from northern Europe and Ireland and had their own styles of craft. From 793 they were harassed by the Vikings of Scandinavia, the most daring and expert seafarers of the age.

King Alfred founded the first recorded English navy around 875, and he designed a new type of ship, considerably larger than the Viking longships that opposed him. 'They were full twice as long as the others; some had sixty oars, and some had more; they were both swifter and steadier, and also higher than the others; they were shaped neither like the Frisian nor the Danish, but so as it seemed to him as they would be most efficient.'[1] Clearly they were fighting ships, not merely troop transports. They were purpose-built warships, not converted or hired merchantmen. There is no real information on how Alfred manned his navy, but it was assumed by his contemporaries that he had the right to call free men to his service. Nobles, peasants and townsmen were liable to be called to fight in the *Fyrd*, or army, and the same applied to seamen. Alfred paid particular attention to the training of his men.

His successors, both Anglo-Saxon and Danish, kept up the fleet in varying degrees of strength. In 1066, Harold Godwinson had the largest fleet yet assembled in England to resist William the Conqueror's invasion force, but he failed to stop it and was defeated on land at Hastings. Under William and the early Norman kings the naval situation was very different.

The Viking menace was much reduced, and the King controlled both sides of the English Channel. There was no great need for a naval fighting force as such, and the King mostly needed ships to transport himself, his troops and his courtiers between France and England. Moreover, the French coast provided its own supply of seamen, so there was no great pressure on English resources. Specialised warships were not needed, and transports could be requisitioned from the merchant fleet when necessary. They were taken over complete with crews, so there was no question of a naval 'lower deck' as such.

Under these circumstances, the Cinque Ports came into prominence. These towns, situated in the south-east corner of England, were obliged to provide the King with ships for fifteen days every year, without charge, in return for certain privileges. Hastings, for example, with its associated ports, 'ought, on the King's summons, to find 21 ships; and in each ship there ought to be 21 men, strong, fit and well armed, and prepared for the King's service'. The king was to give 40 days notice for the fleet to assemble, and

> when the aforesaid ships and the men in them have come to the place whither they have been summoned, they shall there remain in the Kings service at their own cost. And if the king needs their service beyond the 15 days aforesaid, or wishes them to remain there longer, those ships with the men in them shall remain in the King's service so long as he pleases and at his cost; that is to say, a master shall receive 6*d* per day, a constable 6*d* per day, and each of the others 3*d* per day.[2]

Clearly fifteen days was not enough to fight a sea campaign, but it was possible to mount patrols and, with good luck and resolution, it might serve to transport the King and his followers across the Channel. Other ships were provided by feudal tenure; a lord, such as Hugh de Paplesham of Crokham, might hold his manor in return for providing a ship for the King in the same way as another might be expected to fight or lead troops in battle. Such ships, of course, also came complete with crews and all the other necessities.

THE LATE MEDIEVAL NAVIES

Late in the twelfth century several factors combined to change this situation. In 1190 Richard I set out on his crusade to Palestine and decided to take his force by sea rather than by land. This was a very different expedition from a Channel crossing, and it demanded a fleet well beyond the resources of his predecessors. It required a force that could operate over a very long range and seamen who would be prepared to spend months and years away from home, rather than days and weeks. It demanded some real fighting ships as well as transports, for there were several engagements with the Saracens in the Mediterranean, and the crusaders encountered the terrible weapon of Greek fire. Richard raised money for his crusade by means of a tax known as the Saladin Levy, but unfortunately we have little knowledge of how he recruited his seamen, though it is possible that it set some precedents for the next reign. Out of a fleet of more than 200 vessels, Richard provided at least 45 ships at his own expense, and many more came from his provinces in Normandy, Brittany and Poitou. There is no clear evidence that the crews were impressed, and perhaps in the climate of the time it was possible to find enough volunteers for a holy crusade.

Richard's brother John came to the throne in 1199 and built a new kind of navy, out of necessity rather than foresight, for in 1205 he lost control of Normandy to the French King, Philippe II Auguste. The English Channel was no longer under English domination, and a more active defence force was needed. Furthermore, his remaining overseas possessions, in Gascony and south-west France, were more than a few days sailing away, and the fifteen days the ships of the Cinque Ports served without payment would not be enough to transport an army that far. So John was forced to revive the idea of fighting at sea. His fleet had its greatest triumph at the Battle of Damme in 1213, when 500 ships, carrying 700 knights under the Earl of Salisbury, attacked the French off the coast of Flanders. About 300 enemy transports were captured, and some 100 more were destroyed. It was the first of a long line of English victories against the French, and perhaps the first real English sea battle, as it was on a much larger scale than the fights with the Vikings. However, victory was made much easier by the fact that most of the French soldiers were ashore at the time, while the English ships had their full complements.

Medieval sea warfare was an extension of fighting on land, with noblemen in command of the fleet and the seamen in a subordinate (but essential) role. England's next naval victory, off South Foreland in 1217, is described by one historian as follows:

> As soon ... as the English had gained the wind of the foe ... they bore down upon the French rear, and as they came up with it, threw grapnels, and so fastened their own ships to those of their enemies. The crossbow men and

archers of Sir Phillip d'Albini did good work by pouring in flights of arrows. The English also made use of unslaked lime, which they flung forward and which, borne on the wind in powder, blinded the Frenchmen's eyes. Under cover of this the English boarded, and with their axes cut away the rigging and halyards, so that the sails fell upon the French, and increased their confusion. After a short hand to hand combat, involving immense slaughter, the enemy were completely defeated.[3]

There was another battle off Winchelsea in 1350 under King Edward III. The seamen were taken for granted in historical accounts, and the battle was described in terms of land conflict. The King was on board *Cog Thomas*, commanded by Robert Passelow, leading a fleet of against the Castilians.

When the King of England, on board his own ship saw what was happening he shouted to his helmsman, 'Steer for that ship for I want to joust with her.' And his ship was turned towards the leading Spanish ship. The sailor did not want to disobey his orders because it was the King who desired it, even though the Spaniard came on at speed sailing on the wind. The King's ship was strong and manoeuvrable otherwise she would have split; for she and the great Spanish vessel struck with such force that it sounded like thunder and as they rebounded the castle of the King of England's ship caught the [top]castle of the Spanish ship in such a way that the mast levered it from the mast on which it was fixed and it fell in the sea. All those in the castle were drowned and lost. This shock sprung the seams of the King's ship and she began to make water; the King's knights realised this and began to pump and bale but didn't yet tell the King. The King, looking at the ship alongside with which he had jousted exclaimed, 'Grapple my ship to that one; I must have her!' A knight exclaimed; 'Let her go, you'll get a better!' This ship sailed on and another big one came up. The knights grappled the King's ship to it with hooks and chains. The battle began, being fiercely and proudly contended, with archers and stout defence by the Spanish, with skirmishes in ten or twelve places …

The English royal knights made strenuous efforts to take the ship they had grappled with because their own, as I have said above, was in danger of foundering as she had taken in so much water. At last the King and his crew fought so well that the Spanish ship was taken and everyone on board her was thrown over the side. Then they told the King of his peril from the sinking ship and that he should go on board the prize vessel. The King took this advice and went on board the Spanish ship with all his men leaving the other empty.[4]

A medieval king had three ways of obtaining ships for his fleet. He could use purely feudal means, such as the Cinque Ports, or sergeanty. This was based on the holding of land in one form or another, so it was not easy to expand a fleet. However, in the 1220s Henry III did enter into agreements with some ports for extra ships. The Cinque Ports agreed to provide vessels 'besides those which are owed us by way of service'.

The second method was by means of 'arrest', or impressment of ships, as it was called later. The king always claimed the right to take merchant ships into his service, and even Magna Carta went some way to conceding this. Thus in 1227 Henry III demanded that the citizens of Dunwich 'in the fealty by which you are bound to us ... have all the good ships of your port, besides thus which you owe us through your promise, come to Portsmouth well supplied with arms and victuals'.[5]

The third method was for the king to build or buy his own ships. Obviously this was the best way to acquire galleys, and these were important in John's fleet. He also owned some sailing or 'round' ships, though it is not clear how many, or how large they were. As early as 1205 there are references to 'our' longships, meaning the galleys of the King, and in the same year workmen and sailors were impressed to repair the King's ships and gallies, and take them round to Portsmouth.[6] The size of the permanent fleet varied considerably according to the resources and ambitions of whoever was on the throne, but in general the more warlike kings, such as Edward III and Henry V, had the largest fleets. Later monarchs tended to concentrate on sailing ships rather than galleys, and often a king would build a particularly large ship as his flagship. A classic example of this was Henry V's *Grace Dieu*, launched in 1418 of 1,400 tons – it would be nearly two centuries before an English king would build a bigger one.

THE MEDIEVAL SEAMAN

Unlike requisitioned merchant ships, the King's own ships did not come complete with crews. Many of the merchant ships needed larger crews in order to fight – not just knights and archers, but extra seaman to make the ship more manoeuvrable in action. The medieval seaman was a specialist, who had probably spent all his life learning his trade. At Bristol in 1445, three years' experience were needed to become a 'servant', so that 'he be knowen able in connyng of his crafte'.[7] The seaman was not unique, of course, in that all skilled medieval workers needed long training. It took many years to turn a boy into a fully fledged seaman, and so the total supply available to the kingdom could not be expanded easily. The seaman was obviously essential to the military strength of the country, as well as to trade.

Again, the seaman was not unique in the Middle Ages. Britain was not yet an 'island kingdom', for wars between England and Scotland were as common as those in France, and for much of the period the English kings also held possessions in France, while internecine conflicts, such as the Wars of the Roses, were often as intense and as frequent as foreign wars.

There was no attempt at colonial expansion outside Europe, and so sea warfare was far from paramount in the defence and expansion of the realm. The seaman took his place alongside the other specialists who were necessary in war. In later times it would take a few months to train a musketeer or a cavalry trooper, but the medieval archer or knight, like the seaman, needed to learn his craft from boyhood, and to keep in constant practice. The seaman was subject to compulsory military service, but he did not bear a grossly disproportionate share of the burden, as he was to do in later centuries.

The seaman faced many hardships, but he retained a certain dignity. He had many rights against the master of his ship, and in a sense he was the subject of a benevolent autocracy rather than a floating tyranny. He had some protection against corporal punishment, for according to the fourteenth century Rules of Oleron, 'if the master strike one of the crew of the ship, the latter ought to support the first blow either of fist or palm of the hand, and if he strikes any more he may defend himself.'[8] The master was obliged to look after his men if they fell sick, and could not discharge them without just cause. Sometimes he could be subjected to draconian punishments – the reign of Richard I produced an imaginative and strict set of sea laws, by which

> Anyone who should kill another on board ship should be tied to the dead body and thrown into the sea.
> Anyone lawfully convicted of drawing a knife or other weapon with intent to strike another, or of striking another so as to draw blood, shall lose his hand.[9]

But aboard ship there was no class division between the master and the crew. There was no lower deck in the later sense, and not just for geographical reasons, in that most ships did not have more than one deck. More important, a medieval ship was a cooperative. There were no charts or pilot books, so literacy was no advantage. Ships did not venture on ocean voyages, so navigation was done by local knowledge rather than calculation. Chaucer's shipman, for example:

> knew well alle the havens as they were
> From gotland to the Cape of Finistere,
> And every creke in Bretagne and in Spaine.

This knowledge was gained by experience rather than book learning, so in that sense every seaman had a chance of becoming a master. The medieval merchant ship was run more or less as a partnership with the captain: for example, the crew's consent was needed before setting sail. The authority of the master was strong, but there was a sense that he was the senior partner rather than someone from outside. Often members of the crew had shares in the ship, or they were paid by 'portage' by having a space in the hold for private cargo. The Rules of Oleron recognised only three ranks – the master, the lodesman, or pilot, and the common mariner – but by 1488 a typical ship also had a purser, boatswain and cook.[10] Others were added, such as quartermaster and often gunner, and most of them had mates, or assistants. There were no formal conditions for appointment or promotion, which depended on the trust of the owners, or perhaps having a large share in the vessel. Crews were small. As late as 1582, nearly 1,500 ships in the kingdom of England were manned by 16,000 sailors, an average of eleven men per ship.[11] In these circumstances it was not likely that a separate 'officer class' would develop, isolated from the crew. Until the late fifteenth century, rigging was relatively simple, just a single square sail. Voyages were seasonal, and ships did not risk bad weather, though they could never be sure of avoiding it. According to the traditional Scottish ballad, Sir Patrick Spens was shocked to be asked to cross the North Sea in winter:

To Noroway, to Noroway,
To Noroway o'er the foam;
The King's daughter of Noroway,
'Tis thou must fetch her home.

The first line that Sir Patrick read,
A loud laugh laughed he;
The next line that Sir Patrick read,
A tear blinded his ee.

O who is he has done this deed,
Has told the King of me,
To send us out this time of year,
To sail upon the sea?

Most of the vessels in the medieval fleet were pure sailers, 'round ships' in contrast to the 'long ships', or galleys. The standard round ship or 'keel' of medieval northern Europe was a descendant of the Viking ship, clinker-built with overlapping planks, and double-ended. Other types, also clinker-built, included the 'hulk' from the Netherlands in which the planks ran parallel to the keel that then came to an end at the stern post; and the 'cog' from Germany with higher sides and a straighter stem and stern post.

When used for war a merchant ship was fitted with wooden castles at the bow and stern as shown in the seals of the Cinque Ports, and these castles tended to become more elaborate and permanent over the years. By about 1350, ships were fitted with rudders rather than steering oars, so they were no longer identical at both ends. The seals also give us a rare glimpse of the seaman at work, hauling on ropes and an anchor cable, climbing the shrouds (without any ratlines to create a kind of ladder), and working on the ends of the yards.

The English fleet sometimes included galleys, which contributed to the victory at Damme by ramming the enemy and sinking some of his ships, but they were native to the Mediterranean and often found life difficult in northern waters. They were never the predominant vessels in the open waters of the Channel and North Sea, and their use tended to decline over the years. They were, of course, designed solely for warfare, as their enormous crews made them virtually useless for commercial purposes. Edward I ordered twenty in 1294, nominally of 120 oars each but actually much smaller. In 1317, Edward II bought five from Genoa, and later two more were built by Edward III. 'Barges' and 'balingers' were also types of rowing vessel, built in some numbers from 1378 and sometimes used as tenders to larger ships.

Ships fitted for war needed larger crews of seamen, for greater manoeuvrability in action and perhaps to row when the wind failed in action. In a squadron fitted out in 1324, those of 240 tons needed 60 mariners each, those of 140 tons had 35, and of 80 tons, 24.[12] In the 14th century the largest ships were sometimes given double 'eskippamentum', a term that includes the rigging and stores of the ship, as well as her crew, so it is possible that all of these were increased to make her fit as a warship.[13] In 1315 a clerk was sent to Bristol to choose fourteen ships, and 'to select "defensible" men, as well mariners or others, for the equipment of the ships aforesaid, so that each of the ships aforesaid shall be provided with a double shipment of men'.[14]

The warship also introduced a new element, the soldier. When fitted for war a ship usually carried at least one constable, a junior army officer who ranked equal to the master, but after him in the chain of command. He might or might not be in charge of a troop of soldiers to fight the ship, including infantry, dismounted cavalry and archers, who provided the only means of attacking another ship apart from boarding it. There was little space for them to operate, however, so they were carried only in the proportion of two archers to one other, rather than three to one as in land service. Some ships were intended purely as transports. Those to be used as warships were double manned.[15] In 1416–19, Henry V's balinger *Ane* of 120 tons made at least fifteen voyages, with crews ranging from 45 to 145 men and boys. The smaller crews were when she served as a transport, taking artillery to Caen or supplies to Falaise, Honfleur or Rouen. With the larger crews she was serving as a warship patrolling the seas. *Nicholas,* also of 120 tons, served solely as a warship and had a crew of 100 to 120 men most of the time.[16] As to soldiers, in 1417 the carrack *Mary de la Tour* had a crew of about 100 seamen, with 62 men at arms and 134 archers, making the ship very crowded, with 296 on 500 tons.[17]

RAISING THE MEN

It was always possible for the king to raise crews by normal commercial means, by hiring them on competitive terms; but he was far more likely to be short of money, and to use his inherent powers to compel them to serve, often on less favourable terms than they could get from the merchants. Thus the impressment of individual seamen became common under John (though the term itself was not yet in use). The conscription of an individual was a much greater hardship than the impressment of his ship. In the latter case he remained with his old companions, under a master whom he had presumably agreed to serve voluntarily. The ship might become crowded with men at arms and a knight and his retinue, but this was not necessarily a greater hardship than carrying a large cargo. It might face danger in battle, but the seaman was used to risks from the sea in any case. If, on the other hand, he was impressed as an individual, he would often be sent to a strange port and allocated to one of the King's ships, to serve among strangers.

The process of impressment usually began with an order to 'arrest' shipping in the ports. Since the merchant ships that were not taken up were unable to trade, this created a pool of seamen from which some could be impressed. The next stage was to send orders to the king's agents in the ports (reeves or bailiffs in the twelfth century), to provide a specific number of seamen. For example, in 1205 John ordered the bailiffs of Yarmouth, Liddingland, Orford and Beccles to send four officers and 140 sailors to London, where they were to be assigned to the King's galleys. The bailiffs would choose the men from among the seamen in the port and arrange for their transport to the rendezvous. In 1314, Edward II gave his clerks power to go to the ports of the West Country to 'select mariners who are stout and strong at arms equipt to with fitting arms to proceed in the ships above said'. In other cases, men were selected for individual ships. In the same year, the commanders of the ship *Christopher of Westminster* were given 'power to select ... men, mariners and others, "defensibles" and powerful at arms or the defence of the same ship, as shall be most expedient for our honour'.[18]

Over the next two and a half centuries the precedents set in John's reign were followed and reinforced. We know nothing about the thoughts of the medieval seaman, but his actions suggest that he was not always happy about the terms of his service to the King. Of course he was paid for it, normally at 3*d* per day until 1327, 3½*d* until 1370, and 4½*d* after that.[19] It is difficult to compare these with commercial rates, for the merchant seaman was usually paid part of the profits of the voyage. Nevertheless, kings were already getting a reputation for paying low wages, and paying them late, and in 1336 some impressed seamen refused to embark unless they were given part of their wages in advance.[20] There are signs that some seamen resisted impressment by any means available to them. In 1348 fifteen deserters were said to be 'roaming about London', and masters often disobeyed orders to sail to the ports of assembly, while there were reports of officials being bribed to allow particular ships to evade the arrest.[21]

In 1379, during the minority of Richard II, Parliament paid attention to the impressment of seamen for the first time and passed an act 'Against mariners departing the King's service without license'. 'Because that divers mariners after they be arrested and retained for the King's service upon the sea, in defence of the realm, and thereof have recovered their wages pertaining, do flee out of the said service without license of the admirals, or of their lieutenants.' Such desertion was to be punished by one year's imprisonment, and the offender was to forfeit a sum double the amount he had been advanced.[22]

MUTINY

As often happens in the story of the lower deck, we only hear about the common seaman when he is causing trouble. In 1420, for some unknown reason, the officers and soldiers objected to the taking of a muster of 50 men at arms and a thousand archers at Southampton. On board Henry's great ship the *Grace Dieu*, Quartermaster William, Duke of Dartmouth, refused to let the clerk take the names and 'violently seized the roll of sailors' names out of the hands of the clerk and threatened to throw it overboard into the sea'. It got worse after the ship put to sea on what was probably her only voyage, to 'keep the seas' or patrol the English Channel:

a certain William Downynge of Plymouth, Walker, John French of Dartmouth, tailor, Thomas Sydoner, John Boterel, William Dutton, Walter Boterel, John Slee, John Oxxne, Thomas Bowyer of Tavistock and many others in their company rose up against the Earl of Devon their captain and the royal commissioners aforesaid and William Payne master of the said ship and his crew and refused to allow them to keep their station at sea, and force them against their will to sail to St Helen's on the Isle of Wight ...

Thomas Lynnsey, a servant to one of the Commissioners, asked Downynge, 'Why don't you want to obey and make your muster before the master and his assistant as other men in other ships have done?' Downynge replied by ripping Lynnsey's clothes and 'using insulting words'.[23]

THE TUDOR AGE

The custom of impressing seamen had an enormous capacity to survive through the centuries, through all kinds of social, political and technological change. It came to prominence within a few years of the signing of Magna Carta, and it lasted almost until the beginning of the railway age. It survived the abolition of feudal tenures, the Bill of Rights and the Industrial Revolution. It was far from unchanged by these events, and the nature of impressment altered radically over the years, but in one form or another it outlasted different several forms of government.

The first great period of change came after 1485, during what some historians call 'The Tudor Revolution in Government'. Certainly there were changes in state and society that indirectly affected the seaman. The medieval baronage lost much of its political power to the monarchy, which became progressively richer in the first part of the period, wages tending to replace feudal tenure as the basis of the military system. The justices of the peace became the king's agents for local administration, including the recruiting of soldiers and seamen.

There were several developments in the design of ships that affected the seaman's work. A second mast was added to larger ships from about 1400, including Henry V's larger vessels, ranging from the 750-ton *Holyghost de la Tour* to the 120-ton *Ane*. The largest of all, *Grace Dieu* of 1,400 tons, had at least three.[24] Built in response to the large ships known as 'carracks' being built by the European powers, she stretched the clinker-building system to the limit – later ships would be carvel-built, with stronger frames and the planks laid side-by-side to create a smoother surface. The three-masted rig allowed the building of ever-larger ships without making the individual sails unfeasibly big. It aided steering, as sails could be set at different angles to balance the ship, and it was particularly useful in tacking, when the foresail was kept in position, as the head of the ship turned into the wind, to help the bows to move round. Between 1450 and 1570 a topsail was added above the mainsail, and the spritsail was hung under the bowsprit, which projected forward of the ship. Ships were becoming increasingly complex, and the seaman needed extra skills to handle the much more elaborate rigging. As always with an improvement in ship design, it led to greater expectations of what ships could do. Horizons were widened in 1492 when Columbus made his first voyage to America, while the sea route to India was discovered by the Portuguese. Over the next century English sailors would become increasingly involved in the New World. There was a general trend for ships to become larger, and Henry VIII's flagship, the *Grace Dieu*, was of 1,000 tons, and he had fifteen ships of more than 200 tons in his fleet in 1546.

Gunpowder increased greatly in military importance, and this assisted royal power as the King kept its manufacture in his own hands and used it to nullify the walls of the old feudal castles. It had been known in Europe since the thirteenth century and used on ships since the fourteenth. In 1495, Henry VII's *Sovereine* carried 141 guns, mostly serpentines, which were small-calibre, long-barrelled breech-loading weapons. Sixteen of these were mounted in the forecastle, 24 below the 'sommercastell' in the stern, 21 in the sommercastell itself plus 25 on a deck above that, four in the stern and 20 in the poop. In addition there were eleven 'patereros', 'stone gonnes of yron' in the sommercastell and twenty more in the waist, firing stone shot[25]. None of these guns was mounted below decks. Guns usually came with expert gunners who had perhaps learned the trade on land and were often interchangeable between land and sea service. In the 1470s there were Flemish gunners such as Jan van Delft and Hans van Brussel serving alongside Englishmen such as Harry Thompson and the aptly-named Nicholas Armourer. A large ship had a master gunner and forty ordinary gunners.[26] They brought skills in the treatment of gunpowder and in the handling and aiming of guns. In general in the mid-sixteenth century a warship carried one gunner for each major piece of ordnance. They were well-paid professionals, and it was not usually necessary to raise them by impressment.

The key invention was the gunport, which appeared around 1500, and allowed much larger guns to be mounted lower in the ship. It kept the centre of gravity low, but at the same time it could be closed in bad weather or in action. By 1513, fifteen of Henry VIII's ships carried guns in some form. *Sovereign*, with 70 to 80 pieces, had forty gunners; *Sweepstake* and *Swallow* had four each.[27] Guns came in many different forms, and the master gunner was expected to know all of them. The largest were cast in brass and mounted on wheeled carriages – cannon and demi-cannon firing balls of 60 to 41 pounds in weight. There were six different types of culverin, longer guns of slightly smaller calibre ranging from the culverin itself with a ball of about 20 pounds, through the demi-culverin, saker, minon, falcon and falconet with a ball of about ½ pound. Their longer barrels were expected to give greater range, 760 paces from a full culverin in 1587 compared with 400 for a cannon.[28] Some of the smaller pieces were cast in iron, though most were still of bronze. Small iron guns, known as 'port-pieces' and 'fowlers', were made up of iron staves and hoops (hence the term 'barrel' of a gun). They were breechloaders with detachable chambers and were mounted on fixed wooden beds.

The main tactic in a gun battle was to steer the ship to aim the guns, and this could only be done by skilled seamen. The soldiers no longer operated the primary armament of the ship, for the 'great guns' were directed by the gunners with the assistance of the mariners.

It is not always clear how the guns were operated, but it seems likely that each large piece had a gunner in charge to lay it and supervise the seamen who assisted with loading. It was not unknown for a man or boy to be sent outboard to load the piece from there, which was possible because the ship usually reloaded away from the action. Otherwise the seamen hauled the gun in on its tackles, for with restricted space on deck it was not common to allow it to recoil.[29] A gunner might also supervise a group of smaller guns, which did not need such methods and were only used at short range. In the case of a port-piece, the chamber was loaded separately and then wedged into place, two chambers being provided to keep up a high rate of fire.

Seamen tended to become ever more important as the range of operations increased, calling for more navigational skill. This was also the beginning of a class division within them, those with some education and skill in navigation becoming an elite while the others had few hopes of promotion. The proportion of mariners aboard ship tended to increase over the years. At the beginning of the century they made up about two-fifths of the crew, and in 1546 they were still less than half on larger ships. By 1578 they made up at least half the crews on all large ships, and up to two-thirds on some. But in the early part of the century boarding was still the climax of tactics, giving the soldier his main role; according to Thomas

Audley's fleet orders of about 1530, 'In case you board [i.e., come alongside] your enemy, enter not till you see the smoke gone, and then shoot off all your pieces, your port pieces, the pieces of hail shot and cross-bow shot to beat his cage deck, then enter [i.e., board] with your best men.'[30] In other words, gunnery was only used in preparation for the soldiers to board. Nevertheless, it was steadily increasing in importance, which meant that the difference between warships and merchantmen was becoming greater, so that the royal ships began to predominate over hired or impressed merchant vessels. In turn this meant that seamen had to be recruited as individuals to the king's ships, rather than taken over with their own ships.

The increasing size of ships and the new emphasis on gunnery caused the development of more specialised warships at the expense of merely converted merchantmen. Henry VII, the first of the Tudor kings, concentrated on internal affairs and built up only a moderate navy of about a dozen ships. His son Henry VIII came to the throne in 1509 and adopted a much more aggressive foreign policy. The Protestant reformation of 1534 had two main effects – the dissolution of the monasteries put a large amount of money into the King's hands, which could be used to build and man the navy; and the breach with Rome put England in conflict with the main powers of Western Europe, France and Spain. Henry VIII had 58 ships in his fleet in 1546, at the end of one of his wars with France. His reign marks the beginning of a continuous naval policy, and the English fleet was never again to disappear from sight as it had done in the past under the less warlike medieval kings.

MANNING THE FLEET

The Tudor kings accumulated extra powers to themselves, and they did not surrender any of their old feudal prerogatives. Impressment was as common as it had ever been in the Middle Ages. In 1489 the captains and masters of various ships taken over by the King were empowered to 'impress soldiers and sailors'.[31] The practice was just as common in the 1540s, during Henry VIII's war with France. In 1544 it was reported that the King had 'arrested all ships at present in the harbours of this realm, and is about to put in order more than 150 sail'.[32] Robert Legge of Harwich was paid 40/- for himself and two horses, to ride round the ports of Essex 'for presting mariners to Deptford Strand',[33] while Viscount Lisle, the admiral, was given authority 'To take up and provide in all places, as well within franchises and liberties as without, such and as many shipmasters, mariners, shipwrights, soldiers, gunners and other able persons as our said cousin shall think meet for the furniture and manning of the said ships.'[34] In July 1545 it was reported that the Sheriff of Devon had 'laid out certain sums of money for the conduct and prest money of such mariners as be took up to go to Portsmouth'.[35] ('Prest money' was originally from the French 'prêt', or 'ready', and referred to the advance given to a soldier or sailor on his recruitment – it eventually became confused with 'press', meaning to force to serve.) The impressment in Devon was enough to disrupt normal life, and it was reported from Exeter, 'As most of the fishermen here are taken from hence as mariners to serve the King, no fish is to be had, and women are going out fishing, and sometimes are chased by Frenchmen.'[36] Even enemy prisoners could be used on board ship as necessary; according to the instructions to Admiral Woodhouse in 1545, his ships were to 'take all Frenchmen and Scots as good prize, taking the men into their own ships to serve in the same as drudges'.[37]

In 1545 the government issued a proclamation that 'No mariner or soldier or other person serving or prest to serve in the Kings ships land from the same without a testimonial signed by their captain.'[38]. But this is the only hint of any difficulties with the impressment of seamen. The same proclamation raised the wages of seamen from 5/- to 6/8 per month, and this seems to have been enough to allay discontent. For Henry VIII, though he sometimes over-extended his resources, was a comparatively rich monarch after his profits from the dissolution of the monasteries, and paid his men quite well. There was inflation in Tudor times, largely because of the King's own debasement of the currency and the discovery of gold in the New World; but the royal seamen were kept relatively happy. The system of impressment was perhaps less harsh than it had been in the Middle Ages. In 1544 the 'Common crier of London' was paid 8d for making a proclamation 'for certain mariners that had received the King's prest to depart out of London to serve the King upon the Narrow Seas under Sir William Woodhouse'.[39] This may imply that the men were given money well in advance of the call to arms and raises some interesting questions. In the first place, the word 'prest' is used in a slightly different sense, for it means money given to the seaman to hold himself in readiness, rather than ready money. Secondly, if men could be trusted with advance payment and expected to obey the call from the town crier, it suggests that impressment was not at all unpopular.

The Tudors were relatively well supplied with seamen. In 1551 the Venetian ambassador wrote that the English 'have a great quantity of both ships and sailors', and that 'the military discipline of the English ... would be perfectly devised if the soldiers were suitably exercised before being required for active service, as is the case of the sailors, who constantly keep the sea clear of Flemish and Breton corsairs, and especially from the Scots'.[40] A few years later it was reported that the sovereign 'has great plenty of English sailors, who are considered excellent to the navigation of the Atlantic'.[41]

THE CREW OF THE *MARY ROSE*

When *Mary Rose* sank off Portsmouth on 19 July 1545, she was probably carrying around 415 men including, or in addition to, Vice Admiral Sir George Carew and his retinue. If the *Anthony Roll* is accurate, 185 of them were soldiers, 30 were gunners and 200 were sailors. In any case only about 35 of them survived as the ship capsized while turning during a battle with the French. Many of the rest were trapped under the boarding nettings that covered the decks, and those high up in the tops seem to have had the best chance of survival.

Archeology on the site and the recovery of the ship's hull in 1982 has provided us with a glimpse of the life of the crew, though it does not answer all the questions. According to one account they were not a very good crew anyway. When the Admiral ordered some of them to go to one side to right the capsizing they disobeyed, and Carew, in almost his last words, called out to a passing ship that 'he had a sorte of knaves whom he could not rule'. But that was written by Carew's biographer 30 years later and may well be a slander on the dead men.[42] The 179 skeletons recovered suggest that the crew were generally young, including one child, seventeen adolescents under 18, 54 young adults under 30, fifteen in middle age by Tudor standards, and only one man over about 40. Some of them were archers, identifiable by *os acromiale*, the changes in the bones their profession caused. Others were gunners, who developed premature spinal lesion due to the heavy nature of their work. Though there was a barber-surgeon on board, his skills were limited, and the numerous injuries and illnesses of the crew suggest that their life was not without suffering and pain; injuries included three broken noses, three broken ankles and fourteen fractured skulls. Despite their youth, 84% of them had had at least one tooth extracted, as that was the only form of dentistry available. Others bore the pain of cavities, without having the teeth extracted.

We know practically nothing about the inner life or daily routine of the ship, or of any other Tudor warship. We do know that orders were conveyed by an early version of the boatswain's call, though in those days it was carried and used by captains and masters as well. We know little about sleeping arrangements, except for a few cabins that were occupied by the carpenter, barber-surgeons, gunners and the pilot. The crew had a diet of salt beef, pork, peas and ship's biscuit, which they mostly ate from wooden bowls. If they used spoons they were probably made from horn, as few have survived. Each seaman probably carried his own knife for work as well as for eating, and more than 50 of these survive. There is no evidence that they ate at tables, but they may have sat on their sea chests. They drank mostly beer, often out of wooden tankards. Some of the men were supplied with white or green coats for parade purposes, but nothing of these has survived. Leather jerkins were common, in many different styles with no sign of any uniformity. Most of them must have worn shoes, for 157 of these have been found. Only a few were of the low-cut pattern that might have been worn by officers on dress occasions. The rest were of the common high-throated, slip-on type, practical footwear for most manual workers of the day. Off duty the men fished and played backgammon, or nine-men's morris, or dice. There is no evidence that they gambled, and the amount of money found on board was quite small for the size of the community – often it was an almost cashless society on board ship.[43]

Hawkins' Reforms

Several small wars with France followed over the next decades, but by the last quarter of the century that country was torn apart by wars of religion, while England, despite some Catholic opposition, was now firmly under the control of Queen Elizabeth I. In the 1560s the government had evidently made careful plans for naval mobilisation. Forms of warrants were drawn up, to be sent to the constables of the different areas in the event of war. The royal commissioners were to issue proclamations to them to 'charge all mariners and seafaring men within your precinct or liberty to appear before me tomorrow by 8 of the clock before noon; to view and take up (the muster seen) such men as shall be thought meet for her service presently to be done'. Tables were compiled to show the distance, and therefore the rate of conduct money, from each port to Chatham or Deptford. An itinerary was drawn up for the prestmaster, giving 'The ways to travel into the west parts along the sea coast from town to town, village to village with the Queens commission for the presting of mariners for the service of Her Majesty's ships as afore is written, from London and so forth.' A press warrant was to be given to each of the prested mariners –

'This shall be to require and also in the Queen's Majesty's name do charge and command all you whose names be here underwritten that you do immediately repair to Chatham in Kent, and there to present yourselves before the officers of Her Highness's ships, who will place you as it shall seem good unto them.'[44]

Elizabeth's navy remained mostly in harbour, while merchantmen and privateers expanded their horizons, coming into conflict with the Spanish empire in America.

The fleet was reformed under the leadership of Sir John Hawkins, who became Treasurer of the Navy in 1572, bringing a great wealth of nautical

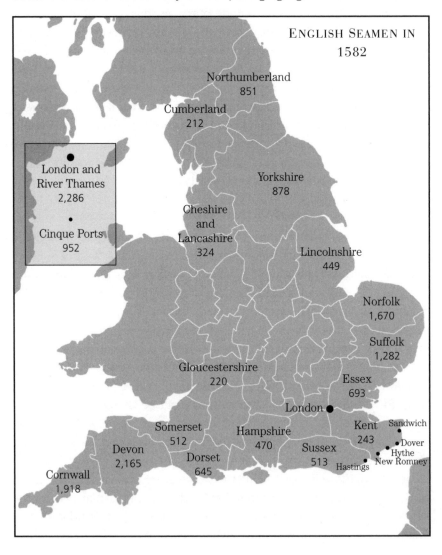

ENGLISH SEAMEN IN
1582

Northumberland
851

Cumberland
212

Yorkshire
878

London and
River Thames
2,286

Cinque Ports
952

Cheshire
and
Lancashire
324

Lincolnshire
449

Norfolk
1,670

Suffolk
1,282

Gloucestershire
220

Essex
693

London

Kent
243

Sandwich

Dover

Hythe

New Romney

Somerset
512

Hampshire
470

Sussex
513

Hastings

Devon
2,165

Dorset
645

Cornwall
1,918

and tactical knowledge gained in his unofficial brushes with the Spanish, as well as considerable administrative skill. He promoted a new kind of fighting ship, relatively low out of the water and with yet more emphasis on gun power than than on boarding. The role of the soldier at sea was further diminished, and England needed her seamen as never before. The Dutch revolted against Spanish rule and were supported by the English state. After a slow build up, largely due to the Queen's reluctance to involve herself in expensive projects, war between England and Spain began in 1585, during which Sir Francis Drake 'singed the King of Spain's beard', by attacking his ships at Cadiz in 1587, and Phillip II of Spain began to prepare his great Armada for the invasion of England.

The English naval administration had taken pains to find the seamen, and record their numbers and places of abode. By a survey of 1582, which was not completely out of date by 1588, England was found to have 1484 master mariners, 11,515 seamen, 2,299 fishermen and 957 Thames wherrymen, a total of 16,255 who were eligible for impressment into the navy. The government's powers over them had been clarified by an act of 1562, which extended the act of 1439, on the presting of soldiers: 'And where doubt has heretofore been, whether the statute in the 18th year of the reign of King Henry VI, heretofore made against soldiers retained which desert from their captains without license, did or ought to extend to mariners and gunners serving on the seas, taking wages of the King and Queen of this realm ... hereafter shall extend, as well to all and every mariner or gunner having taken or shall take prest or wages to serve the Queen's majesty ... as the same did or doth any soldier.'[45] This was a clear enough statement of the state's power to impose discipline on seamen after they had accepted an imprest; but the power to make them take the imprest in the first place still rested in common law, as it always had.

Hawkins' administration made sure that sea service would not be too unpopular. In 1585 he successfully argued for both a reduction in the numbers of seaman required for each ship and for an increase in pay:

> By this means Her Majesty's ships would be furnished with able men, such as can make shift for themselves, keep themselves clean without vermin or noisomeness ... The ships would be able to continue longer in the service that they should be appointed to, and would be able to carry victuals for a longer time. There is no captain or master exercised in service but would undertake with more courage any enterprise with 150 able men than with 300 of tag and rag, and assure himself of better success.[46]

The basic wage of an able seaman was increased to 10/- a month. The rules for manning were set forth, based on the size of the ship rather than the needs of the armament:

> For service in warlike manner the ship is to be rated by her tonnage in dead weight, and to allow for every 5 tons 3 men, of which number the ⅙ part to be soldiers, and the ½ part of the rest gunners, the residue mariners.
> That is to say, for a ship of 500 tons:
> Soldiers, 100
> Gunners, 28
> Mariners, 172.[47]

THE *GOLDEN LION*

On board ship, things did not always go smoothly. *Golden Lion* was part of Drake's fleet of 25 ships for the attack on Cadiz in 1587. *Golden Lion's* captain, William Borough, complained that Drake was too autocratic and took little heed of the advice of his captains; Borough was supplanted by John Marchant, but he remained on board. There were some doubts about the quality of the officers and crew. It was claimed that 'not a man in the gunner room was of any skill and knowledge', while the ship's company was made up of 'fishermen and simple fellows of little value and easily to be led'.[48] On 27 May the ship left the fleet with the pinnace *Spy* to investigate a strange sail, which turned out to be a barque from Dorset. Marchant ordered the spritsail taken in so that the ship could rejoin the fleet and the master, William Bigatt, went forward to set the crew to do it. He 'called unto the companye as yt is the use of sea menn for to doe'. He got no answer but assumed they would get on with it and went aft. After a while he went forward again and found it had not been done. He called Quartermaster John Terrye to the mast and asked why. 'He answered me that the companie said theye would not take yt in. No! said I, what is the cawse? Whoe be they that they saye they will not? He answered, they all in generall saye soe.'[49]

At this point the crew produced a letter to Marchant, 'as you are a man and beare the name of captayne over us':

> let us not be spoiled for want of foode, for our allowaunce is so smale we are not able to lyve any longer of it; for when three or foure were wonte to take a charge in ahnde, nowe tenne at the least, by reason of our weake victuallinge and filthie drinck, is scarce able to discharge it, and yet growe rather weaker and weaker ...
> For what is a piece of Beefe of halfe a pounde amonge foure men to dynner or halfe a drye stockfish for foure days in the weeke, anod nothing ells to helpe withal – Yea, wee have helpe, a little Beveredge worse than pompe water.

Clearly the crew did not believe that the fact of being pressed into the navy eliminated their rights – 'Wee were preste by her Ma [jesty's] presse to have her allowaunce, and not to be thus dealt withal, you make no men of us, but beastes.' Furthermore, because of the lack of food their fighting capability had declined since the attack on Cadiz:

> Our hartes were then so boldened and our stomackes so coragiouslye bent, that if theye had byn tenne to one we rather had wished to fighte than to goo to dynner. But nowe, most unfortunate and unluckie chaunce fallen amongst us by the weakeninge of our [limbs], and feblenes of our bodyes, we are not able to abyde the force of them as nowe, and thoughe they be but one to one, the more is our greife.[50]

Marchant came on deck and ordered the crew to strike the sails, but they took up positions on the masts and yards and refused to move. He approached the helmsman, Nathaniel Crowe, and ordered him to alter course. Crowe replied that 'there was such a press of his company that he could not stir the same',[51] though he later claimed that was a joke; in any case, Captain Marchant was put on board *Spy*, and *Golden Lion* set course for home. It was never quite established whether Borough was behind the mutiny or whether the crew's grievances were genuine and the mutiny was spontaneous. But it was not just a lower-deck affair. Though Crowe emerged as one of the ringleaders, it was supported by gunners and quartermasters, and the new commanders had the skill to navigate the ship home.

FIGHTING THE ARMADA

Mobilisation against the Armada began in October 1587, with a 'general stay … of all vessels able to cross the seas, to be employed for Her Majesty's service as occasion shall require'.[52] The vice admirals of the various counties were ordered to raise specific numbers of mariners, and even the merchant captains in the employ of the crown had some powers of impressment – 'A placard of assistance for Captain Bullingham to imprest and take up mariners, sailors and men for the service of these ships that were set [forth] by the merchant adventurers.'[53] The old system of naval recruiting was at its best in 1588. Morale was high, and there was a sense that this was a national rather than a dynastic war. For once the threat of an invasion from Scotland was removed, for the Scots had had their own Reformation and, despite their many differences with the English, were not likely to support a Catholic invasion. In this war the navy was to become the main defence of the country for the first time. As early as 1570 one Montgomery had written (with geographical inaccuracy) that 'this isle of England, being environed with the sea and having on every side good ports and landing places, of safety ought to be defended hereafter, that is to say with ships and blockhouses.'[54]

There was no great difficulty in raising the men, and Howard of Effingham, the Lord High Admiral, was pleased with their quality. In May 1588 he wrote, 'My good Lord, there is here the gallantest company of captains, soldiers and mariners that I think was ever seen in England.'[55] In July, on the eve of battle, he reported, 'I never saw nobler minds than be here [in our] forces.'[56] He was equally satisfied with the quantities of men. When Sir George Carey sent him a shipload of mariners and soldiers, 'he returned them to me this afternoon with great thanks, willing the captain to tell me that he had as many men as he desired or could well use'.[57] The fleet went on to defeat the Spanish Armada, though the protagonists of gunnery had wildly exaggerated their case, and storms did far more damage to the enemy ships than did the English guns.

But by the end of the year the defects of the system were beginning to become plain. Even as he was praising the quality of his men in 1588, Howard added, 'it were pity they should lack meat, when they are so desirous to spend [i.e., expend] their lives in Her Majesty's service.'[58] By August supplies were falling drastically short. According to Howard, 'Sickness and mortality begins wonderfully to grow amongst us; and it is a most pitiful sight to see, here at Margate, how the men, having no place to receive them here, die in the streets ... It is like enough the like infection will grow throughout the most part of our fleet; for they have been so long at sea and have so little shift of apparel, and so few places to provide them of such wants, and no money wherewith to buy it, for some have been – yea the most part — these eight months at sea ... Good my lord, let mariners be prest and sent down as soon as may be; and money to discharge those that be sick here.'[59] As well as disease, discontent began to spread among the seamen as their pay was delayed. The Queen's treasury had been put under considerable strain. After the windfall from the monasteries had been exhausted, the Tudor state did not have the financial resources to prosecute a hard and long war without subjecting its seamen to great hardship. But Drake and Hawkins did set up the Chatham Chest, which was to receive 6d a month (the 'seamen's sixpences') from all English sailors and use the money to support those who were injured or disabled, while a small naval hospital was founded at Chatham to support ten disabled men.

FIGHTING A LONG WAR

Despite the English success against the Armada, war went on for the rest of Elizabeth's reign, for more than fifteen years. Year by year fleets were sent out, and year by year the quality and morale of the crews became worse. The first effect was to teach the most qualified seamen to avoid the royal service – a lesson they would not forget over the centuries. According to Sir Walter Raleigh, writing early in the next century, 'many times they go with great grudging to serve in His Majesty's ships, as if they were to be slaves in the galleys, for so much do they stand in fear of penury and hunger, the case being clean contrary in all merchants ships.'[60] Furthermore, the actual system of impressment began to break down, with allegations of corruption. According to Raleigh, 'As concerning the musters and presses for sufficient mariners to serve in his majesty's ships, either the care therein is very little, or the bribery is very great; so that of all other shipping his majesty's are ever the worst manned ... it is grown a proverb among the sailors, that the muster masters do carry the best and ablest men in their pockets.'[61] In 1597 the Earl of Essex wrote about 'the monstrous abuses of the press masters, that furnished us with men of all occupations, some of whom did not know a rope and were never at sea, and let all the good men go at 20/- a piece'.[62] Officers complained of 'men unserviceable taken up by the press masters in mariners clothes, that know not one rope in the ship, yet all the ships are so ill manned that if here and at Plymouth we be not better supplied, we shall scarce know how to sail the Queen's ships.'[63] Even the seamen who were recruited were prone to desertion. In 1602, William Monson complained, 'it is an incredible thing to inform your honours of the number of sailors that are run away since our coming home.'[64] He suggested some measures against this, and wrote to 'the chief officers of the towns where any presses have been that if they find any prest men returned from Her Majesty's ships without a discharge under my hand, that they shall apprehend him and cause him to be conveyed to the gaol, to be tried according to the statute'. The royal orders became more strict and applied to a wider range of men – in 1599 mariners from 16 to 60, instead of 18 to 50, were called, and were 'charged upon pain of death to make their present repair unto Chatham'. Each vice admiral was 'to appoint some discreet and trusty persons to come in their company, to hasten them in coming hither, and see that none of them do run away'.[65]

Once the men were on board there was often tension between the different parts of the crew, and in 1589 captains were ordered to have 'especial regard that no contempt be suffered between the mariners, soldiers, or companies'.[66] But the position was far better than in Spanish ships, where, according to Hawkins:

> Their soldiers watch and ward, and their officers, in every ship round, as if they were on shore; this is the only task they undergo, except cleaning their arms, wherein they are not over-curious. The gunners are exempted from all labour and care, except about the artillery ... the mariners are but slaves to the rest, to moil and to toil day and night ... and not suffered to sleep or harbour themselves under the decks. For in fair or foul weather, in storms, sun, or rain, they must pass void of covert or succour.[67]

This was very different from Drake's ideal that the crew should 'all be of a company' and that gentlemen must 'haul and draw with the mariner'.

In 1591 the Queen tried an older expedient, by summoning the ports to provide ships fully rigged and manned. In reply, the government received a catalogue of excuses – 'The port of Padstow can by no means perform, having no ship or bark exceeding 23 tons.' The mayor and aldermen of Bridgewater replied, 'Our town depending heretofore altogether on trade, is at this present greatly impoverished, so that we are not of ability to do that which we would in regard of Her Majesty's service.' 'Though all for the most part willing, yet being all poor they do stand so much upon their inability as that out of them all not above £50 can be drawn ... The charge for a ship for that service cannot be less than £1000, which will be too burdensome for the port of Yarmouth to undergo.'[68] Clearly this was not a very satisfactory way of fitting out a fleet.

One innovation of this period that had a longstanding effect was the introduction of the hammock, which was first found in use by the Caribs in the West Indies. A warrant of 1597 authorised payment for 300 bolts of canvas 'to making hanging cabons or beddes ... for the better preservation of their health'.[69] It is not clear where seamen slept before that: probably on straw palliasses, perhaps contained within wooden boxes. Hammocks were issued only between two men and only on ships on foreign service until well into the next century, but they provided a simple solution to sleeping large numbers of men in cramped conditions.

HAWKINS IN THE *DAINTY*

Sir Richard Hawkins' voyage of 1593–4 in *Dainty* provides an illustration of relations between captain and crew. He was a good navigator but perhaps less ruthless than his father Sir John, or Drake himself. On the passage out of the Thames there was a minor accident and his men were 'so daunted that they would not proceede with the Ship any further'. Hawkins observed, 'Mariners are like a stiffe necked Horse, which taking the bridle betwixt his teeth, forceth his Rider to what list mauger his will: so they hauing once concluded, and resolved, are with great difficultie brought to yeelde to the raynes of reason.'[70] When they were given shore leave in Plymouth, they behaved like sailors of all ages:

> And so began to gather my companie aboord, which occupied my good friends and the Iustices of the Towne two days, and forced vs to search all Lodgings, Tavernes and Ale-Houses. (for some would ever be taking their leaue and never depart:) some drinke themselves so drunke, that except they were carried aboord, they of themselues were not able to goe one steppe: others knowing the necessitie of the time, fayned themselues sick; others, to be indepted to their Hostes, and forced me to ransome them; one his Chest: another, his Sword; another, his shirts; another, his Carde and Instruments for Sea.[71]

For as Hawkins observed, it was 'a common calamatie among the ordinary sort of Mariners, to spend their thrift on the shore, and to bring to sea no more Cloaths than they haue backs'.[72]

Once at sea, Hawkins took good care to keep his men occupied during what he called 'an idle Navigation'. In addition to the normal system of two watches, 'the halfe to worke whilest the others slept, and take rest', he had three working days,

> which appertayned to each to be employed in this manner: the one for the vse and clensing of their Armes, the other for roomeging [rummaging] making of Sayles, Netting, Decking, and Defences for our Shippes: and the third, for clensing their bodies, mending and making their apprarell, and necessaries ...[73]

Approaching the Equator, his men showed symptoms of scurvy, 'a kind of dropsie'. He knew of many theories about the disease – 'The cause of this sicknes, some attribute to sloath; some to conceite.' He favoured the idea that it was caused by excessive heat among men from colder climates, but in fact he was close to the real solution – 'sower Oranges and Lemmons', which he issued on occasion. Hawkins took better care of his men than Drake and suffered far fewer deaths from illness. In order to reduce the effects of cold nights, he issued his men with 'Rugge-gowns' or warm coats. There was only enough for one watch, but 'he which watched had ever the gowne: for they which watched not, were either in their Cabins, or vnder the decke, and so needed them not'.

Against his better judgment, Hawkins was persuaded by the master to let pitch be heated in the galley. It caught fire and a seaman wearing gloves lifted the pot off the fire but was soon forced to drop it, spreading the burning pitch on the deck. Hawkins was roused from his cabin and ordered the men to tie ropes to the gowns and cast them in the sea, then haul them up and dowse the fire.[74] Giving thanks for their deliverance, he persuaded the men to give up swearing, 'which amongst the common sort of Mariners, and Sea-faring men, is too ordinarily abused'. He had a small cane made, which was to be kept by the last man caught swearing, until he could find another to pass it on to. The man who held it in the evening or at morning prayer was to have three blows with it from the captain or master.[75]

At last they encountered a much superior Spanish force and a long fight began: 'the fight continued so hot on both sides, that the Artillery and Muskets never ceased playing. Our contraries, towards the euening, determined the third time to lay vs abourd.' The enemy were to 'pay deerely for their rashnesse' and had at least 36 men killed and wounded. But Hawkins' men were worn down – 'In these bourdings, and Skirmishes, diuers of our men were slaine, and many hurt, and my selfe amongst them received six wounds.' Some suggested surrender, but Hawkins, suffering from 'the torment of wounds', made a speech: 'Came we into the South Seas to put out flags of truce?' This rallied the men and,

> they persevered in sustaining the fight, all this night, with the day and night following, and the third day after. In which time the Enemie never left vs, day nor night, beating continually vpon vs, with his great and small shott. Saving that every morning an hower before breake of day, hee edged a little from vs, to breath, and to remedie such defects as were amisse; as also to consult what they should do the day and night following.

By that time 19 men out of 75 had been killed, and nearly 40 wounded, so surrender was inevitable though sheer exhaustion.

THE END OF THE WARS

Back home, the seaman was no longer the hero of the hour. In 1592 his status was so low that that it was considered useless to put them on oath, as 'we hold it lost labour and offence to God'.[76] By the time Elizabeth died in 1603, virtually no goodwill remained between the naval administration and the seamen. The former claimed that the seamen were feckless, greedy and treacherous; the seamen knew from long experience that the crown was a bad paymaster and a poor provider. Seamen's wages did not keep up with the rates paid by privateers, and good seamen had little wish to serve in the Royal Navy. The problem was essentially caused by lack of money, and none of Elizabeth's successors were to be much happier in that respect. But Elizabeth's own navy was very small by later standards – 42 ships at most, compared with a thousand in the days of Nelson. The problem would become far greater in later years.

King James VI of Scotland inherited the English throne on the death of Queen Elizabeth in 1603. Though Scotland remained a separate state, with its own parliament and a tiny navy, it was now accurate to talk of an 'island kingdom'. There were to be plenty of Scottish revolts over the next century and a half, but the island was more united than ever before, and this, of course, increased the importance of the English navy. The new King, however, was a peace-loving man, and soon ended the war with Spain. He carefully avoided too much involvement in foreign wars for many years, and allowed the navy to fall into decline for the first fifteen years of his reign. He did, however, build one very large ship, *Prince Royal*, which was in some senses the first three-decker.

Peace did not necessarily mean an end to impressment in the seventeenth century, for kings were starved of money and tried to do things as cheaply as possible. In 1604 seamen were pressed to convey the new ambassador to Spain, and twelve more were taken up to man a ship carrying a gift of horses to the Spanish king. In the same year the mariners of Kent were called to go to Chatham for one day, to put on a show for the King's visit. They were to turn up 'in their best and most decent apparel', in order to 'man the ships and row His Majesty on board'. They were to be given board and victuals, but there is no mention of pay. They were to return home the same night.[77]

While the English navy was weak there was an increase in piracy, and occasionally the King tried to do something about it, still with a liberal use of his right to impress. In 1613, for example, the Mayor and officials of Exeter were ordered to impress ships, mariners, stores and other necessities for the suppression of pirates. Instead of payment they were to be given the right to keep the goods seized from the pirates.[78] These methods had little success, and corsairs, based at Dunkirk and in North Africa, continued to make the Channel unsafe throughout the first four decades of the century.

In 1618 James appointed a Commission of Enquiry to reform his navy, and under the Duke of Buckingham several new ships were built. It was assumed that even in peacetime volunteers were not likely to come forward for the navy, and impressment was still normal. Among the charges 'to employ a sufficient guard upon all our coasts in these peaceable times' was £36 for 'prest, conduct and presting charges of 240 men to be taken at London and places near Chatham at 3s the man'.[79]

The early Stuart monarchy, as represented by James I and his son Charles I, found impressment a very useful tool, for the two reigns shared two essential characteristics: the poverty of the crown, and the monarch's belief in the Divine Right of Kings. Already by the end of Elizabeth's reign the royal coffers were nearly empty, and the wealth of the early Tudor years had long since evaporated. Crown lands had been sold, and the sovereign's own sources of income were gradually reduced, while price inflation or economic depression continued to erode what was still available. One way round this was to ask Parliament to levy new taxes; but this, of course, conflicted with the Kings' perceptions of their divine right to rule without interference. Relations between King and Parliament declined steadily throughout the period, and the crown tried to go on without calling a parliament. This meant that they had to revive and use their old feudal rights as far as possible. It also meant that, with some exceptions, their foreign policy was not very aggressive.

Life on Board

There was an increasing tendency to appoint courtiers and noblemen with little sea experience to take command of royal ships, and this was perhaps why a number of nautical dictionaries and reference books were written around 1630. Indeed Nathaniel Boteler's *Dialogicall Discourse Concerning Marine Affaires* takes the form of a dialogue between a newly-appointed Lord High Admiral 'of eminent birth' and an experienced captain.[80] Sir Henry Mainwaring produced a nautical dictionary. John Smith, the founder of Virginia, published his *Sea Grammar* in 1627, though he had less inside knowledge of the King's navy than the others.

Sir William Monson gives us our most detailed picture of life on board ship. Though written in the 1630s, much of his tract refers back to the late Elizabethan period. The main distinction on board was not between the quarterdeck and the lower deck, but between 'abaft' and 'afore the mast'. As Mainwaring put it,

> the whole ship's company is divided, both in respect of the labour and command, into two parts; the boatswain and all the common sailors under his command, to be before the main mast; the Captain, master, master's mate, gunners, quartermasters, trumpeters, &c., to be abaft the mainmast.[81]

Monson provided a list of officers, though he does not use the term in any modern sense, but simply as those who held certain offices, however temporary. Near the bottom was the swabber, who was to 'keep the cabins, and all the rooms of the ship, clean within board'; he was assisted by the liar, the first man caught in a lie each Monday morning, who was to clean the ship 'outboard' – that is, the sanitary waste.[82]

Of the more senior and respected officers, the captains of king's ships (as distinct from privateers) were to be 'gentlemen of countenance and means, maintain their diet at their own charge' – though Monson implied that this was not always the case since Queen Elizabeth's time. The new rank of lieutenant was 'an employment for a gentleman well bred, who knows how to entertain ambassadors, gentleman and strangers when they cone aboard ...'[83] The master, on the other hand, had some experience of 'afore the mast', for according to Monson he 'ought to pass through all the offices and degrees of a ship, before he attain his place of master'. His job was to navigate the ship and to 'oversee carefully such business as concerns the safety of the ship' – raising anchor, tacking and carrying out all difficult manoeuvres. The other officers who lived aft included the surgeon, the purser, the gunner, the trumpeter, the coxswain, the cooper, the corporal and four quartermasters. The latter were responsible for stowing the hold and its effect on the trim of the ship, and for taking charge of the steering during watches. Monson makes the distinction between the 'captain, master, or other chief officer, or any of their lieutenants' on one hand and 'any other inferior officer' on the other; striking anyone in the first group was punishable by death, while striking an inferior officer was only on 'pain of further punishment'.[84]

The boatswain was the only officer who lived among the sailors and had almost certainly risen from their ranks himself. 'As the master is to be abaft the mast so the boatswain, and all the common sailors under his command, are to be afore the mast.'[85] He was allowed to choose several mates to assist him, 'his place being more laborious than one man can perform', though unlike the quartermasters none of them was listed among the officers, and they had no greater share of the prize money than a common seaman. As well as being responsible for the rigging of the ship, the boatswain was the real leader of the crew. He would organise the men in watches and messes, and supervise them, under the master, during difficult manoeuvres.

As the master commands the tacking of the ship, the hoisting or striking the yard, the taking in or putting forth the sails, upon the winding of the master's whistle the boatswain takes it with his, and sets the sailors with courage to do their work, every one of them knowing by their whistle what they are to do.[86]

The boatswain was also a disciplinarian:

He is (in the nature of a Provost Marshal at land) to see all offenders punctually punished, either at the capstan, or by being put in the bilboes, or with the ducking from the main yard-arm; accordingly as they are censured by the Captain, or by a Martial Court.[87]

Besides the boatswain's mates, the petty officers included the yeomen of the tacks and the sheets, who were responsible for seeing that these ropes ran free during difficult manoeuvres such as tacking.[88]

The complement of an individual ship might be decided in one of two ways – by a formula related to its size, such as one man for every four tons, or according to the number and size of her guns – 'some would have this proportion taken to be taken and made considerable to the number and quality of the great guns that the ship is to carry, with an answerable allowance of spare hands for that management of sails.'[89]

One source of tension on board was that the sailors often had more work to do than soldiers: 'Divers sailors ship themselves as soldiers because they will not take their turn at the helm but at their pleasures.'[90] In Elizabethan times the gunners had not regarded themselves as part of the crew at all. 'All these [gunners] refuse to do any labour [apart] from their calling. For, when a captain hath commanded them in time of need, they have detained him in the gun-room prisoner until he hath yielded unto their sea orders.'[91] This was beginning to change, and gunners were more likely to be selected from among the seamen. In battle the separation between the gunners, soldiers and seamen was no longer absolute: 'a man may step from a gun to a rope, or from a rope to use small shot, and the like.[92] Indeed it was the duty of the ship's corporal to 'see that the soldiers and sailors keep their arms neat, clean, and yare, and to teach and exercise them every calm day ...'[93]

CHARACTER

The character of the seaman was described, with slight exaggeration, by Richard Braithwaite in his *Whimzies* of 1631. Since he mostly saw the seaman ashore, he was all too aware of his drunkenness, which he mentioned several times. 'The sea cannot roar more abroad than he within, fire him but with liquor ... He ever takes his worst rest when he goes to bed most sober. He will domineer furiously in the height of his potation, but he is quickly cudgeled out of that humour by the master of the house of correction.' But Braithwaite was aware of his skills, 'for he can spin up a rope like a spider and down again like lightning. The rope is his road, and the topmast his beacon.' He was at home aloft in his ship. 'He partakes much of the chameleon, when he is mounted the top-mast, where the air is his diet-bread.' His clothing was distinctive. 'One would think his body were wounded, for he wears pitch-cloth upon it; but that is invulnerable, unless a bullet casually finds a loophole and that quite rips up his sailcloth.' Without it he looked less impressive: 'What a starveling he is on a frosty morning in his sea-frock which seems as if it were shrunk from him and grown too short, but it will be long enough before he gets another.' He was not too concerned about hygiene. 'He is most constant to his shirt, and other seldom-washed linen.' He was used to bad food, for 'he hath an invincible stomach, which ostrich-like could well-near digest iron'. He could endure discomfort. 'He makes small or no choice of his pallet; he can sleep as well on a sack of pumice as a pillow of down.' He enjoyed the comradeship of the sea. 'He is many times so long on sea, as he forgets his friends by land. Associates he has, and those so constantly cleaving, as one voice commands all. Stars cannot be more faithful in their society than these Hans-kins in their fraternity. They will brave it valiantly when they are ranked together, and relate their adventures with wonderful terror.'

The seaman was, of course, much travelled. 'He has coasted many countries, arrived in sundry havens, sojourned in flourishing cities, and conversed with various sorts of people.' He faced danger all the time. 'Death he has seen in so many shapes, as it cannot amaze him, appear it ever so terrible to him.' 'The breadth of an inch-board is betwixt him and drowning, yet he swears and drinks as deeply as if he were a fathom from it. His familiarity with death and danger hath armed him with a kind of dissolute security against any encounter.' All this made him live for the moment with no thought of the future. 'They sleep without fear of losing what they enjoy; and in enjoying little, they share in the less burden of cares.' 'They taste all waters and all weathers; only the gale of prosperity seldom breathes on their sails; neither care they much for any such companion.' He had scant interest in religion. 'He converseth with the stars, observes their motions, and by them directs his compass. Singular notions derives he from them; meantime he is blind to Him that made them.' As a result, 'In a tempest you shall hear him pray, but so a-methodically as it argues that he is seldom versed in that practice. Fear is the principal motive of his devotion; yet I am persuaded for form's sake, he shows more than he feels.'[94]

ROUTINE

At sea the sailors were divided into two watches, known as starboard and larboard, one commanded by the master himself and the other by his mate. Each period on duty, also known as a watch, usually lasted four hours. The 'watch was set' at eight o'clock in the evening: that is, those off watch were free to go below, to sleep or enjoy some leisure. According to John Smith (who had much less direct experience of warships than the others),

> at six a'clocke sing a Psalme, say a Prayer, and the Master with his side begins the watch. Then all the rest may doe what they will till midnight; and then his Mate with his Larboard men, with a Psalme and a Prayer, releeves them till four in the morning. And so from eight to twelve each other, except some flaw of winde come – some storm or gust – or some accident that requires the helpe of all hands, which commonly, after such good cheere, in most voyages doth happen.[95]

During the watch the men had to 'trim sails, pump and do all duties for four hours'.[96] Every skilled seaman was expected to take a turn to steer the ship under the quartermaster. Larger ships steered by means of the whipstaff, which meant that the helmsman himself had a very restricted view. This was not a problem in the open sea when the ship was steered by the compass, but in other cases the quartermaster's orders were vital. He would use terms like 'port the helm', 'starboard the helm', 'amidship' and 'right the helm'. But it was best not to interfere too much

> in chases or in narrow channels, where the course lies not directly upon a point of the compass, there the master, mate or some other standing aloft doth give direction to him at the helm and this we call *conding* or *cunning*. Sometimes he who conds the ship will be speaking to him at the helm at every little yaw; which the seafaring men love not, as being a kind of disgrace to their steerage; then in mockage they will say, *sure the channel is narrow he conds so thick* ...[97]

Normally there were two quartermasters in each watch, and they took it in turns 'to keep a station upon the quarterdeck or half deck or at the round-house door, or wheresover they may best look to him at the helm and direct him'.[98]

The crew was divided into messes of four men each for victualling purposes, though this might be increased if food were short, for example in 1589 when 'the whole country hereabout is by no means able to afford this great army so much victuals as daily in the same is spent, it is therefore thought behoveful that the whole companies, of mariners as well as soldiers, do sit six of them to every one mess ...[99]

The duty of the ship's cook was to

> dress meat according to the number of the messes of men he hath aboard. And this meat he is to receive from the steward by tale, and some of it by weight; and, being cooked, he is to deliver it to such persons as are chosen by every mess for the fetching of it away from him.[100]

Every man and boy was allowed a pound of bread every day, with a pound of beef or pork. The others were fish days, in which each mess was allowed 'a side of salt fish, either haberdine, ling or cod' along with seven ounces of butter and fourteen ounces of cheese, except on Fridays when there was no cheese. Every man and boy was allowed a gallon of beer a day, a quart each in the morning, at dinner, in the afternoon and at supper.[101]

By this time most of the men slept in hammocks, but cabins were not unknown, and Boteler complained:

> And though the common seaman liketh it well enough, as coveting store of cabins, yet are these cabins no better than nasty holes, which breed sickness, and in a fight are very dangerous, as causing much spoil with their splinters; so that in all long voyages, especially to the southwards, the lodging of the common men in hammocks is far more wholesome and preferable.[102]

If they did have cabins, it is likely that they were accommodated in pairs in a tiny space. Smith advised, 'care should bee had that there be not two Comrades upon one watch, because they have the more roome in their Cabbins to rest.'[103] In 1635, Admiral the Earl of Lindsey ordered that 'no bed of straw be kept on board in battle'.[104]

In harbour each watch was divided in two so that only a quarter of the men were on duty at any given moment. Shore leave was highly restricted, and in the 1630s captains were 'peremptorily commanded not to suffer any of their men to go to the shore, whilst the ships lay in the harbour or near the shore, which hath sometimes been two or three months together and more ...' This was intended to prevent the men from deserting, but according to Boteler it had the opposite effect,

> by reason of many shore boats that haunted the ships lying so near the shore, and often stole aboard them in the night, in despite all the care to the contrary, wherein the mariners stole passage to the shore even from their very watches, and being thus gotten thither, and having spent the little money they carried with them, they began (as they grew sober) to be so terrified with an apprehension of

the punishment which they expected to undergo if they returned to the ships from whence they came, that they utterly forsook the service …[105]

Monson advised seamen going on shore leave to mend their ways, more in hope than expectation:

> But whether it be the sea that works contrary effects to the land, or whether it be a liberty you feel ashore after you have been penned up in ships, like birds in a cage, or untamed horses when they are let loose; certain it is, neither birds nor horses can shew more extravagant lewdness, more dissolute wildness, and less fear of God, than your carriage discovers when you come ashore and cast off the command your superior officers had over you.

However, he had to accept that, 'He that could as easily reduce the ordinary seamen to civility and good behaviour ashore, as to be under the government of a discreet commander at sea, were more than a man.'[106]

The work of the seaman became even more complicated with bigger ships – *Sovereign of the Seas* of 1637 had 10,998 fathoms or 12½ miles of rigging. More than 230 different ropes were listed, most of which were at least duplicated on both sides of the ship. Others, such as shrouds, were used in larger numbers. Sizes ranged from an inch to sixteen inches in diameter, and that did not include the anchor cables or the gun tackles.[107] But it was not just a question of skill. 'The bred seaman is for the most part hardy and undaunted, ready to adventure any desperate action, good or bad; as prodigal of his blood, into whatever humour his commander will draw him unto if he loves him or fears him.'[108] Yet he was still seen as a child, and Monson, among others, referred to those who had not risen to petty officers as 'younkers', one stage above the ship's boys.[109]

The life of the early Stuart seaman featured many elements that would be familiar to later generations – a division between fore and aft, working in four-hour watches, sleeping in hammocks, collecting food for each mess from the cook, eating salt beef, pork and ship's biscuit, very restricted shore leave, desertion and so on. But one feature that differed quite considerably was punishment. There was no mention of flogging in the works of the 1620s and '30s. Instead, there was punishment at the capstan, which could be used as a form of torture. A capstan bar was thrust through the man's sleeves and he had a weighted basket hung about his neck, 'In which posture he is to continue until he be made either to confess some plot or crime whereof he is pregnantly suspected, or that he have suffered such condign punishment as he is sentenced to undergo …' Alternatively he could have his ankles locked in the bilboes, 'a kind of stocks made for that purpose, the which are more or less heavy and pinching, as the quality of the offence is found to be, upon open proof.' More serious was ducking from the yardarm, in which the man was dropped into the sea up to three times, 'and if the offence be very foul he is also drawn under the keel of the ship, which is termed keel raking.' For even more serious crimes, 'in capital causes, such as murders, mutinies and the like, these punishments are so transcended that instead of a ducking at the main yard there is hanging to death executed in the same place.'[110]

IN BATTLE

Battle tactics still looked back to the days of the Armada, with the ship being turned round to bring groups of guns to bear. The process is described by Boteler:

> In the first place, your chase guns are to be given; and coming up somewhat nearer, your whole broadside in order, as your pieces will be brought to bear. This done, you are to run a good berth ahead or beyond your enemy's ship, if it may be, and then edge up into the wind; and to lay your foresail and main topsail (which are called the fighting sails) on the backstays.

This was followed by a second charge:

> you are to edge in with him, and in your way, if you find any store of men upon his decks, you may give a volley of small shot as before; and presently upon it (being gotten up side by side with your enemy ship) you are to fire your bow pieces upon her, and then your full broadside; and letting your ship fall off with the wind, late fly with your chase [bow] pieces, all of them and so your weather broadside The which being done, bring your ship about, that your stern pieces may also be given.[111]

After that, the ship would withdraw to load and come back for another attack and finally board the enemy once his strength had been depleted.

These tactics were beginning to change, however. Boarding was no longer considered viable, and in 1628 the Commissioners of Trinity House reported,

> As for boarding a king's ship, the only case is that of the *Revenge* in the time of queen [Elizabeth]; the enemy lost then as many as 100 men and at last gained her, only 'by composition.' Seamen in merchant ships fear not boarding, even though the crew number only 40 or 50. The king's ships, with 200 or 250 men and well furnished have much less cause for fear.[112]

At the same time there was a silent revolution in gunnery during the first half of the seventeenth century. A very simple device, the train tackle, was fitted to the rear of the gun to restrain it while reloading, and it became much easier to keep up a constant fire. It was also possible to aim the guns to a certain extent by pulling the tackles on either side. Mainwaring wrote:

> Bowse is a word they use when they would have the men pull together, and is chiefly used by gunners when they haul upon their tackles to thrust a piece out at a port. They will cry *Bowse hoa*; that is, pull more upon the tackle, and then they know to pull together; and also when there is occasion to pull more upon one tackle than the other, they will say, *Bowse upon* that tackle.[113]

All this meant that more seamen were deployed on the guns in action to aim and to keep up the rate of fire. In 1619 in *Speedwell*, 18 gunners and 48 others were allocated to the great guns, a total of 66, compared with 50 to sail the ship, 50 on the small-arms and 24 others, so that less than a third of the crew were on the guns.[114] By 1633 *Vanguard* had 130 men out of a complement of 250 with the 'gunner and his party', with five in the powder room. There were 46 men with the 'boatswain and his company', mostly to handle the sails, plus four more on the steering. Forty-five men, presumably soldiers, formed the small-arms party, while the carpenter led a group of six to carry out repairs. The rest of the company included the captain and lieutenant, the master and his mate, and stewards, cooks, surgeons and trumpeters.[115]

At the same time there was a change in ship design, as insecure monarchs such as Charles I vied with one another to build the most

CREWS OF SELECTED SHIPS, 1599–1800

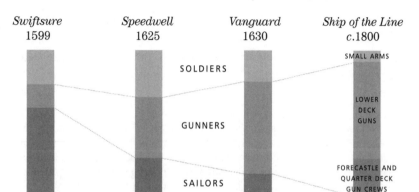

prestigious ship. His most famous, *Sovereign of the Seas* of 1637, was the first full three-decker and the first to carry 100 guns. This could only be done by cramming in as many as possible, using space that had been reserved for small-arms parties in the past. It was pointed out that such large ships would find it difficult to turn in battle and would have to continue with the guns on the same side, while only a small proportion of them, if any, would fire fore and aft. At the other end of the scale, there was a demand for small ships to fight pirates and privateers; these needed to be long and narrow, and less able to turn. More or less by accident, ships would come to rely more and more on the broadside and on the rate of fire of its individual guns, which would depend very much on the skills and enthusiasm of the seamen.

THE CADIZ EXPEDITION

Apart from a few expeditions against pirates, the navy remained at peace until near the end of James's reign, when war broke out with Spain. Serious hostilities began soon after his death in 1625, and a major fleet was fitted out for the first time in many years. It was not difficult to find the seamen, for the government had kept up regular censuses of the coastal counties; in 1618, for example, a very detailed list of the men of South Devon had been drawn up.[116] Persuading them to serve in the navy was rather more difficult. A proclamation, first issued in 1623 and reissued in 1625, urged that 'all such persons having our prest money given or tendered unto them, do dutifully and reverently receive the same and repair on board our ships at the times to them assigned'.[117] In March 1625 there was a proclamation 'for better furnishing the navy and shipping of the realm with able and skillful mariners, forbidding all shipowners to employ seamen who have entered foreign service, disobeyed the imprest, or abandoned the service'.[118] Ships from the West Country were forbidden to leave for Newfoundland until the King had found sufficient men for his own fleet.[119]

When Charles I came to the throne in 1625 he began to take more active steps in a war with Spain, planning an attack on Cadiz. The Duke of Buckingham, Lord High Admiral, sent instructions out to the constables of the various towns. They were 'to warn and summon all mariners and seafaring men, as well fathers and masters as sons and servants, to appear personally before you at a certain day and place'. Based on this, each constable was to deliver 'A roll or book of the proper and surnames of all the mariners and seafaring men dwelling or abiding within the several precincts' and send it to the Navy Office. Any seamen who failed to appear were 'to answer their contempt'. The constable was to impress 'Such only as are seamen or fisherman, or that are practised in seafaring, and no unskilful, weak, decrepit, impotent, maimed or unfit persons'. He was to 'take but one or two men at most out of the company of any small bark, and generally to use such discretion in the choice that His Majesty may be served, and yet trade and fishing as little hindered as may be'. Fathers were to be held responsible for the conduct of their sons, and masters for their servants. A list was to be drawn up of the pressed men, 'describing therein the persons by their age, stature, complexion or other pregnant marks'.[120]

Despite this, there were plenty of complaints about the quality of the men. One official wrote: 'The number of lame, impotent and unable men unfit for actual service is very great.'[121] Even before the fleet set out, disease was rife among both sailors and soldiers. The ships had been neglected for years, and hulls and fittings were in terrible condition. The expedition, which attempted an attack on the Spanish port of Cadiz, became one of the greatest disasters in the history of the British navy.

It was disease, incompetence and bad provisions that caused the problem, rather than enemy action. The military side of the expedition was badly handled, while sickness almost destroyed the crews of some of the ships – *Anne Royal* had 130 dead and 160 sick out of a total crew of 800. One of the commanders wrote of 'the greatest part of the seamen being sick or dead, so that few of them have sufficient men to bring their ships about', and said there was 'a miserable infection among them, and they die very fast'.[122]

The fleet returned, and a series of mutinies began. It was reported, 'The mariners prest for Cadiz, and others retained in the Kings ships, for that they never received their pay, came in troops to London at divers several times, and threatened the Duke of Buckingham, and once they made an attempt against his gate to pull it down, but at last they were pacified, and had their pay out of the loan of subsidy money, and discharged.' But this was early in 1627, more than a year after the expedition.[123] The political credibility of the government had sunk, and the seaman's reluctance to serve the King was greater than ever before.

Later in 1627 there was another expedition, to support the Protestants of La Rochelle, who were in revolt against the French king. The ramshackle machinery was put in motion again, with equally depressing results – 3,800 seamen were raised, many died, all were paid late or not at all, and hundreds faced starvation. After the return of the expedition one captain wrote of the 'miserable condition of the men, who have neither shoes, stockings nor rags to cover their nakedness ... all the seas are so infectious that I fear if we hold the sea one month we shall not bring men enough home to moor their ships'.[124] In 1628 there was an attempt to send out another expedition, and it was said that 'the mariners being at Plymouth and almost ready to set to sea, being unpaid nine months, and seeing their best victuals sold away, they began to mutiny, in which mutiny there were three slain, and after the tumult was somewhat appeased many of them ran away'.[125] Dawtrey Cooper, the captain of *Pelican,* wrote:

> And whereas the King's allowance is 4 gallons of beer a day to a mess, we have ever since the 25 September put 5 men to 2 gallons a day, and yet they had drank water sooner but for some few prizes which were taken by some of our fleet laden with wine and aquavitye. Besides we had been in much distress for want of victuals had we not been supplied with the victuals that should have gone into Rochell. Likewise our wood by this time was so far spent that in less than a fortnight we must have eaten our meat raw or burnt part of our ships, but it pleased God to provide us wood ... by the wreck of some of our own ships.[126]

It was even worse for the soldiers, as Cooper found when they evacuated La Rochelle:

> So lamentable a spectacle I never beheld till now, for most of those poor men were so starved that they had not the strength to come into the ship but as we handed them in, nor able to stand being there, but lay atop of one another, and as fast as they took in either meat or drink, it went and came for them again in most noisome manner, many of them after dying even with meat in their mouths.[127]

The Duke of Buckingham was assassinated by a disgruntled survivor of the expedition, and with him the aggressive policy ended. Charles's relations with Parliament got even worse, and 1629 he dissolved it and decided to rule without it.

SHIP MONEY

For several years the navy was almost unused, but some kind of force was needed to protect English interests on the seas. Barbary and Dunkirk corsairs continued their raids on shipping and on the coasts, while Dutch fisherman used the areas of the North Sea that the English King claimed as part of his territory. In the absence of any large sums of money, the King decided to revive his feudal prerogatives in order to fit out a fleet. In 1634 he issued 'ship writs', which demanded that each of the larger port towns should fit out and man a quantity of ships of specific sizes. London was to supply a ship of war of 900 tons, 'with 350 men at the least, as well expert masters as very able and skilful mariners', a ship of 800 tons and 260 men, four more of 500 tons and 200 men, and another of 300 tons with 150 men.[128] There was no serious doubt of the sovereign's right to demand this – it had been done by Queen Elizabeth as recently as 1591 – and, despite some grumbling, the fleet was put to sea in 1636.

However there were many difficulties with such an approach. The gap between men of war and merchantmen was continually widening, and Charles was already building his great ship, *Sovereign of the Seas*, with more than 100 guns. Warships were growing in size faster than merchantmen, and it was not easy to find suitable ships among the resources of the port towns – only London actually supplied ships and men in 1635, the other places agreeing to a money payment instead.

In 1636, King Charles extended the policy of issuing 'ship writs' to the inland towns and counties. Recognising that many towns were too small to provide a ship on their own, and that inland places could not easily find ships in any case, he allowed money payment in place of the actual provision of a ship. Thus, for example, Cornwall was to provide a ship of 650 tons and 260 men or a sum of £6,500. Buckinghamshire, an inland county, was to supply one of 450 tons and 180 men or to raise the sum of £4,500.[129] The smaller towns were not given the option of providing a ship: Derby was to pay £175, Hereford £220, Chesterfield £50 and Huntingdon £40, for example.[130] The new policy was not supported by any constitutional precedent. John Hampden, a gentlemen of Buckinghamshire, refused to pay the levy of Ship Money and fought the issue through the courts. Eventually he lost his case by the narrowest of margins, but the issue became a *cause celebre* and stimulated opposition to the King as nothing had done for centuries.

The old method of impressment, relying heavily on local officials such as sheriffs, bailiffs, mayors and constables, had not worked well in the past. None of these men could be expected to have any knowledge of the sea and to be able to pick out good mariners. Even the vice admirals, despite their title, did not necessarily have any great maritime experience. Furthermore, all these officials were locally based and often afraid of upsetting local opinion. They went through the motions of mustering seamen and either made excuses for not finding enough or sent unfit or unskilled men. Charles attempted to move away from the old system. The authority of the local officials was still needed to muster the men, but the actual choice was left to 'prestmasters', experienced seamen, usually boatswains, who were 'chosen of purpose for their long experience at sea, the better to distinguish mariners from others'. They were sent to the various ports to pick out the seamen at muster.[131] Given goodwill on all sides it might have succeeded; but in 1636 neither the seamen nor the local officials wanted to make it work, and the prestmasters proved to be very unsuitable men for the tasks allotted them. The gentry and merchants resented the power given to men of such humble background. There was a universal complaint from captains that 'The making mean prestmasters doth occasion abuses.'[132] The local officers were equally unhappy, and 'the magistrates and gentlemen of quality in many parts found themselves aggrieved to associate with such mean persons as our prestmasters'.[133] This was not helped by the prestmasters themselves, who seem to have let power go to their heads. At Weymouth, Thomas Nash gave the mayor a warrant to assemble all the mariners in the town. Most of the seamen hid themselves, and the mayor was only able to assemble sixteen or seventeen before the Rose and Crown inn. They waited twelve hours, but no prestmaster appeared. The following evening Nash turned up 'much distempered with drink' and got the mayor and constables out of bed. He 'reviled all the constables and the late mayor, and having thus neglected the service, he pressed many insufficient men who afterwards returned'.[134]

On the whole the men sent by the prestmasters were no more suitable than those the local officials had produced. The old officials could be seduced away from their duty to the King by local opinion; the prestmaster was likely to neglect his duty for more straightforward financial incentives. A common seaman would not be able to find enough money to bribe a mayor or a vice admiral, but an ex-boatswain was well within his means, and it was said that the going rate for being passed over at the muster was £1.[135]

The captains of the King's ships complained bitterly about the quality of the men they received. Captain Kirke of *Repulse* stated, 'at his first coming on board he found the ship very ill manned, and enquiring of the men where they had served, they answered that they were pressed upon spite and had never been to sea before.' Captain Carteret said, 'that near a third part of his men had never been at sea in a ship, and of 150 men he could not find 12 (besides officers) able to take their turn at the helm, which he can impute to nothing but the default of the prestmasters.' Captain Rainborough wrote, 'I have heard of many that have taken money to discharge good men that they have prest, and I myself, being once prestmaster for Dorsetshire, had six pieces put into my hand by a man to clear him, yet I made him serve, and was extraordinary railed at because I would not clear men for money'.[136]

Men aboard merchant ships were also impressed. Edward Clark, master of *Indifferent* of Ipswich reported that his ship was first been boarded in Tilbury Hope and four men taken off, which he regarded as not unfair. The next day the boatswain of *Great Neptune* came on board to look for more. Only four men and a boy appeared on deck, and the boatswain demanded to see the rest, to which Clark replied that these were all he had left. The boatswain decided to take the boy, although Clark pointed out that he had only been three months at sea. At this, 'the boatswain offered to strike Clark with his truncheon. Clark took the same from him, and threw it upon the hatches. Presently after the boatswain struck Clark on the head with his fist; Merrington [the ships carpenter], seeing Clark so abused, told the boatswain if he struck Clark again he would be foul on him, yet the boatswain laid violent hands on Clark.' The boatswain eventually pressed the mate of the ship, and then released him the day after.[137] Clearly, violence was becoming part of impressment, though it was not yet accepted by all involved.

On the whole, impressment from ships was more efficient than that conducted on land, for at least it could be guaranteed that the men were seamen – in March 1636, *Anne Royal* and seventeen other ships brought in 1,886 men for the fleet. On the other hand, it was disruptive of trade, and one master of a merchant ship complained, 'Out of his 20 mariners, four have been pressed, others have run away, and for danger of the rest to be prest when he has passed Gravesend, he dare not proceed on his voyage.'[138]

The seaman was beginning to learn tricks to avoid impressment. Some, it was said, 'upon rumour of a press, and after some warning, absent themselves, and lurk in private men's houses, remote from the maritime towns, until the press be past.'[139] Others took the prest money and failed to appear. The Navy Board was concerned that 'many that are pressed appear not, but by stealth ship themselves away upon merchant voyages, and render to the press masters wrong names and false places of abode'.[140] More deserted after they had been taken on board the King's ships. *St Andrew* had 150 pressed men put on board and 120 deserted, while none of the twenty gunners pressed for the ship actually appeared on board.[141] Charles's Ship Money fleets did put to sea, but it is not surprising that they achieved nothing.

SOURCES OF SEAMEN

Although ship money had divided the King from his subjects, and the seaman's reluctance to serve in the Royal Navy was now greater than ever, there was a growing feeling that England really needed a navy that would serve the interest of the people as a whole rather than just the King. There was concern about the growing need for seamen, and some consideration on how their numbers could be increased and the resources of the nation better used. Captain Nathaniel Boteler considered that there were six groups that could provide recruits for the navy. First, and least useful, were the Thames watermen, who rowed passengers between London Bridge and Westminster. According to Botleler they were 'expert oarsmen, and this is one step (though the lowest) towards the attainment of this mystery'.[142] Others held that no ship should have more than 5% of her complement made up of such men, though they could soon be trained into seamen.

Inshore fisherman were the second source. They did not know how to handle big ships, but, 'besides their sea legs and sea stomachs, which they have very perfect, they have some few ropes and sails to handle. And passing well foresighted they are, of sudden gusts, flaws of wind and all changes of weather.' Sea fishermen were the third source. These included the men of the Newfoundland trade, which was then growing rapidly. 'And these, as they are bolder men so they have bigger vessels, with all the ropes, sails, masts and yards that belong to a big ship.' They were to be encouraged, 'so as to breed a seminary of good seamen'.

The Newcastle coal trade with London was large enough to form the fourth group. It used full rigged ships and trained proper seamen among the sandbanks of the Thames Estuary. Its cardinal advantage was that its ships were never far from home, and its men were always available quickly in time of need. The fifth group included the rest of the merchantmen. Ships that traded in the Mediterranean, the Baltic and to India produced 'accomplished mariners and navigators'. Finally, the perfect crews for men of war could only be trained aboard the King's own ships. 'For herein they may not only attain to whatsoever can be taught in any of the former schools, but to an addition of being as well sea soldiers as seaman. Here they may learn discipline and obedience; the use of arms, and chiefly of the fiery weapons, the skill of the sea gunners art, which is different from that on the shore in many particulars.'[143] The seaman, rather than the gunner or the soldier, was now the principal fighting man aboard ship, as well as the man who hauled the ropes and steered the vessel.

The Legality of Pressing

But Charles I was never in a position to use these potential seamen to the full. In 1640 a Scottish revolt forced him to call a parliament again after eleven years. He dissolved that very quickly, but defeat by the Scots soon forced him to call another and to submit to all its demands for a time. By the spring of 1641, Parliament was the effective government of the country, and it wanted to cut the King down to size. It abolished many of the old feudal prerogatives, partly out of a concern for civil liberties but largely in an attempt to make him impotent. Ship Money was declared illegal, and any funds remaining from it were to be repaid. In the circumstances, it would be surprising if Parliament had not turned its attention to impressment, a power that was clearly filled with injustice, and which was abused as often as not.

The House of Commons had such a debate in April 1641. A fleet had been prepared largely, it was said, to defend the country against the Barbary corsairs. Sir Henry Vane, Treasurer of the Navy, asked for the right to impress, for 'they now wanted only mariners to man the said ships, and they would find few or none, so as unless this house took some course that mariners might be prest', the money already spent on fitting out the ships would be lost. It was not the first time Vane had raised this point, and there was much opposition to it. 'Divers spoke up to this motion, and would by no means have any mariners prest, as being against the laws and liberties of the subject. They admitted that the wages might be increased, and their paying better used than formerly ... Others spake often, and most declined the way of bill, and wished that we might make no such precedent, for it might perhaps be defiled at another time.' A few members took the opposite view, and argued that urgent necessity was enough to override these considerations:

> I moved that this was a difficult issue to be discussed, in respect of the necessity of the defence of the kingdom. For it was made clear that by the laws of England there is but one liberty and one servitude, and the meanest freeman hath as great an immunity from this service of having his body employed against his will as the greatest peers of England, so as we cannot now permit the necessity of enforcing any man to serve. But in case the kingdom be in danger, and there be no other way left to provide for all our safeties but by pressing of mariners, then if there be no way left to press them but by drawing and passing a short bill speedily for the pressing of such a number only as are now needful for the manning of the present navy. This being done by public consent of the kingdom, will be rather a confirmation than a diminution of the ancient and

hereditary liberties of the subject of England. For the very passing of this bill will be a declaration that by the law of England without it, the persons of the subjects of England are free from pressing.

If the bill was passed with a time limit, it was hoped to prevent pressing being used indiscriminately in the future. But these arguments cut no ice with the house, and the issue was shelved. [144]

Parliament returned to the question later in the same year. By this time relations with the King were very bad indeed, and many members must have been aware that the fleet might be used for a civil war instead of a foreign conflict. This time they did pass an act allowing impressment, though it contained several safeguards in the hope of protecting both trade and liberty. The act was to last for just over a year, from November 1641 to December 1642. Impressment was not to extend to masters, mates, carpenters, boatswains or gunners of any ship in employment, nor to more than one in ten of ships outward or homeward bound. It was only to apply to men aged between 18 and 50. On the other hand, the act made clear, for the first time in statute law, the government's right to take up seamen against their will: 'If any ... shall willfully refuse to be impressed in or for the said service, or shall voluntarily hide and absent himself at the time of such press to avoid the said service', he was to be punished with the relatively mild term of three months' imprisonment.[145]

Within three months the act had been found ineffective 'by reason of sundry restrictions and doubtful limitations'. A new act was passed, giving exemption only to masters, mates and carpenters 'of any ship or bark that is in employment at the time of the said act'.[146] However, by the time the new act came into force the King had withdrawn from London, and the country was on the verge of conflict. In August he raised his standard at Nottingham, and both sides began to organise their armies. The seamen of the English navy, after their many disappointments and broken promises from Charles, would have to choose which side to support in a civil war.

2

CIVIL WAR and DUTCH WARS
1642 to 1689

THE SEAMEN AND PARLIAMENT

On 4 January 1642, King Charles I led a party into the House of Commons in person to arrest the five most troublesome of its members, but his coup failed – 'All my birds have flown,' he observed. He withdrew to Hampton Court on the 9th, and two days later the five members left the City of London and returned to Westminster in triumph. They joined a decorated barge at Three Cranes Wharf, a quarter of a mile upriver from London Bridge, and were met by a party of 2,000 seamen from Chatham. 'From London-Bridge to Westminster, the Thames was guarded by above one hundred lighters and long-boats, laden with nablettes and murders, and dressed up with waist clothes and streamers, as ready for fight.'[1] There were '30 or 40 long-boats, with guns, flags, &c., and a great number of citizens and seamen in other boats and barges, and so they were conveyed to Westminster'. The seaman's aim, they said, was to guard the king and his palace. They

> came as well to protect Whitehall, had his majestie been there, as the parliament house. But a rumour being spread amongst us, that that great council was in feare to be dissolved, and knowing too well the happiness of this kingdome consists in these sessions … we, seeing and hearing the whole city to be in complete arms, presently turned fresh-water soldiers; and, with as sudden expedition as we could, attended by water their progress thither, and joined our thunder of powder with the city muskets …

The seamen took great care to explain their position. They asserted that their presence was 'an act of our own free and voluntarie disposition', and they had not come under pressure from Parliament, though their letter was far too literate and politically sophisticated to be the work of the average seaman, and they may have had outside help of some kind. They believed 'That great vessel, the parliament house, which is so richly fraught with no less value than the price of a Kingdom, is fearfully shaken, and in great danger.' They cited their experience at sea as reason for their support for the English system of government as they saw it:

> We, who are always abroad, can best tell no government upon earth is comparable to it; especially for the keeping of a crown upon the king's head; for the procuration of the subjects' loyaltie, and unfeigned fidelity to their monarch; for the flourishing of traffique and merchandizing (this kingdom's right hand) the continuation of which is, was, and must necessarily be, by parliaments.
>
> Witnesse the heavie and lamentable distractions in France, Spain and Germanie, for want of them and the like government.

The Parliamentary cause was greatly strengthened, and some of the masters and mariners were called before to House of Commons and thanked for their support:

> That the house did take special notice of the performance of this service of theirs, to this house, and to the commonwealth, and gave them thanks for it, and desired them to communicate the same to the rest of the seamen and mariners.[2]

With a single blow, the King had lost control of London and the support of the seamen.

Parliament put the Earl of Warwick in charge of the fleet at the Downs, and at the beginning of July he found himself in 'a great strait ... between two commands that had so much power over me'. Nevertheless he decided to support Parliament and called his captains to a council of war. All except five supported him, and four of these gathered their ships together for defence. Next morning Warwick moved his own ships into position around these four, which caused two of them to surrender. Warwick fired a gun over *Garland* and *Expedition* and sent out his ships' boats to surround them. Everything was set for a bloody confrontation when Warwick called on the two captains to surrender. Then the seamen in the boats took matters into their own hands:

> Their answer was so pre-emptory, that my masters and sailors grew so impatient with them, that (although they had no arms in their boats at all, yet God gave them such courage and resolution, as, in a moment) they entered them, took hold of their shrouds, and seized upon those captains, though armed with their pistols and swords; struck their yards and topmasts, and brought them both to me. The like courage and resolution was never seen among unarmed men, so all was ended without effusion of blood ...[3]

According to a leading Royalist, 'the devotion generally of the seamen' was 'so tainted and corrupted to the kings service, that, instead of carrying away the ships, the captains themselves were seized, taken and carried by their own men to the Earl; who committed them to custody, and sent them up prisoners to the Parliament.' According to the same authority, this left 'His Majesty without one ship of his own in his three kingdoms'. It was 'of unspeakable ill consequence to the king's affairs, and made his condition much the less considered by his allies and neighbour princes; who saw the sovereignty of the sea now in other hands'.[4]

THE CIVIL WAR

The war that followed was mainly fought on land, but Parliament still needed a navy to deter any foreign intervention, to stop Royalist gun-runners, to prevent movement of Royalist forces from Ireland to England, to intervene in sieges of coastal towns such as Lyme and Plymouth, and to protect their commerce and supplies against privateers and pirates. Parliament invariably used 'both carrot and stick' to recruit its seamen. Early in 1643 wages were raised from 15/- to 19/- per month, but at the same time the act of 1642 in favour of pressing was renewed for another year, and it was to continue being renewed until 1660. By a proclamation of April 1643, alehouse keepers and innkeepers were forbidden 'to harbour or entertain any mariners, seamen, watermen and co., prest into any of His Majesty's or merchant ships employed in the service, after the beat of the drum and proclamation made to give them notice to repair on board the several ships to which they belong'.[5] This suggests a relatively mild form of impressment, reminiscent of the time of Henry VIII. Presumably seamen were given the prest money in advance, to be called by the beat of a drum and the reading of a proclamation around the town.

During the Civil War the fleet consisted of about 6,000 men for the summer campaigns, and about 2,000 in winter. A few new ships were built, but these were mostly small, fast frigates, so the navy needed about the same number of seamen as in the days of the Ship Money fleets. Parliament was generally better organised and had far better financial resources than the King, so it could pay its seamen more and feed them better. As a result, recruitment was not too difficult, though it relied on impressment as well as volunteers. According to a warrant issued by Warwick early in 1645, the service of the coming year 'may require a greater proportion of men than may voluntarily offer themselves; these are by virtue of an ordnance of both houses [of Parliament] to enable and authorise you ... to impress and levy such and so many mariners, sailors, watermen, surgeons, gunners, ship carpenters, caulkers and hoymen ... as you may consider requisite and necessary for that service.'[6] That year prest masters were sent out to Suffolk and Essex to recruit 500 men. They found that 'such was the willingness of the seamen and watermen to serve the Parliament, that the ships are all manned long since, and at sea; and we writ letters to the prest-masters to stay their hand; and those of that were pressed, came to Chatham 358 men, besides watermen.'[7]

During the early sea fights at least, captains still found it useful to consult their men. When Captain Smith of *Swallow* caught up with the Royalist *Fellowship* near Milford Haven in 1643, he called together his officers then the ship's company and told them that 'the ship was rich, having aboard divers goods belonging to the merchants of Bristol, to preserve them from plundering'. When he put the question to his men, 'they cried all, as one man, "God bless King and Parliament" and that "they would stand by me to the last man"'. He tried to negotiate with the Royalists, but their captain only offered 'the King's grace and mercy' if the crew of *Swallow* would follow him. Captain Smith silenced him angrily and accused him of piracy. Both ships grounded and *Swallow* fired a few warning shots, but Smith had a less violent method:

> in the mean time I had sent a letter to the master and ship's company, that if they would deliver up the two other captains, with the ship, I did promise them all free entertainment, and that they should have their wages paid, and all such goods as they could make appear justly to belong to them. Upon receipt of which letter, the master and mariners did deliver the ship without the loss or hurt of any one man (God be praised).[8]

When it did come to a fight, some of the seamen were just as mercenary. In 1645 when *Constant Warwick*, *Expedition* and *Cygnet* engaged a Royalist ship under Captain Mucknell, Captain Gilson grappled *Constant Warwick* alongside her and offered ten pounds to any man that would take down the Royalist flag. Two men volunteered, but one fell into the water and was drowned. The other got on board and climbed the shrouds, but *Warwick*'s grapple gave way and the ships separated. The man hid himself then leapt overboard. He swam to *Warwick*'s boat, which was being towed astern, and cut it loose to take it back as a prize to his own ship. He was rewarded with a gratuity; but Mucknell escaped.[9]

In an amphibious operation, men were landed to take the Isle of Wight in 1642, when only the central stronghold remained in Royalist hands.

Colonel Brett with other cavaliers held Carisbrooke Castle, whereupon we took consideration how we should dispossess the new made Governor, and with unanimous consent we landed 400 men from the ships, who went into a full resolution not to return, until they had made the Colonel conformable to the ordnance of Parliament.[10]

During the siege of the crucial fortified town and port of Hull in the following year, the Parliamentarian defenders got wind of an attempt to hand the city over to the Royalists. As a result, 'Captain Moyer sent Ripley 100 men out of his ships, to help surprise the three block-houses, which was done in a trice …'[11] Helping defend Lyme against the Royalists in 1644, the sailors showed their characteristic generosity to the inhabitants:

> The condition and courage of the besieged did so prevail with our seamen, that on Saturday last, out of their poor overplus, they sent them above 30 pairs of boots, 100 pair of stockings, 100 pair of shoes, some linen and old clothes, and some quantity of fish and bread, that they had formerly saved out of their sea allowance. They did also unanimously give one fourth part of their bread for the next four months, amounting to 9,000 weight, which their hard labour and constant duty might advise them to have reserved rather for their own bellies.[12]

However, by 1646 there were signs that the seamen were becoming less keen on land service. During the siege of Bunratty Castle, Captain William Penn

> sent for Captain Line and Captain Coachman, willed them to gather a fresh crew for the relief of their men above, which having considered of, as very necessary for the strengthening of the garrison, they went on board their ships to effect; and so, with some difficulty, which cannot be avoided when men are enforced to land-service.[13]

This was an early sign of a growing rift with the army, which was coming under the dominance of the fanatical 'independents'. There was also growing discontent on board ship, and in 1647 the crew of *Bonaventure* 'did in a very disorderly and mutinous way demand their pay from the said Captain Crowther and contrary to their duty desert the ship'.[14]

THE SAILORS SUPPORT MODERATION

The first Civil War ended in 1646 after the land battle of Naseby, and the King, who surrendered to the Scots, was handed over to Parliament and imprisoned by them. Up to this time Parliament had maintained the fiction that it was really fighting to save the King from his pernicious advisors, but this became increasingly difficult, and the winning side became divided over what to do with him, and the extent of the social revolution that was to follow the victory. The seamen had supported Parliament strongly in 1642, but they did not wish to overthrow the King completely. When in 1648 Parliament began to issue orders in its name alone, the seamen became suspicious – 'We have been long pressed in the king's name, though against his will and interest.'[15] They disliked the growing political power of the New Model Army, as did most of the population. They objected strongly when Colonel Thomas Rainsborough was appointed as vice admiral in charge of the Channel Fleet at the Downs. Not only was he an army officer and an outsider, he was a man of 'insufferable pride, ignorance and insolency' who 'alienated the hearts of the seamen'.[16] He was regarded as an extremist and leveller, 'a man of most destructive principles both in religion and policy and a known enemy to the peace and ancient government of this kingdom'.[17]

The people of Kent rose against the government and made contact with the fleet at the Downs. On 27 May the sailors, led by Boatswain's Mate William Lendall of the flagship *Constant Reformation*, took control of the ships and displaced Rainsborough, who was ashore at the time. They summoned the captains on board the flagship, but Captain Penrose of *Satisfaction* refused to come, and a party of 40 armed men went to fetch him. 'Captain Penrose asked who was that Vice-Admiral. They replied, that his name was Lendall. Then Captain Penrose said, he knew such a man to be a boatswain's mate, but no otherwise, and was resolved not to go with them.'[18] Instead he was sent to London with the 'Declaration of the Navy, with the oath taken by the officers and common men of the same'. They demanded that Parliament should negotiate with the King; that the army should be disbanded, that 'the known laws of the kingdom may be established and continued', and that 'the privileges of parliament and liberty of the subject be preserved'. The petition was perhaps too literate and politically sophisticated to be the work of the lower deck alone, and no doubt many of the officers had a hand in it, but it was the seamen who were in ultimate control. For once, they were not revolting about poor pay or victuals, but they held the fate of England, and ultimately Scotland and Ireland, in their hands.

The Kentish revolt was soon crushed by Fairfax's army, but a naval rising could not be put down in that way. The sailors considered the possibility of sailing to the Isle of Wight where the King was imprisoned, or blockading the Thames to stop the trade of London, which would have been a very effective strategy. Instead they sailed to Holland, where the Prince of Wales was in exile. In the meantime, the Earl of Warwick was restored as the commander of the ships that remained under Parliament's control. He had fought with the seamen all through the Civil War, and he was a moderate Parliamentarian. He managed to rally at Portsmouth the ships that were wavering in support of the rebels and, despite many difficulties, put together a new force. Early in September he headed down the Thames with a newly manned fleet.

> We had by this time a very great experience of the mariners' affection; those aboard my ship applying themselves to a preparation for fight with the greatest alacrity that I ever saw, there being not one of them that discovered the least averseness to engage, or unwillingness to lay down his life for the enemy's reduction; which (as the Captains informed me) was likewise the general temper of the rest of the fleet.[19]

Meanwhile the rebels had accepted the popular Sir William Batten as their commander, while the see-saw career of William Lendall led him to be dropped from vice admiral to lieutenant in the Royalist navy. Prince Charles came on board and used his charm to the full – 'his princely carriage with them hath made so deep an impression on the whole seamen that he is master of their very souls: and all men rejoice beyond expression to see such admirable fruit in so young a plant.'[20] They still had their difficulties. They returned to the Downs and took some merchant ships but failed to apply a full blockade, and the Royalist policy of extracting ransoms did not please the seamen:

> Batten and Jordan, spent the time in making bargains with the merchants to discharge their ships, hardly a ship coming in but was kin to one of them; this displeased many among us, and made the sailors mad, insomuch that they upbraided them to their faces with treason and corruption, under which our steadiness suffered also.[21]

It was decided to return to Holland. The seamen now knew that their revolt was not going to produce a quick solution. They were far less committed to the King than their new leaders and feared they would be cut off from home and family. Some of the ships' crews demanded to sail up the Thames in a 'very arrant mutiny'.

The Portsmouth squadron arrived and anchored outside the estuary. It was not clear whose side they were on, and Prince Charles claimed that Batten was sweating with fear as they saw Warwick's ships coming towards them, not knowing whether the sailors intended to fight or hand them over to the government. According to one Royalist,

> We said little to them, which many understanding persons are angry at, being confident we might have taken them upon our bare demand, we being many more and under sail, and they at anchor. Nay, I heard a good old seaman say, that he who persuaded us to that neglect was either a coward or traitor.[22]

Both sides were unwilling to risk a battle among the sandbanks of the estuary, and neither was totally sure of the loyalties of its crews. The Royalists retreated back to Holland, Warwick following slowly and cautiously.

Warwick could now raise twenty ships to blockade them in Hellevoetsluis. The King's nephew, Prince Rupert, was appointed commander there, but he was seen as an uncompromising Royalist and was not popular with the seamen, who had begun the revolt in favour of conciliation. 'Prince Rupert ... had with notable vigour and success suppressed two or three mutinies, in one of which he had been compelled to throw two or three seamen overboard by the strength of his own arms.'[23] This brought the men into 'some sort of awe and obedience', but it was not a recipe for success. Some of the ships defected back to Parliament, and

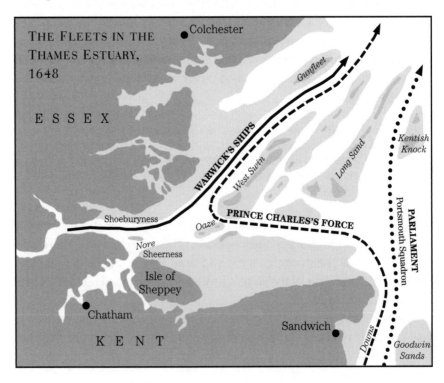

THE FLEETS IN THE THAMES ESTUARY, 1648

many of the seamen deserted. The seamen had started their revolt as an attempt to end the conflict, but they lacked any political initiative of their own, as seamen nearly always do. In the end they had just switched from one side to the other. In December the seamen were silent when the government of England passed into far more extreme hands, as Colonel Pride purged the House of Commons of moderate members. The moderate Warwick was dismissed, and the King was put on trial and executed in January 1649.

The new republican regime remained nervous about the loyalty of the seamen. When the fleet was assembled at the Downs in April for another summer campaign, some of the men refused to sail without a say in the control of the fleet. They had to be addressed by the puritan chaplain Hugh Peters, who went on board each ship and made unforgettable sermons asking the 'courageous and daring' seamen 'whether they were well resolved to their voyaging against the Prince's ships' and to comply with the Admirals. At once they cried out as one man, that they would live and die with the admirals' against the enemies of the Commonwealth.[24] The admirals then circulated an 'engagement better to discover the Mariners affections', and 540 men on board *Triumph* signed it before it was passed to other ships.[25] Patriotism had taken over, and the men sailed out to take Prince Rupert's privateers. Only one more ship, the tiny *Hart*, would mutiny for the Stuart cause during the whole life of the republic.

THE NEW NAVY

Though it was victorious, the Parliament was far from secure. The Scottish Parliament was not entirely in support of the English one, while the Royalists held many outposts, such as the Scilly Isles, and Ireland was in revolt against English rule. The republic would never be entirely at peace during the years of its existence. Ships rather than armies were needed now, as most of the state's enemies were overseas. Very soon after the execution of the King, Parliament began to build several new ships, the beginning of a programme which was to have major consequences. In a sense, this was the true 'take-off' point of the British navy. It had had its ups and downs over the last two and a half centuries, reaching its peaks under Henry V, Henry VIII, Elizabeth and Charles I. The navy had always maintained some kind of existence since the days of Henry VII, but there was no real tendency for it to increase in size: Charles I's fleet was no bigger than that of Henry VIII and probably not bigger than Henry V's. This was to change in the middle of the seventeenth century. In 1642,

Parliament had inherited a fleet of 35 effective ships, capable of employing about 7,300 men if fully manned. By 1652 it had doubled, to 102 ships and 12,500 men. By 1660 the fleet consisted of 157 ships employing 21,910 men – it had virtually trebled in size in eighteen years. The fleet would continue to grow in every war fought over the next two centuries, but never again would it have such a large proportional increase in so short a period. A fleet of 6,000 men could be maintained without too much upheaval, provided finance was forthcoming, the government had popular support, and the war did not go on for too long. After 1649 none of these conditions would apply, and the fleet would need far more than 6,000 men.

The republic continued to use 'both carrot and stick' to enforce discipline. In the wake of the mutiny, new regulations were put in force in 1649. To enforce discipline yet further, the Articles of War were passed by Parliament in 1652. These were far more severe than the rules that had governed medieval fleets. Twenty-five out of 39 articles carried the death penalty, and in thirteen of these it was mandatory. They offered the seaman no redress against his superiors as the medieval sea laws had done; instead it was decreed, 'If any officer, mariner, soldier or other person in the fleet shall strike any of his superior officers, or draw or offer to draw or lift up any weapon against him, being in the execution of his office, on any pretence whatsoever, every such person convicted of any such offence by the sentence of a court martial shall suffer death.'[26]

On the other hand, the seamen's financial position improved. The act of 1649 for extending the right to impress was also intended 'for encouragement of officers and mariners'. The captain and crew of a captured ship were to be given one third of the profits when she was sold. They were also to divide the gun money paid by the state: £12–£20 was given for each gun aboard the prize. Wages were increased, and allowance was made for different grades of seamen. From 1 January 1653, able seamen, 'fit for the helm and lead, top and yard' were to have 24/- per month. Others 'not capable of performing the duties aforesaid' were to continue at the rate of 19/- established during the Civil War. 'Gromets', or unskilled men, were to have 14/-, and boys 9/-.[27] Conduct money was increased to 1d per mile, then to 1½d. The government was clearly aware of the need to increase its store of seamen. By the use of 'gromets' it showed its willingness to take on unskilled but mature men, willing to learn the trade. Apparently captains did not always accept this, and in 1659 one reported, 'Several volunteers came on board the *James* in the Hope, under the notion of seamen, but not able to do the work.' He intended to discharge them, rather than put them on the lower rate of pay.[28]

ON BOARD AND ASHORE

Despite the new Articles of War, discipline on board ship was not necessarily savage or tyrannical. The Articles were aimed at officers as well as men, after a good deal of indiscipline among the captains during the early stages of the Dutch War. They were rarely enforced to the full. Only one man was hanged under them for an offence on board ship, though others were sentenced then reprieved.[29] In fact, sailors were persistent in demanding what they saw as their rights. There were tyrannical captains, such as Robert Wyard of *Adventure*, whose crew claimed he was

> ever beating and abusing the seamen, breaking some men's heads and arms and kicking some in the mouth; and cocked his fowling pieces at the boatswain, and threw a crossbar shot at him, like to have killed him in his cabin, beating others with horsewhips and canes, and calling men rogues, rascals, whores, birds, whoresons and the like, so that men lived all the voyage more like slaves than state's servants.[30]

Wyard did not escape unpunished. Some of his men marched to London to complain to the Admiralty, who took their side. This was not unusual, and several other captains were dismissed because of their cruelty. Cowardice and incompetence were equally despised in a captain. After John Best of *Adventure* was seen to trim his sails to avoid catching an enemy in 1656, his crew adopted the derisory chant, 'A man of war ahead, a man of war ahead'. He was also a drunk and a bully, and many of his men deserted. He was not reappointed by the Admiralty. [31]

The seaman was brave but believed he had a right not to have his life sacrificed needlessly. In 1652 the men under Richard Badiley refused to fight against a much superior Dutch force in the Mediterranean, claiming that 'the state has better ships, but we have no more lives'. But there was a flat calm the next day, and the action was not resumed, so the matter never came to a head.[32] During the decade or so after their passing by Parliament, the Articles of War remained largely aspirational, and confusion was never far under the surface of the navy.

Despite the puritan ethic of the state, the seamen continued to find ways to enjoy themselves, and a Quaker complained to them of 'your mirth and your melody, your jesting and your folly, your laughter and your vanity, your pastime and your singing'.[33] Women were often invited on board, legitimately or not, and the seaman ashore was accused, as in all ages, of 'licentiousness and lasciviousness'. Despite being a single-sex community, there is no evidence that homosexuality among adults was common, though of course the only cases we know about are those that came to the attention of the authorities. Paedophilia was not unknown. A seaman who invited a boy into his hammock in *Peregrine* was quickly reported and sent for trial. In 1654 two youths were sent ashore for 'the most horrid buggery' with each other after they had been reported by their comrades. The master of *Great Charity* had a habit of inviting youngsters into his cabin and plying them with brandy, and the master of *Amity* also preyed on the ships' boys.[34]

The seaman also enjoyed himself when given leave:

> And being permitted to go a shore, either about your business or to see your friends, or to refresh your bodies, or the like, even at such times do you most shamefully abuse your selves, by drinking excessively till you make your selves more like beasts than men ... when you have so abused your selves with wine, strong waters or strong beer, then you cannot govern yourselves, but oftentimes doth that which you ought not to do, and thereby trangresseth the law ashore ...[35]

EDWARD COXERE

The main work of training seamen remained with the merchant service, and the state realised that it needed to be encouraged and protected. To achieve this Parliament passed the first Navigation Act in 1651. Many goods and commodities were only to be imported on British ships 'such as do truly and without fraud belong to the people of this commonwealth, or the plantations thereof ... and whereof the masters and mariners are also for the most part of them people of this Commonwealth'.[36] This was to remain the basis of British commercial policy for nearly two centuries, throughout the age of naval expansion. But the most immediate effect of the act was to infuriate the Dutch, who did most of the carrying trade of Europe. War with the United Netherlands, the most prestigious maritime power in the world, began in 1652.

Edward Coxere began his career as a merchant seaman very tentatively around 1648:

> I not settling my mind to a trade, my lot fell to the sea. I was sent with James Moran in the *Malaga Factor*, a new ship, on trial to be his prentice if I liked the sea. The voyage proved to be very short, but seven weeks from the Downs to the Downs; as it was short, to me it was unpleasant. Though the wind was fair the seas was very boisterous by reason of the high winds, insomuch that I was mostly very sea-sick, which did so discourage me that I concluded not to live

that miserable sea-life. But this was not all; but to harden me to the sea the master would run after me with a rope's end, more to scare me than to hurt me, as since I perceived; the master's mate would run after the master, as if he would hold him. Though they ever did it in jest, I took it in earnest, that I thought if ever I got ashore he should look [for] a prentice, for I did not like such kinds of sea tricks; for when it was foul weather I was sick, and when fair then he scared me with a rope's end.[37]

Despite this, he joined the 60-gun *St George* as servant to Lieutenant William Tattnoll and soon encountered one of the most terrifying experiences known to seamen. As the powder in the gun room was accidentally set alight, there was complete panic in which 'the captain was no more regarded than the cook'. 'So dreadful was it that the men who could swim leapt overboard into the sea to swim to the boats that were at the stern of the ship.' As to Coxere himself,

> I was got on the top of the stern of the ship. I perceiving the men made to the boats, I got over the stern to get down by a rope into the boat, but by the way my foot got foul of something which was like to have proved very much to my damage, the men making such way to get into the boats to save their lives. But it so happened that I got clear and got into the boat, where the captain soon gat after and, the boat full of men, we soon rowed the boat from the ship. Where we looked on with sorrowful hearts, expecting they that were aboard would a been blown up every minute.[38]

In fact the ship survived, as did Coxere's brother John, who was still on board when the fire was overcome.

THE FIRST DUTCH WAR

Even in 1650 and 1651, when the naval effort was relatively small, it was sometimes difficult to find seamen. Competition between captains was quite fierce, and in April 1650 it was discovered that some men impressed for *Swiftsure* at Hull were on their way to join their ship when they were pressed for another ship at Tilbury.[39] It was not possible to find many men without pressing, and May 1651 a captain wrote that seventeen men had volunteered for *Recovery* and thirteen for *President*, but that he would have to press for more, as very few would volunteer.

When the First Anglo-Dutch war broke out in May 1652, Parliament was already planning for a summer fleet of 6,000 men. This was quickly increased by another 1,000, and orders were given to impress men from homeward-bound merchant ships. Morale was quite high, and volunteers were still forthcoming – when the Dutch fleet appeared off Dover, 200 seaman of that town offered to go on board the English fleet for the battle that followed.[40] Even so, it was not always easy to meet the needs of the fleet. In July, Admiral Blake wrote, 'The greatest want now is men, which we hope will be supplied shortly.'[41] Two hundred soldiers were raised in London and sent to the fleet in the Downs; there was some doubt about their discipline, and it was desired that Lieutenant General Fleetwood 'appoint some competent number of officers to ... conduct the said men thither, and see them put aboard, to end such disorders as happened amongst the soldiers who were last sent aboard'.[42] Some new supplies of seamen were available, and a few Scottish fishermen were pressed.

It was decided to send out an enormous fleet of 16,000 men in 1653. Such a force required some advance planning, which had already begun at the end of the previous year. The act increasing seamen's wages and guaranteeing them a share of the prize money was passed through Parliament, and it was read out in all the seaports. At Dartmouth, for example, the mayor 'caused the same to be published in the market place, where all proclamations are proclaimed, and have also caused it to be published by beat of drum throughout the town, and have set up the same that all seamen may take notice of it'.[43]

Nevertheless there was a great deal of reluctance among the seamen. At Dover the prest master 'caused about fifty seamen to be imprested for the service, and appointed them to come to receive conduct money; and only twenty of them came to receive it, and they, after the receipt thereof, do most peremptorily refuse to go, being, as I conceive, animated therein by some interested in private men of war, of which there are so many here that we cannot expect that any considerable party can be raised by the state while they are appointed'.[44] Privateers always sounded attractive to seaman when the war was against a rich maritime power like the Dutch, and more money could be made by raiding merchant vessels than by fighting the enemy fleet, while the risks were rather less.

The seamen of other towns were equally unwilling. The mayor of Poole was ordered to find 66 seamen but could only get hold of 30. He found much difficulty in the work, 'most men not only endeavouring to absent themselves from the press, but also not appearing after they have received the state's money'.[45] At Deal, on the other hand 'the major part of the seamen of this town do express their readiness to serve the commonwealth' on the terms given in the new act. In Yarmouth volunteers could still be found. The prest masters sent 200 seamen, 'the most of which men were impressed ... and a good part of them came in voluntarily and offered themselves in the service, and were very proper men, and well deserving'.

Men could be found for the navy, but it was hard work. Gravesend, on the Thames, was particularly fruitful, and in February 1653 the prest master 'caused a narrow search to be made this day twice through the town', producing 60 men.[46] They could also be found aboard ships in the Thames: 'I got the commanders of the respective ships aforementioned to go along with me and take their ship's boats with them, and search every wherry or merchant ship in the river for seamen coming down that tide of ebb, which was accordingly done, whereby there was procured about 70 seamen.'[47]

Around this time Edward Coxere was a seaman on a merchant ship in the Thames, being paid at a rate of 41/- a month. A boat from a man of war came alongside, and the seamen, knowing what was afoot, ran to hide themselves. Coxere was grabbed by one of the press gang but struggled free and ran to the gun room, aft on the lower deck. He climbed out of a gunport and into the ship's longboat, where he hid until safe. 'One may judge of the fear I had on me then. I had no way but to thrust myself as far as I could under the fore sheet of the boat, and there I lay until the boat drove away again to the ship's stern.'[48] He escaped on this occasion and was discharged from the ship, and made his way back home to Dover. He travelled on by-ways to avoid the press and got there after some adventures; but 'instead of taking some pleasure with my friends I was still terrified with the press, and could not walk the streets without danger, nor sleep in safety'. Tired of this kind of existence, he and his brother decided to volunteer for the navy.[49] After that, Coxere had a varied career even by the standards of an eighteenth century seaman:

> I served several masters in the wars between King and Parliament at sea. Next I served the Spaniards against the French, then the Hollanders against the English; then I was taken by the English out of a Dunkirker; then I served the English against the Hollanders; and at last I was taken by the Turks, where I was forced to serve them against English, French, Dutch and Spaniards, and all Christendom.[50]

Unfortunately for the historian he became a Quaker and was reluctant to say any more about his military life.

The Newcastle collier fleet was highly regarded as a source for seamen, but its crews had learned how to evade the press. It was found that many ships were dropping off parts of their crews in Essex and Suffolk before they reached the Thames. But in April the Newcastle convoy was escorted by men of war, and after it had entered the Thames the crews of the colliers were impressed. 'We have had much ado to keep the men that belong to the colliers from running away; this day we espied a boat with six men running away; we saluted them with a gun and so they came to us. We have our complement of men, and more than overplus we shall spare for any of the state's ships. We cannot give you the exact number of them because we continue our press.'[51]

Despite these efforts, the fleet remained undermanned, and by March 1653 the press gangs were resorting to increasingly desperate methods. There was a report that 'We have so fleeced this river [the Thames] that there is not an able man to be found'.[52] Another report claimed, 'We began to press, and for three days and nights continued pressing all sorts of people (whether gentlemen or others) that came in our way. The watermen and seamen were pulled out of bed from their wives, and we sent them to the fleet in barges, two whereof being overladen and the wind high, were cast away below Gravesend and all the men lost, which was a sad omen to the rest, who went as unwillingly as they would have done to the gallows; from whom we cannot expect much service.'[53] This was perhaps the first example of a 'hot press', from which no one was safe. But it is not likely that many of the landsmen swept up in such a process were retained. Admiral Bourne wrote to the Admiralty, 'I have observed aboard the ship this day many that are sent down are very unservicable, divers housekeepers, [i.e., householders] and landsmen that I find were never at sea and others that are merely a burden to the service but gathered up and sent away.'[54] The manning problem was largely solved by using soldiers, and it was proposed that 5,000 should be carried. The commanders of the fleet were unhappy about such a high proportion, who would 'probably know nothing of either land or sea service', and they would need 'able and sufficient seamen to direct the former unskilful men'.[55]

The navy was eventually manned and won several notable victories in 1653, particularly at the Battle of the Gabbard when more than a hundred ships in the fleet formed a single line of battle for the first time:

> the English found the Dutch fleet in at the height of Dunkirk, and when they approached them, they stayed upon a tack, having the wind, within twice cannon shot about half an hour, to put themselves in their order they intended to fight in, which was in file at half cannon shot, from whence they battered the Hollanders furiously all that day, the success whereof was the sinking of two Holland ships. Towards night Tromp got the wind, but soon lost it, and never

recovered it the two following days during which the fight continued, the Dutch steering with a slow sail towards their own coast. The second day the English still battered them in file, and refusing to board them upon equal terms, kept them at bay but half cannon distance, until they found some disordered and foul one against another, whom they presently boarded with their frigates ...[56]

These new tactics had a profound effect on the way the navy was run. Stricter discipline was needed among the officers to maintain the line. Larger ships were needed for the line of battle – it was no longer possible for a few small ships to attack a larger one as Drake had done. The broadside was established as the main naval tactic, and it was common to fight with one side of the ship only, so that seamen had to become expert at loading and firing, rather than turning their ships as they had done against the Armada. And boarding, if it took place at all, was only likely once an enemy's line had been broken and he was more than half defeated.

Meanwhile Oliver Cromwell came to power as Lord Protector in 1653 and was largely responsible for ending the war with the Dutch. Peace was made early in 1654, on English terms. The First Dutch War was a purely maritime war, and it did much to increase the importance of the seaman in national defence. It was fought against the largest maritime power of the time, and won. It set the pattern for much that was to follow, including the intense use of national resources to man the ships and the increasing use of violence in pressing. Cromwell favoured a more traditional conflict with Spain, which he hoped would be cheap, popular and profitable. In 1654 he sent out an expedition against Hispaniola, the naval side commanded by William Penn. But the war was never as successful as Cromwell had hoped. Penn captured Jamaica instead of Hispaniola and was put in the Tower of London for a time. The Spanish reacted with quite an effective campaign against British shipping, and that kept the navy busy for years. The nation, and in particular the seamen, became increasingly war-weary as time went on. Financing the war was also a problem: the Commonwealth had its windfall when it confiscated the estates of Royalists, but that did not last for ever, any more than the money from Henry VIII's dissolution of the monasteries had done. There were delays in the payment of wages, and seamen sometimes rioted to demand their money. And all through the years of the Protectorate, impressment remained in use; though never approaching the scale of 1653, it was a continual nuisance to seaman and shipowner alike.

In April 1657, Thomas Lurting was boatswain's mate of the 48-gun *Bristol,* part of a fleet under Robert Blake that attacked Spanish treasure galleons anchored in what they thought was a secure position off Santa Cruz, Tenerife. They came up under the stern of the flagship to get orders and were told to attack 'where we could get room'. As a result *Bristol* found herself closely engaging two Spanish flagships and some forts on shore, and all the crew's seamanship and gunnery skills were needed:

> And when we had brought up our ship, and we were about a cable's length from the vice-admiral, just in his wake, or in the head of him; then our captain called to me, to make ready, or to veer nearer the galleon; 'For I will,' said he, 'be on board the vice-admiral.' So we veered to be on board of him; and so fast we veered towards him, he veered from us, until he came about musket shot of the shore. Then the captain called to me, to get a hawser out of the gunroom port, and clap a spring on the cable; when done, we veered our cable, and lay just cross his hawse, about half musket shot from him; then we run all the guns we could on that side towards him, which were in number 28 or 30, and all hands went to it in earnest.

The intense fire soon had its effect, and the galleon was apparently hit in the powder room by the second broadside, blowing up with the loss of all hands. *Bristol* turned her fire on the main flagship, which was attempting to manoeuvre into position to destroy her. Instead, 'we perceiving, plied him very close with about 28 or 30 guns, and the third broadside, all his men leaped overboard, and instantly she blew up'.

Lurting then took command of a longboat to take charge of a grounded Spanish ship. It was thought to be abandoned, but some guns were fired from it and missed the boat. Lurting was about to set off again in a pinnace with two men to burn some galleons, when the captain ordered him to take five more; they succeeded in burning three ships. On the way back they were fired on by Spanish forts, and two men were killed. 'I sat close to one that was killed, between him and the shore, and close to him that was shot in the back, and received no harm.' Back in the ship, he was helping with the rigging: 'And I was on the clew of the main tack on board, and a shot cut the bolt rope a little above my head.' Having had four narrow escapes in a row within six hours, Lurting attributed them to God's will and was converted to Quakerism by some soldiers on board.[57]

THE NAVY AND THE RESTORATION

By 1659 Cromwell was dead, and the country was divided about what sort of regime was to succeed him. The impressment effort was meeting increasing resistance from the people, and at Ipswich it encountered serious local opposition. The prest master, Captain Edmund Curtis, was told by the local bailiffs that there were few seamen in the port, only masters and mates who were exempt from pressing. He did not believe this, as he saw that there were more than a hundred ships in the river. Next day, without giving advance notice to the bailiffs, he came at the head of an armed press-gang to seek out the seamen, 'but when our people began to press, and had taken a man or two, the town's people fell upon our men, and rescued them, by which means there was likely to have been blood spilt had not our men been civil.'[58] Presumably this inspired a new clause added to the annual impressment bill that year: 'all and every person and persons that shall oppose or resist any of the officers intrusted for impresting as aforesaid, in the execution of that service, or abet or set on any others to do so, shall for the same offence suffer the penalty of death.' [59] But relations with the seamen had reached a new low. Things had deteriorated drastically since the seamen had marched to the support of Parliament in 1642.

In 1660 the seamen, like the bulk of the population, supported the return of Charles II as king. *Royal Charles* (ex-*Naseby*) was the flagship of the fleet sent to Holland to bring him back from exile. Young Edward Barlow was on board *Naseby* to witness the King's reception on his first visit to the fleet.

> At his first coming to the ship's side all the men in the ship gave a great and loud shout, many of them hurling their caps or hats into the sea as a token of their joy to see His Majesty. That done, and he coming on board, we fired above 70 pieces of cannon, three times, one after another ... and all the admirals having fired then began all the rest of the fleet to fire, they all firing together, which made a great rattling in the sky as though it had been a great storm or tempest of thunder and rain.[60]

Two days later the King and his brothers arrived for the voyage to England, and again Barlow was a witness:

> His Majesty, knowing that all things were ready, came on board accompanied to the water-side by many of the chief lords in Holland and a guard of soldiers on both sides of the way as they came: and when they came to the water-side, there was the Lord Montague's barge, our Admiral ready to receive him in; and many of the country's boats were prepared to carry the lords and nobles on board, the boats being decked as fine as possible with other boats also of soldiers to guard them: and when the boats came to the ships the soldiers shot off a volley of small shot for a salute, so His Majesty came on board of our ship; his brother, James, Duke of York, on board of the Vice-Admiral; and the Duke of Gloucester on board of the Rear-Admiral; all the

ships receiving them with great joy, firing all their ordnance three times round as before. And the lords and nobles of Holland that accompanied, taking leave of His Majesty and the two Dukes, returned on shore again, and the soldiers which were in the boats saluted with a volley of small shot, which were answered with our great guns.

And things being ready we weighed our anchor and set sail with joy for England, bringing again with great joy and peace those which were driven out with war and the sword.[61]

One of the passengers was Samuel Pepys, cousin and secretary to Edward Montagu, the admiral. On the way out he had watched the crew of *Naseby* removing the republican decorations and insignia as offensive to His Majesty, and on the way back the ship was re-named *Royal Charles*. Pepys watched as the King and his brothers disembarked together off Dover to eat a seaman's breakfast, 'only to show them the manner of the ship's diet, they eat nothing else but pease and pork and salt beef'.[62]

EDWARD BARLOW

Edward Barlow was born inland in Prestwich, near Manchester, in 1642. He had never seen a ship until he went to London in 1657: 'I looking below the bridge upon the river, and seeing so many things upon the water with long poles standing up in them and a great deal of ropes about them, it made me wonder what they should be, not knowing that they were ships, for I had never seen any before that.'[63] Despite his inexperience he was indentured as an apprentice to the chief master's mate of the flagship *Naseby* and joined the ship; 'and that night I was put into a cabin to sleep, a thing much like to some gentleman's dog-kennel, for I was forced to creep in on all fours, and when I was in and set upon my breech I could not hold my head upright; but being very weary I slept indifferent well.'[64]

Barlow's career was not quite as varied as Coxere's, but he certainly had his ups and downs. As apprentice to a well-placed master's mate, he might have done well, but he did not get on with his master's wife on shore, and he had constant misfortunes at sea. Though he had started in the royal service, he drifted in and out of the merchant and royal navies as economics and the press gang dictated. His diaries only say a limited amount about life on board the seven warships and twenty merchantmen he served in; mostly they describe the places he visited, the battles he witnessed and complain constantly, but revealingly, about the hard life of the seamen, for example in the 26-gun *Augustine* in 1661:

We seldom in a month got our bellyful of victuals, and that of such salt as many beggars would think scorn to eat; and at night when we went to take our rest, we were not to lie still above four hours; and many times when it blew hard were not sure to lie one hour, yea, often were called up before we had slept half an hour and forced to go up into the maintop or fore top to taken in our topsails, half awake and half asleep, with one shoe on and the other off, not having time to put it on: always sleeping in our clothes for readiness; and in stormy weather, when the ship rolled and tumbled as though some great millstone were rolling up one hill and down another, and had much ado to hold ourselves fast by the small ropes from falling by the board; and being gotten up into the tops, there we must haul and pull to make fast the sail, seeing nothing but air above us and water beneath us, and that so raging as though every wave would make a grave for us; and many times in nights so dark that we could not see one another, and blowing so hard that we could not hear one another speak, being close to one another; and thunder and lightning as though heaven and earth would come together ...[65]

On another occasion in the 50-gun *Yarmouth* of Genoa in 1669,

the day following we had a cross wind, blowing very hard and splitting our sails in pieces; and we being forced, poor men, to go up into the tops in the dark nights to put to our yards other sails, when it blowed and rained, with thunder and lightning as though Heaven and earth would come together, and then were we to hang by our eyelids up in the air, when the ship rolled and tumbled so that we had much ado to hold ourselves fast from falling overboard, above us seeing nothing, and underneath us the raging of the sea, each wave ready to swallow the ship and all up.[66]

Not all the horrors were natural:

if I went to sea when I should be grown in years ... I should be little better than a slave, being always in need, and enduring all manner of misery and hardship, going with many a hungry belly and wet back, and being always called 'old dog', and 'old rogue', and 'son of a whore', and suchlike terms, which is common use amongst seamen, and that would be a great grief for an aged man ...[67]

But he failed to rise above it – he was shipwrecked, pressed, taken prisoner by the Dutch and cheated by his employers. 'And thus a poor man is abused with proud and ambitious masters, finding no recompense, having no money to try the law ...'[68]

THE RESTORATION NAVY

Under Charles II the navy became even more important. Parliament had suffered from the political power of Cromwell's New Model Army, and had developed a fear of standing armies that was to last for nearly two centuries. The King was allowed only a small force of personal guards, so that the navy became, more than ever, the main defence of the realm. The King himself, though he would not have been averse to a large army, was deeply interested in his navy and paid much attention to its affairs. According to Samuel Pepys, who knew him well, he was the king 'who best understands the business of the sea of any prince the world ever had'.[69] His brother, the Duke of York, was even more concerned with the detail of naval affairs. He had been nominally Lord High Admiral since his childhood and took up his duties properly in 1660. He did not treat the post as a sinecure; he even commanded the fleet in person on one important occasion.

There was no longer any prospect of the King reviving a feudal tax to finance his affairs, so to a certain extent he had to follow the wishes of Parliament if he were to remain solvent. The new Parliament, elected in 1661 on a wave of Royalist euphoria, was nevertheless determined to get rid of more of the King's feudal prerogatives. The 'Act Abolishing Feudal Tenures' removed the King's right 'of making provision of purveyance of victual, carriages, or other things for His Majesty', but it said nothing about the impressing of seamen. The act of 1642 had long since expired, and acts passed in the absence of the King were no longer recognised. There were some who doubted whether pressing of seamen remained legal in the circumstances.

All went well for the next four years, as the navy fitted out small squadrons against Algiers and for local patrols. One official wrote, 'We find now there is no need of pressing seamen, they being solicitors to be admitted into the service, which may rather be imputed to the small employment the merchants have for them (compared to what they had heretofore) than to the greatness of their pay.'[70] However, the captains in service do not seem to have had any doubts about the legality of pressing, and Thomas Lurting, now a merchant seamen, was pressed several times. As a Quaker he used passive resistance:

> Another time (in the year 1662) going to Harwich, laden with corn; and no sooner we came to anchor, but a press-boat came on board us; and the first man they laid hands on was me, saying, 'You must go with us.' 'I hope not', said I. They swore that I was a lusty man, and should go. Then they laid hands on me, and lifted me into their boat, and carried me on board the ship *Mary*, one Jeremiah Smith commander, who was a very loose and wicked man; so when I came to the ship side, they bad me go in; the which I had not the freedom to do so; then they tied a rope about my waist, and with a tackle hoisted me; making a noise, as if I had been some monster, and lowered me down upon the main-hatches …

After days of ill treatment, he was called before the captain, who offered to compromise and let him pass on his orders: 'Thou shalt stand by me, and I will tell thee what I will have done, and though shalt call the men to do it; or else thou shalt stand by the fore-braces, and I will call thee to do so and so; and this is not killing of men, to hale a rope.' Lurting refused, and Smith offered 'an employment ... which will be a great piece of charity, and a saving of men's lives, thou shalt be with the doctor, and when a man comes down, that hath lost a leg or arm, to hold the men, while the doctor cuts it off; this is not killing men, but saving men's lives'. Lurting still refused, and the exasperated captain finally dumped him on shore.[71]

The period saw a great improvement in the standard of record keeping by the administration, which is of great benefit to the historian. Samuel Pepys, Clerk of the Acts to the Navy Board from the Restoration, claimed most of the credit for this and deferred only to his Royal master, James Duke of York. Certainly it was James who issued detailed instructions to his captains in 1663, giving some detail of shipboard life as he hoped it would be, and perhaps merely regularising standard practices. On coming on board, each new man was to have his name entered in a muster book, which was to be sent to the Navy Office every two months to control his pay. Before leaving harbour, the captain, master, boatswain and gunner when appropriate were to pick out 'who are to be inferior officers, and also able seamen, grommets and boys, expressing the same upon the sea book without partiality and favour'. No one was to be rated as able seamen 'who has not continued seven years at sea (usual intervals between voyages excepted) and unless he can perform the whole labour and duty of an able seaman, and to be 24 years of age'. The men were to be allocated their stations.

> Before your ship goes out of the harbour, you are to take care for quartering your men, appointing sufficient number of suitable men for the great guns, small shot, trimming of the sails, etc., as is usual, that so every man upon occasion of service may know his particular duty and station. And you are not only to cause a table fairly written of all the men's names to be hanged up in the steerage and their respective quarters, but also to cause a small bill to be fixed in every quarter of the ship containing the names of such men as are to that quarter.

The captain was also to keep the ship's company in 'good order and discipline' and 'on board always in readiness for service'. No one was to leave the ship without the express permission of the captain or lieutenant, to make sure that the ship was always ready for service and 'for preventing of debauchery when absent'.[72]

THE REVIVAL OF PRESSING

In 1664, as another war with the Dutch threatened, the government decided to fit out a dozen major ships in preparation. From the dockyards, it was complained that to get the ships ready without the power to impress seamen was 'to make bricks without straw'.[73] The ships needed 1,870 men, but it was decided to ask for 2,000 at least, 'as some will fail, and few will come voluntarily when there is a press abroad, because they will have prest and conduct money'. Eventually warrants were issued for 2,500, including carpenters, caulkers, ropemakers and other shore-based workmen.[74] Pepys was pleased and wrote in his diary, 'of necessity there is a power to press seamen, without which we cannot really raise men for this fleet of 12 sail. Besides that it will assert the King's power of pressing, which at present is somewhat doubted, and will make the Dutch believe that we are in earnest.'[75]

Edward Barlow tried to avoid naval service. 'There being a press for seamen, I thought it best to ship myself in a merchant ship called the *Maderosse*, which was bound to Guinea ... I had a ticket given me to keep me clear from the press ... And the press increasing so that few could walk the streets who had not tickets to show, and the ticket keeping me clear until such time as our ship was ready to sail.' *Maderosse* went out and anchored at the Downs, where it met part of the fleet led by the Duke of York. The protection proved useless: 'he ordered our voyage to be stopped and proceed no further, and caused all the men that were in the merchant ships to be put into men-of-war and frigates that wanted men.' Barlow was one of 40 men put on board *Monck*, a third rate of 58 guns, and eventually he became proud of a ship 'which deserves to be set in a ring of gold for the good services she has done, being a ship where I escaped many great dangers, and she shall have my good word as long as she is a ship'.[76]

In 1665 the war started in earnest, and the government began to prepare for a fleet of 20,000 men. Press warrants were issued, but in some areas there was enthusiasm for the war. From Norwich it was reported, 'There has been a press for seamen in all the towns of the country; by the countenances of the men, they seem very willing to be employed. A company of 40 marched through the town, with drums beating and other expressions of joy at their taking water. There would be volunteers enough against the Dutch, if they were to be fought at home and not at Guinea.'[77] At Yarmouth, 'The press goes hotly along the coast; throngs are mustering up and down the streets, frolicing away their press money, and saying, when their friends try to dissuade them from going, that they could not serve a better master.'[78] But later the Commissioner at Chatham complained that the men from Yarmouth, as well as those from Whitby and Scarborough, were not all seamen, which might help to explain their enthusiasm.[79] In Newcastle the press was said to be very efficient, 'knowing the haunts of most of the seamen of the town'. Furthermore, 'as none can escape the prestmasters, many come in as volunteers because they will not be pressed; there are hundreds of stout young keel and barge men, who could do good service, and hundreds would go as volunteers, if they may be employed.'[80]

MARINES

Another expedient was to extend the use of soldiers aboard ship. The war was almost entirely maritime, and Parliament was already suspicious of armies, but this did not prevent the recruitment of soldiers to serve at sea. In October 1664, King Charles signed an order in council to found The Duke of York and Albany's Maritime Regiment of Foot, regarded as the ancestor of the Royal Marines. His Majesty directed that 'twelve hundred Land Souldjers be forthwith raysed, to be in readinesse, to be distributed in His Majesty's Fleets prepared for Sea Service'.[81] Their exact function was not made clear. Certainly it had always been common to carry soldiers on board warships, but their importance was declining, and the new-style battles were fought at longer range: their muskets were not likely to be useful until the issue was already decided. Certainly the Duke of York was keen to have a land force of his own in addition to his command of the navy, while the administration was no doubt aware that this was a way of getting round Parliament's hatred of standing armies. Moreover, it was a way of getting landsmen on board the ships of the fleet without upsetting the seamen. Soldiers now had a purely subsidiary role at sea, but they could fill up gaps in the complement, fire small arms at the enemy, carry out some of the less skilled duties in working the ship, and sometimes act as a force against the recalcitrant seamen. In 1665, Pepys went to Southwark 'to get some soldiers ... to keep the press men on board of our ships'.[82] Recruiting and training were quite fast, and at least 300 men were afloat by January. There was no definite establishment of marines on board each ship, but places were taken up as men came forward. They seem to have been a mixture of veterans and new recruits, and from the *Royal Charles* in April it was reported:

> The old soldiers which have been allotted to the fleet have done wonderful good service towards the manning them, the Commanders being desirous to change whoe goe under the name of Seamen for those Soldiers but of the new Raysed men they are all afraid.'[83]

Unlike the seamen, the marines wore uniform, yellow coats until about 1686 when they adopted the red of the infantry. They had the same style of organisation as the army, with colonels, majors, captains, lieutenants, sergeants and corporals. They saw much action in the great battles in the North Sea, and were already serving ashore as well in the defence of Landguard and Sheerness forts against the Dutch in 1667. They were to have have their ups and downs over the next ninety years or so – sometimes they were disbanded in peacetime, sometimes they were under the control of the army, sometimes the navy – but they had begun a history that would parallel and complement that of the Royal Navy.

WHY DID THE SEAMEN HATE THE NAVY?

In view of all the difficulties, Pepys took some trouble to find out why seamen were so anxious to avoid naval service. One problem outside the navy's control was the law of supply and demand – 'as pressing in men for the King raises the wages of seamen in merchant ships, as from 21s their late common wages to 30 and 35, and from 40 and 45 the voyage to Newcastle in colliers to be 50 and 55s.'[84] Once in, men were kept too long in the King's service and often transferred between ships against their will.

> That among other discouragements which seamen meet withal in the King's service, a great one is their being turned over from ship to ship, not only as it brings difficulties upon them in the procurement of their payment … but as it occasions their continuance in the service from voyage to voyage, to the robbing them of the satisfaction which most of them expect from many other reasons in being at liberty at the end of the voyage to dispose themselves as they see fit …[85]

Men who were discharged from a ship for one reason or another were issued with tickets that could be cashed in later. This led to many abuses at all stages in the process – by the captains, by the ships' clerks and at the Navy Office. Men often had to wait years to claim the money and perhaps present themselves several times if they had served on more than one ship.

Twenty-five years of naval administration and a few sea voyages gave Pepys some insight into the character of the English seaman. He believed that 'Englishmen, and more especially seamen, love their bellies above everything else', and an administrator should take good care for their victuals. They would 'do more bodily labour on their ships than the common seamen either of Holland or France, as being better fed and really stronger'. His friend and assistant Richard Gibson pointed out that '... courage arises much from the nature and plenty of our diet; and that the English sailors have better allowance of diet than any other nations ...' He also noted that 'our English seamen are generally greater ramblers and effect more variety of voyages than any other nations'. They were 'the most adventurous creatures in the world, and the most free of their money after all their dangers when they come to receive it'. Compared with a soldier, a seaman was not only in danger in the heat of battle, but 'the work and labour and hazards are most of them constant to a seaman, besides what he meets in a fight'. Moreover, 'A seaman has something to learn all the days of his life, either of sands, shoals, currents of other things; whereas a land man's trade is all certain and digested.' The seaman's life was for young men.

> What can show more the difficulty of the seaman's life than that no man will stay in it longer than he has got an estate that is competent like our ordinary masters of ships, and that no man that has any kind of learning that he can get a living with, will stay there or go thither, but keep on shore. So the whole generality of those that go and stay there are either poor and illiterate or desperate people, or at least such as being by force or chance brought thither by times are by customs hardened in it, and, knowing no better way, continue it.[86]

THE SECOND DUTCH WAR

Edward Barlow was in *Monck* when she was part of Lord Sandwich's fleet of 109 ships at anchor in Southwold Bay on 1 June 1665:

> We had not rid above two or three hours but the men at the topmasthead on board of the General had spied the Hollands fleet, being in sight five leagues off. Our General firing a gun and making a sign that they saw them, the whole fleet presently weighed anchor, and making all things clear and ready and heaving all lumberment overboard to clear our decks and guns, so plied towards them, they being to windward of us. But that night we did not come near them.[87]

The two fleets met on Saturday 3 June and fought hard all day. In this, the Battle of Lowestoft, the English fleet won a considerable victory, but the retreating enemy was not pursued, due, some said, to treason in the Lord High Admiral's staff. Barlow does not seem to have been aware of these accusations, though he was always ready to believe rumours of treason when he heard them. He railed against those who 'grudged to see their own nation flourish, striving with what they could to bring in a papist power ...'[88]

In 1666 the English fleet was mobilised again, and this time even greater efforts were needed. France had entered the war against England, with a substantial naval force. Plans were made for a fleet of 35,000 men, far more than ever before. It would not be easy to find so many. Parliament had been enthusiastic enough for war but was less keen on voting the money to finance it. The members could not understand how much prices had risen, and suspected that the money was finding its way to royal courtiers and mistresses. Certainly the court of Charles II was never free of corruption, but the war cost far more than Parliament was prepared to give. The result was that the financial credit of the government was already very low among seamen, merchants, and shipowners.

Cooperation from the local magistrates was even less than in the past. From Yarmouth it was reported that there were twenty men available, but the magistrates kept them in prison for want of a warrant from Lord Townsend. At Ipswich the deputy lieutenants and justices were 'remiss and unwilling to move', allowing men to 'skulk in the country'. At Aldeborough the men ran inland on the approach of a man-of-war.[89] In the absence of any laws either allowing or forbidding impressment, some elements in the navy took matters into their own hands, and the situation became chaotic. The gangs in London seem to have grabbed anyone in sight who was not obviously a gentleman, and Pepys wrote, 'It is a pretty thing to observe that both there and everywhere else a man shall see many women nowadays of mean sort in the streets, but no men; men being so afeard of the press.'[90] Even the Navy Board's own employees were not safe. According to Pepys, 'it is now become impossible to have so much as a letter carried from place to place, or any message done for us. Nay, out of victualling ships full loaden that go down to the fleet, and out of the vessels of the officers of the ordnance, they press men; so that for want of discipline in this respect, I fear all will be undone.'[91]

There were genuinely pathetic scenes as the pressed men were sent to the fleet. In July, Pepys spent a night at Tower Wharf supervising their departure, and wrote in his diary,

> But Lord, how some poor women did cry, and in my life never did see such natural expression of passion as I did here – in some women's bewailing themselves, and running to every parcel of men that were brought, one after another, to look for their husbands, and wept over every vessel that went off, thinking they might be there, and looking after the ship as far as ever they could by moone-light, that it grieved me to the heart to hear them.

He was concerned about the legality as much as the sadness of the situation – 'to see poor patient labouring men and housekeepers, having poor wives and families, taken up on a sudden by strangers was very hard; and that without prest money, but forced against all law to be gone. It is a great tyranny.'[92]

In December 1666 there was a serious riot at Dartford on the Thames. A master's mate and about ten seamen from *Bonaventure* came ashore to impress men. They had taken a few when a gang of about 40 or 50 merchant seamen came down the hill, armed with clubs, pistols, swords and stones. The master's mate threatened to use his pistol on them, but he was overpowered and the pressed men set free. It was decided that there was 'no legal ground of proceeding against the inhabitants of Dartford'.[93] In another violent incident, Lieutenant William Golden and five men of *Henrietta* called at a house in Whitechapel 'to try to obtain men for the ship without violence or pressing'. They were attacked by 40 or 50 men with swords and clubs, and the lieutenant received a mortal wound. But no one was prosecuted.[94] The government's whole legal position was based on bluff – on the hope that none of the men affected by pressing would be able to challenge the procedure through the courts.

The naval war was fought very intensely during 1666. In May the English fleet was divided, one part to meet the French and the larger to meet the Dutch. This proved to be a disastrous strategy, and yet again there were rumours of treason in high places.[95] According to Lieutenant Jeremy Roch of *Antelope*, 'And thus began the most terrible, obstinate and bloodiest battle that ever was fought on the seas ... The day was very hot, more ways than one, for between the flames of the burning ships, the fiery flashes from the guns, with the beams of the sun, we seemed to be in the Fiery Region.'[96]

The larger section of the fleet fought a superior Dutch force for four days at the beginning of June and suffered heavily in both ships and men, though it was not completely defeated. Lieutenant Thomas Browne of the 40-gun *Mary Rose* noticed the effect that battle had on seamen, however reluctant they had been to enter the service in the first place. He wrote to his father,

I thank you for your directions for my ears against the noise of the guns, but I have found that I could endure it, nor is it so intolerable as most conceive, especially when men are earnest and intent upon their business, and unto whom muskets sound like pop guns. 'Tis impossible to express unto another how a smart sea-fight elevates the spirits of a man, and makes him despise all dangers. He that so often stands in the face of a cannon will think nothing terrible.[97]

In *Monke*, Edward Barlow was wounded:

we had not engaged above an hour but that an unlucky shot that came from the Hollands came through the ship's side, hit me on the hollow of my ham on the right leg, it striking me lame for the present, but I praise the Lord it was spent before it hit me, or else it would have carried my leg away, but it did me no great harm ... but my leg swelling so that I could not go on, I was forced to go down amongst the wounded men, where one lay without a leg and another without an arm, one wounded to death and another groaning with pain and dying ... which is a sad sight to see ...[98]

After the battle he was given treatment.

And coming up to Chatham, we hauled into the dock on the Sabbath day, being the tenth of the month. And sending our sick and wounded ashore at Rochester, I went for one, for my leg that was shot was not well. And being carried up to Rochester, we were sent some to one house and some to another, His Majesty paying seven shillings a week for every man for his diet and looking after, there being a kind of hospital where they lay that were worst wounded, and a doctor to dress them, which we went to every day from the other places when we wanted any dressing.

My leg being upon the mending and our ship and all the rest of the whole fleet being fitted and preparing all things ready; so I staying three weeks at my quarters, and my leg being well and the ship almost ready to sail, I got a discharge from the doctor and came on board.[99]

He was back in his ship late in July when the whole English fleet met the Dutch off North Foreland. Barlow's account has been lost, but Lieutenant Roch was exultant.

Here was a glorious prospect of 2 fleets, drawn up in such order as perhaps was never observed on the sea before, for here every ship fought single so that valour was not oppressed, nor could cowards well avoid fighting. Now the English shouted for joy that they had this day the opportunity to try out with the Hogens on equal terms.[100]

The English won and exploited their success by raiding and destroying a large group of Dutch merchantmen anchored off the island of Terschelling.

But soon afterwards the Great Fire of London broke out. Yet again it was rumoured that traitors were at work, perhaps connected with the Catholic Duke of York. Barlow saw action once more in August off the south coast when there was a close encounter with the French fleet:

> and it being almost night and most of our ships at anchor and their topmasts down, they could not get themselves ready to follow them in time to do any good. Yet the first of them, coming amongst us, was taken; it coming my share to fire one piece of cannon at him. And being amongst four or five of us, there was no other way for him but to yield his ship to us, yet he fought very stoutly before he yielded.[101]

She proved to be *Rubis*, 'burthen about a thousand tones, built for the East India trade, forty brass guns, 14 iron, six pederos'.[102]

The government's handling of the seamen proved disastrous. There was no money to pay or feed them, and on some ships the wages were more than four years in arrears. Those still on board ship mutinied or deserted, while those who had been discharged rioted in London, demanding their pay. Pepys was disturbed by 'the horrible crowd and lamentable moan of the poor seamen that lie starving in the streets for want of money'. But the government was almost bankrupt and unable to do anything about it. Charles II's honeymoon with his people was over, and the seamen would never trust him again.

In 1667 a third great disaster, after the plague of 1665 and the Great Fire of 1666, struck the country. It was decided that there was no money to fit out a fleet that year, and only small patrols were to be organised. The Dutch responded by raiding the English fleet laid up in the Medway with only shipkeepers on board, capturing *Royal Charles* and destroying several large ships. To add to the humiliation, many observers reported that they heard English voices among the Dutch fleet, of men who had deserted to the other side for want of pay and victuals. It was the English navy's worst moment, and it increased disillusion with the government. Peace was made soon afterwards.

AFTER THE WAR

Barlow had enough to do to get his money at the end of the war in 1667:

> So lying at Portsmouth about six weeks, we had orders to be paid, and on the 14th November we were paid, I having been in her three years and two days, from the beginning to the last of the war.

Having ten months pay at Portsmouth, we had a ticket for five more, which was to be paid at London. And the day following after we were paid, putting our chests and clothes in a wagon ... we began our journey to travel up to London; coming the first night at Petersfield, and the next night to Guildford, and the next night to Kingston-upon-Thames, there taking water in a wherry and so coming down to London.[103]

Pepys, with his position within the Navy Board now strengthened, took the chance to reorganise many aspects of the administration, while he and many others took cover during the enquiries into the Medway disaster.

In general, the government was reluctant to use impressment in peacetime, but it was occasionally necessary. In 1668, Barlow was pressed again. On returning from a voyage to the Canary Islands the merchant ship *Real Friendship* anchored off Margate,

and the next morning we saw a frigate at anchor, we being very fearful of her that she wanted men and would press, so the flood of tide coming, we weighed our anchor, and coming up to her, her boat came on board, being manned with ten men, and they told our master they wanted some men; and our master told them that he had but few men as his ship was very leaky ... Yet nothing would content them, but they said the King's ship must be manned, so they took two men, myself and one more, carrying them on board with them on their ship, which was a frigate called the *Yarmouth*.[104]

Much still depended on the qualities of the captain. *Foresight*, under Captain Hayward, and *Jersey*, under Captain Beach, both sought crews together in the Thames in 1669 for a voyage against the Barbary corsairs. Hayward had no difficulty: he needed no pressed men – on the contrary he had to turn a hundred away, according to his steward. When a dozen of them complained about victuals, he simply dismissed them and took on more. Meanwhile Captain Beach was sending out press gangs all along the river, 'and yet he is unmanned; those he has endeavouring to run away from him and adventuring to swim ashore, in which two or three have been drowned, whilst in the meantime he keeps sentinels day and night in his ship with their cutlasses drawn to prevent them.'[105]

THE THIRD WAR

In 1670 King Charles reversed his foreign policy. By the Secret Treaty of Dover he made an alliance with the French king, promising to declare his conversion to Roman Catholicism and to support French foreign policy in return for financial subsidies. One result of this was the Third Anglo-Dutch

War, which began in 1672. The French army was to invade by land, while the French and English fleets were to combine to blockade the Dutch and destroy their fleet. The sea war was to begin with an attack on a Dutch convoy coming home, richly laden, from Smyrna.

Preparations began on 9 January, with an order for the pressing of 1,000 watermen to be chosen from those who had already served at sea. By mid-February press warrants had been issued through then usual channels to the towns and counties. There was an embargo on all shipping, and the King issued several proclamations to aid the impressment. In March he ordered that 'whereas many seamen have left their abodes and removed to obscure places in the inland counties, to escape the press', all seamen who were not already enlisted were to 'render themselves to the Navy Commissioners to be received into the service'.[106] The lord lieutenants of the counties were to impress them and 'send them under sufficient guard with careful conductors unto the said commissioners of the Navy'.[107] Another proclamation withdrew all protections against impressment and allowed merchant ships to be manned with foreigners in place of the pressed men. Even tickets given to men on leave from warships were not to be recognised, and the King threatened 'the utmost severity of the law against those who conceal sailors'.[108] In the various towns and counties, constables and others went round the houses of known seamen leaving orders to turn themselves in.[109]

Attempts were made to raise men in both Scotland and Ireland. In March the frigate *Forrester* and ketch *Hatton* were sent to Kinsale to press men, who were shipped to England. In May the frigate *Pearl* arrived back with 300 more pressed men.[110]

Scotland was ordered to provide 500 men – not a large number in view of the rumours that three times as many were serving as volunteers with the Dutch.[111] The seamen were raised among the various maritime towns, though they were resentful when they discovered that they were to be dispersed among the various ships and wanted to serve together. They were marched down to Newcastle under the escort of twenty horse guards under a 'discreet officer', to 'endeavour to try to prevent any of them from running away, or any disorder by them on the march'.[112] At Newcastle there was a fight between them and the locals, and one Scot was dangerously wounded.[113]

It was increasingly difficult to raise the men in England. In Bristol, 'Many seamen hide themselves and get out of the city'.[114] From Kent it was reported that seamen were rambling about the country. Fifteen passed through Rochester, pretending to be shipwrecked, but this did not fool the local officials, who pressed them.[115] From Sheerness it was suggested that the King should impress 'all ploughmen and farmers sons and servants', as this would force them to deliver up the seamen who were hiding in the countryside.[116] At Plymouth there was but a 'slender appearance' of pressed men, and warrants for contempt were issued to those who did not come.[117]

Even worse, the press was meeting with violent resistance. While engaged in pressing men in Mousehole and Newlyn, one Cornish official was 'going home at night when three or four of them fell on me, and with clubs beat and abused me, and endeavoured to throw me over a great high cliff, and had a rope with them ready fitted to hang me, and tore all my cloak in pieces'. He returned soon afterwards, and 'immediately repaired to a notary, and gave out my warrants, and sent my servant purposely with my horse to Newlyn to the constable with my warrant to impress seamen. The town seeing my horse, fell on my man and knocked him off, broke his head, and threw him over cliff, that he was taken up dead, so that for the present go no further with the other warrants.'[118] The seaman, often treated like a criminal by the authorities, was beginning to respond by behaving like one.

In May the government decided to solve the dilemma by a kind of limited impressment, and the King issued another proclamation. 'Being informed of the great abuses continued to be committed in concealing seamen from the press, and more particularly by the acts and connivance of the masters of coal ships from whom we had reason to expect a considerable supply of men upon the arrival of this last fleet, we have thought fit to signify our pleasure … that … you send for the masters of all colliers and other vessels in the river [Thames], especially those lately arrived in the river, and oblige them severally to produce and bring into our service every third man of those they had left on board them, or as many other good men, to be prest into our service.'[119] Clearly this left a number of loopholes, and a year later it was decided to take two good men from every ship, by again summoning the masters of all the ships in the river. A warrant was issued to 'cause so many of the masters of the merchant ships and vessels as are to be found in the River of Thames, so to be imprested and serve personally on board such of His Majesty's ships of war as they shall be directed to … without excusing upon any occasion whatsoever, other than their supplying two able seamen to serve in the room of each master so desiring to be excused'.

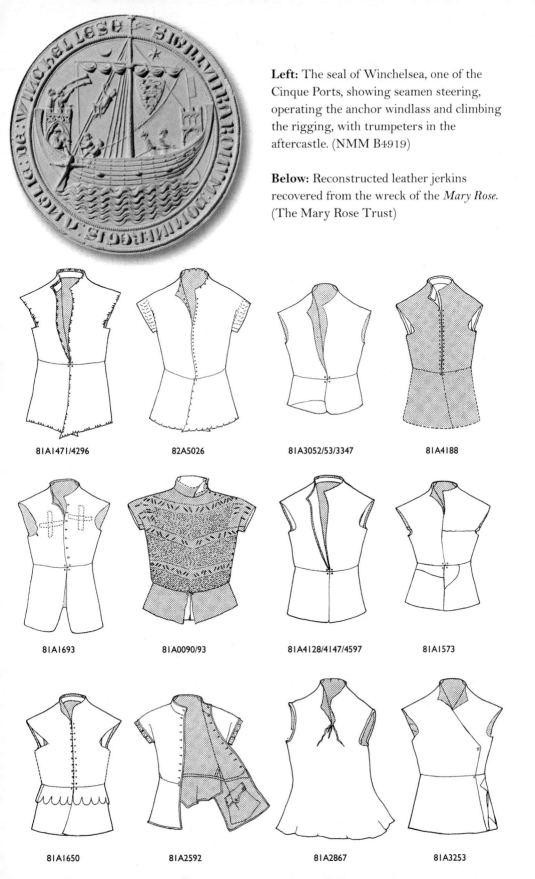

Left: The seal of Winchelsea, one of the Cinque Ports, showing seamen steering, operating the anchor windlass and climbing the rigging, with trumpeters in the aftercastle. (NMM B4919)

Below: Reconstructed leather jerkins recovered from the wreck of the *Mary Rose*. (The Mary Rose Trust)

81A1471/4296

82A5026

81A3052/53/3347

81A4188

81A1693

81A0090/93

81A4128/4147/4597

81A1573

81A1650

81A2592

81A2867

81A3253

Above: The *Golden Lion*, c 1588. It is not a very accurate portrait of the individual ship, but shows a typical warship of the times. (NMM 1091)

Below: The attack on the Ile de Rhe. (NMM PU5047)

Above: The *Constant Reformation*, one of the ships which revolted to the Royalists in 1648, drawn by Van de Velde in Dutch waters. (NMM PZ7253)

Below: Edward Barlow goes to sea from his home in Prestwich near Manchester. (NMM B1686-004)

The second part where ye two fleets begine to ingage about halfe an hour after eight in the mor

Above: Wenceslaus Hollar's panoramic view of London shows Three Cranes Wharf just below the right-hand edge of St Paul's Cathedral. Whitehall can be seen in the distance on the left-hand side of the print. (Public Domain)

Below: A battle of the Third Dutch War, showing how the lines of battle tended to descend into a melee after time. (NMM PT2530)

Above: A painting, based on a print by Thomas Phillips, showing a longitudinal section of a first rate around 1690. The officers' quarters towards the stern are delineated much better than the crew's quarters, but it does show the galley stove encased in brick, and a vertical tube behind the figurehead which was the main toilet facility. (NMM BHC0872)

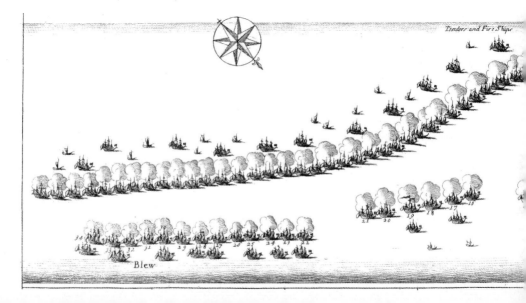

Below: The Battle of Beachy Head, with the Dutch squadron on the bottom right fully engaged, and the English centre fighting at long distance. The *Anne* is no. 22 in the English line, at the head of the rear squadron. (Richard Endsor Collection)

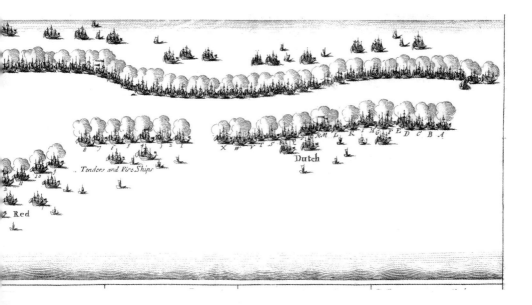

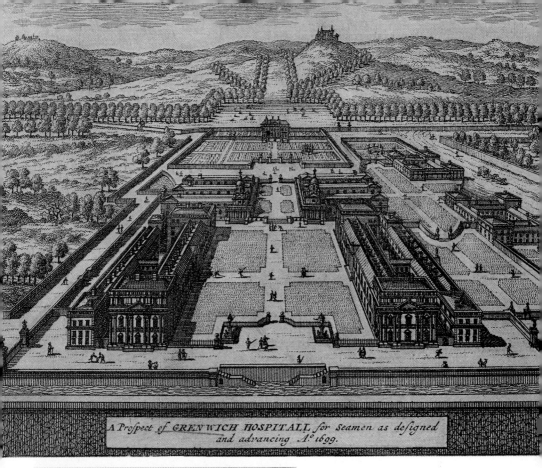

A Prospect of GRENWICH HOSPITALL for seamen as designed and advancing A.º 1699.

The British Hercules

Above: Greenwich Hospital as designed, with the Queen's House (now part of the National Maritime Museum) behind and the Royal Observatory on top of the hill. (NMM PU2173)

Left: *The British Hercules,* showing a seaman awaiting orders to attack the Spanish. It is a good representation of seamen's dress at the time, though beards were extremely rare and this one is probably only there to keep up the classical allusion. (The Trustees of the British Museum)

Thus the master himself was made responsible for finding men and was virtually blackmailed into it.[120] Also in 1673, the government introduced the system of bounties, which was to become important later. Men entering for the largest ships, the first and second rates, were to be given six weeks' extra pay, while those entering third rates were to have four weeks'. Moreover, they were not to be transferred to other ships without their consent.[121]

The war effort was neither successful nor popular. The attack on the Smyrna convoy took place on 12 March, but it went off at half-cock, giving the Dutch a good cause without doing their commerce real damage. The French advance into the Netherlands was initially successful but slowed down after William of Orange came to power and began to mobilise the people and open the dykes to flood the land. Charles II respected the French King, Louis XIV, but the people saw him as an absolute Catholic monarch, exactly what they hated, and what they feared Charles himself wanted to become. Relations with the two allies were not improved in May after the Battle of Solebay, when the French squadron left the English fleet to take the brunt of the Dutch attack. Charles had gambled on a spectacular victory to restore his position at home, but instead he became bogged down in a war which showed no sign of victory. Three battles were fought off the Dutch coast in 1673, but none could be claimed as an English victory. In 1674 the King was forced to make peace, his prestige more damaged than ever, and leave the French to fight alone.

In 1677 there was a change of policy. Parliament wanted to prepare for a war with France, and an expedition was to be fitted out against the North African Corsairs. The matter was discussed at the Admiralty, and 'His Majesty being informed by Mr. Pepys that though press warrants for seamen have been very rarely granted in time of peace, yet such is the scarcity of men now to be had, through the greatness of the merchant service and wages, that the commanders of the ships now going forth do generally declare that without the help of press warrants they shall not be able in any reasonable time to get their ship to sea.'[122] Press warrants were issued, but, in contrast to earlier years, they were to be used with great circumspection. Captains were to 'give strict instruction to those who shall have execution under you of the said warrant, they do in no wise interrupt the said mackerel or fisher boats, the support of the said fishermen and their families, together with the supply of the Cities of London and Westminster and parts adjacent during the said season depending wholly thereon'.[123] By June the King had decided not to continue the warrants any longer because of the fear that 'clamour will (though unjustly) be raised upon it, and the pressing of men and interruption of trade'. The captains were to direct their efforts towards 'improving men they have', rather than finding more.[124] Parliament had just voted for the building of 30 new, large ships, and much effort was directed towards the impressment of shipwrights and other artisans who were to build them.

THE SHIP OF THE LINE

In the 1660s, for the first time, we have detailed knowledge of the geography of the ships of the King's navy. Plans of individual ships are rare, but Anthony Deane's *Doctrine of Naval Architecture,* written for Samuel Pepys in 1670, shows how to design and fit a generic two-decker ship of the line. It is supplemented by the drawings and paintings of the van de Veldes, father and son, who came over from the Netherlands in 1675 to found British marine painting, and by scale models which were usually executed in great but selective detail.

Since the First Dutch War, the two types of warship, the great ship of Charles I and the frigate of the Commonwealth, had tended to converge. The success at the Gabbard (2–3 June 1653) led to the concept of the ship of the line – a ship that was large enough to keep its place in the line of battle against whatever the enemy might put opposite it but nevertheless with reasonably good sailing qualities for other activities. Almost accidentally, *Sovereign of the Seas*, with its heavy gun-power, had been a suitable ship, and many other three-deckers were built by both the Commonwealth and the restored monarchy, though none so large as *Sovereign of the Seas*.

Most ships of the line were the more economical two-deckers, beginning with *Speaker* (later renamed *Mary*) of 1649. There was rapid development of the type in the 1660s, each new class being slightly larger than the one preceding it. Ships were now rated according to gun-power, though there were many overlaps and discrepancies because several generations of ships were in service at once. (These ratings were largely used to regulate the pay of certain officers and warrant officers and had no direct effect on the lower deck.) In 1676 the first rate included eight three-deckers of 90–100 guns, the second rate had nine ships of 64–84 guns, 20 of the the two-deckers of the third rate had 60–74 guns, and the 40 fourth rates had 30–54 guns. All of these were considered fit for the line of battle. The smaller ships of the fifth rate had 28–32 guns; the sixth rate had 16–18.[125]

In 1677, Pepys appeared in the House of Commons to argue for the building of 30 new ships of the line, and he presented the navy as a national asset, not just the King's own possession – 'All our safeties are concerned in it,' he told the House.[126] One of the new ships, *Britannia*, was to be a 100–gun first rate; there were nine three-decker second rates of 90 guns and twenty two-decker third rates of 70 guns. Together they represented the maturity of the ship of the line, after a quarter of a century of development.

For the first time it is truly possible to talk of 'the lower deck' as where the seamen lived. The old distinction between forward and aft did not entirely disappear – as late as 1799, Nelson could write, 'Aft the more honour, forward the better man.'[127] Officers still lived on four different levels at the stern of a two-decker, the master and lieutenant high up on the quarterdeck, the captain on the upper deck, the gunner and surgeon on the lower deck, and the purser and his steward on the orlop deck below the waterline. All this was established by regulations of 1673. Fresh in the official memory was the case of Daniel Andrews, who had been turned out of his master's cabin in *Plymouth* by Captain Le Neve and had complained to the Navy Board about it.[128]

The after part of the upper deck was largely filled with officers' cabins, and none of 'the lower deck' lived there apart from servants. The area forward under the forecastle was dominated by the galley, but it had room for small cabins for the cook, the boatswain's mate and the carpenter's

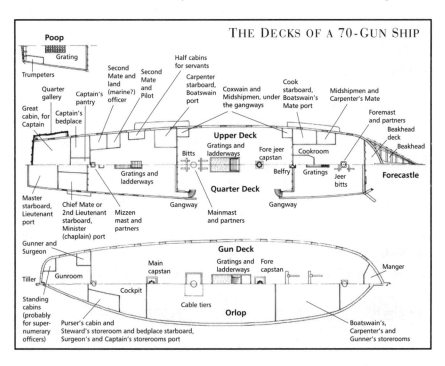

THE DECKS OF A 70-GUN SHIP

mate, all of lower-deck origin, and it is possible that some of their assistants may have slung their hammocks in the space between. The area between the quarterdeck and the forecastle was known as the waist, open to the elements and unsuitable for accommodation.

Deep in the hull, below the waterline and just above the hold, was the orlop deck. Apart from the officers' cabins and store rooms aft, it was dominated by the cable tier, where the huge ropes, up to eight inches in diameter, were coiled and allowed to drain of water after the anchor was raised. It is possible that some of the men slept there, despite the damp and airless conditions. Forward of that were the store rooms for the boatswain, gunner and carpenter, secure areas where men would not have been allowed to sleep.

This left the lower deck, or lower gundeck, between the orlop and the upper deck and a few feet above the waterline to allow the guns to operate. The division between officers and men on this deck was no longer at the mainmast as in the past but farther aft, near the mizzen mast, where a partition sealed off the gunroom. On a 70-gun ship of around 1670, this space was about 120 feet long and 32 feet broad at the maximum breadth of the ship, but it narrowed somewhat towards the bow and stern. It contained perhaps a dozen guns on each side, and down the centreline was a row of features necessary to the sailing and running of the ship – the three masts, two capstans, gratings and hatches, ladderways, the great wooden bitts, which restrained the anchor cable when it was in use, and an area right forward known as the manger, which was largely there to trap water coming in through the hawse holes in the bows. The greatest usable space on each side between the guns and the hatchways in midships was about eight feet. There was a little less than six feet between each pair of guns, but that space was restricted towards the sides of the ship, where great inverted L-shaped wooden knees helped brace the structure. The height of the deck, from plank to plank, was up to seven feet but the depth of the deck beams, 10½ inches, and the 2½-inch thickness of the planks had to be deducted from that, so the actual headroom was less than six feet at best. The lower deck was often damp, noisy, dark, and fetid if the gunports had to be closed in bad weather. This was the space in which around 220 seamen – up to 350 in wartime –might eat, sleep and take their recreation.[129]

In theory it might have been less crowded in a three-decker, which had perhaps 650 men but two decks to accommodate them on, both longer and wider than those of a third rate. In practice the admiral's cabins took up about two-fifths of the middle deck, while the spaces between the guns were filled with tiny cabins for staff officers, servants and perhaps petty officers – James, Duke of York, came on board *Prince* with 150 in his retinue in 1672.[130] It is not clear if the spaces between the ports were fitted with tables for the seamen's meals in those days. Possibly they just sat on their sea chests, though some of them may have been be dismantled at sea; in *Assistance*, Henry Teonge noted that 'we overhaul the men's chests, and order only two for a mess, and the rest to be staved, lest they trouble the ship in a fight'.[131]

The ration of food was almost identical to that described by Monson in the 1630s. There were plenty of individual complaints about it, but on the whole it was adequate.[132] The galley stove was now situated well forward, under the forecastle in a two-decker and a deck lower in a three-decker. It consisted mainly of a 'copper kettle' in which the food was boiled. One found in the wreck of *Stirling Castle* of 1679 is illustrated below. It had a lid on top, a tap to drain off the water and was surrounded by a brick fire hearth. Medical accommodation was still rather primitive when James Yonge joined *Mountague* in 1661. The surgeon's quarters consisted of 'a platform in the after part of the hold laid over with beds to put the wounded men on, and under the scuttle they were to come down and lay a heap of cloths for their soft and easy descent, to be dressed'.[133] It seems that the hammock was almost universal for the seaman's bed place by this time – the Navy Board contracted for thousands of them early in 1665, as they prepared for the Second Dutch War, for prices ranging from 1/2*d* to 2/4*d* each.[134]

THE
STIRLING CASTLE
KETTLE

For toilet facilities, the simplest choice was to urinate over the side, but James Yonge got into danger with this: 'I narrowly escaped drowning, for going into the main chains to exonerate nature, the ship yared to port and heeled so deep to starboard, the side whereon I was, that I were dipped head and ears, the afright of which, together with the surface motion of the sea, had almost forced me from my hold.'[135] 'Pissdales', shaped like modern urinals, were often fitted to the side of the ship in the waist by about 1680, and they offered no privacy. The heads, or the space behind the figurehead, was the standard place for the seamen, and by that time it was often fitted with square boxes with round holes, known as 'seats of ease'.[136]

GUNS AND GUNNERY

In the past the ship was built first, and guns were fitted as available. The ships of 1677 were perhaps the first to be designed around specific types of gun – cannon of seven, or 42-pounders, for the first rate *Britannia*, and demi-cannon, or 32-pounders, on the lower decks of the 90- and 70-gun ships. Lighter guns were used on the middle and upper decks and quarterdecks and forecastles. They retained their ancient names but were more standardised in calibre – culverins, or 18-pounders, demi-culverins, or 9-pounders, sakers or 5-pounders. New interim calibers were in service, 24- and 12-pounders, mostly captured Dutch guns from the three wars.

Guns were now made of iron rather than brass, except for older ones used in flagships. The largest had a 42-pound ball, which was difficult for a man to handle in action. There was a choice of several types of balls for use against rigging or personnel, including double-headed, bar, partridge, chain and hammer. Each gun was now allowed to recoil when fired, and fairly large numbers of men were needed to run it out after loading.

There was no longer any attempt to separate gunners from seamen in crew lists after about 1650, and it can be presumed that gunners were trained within the navy – every man was expected to serve in a gun crew if needed, and selected men would become gun captains and perhaps join the gunner's crew as 'quarter gunners'. Henry Teonge describes the fighting order of *Assistance*:

> our trumpets sounding – pendant, all colours flying; our guns all run out of their ports; garlands lay in all places filled with shot, round and double-headed; tubs full of cartridges and wads stood by, and cowls full of water, etc; and a file of musketeers stretched from the stand to the great cabin.[137]

According the 1677 Establishment of Men and Guns, seven men were allocated to a cannon of seven, but as it was not common to fight both sides at once in the days of the line of battle, that meant 14. Likewise five men per side were allocated to a demi-cannon or a 24-pounder, down to three for a saker or minion and two on a 3-pounder. A large third-rate had 130 men on the lower deck guns, 104 on the 12-pounders on the upper deck, 48 on the sakers on the quarterdeck and forecastle and eight on four 3-pounders. In addition, there were twenty men to 'carry powder for all the guns' and six more to 'fill and hand powder' in the magazine. Seven men formed the surgeon's crew in the hold, four more were with the carpenter to repair leaks, and three were with the purser in the hold. There were 45 men, probably marines, for the small shot or muskets, and 55 seamen to stand by the sails, with fifteen more in the boats and tops, to make up a total complement of 445. As with many figures for the Restoration navy, these should be treated with caution, and as a general guideline Pepys considered the establishment to be 'solemn, universal and unalterable', but it was rarely applied in practice and was in fact changed in 1685 because the supply of guns could not keep up with it.[138]

OFFICERS

Seamen needed good leadership. Captains Christopher Myngs and Charles Wager 'would not only indulge their company by turns with going on shore, but joining in their sports on board, and yet none more beloved more followed, better obeyed, or having the King's work better preformed'. Many other captains had to press very few men, while the seamen would 'openly declare their abhorrency' to some captains whom Pepys declined to name.[139] A bad example was Captain Charles Royden, who once 'commanded his boatswain in the Strait to beat a poor sailor before the ship's company for nothing but running against him as he was busy handling some ropes in haste in the ships business'. A change of command could have a good effect. Admiral Herbert had left his flagship with 'the company the greater part sick in his ship, one or two having for some time died out of it in a day. But when W[yborne] came to get the ship clean (which he found very nasty) and look after the men and get them fresh clothes, they grew all well, so that he buried but 4 or 5 in all his voyage home; the seamen blessing God for the change of commander.' Captain Villiers observed to him that 'nothing makes seamen more willing to serve a commander than their knowledge of the care of that commander to have all good men, that so their labour may be equally borne by all; whereas an ignorant, careless or corrupt commander will favour this or that officer or others with useless servants that can do no part of the work, and then not to, all the pains must lie on the few good hands.'

The led Pepys to think about the best type of officer to set over them – whether a 'Wapping man' or a gentleman. The issue of 'gentlemen captains' – Cavaliers with little sea experience who had been brought into the navy after the Restoration – was one that divided the navy. Pepys agreed that 'gentlemen ought to be brought into the Navy, as being men that are more sensible of honour than a man of meaner birth ...'[140] but he found the present group to be both ignorant and arrogant. He was told of,

> the severe and disobliging deportment at this day of most commanders to their seamen, expressed either in beating them, in the multitude of their servants, friends and retinues, to the rendering the labours the heavier to the few that are seamen, and dividing the pay of the midshipmen and under-officers to their barbers, fiddlers and other creatures of their own ...'[141]

This reduced the promotion prospects of the ambitious seaman, the sort of man who might expect to become a mate and eventually a master in the merchant service – 'an Englishman of any capacity at sea is every whit as sensible and ambitious of honour as at land: so no man can think that a seaman can ever hope to lay up anything considerable for the support of his family till his service shall recommend him to a command ...' But in the navy as it was now run, 'the whole race of seamen ... find themselves reserved only for the toil and hazard of the trade, while they shall observe themselves excluded from the best rewards of it'.[142]

He concluded that he needed a combination of the two, for he could also see that the 'tarpaulins' had made their contribution – 'here may be room to examine whether as great actions in honour have not been done by plain seamen ...' The solution, in 1677, was to set up an examination for the rank of lieutenant and at the same time to encourage the entry of young gentlemen. In the past the rank of midshipman had been ambivalent in status, a 'Bastard breed', as Pepys called it. It was usually for young men over the age of 21 who might become gunners or boatswains. Now it was for trainee officers, mostly under twenty. It was observed that the reforms would 'unite the officers and destroy the distinction between gentleman and tarpaulin, for as all tarpaulins are made gentlemen by accepting the King's Commission, so every gentleman having performed this duty cannot be denied to be as capable of employment as any'.[143] For a man of the lower deck, the reforms would eventually lead to a better standard of competence among his officers, but it also tended to reduce his opportunities for promotion. Plenty of officers would be promoted from the lower deck in the century and a half to come, but not in the same way as the tarpaulins had made it under the Commonwealth. Underlying it all, as well as class distinction, was the greater need for education in an officer, as navigation became more complex and account-keeping more strict.

LIFE ON BOARD

Henry Teonge, a naval chaplain, provides a vivid picture of life on board the ships *Assistance*, *Bristol* and *Royal Oak* in peacetime during the 1670s. Despite his clerical status, he was amused rather than shocked by the women in the crowded mess decks while the ship was at anchor in the Downs:

> You would have wondered to see here a man and a woman creep into a hammock, the woman's legs to the hams hanging over the sides or out at the end of it. Another couple sleeping on a chest; others kissing and clipping; half drunk, half sober or rather half asleep.

The women were forced to disembark when the ship sailed. 'By 6 in the morning all our ladies are sent on shore in our pinnace; whose weeping eyes bedewed the very sides of our ship as they went over into the boat.'[144]

Teonge preached his first sermon in the Downs, 'where I could not stand without holding by both the pillars in the steerage; and the Captain's chair and others were ready to tilt down – sometimes backwards, sometimes forward. All our women and old seamen were sick this day; I was only giddy.'[145] After that he preached his Sunday sermons regularly, except when interrupted by bad weather or 'the business of the ship'. On one occasion, 'In sermon-time came a very great school of porpoises on both sides of our ship, many of them jumping their whole length out of the water, causing much laughter.'[146] At other times he had to bury members of the crew, out of the gunroom port. Sixty men died during the *Royal Oak*'s voyage out of a nominal crew of about 310.[147]

Teonge noted a variety of punishments on board. As well as the cat-of-nine-tails for flogging, he witnessed a punishment for theft:

> This day two seamen that had stolen a piece or two of beef were thus shamed: They had their hands tied behind them, and themselves tied to the mainmast, each of them with a piece of raw beef tied about their necks in a cord, and the

beef bobbing before them like the knot of a cravat; and the rest of the seamen came one by one, and rubbed them over the mouth with the raw beef; and in this posture they stood two hours.

The ancient punishment of ducking was still in use:

> This morning one of our men, viz. Skinner, a known cuckold, for going on shore without leave had his legs tied together, his hands tied to a great rope, and stood on the side of the ship to be hoisted up to the yardarm, and from thence to drop down into the water three times. But he, looking very pitifully, and also by the gentlemen's entreaties to the Captain for him who alleged that he had injuries enough already as having a wife who was a whore and a scold to injure him at home, *ergo* had the more need to be pitied abroad, was spared.[148]

But later in the voyage 'one Arrosmith' was indeed ducked from the yardarm 'for lying ashore without leave'.[149]

Teonge enjoyed good living and was not upset by the seaman's lack of religion, as in an anecdote by Pepys's friend Richard Gibson:

> when Capt. Heling in the *Mary* ... was driven at Port Mahon to make his men do some work necessary on a Sunday he would have invite them thereto by saying that after they had done it, they should go to prayers and then be at liberty all the rest of the day, they answered one and all that if they must go to prayers they had as life work. Whereupon in punishment Capt. Heling made them work the whole day.[150]

THE SEAMEN AND THE REVOLUTION

Over the next few years the navy was immobilised by a political crisis that brought the country to the verge of another civil war. Pepys was dismissed from the Admiralty, and the new commissioners, drawn from the opposition in Parliament, were said to be 'wholly ignorant thereof', with Charles 'sporting himself with their ignorance'.[151] Charles had regained his authority by 1684 and had Pepys re-appointed, with considerable authority, as Secretary of the Admiralty. Charles died not long afterwards and was succeeded by his brother, the Duke of York, now a Roman Catholic, who took the title of James II. His religion made him unpopular, as did his attempts to build up an army and to increase his power. In 1688 it was feared that his nephew, William of Orange, might use the Dutch fleet to invade England and assert his own and his wife's claim to the throne. To resist this, Pepys supervised a mobilisation of the fleet.

The Dutch preparations were known in England by the middle of August, but it took a month to persuade the King that a fleet must be fitted out. It would be quite a small force by recent standards, using no ship larger than a third rate and needing only 15,000 men at its greatest extent; but impressment would clearly be needed to raise that number. On 19 September captains were ordered 'to betake themselves all means in their power for the completing of what they want of their complements',[152] and on the 24th a parcel of press warrants was issued for distribution among the captains of the ships most in need of men. By early October there was still a grave shortage, and at Portsmouth *Plymouth* and *Dreadnought* could not raise even their minimum complements. Soldiers were to be used to help bring them round to Chatham. Similarly, the captain of *Rupert* was to take his ship along the Thames 'with the assistance of your own people and such soldiers as will be sent to you from Rochester'.[153]

In view of the government's unpopularity, it was necessary to be very careful. Pepys wrote to Admiral Strickland that 'it will be a matter of great grievance and complaint if the fishermen of Yarmouth should be interrupted by taking away their men while the present season continues', and he was to avoid pressing them if at all possible.[154] Many of the captains were against James's policy, and Pepys hints that some of them were not doing their best. On the other hand, 'The trusty Captain Tennant, in getting his ship in a condition to join your lordship again, was so laudable, and indeed exemplary to others (if they would please to take notice of it) and at a juncture wherein his so doing was of so much importance to the King that it would almost have excused the carrying a priest away from the altar.' However, Tennant had been over-zealous in pressing some riggers from Chatham dockyard. Pepys warned him of 'the consequence this action has already drawn to the prejudice of [His Majesty's] service, and must in all likeleyhood both continue the greater upon it, if these men should not be timely returned'.[155] Governments were not always so sensitive about pressed men.

The fleet put to sea at the end of October, though it is doubtful if it was fully manned or anywhere near it.[156] When James sent Catholic priests to say mass on board ships there was a hostile reaction from officers and crews. There was disaffection in all ranks, and when contrary winds prevented Dartmouth getting out of his anchorage at the Gunfleet, off Essex, in order to meet the Dutch, the seamen showed no signs of disappointment. William of Orange landed his army at Torbay, began to march towards London and was welcomed by the majority of the population. James fled the country. William and his wife Mary became joint monarchs, and a new era in political and naval history began with this, the 'Glorious Revolution' of 1688–9.

Under Charles II and his brother, the number of ships in the navy had not increased enormously – from 154 in 1660 to 173 in 1688. However, the new ships were much larger – 21 three-deckers of 90 guns or more, and 31 large two-deckers of 64–74 guns had been built in these 28 years. The fleet of 1660 had needed a maximum of about 22,000 men; that of 1688, if fully manned, would have needed 42,000. The navy had fought in many hard battles and built up a cadre of officers with unparalleled combat experience, and its administration had been brought to a fine point after the disasters of the Second Dutch War, largely through the efforts of Pepys. But the English navy did not yet rule the seas, and none of its recent wars had ended in victory, largely because of the confused politics and national disunity that had characterised the last two reigns. This was to change after 1688. But the system of impressment, already discredited, was to survive for much longer.

3
EUROPEAN WAR
1689 to 1739

The Wars with France

The 'Glorious Revolution' of 1688 was the last great constitutional change while the press gang was in active use. The Revolution was not nearly as far reaching as its name might suggest to the modern mind – it did not overthrow the social order; but it confirmed the power of parliament and its right to sit even against the wishes of the king. One of the new parliament's first measures was the Bill of Rights, 'An act declaring the rights and liberties of the subject and settling the succession of the crown'.[1] John Locke, the philosopher of the Glorious Revolution, wrote that 'a man is naturally free from subjection to any government', and 'Every man is born with a double right; first, a right to freedom in his person, which no other man has a power over, but the free disposal of it lies in himself.'[2]

On the face of it, this was enough to deny the right of the government to press seamen; but the Revolution was followed almost immediately by a war with France, now the strongest naval power in the world. It was more intense, and longer, than any of the other wars of that century, and the very survival of the constitutional monarchy depended upon winning it. The war, known variously as the War of the League of Augsburg, the War of English Succession, the Nine Years War and King William's War, began officially in May 1689. Of course, England had fought France many times before, most recently in 1667, when they had been allies of the Dutch. But this new conflict was different from any of the earlier wars and much greater in scope. It was not just a dynastic war between kings but a true European war involving many different states, as well as issues of religion and ideology. Under the strong rule of Louis XIV, France had built up a great army and a navy that in 1689 was larger than either the English or the Dutch. 1689 saw the beginning of the British policy, which lasted into the twentieth century, of supporting a coalition against the strongest nation in Europe, in order to maintain the balance of power. She contributed naval power, money and a certain quantity of troops to the struggle, leaving others to provide most of the cannon fodder.

In the circumstances, there was no possibility of a far-reaching reform of the naval administration, especially since most of the old administrators, and almost all the naval officers, remained at their posts. Despite the concern for liberty, the navy needed men – and needed them quickly. Old methods, however unfair, inefficient and unpopular, had to be retained. Thus impressment survived yet another political change. Indeed, the precedents set in the 1690s – which at the time often seemed to be desperate improvisations – became enshrined as standard practice over the next century and a quarter.

The standard of record keeping tended to improve, and fewer records were lost because there were no more civil wars and revolutions. From about 1690 onwards it possible to trace where almost every warship was at any given moment, within the limits of navigational accuracy. Practically every officer, seaman and marine is recorded in the ships' muster books and pay books, and with some effort it is possible to trace the career of an individual man from ship to ship. We know the name, or at least the pseudonym, of almost everyone who served on the lower deck from this point on. But we know comparatively little about the inner life of ships for this period. Logs give some detail of punishments and issue of food, and muster books show the cost of clothing and tobacco issued to individual men, but there are no full-scale lower-deck memoirs until the 1750s. The only exception is Matthew Bishop whose status was rather ambiguous. There are no more nautical dictionaries until Thomas Blanckley's *Naval Expositor* of 1750, and that deals more with the technicalities of shipbuilding and seamanship than with ship routine and organisation. Instead, out-of-date works such as Boteler's *Dialogues* and Smith's *Sea Grammar* were published or republished in the 1680s and 90s, giving a very misleading impression.

Despite the continuity of the institutions, the period after 1688 was a new epoch in British history. It would be another twenty years before the prime minister would begin to emerge as the real leader of the government in place of the king, but he gained his power from the support of parliament, and that body became supreme and practically inviolable in 1689. Parliamentary government was relatively liberal by the standards of the times, despite several obvious blind spots, of which impressment was one of the most notorious. 1689 also began the era of war with France, which was to dominate the international scene over the next 125 years.

The growth of the empire was mostly driven by private enterprise and was not closely related to political events, but certainly the period after the Glorious Revolution was one of great colonial expansion, in North America, the West Indies, India and later in Australia and South Africa. Trade also grew enormously. Despite the increased building of canals and turnpike roads in the second half of the eighteenth century, most goods were still carried by sea, even if they were not to be exported. Finally, 1707 saw the parliamentary union of England and Scotland, which sealed the kingdoms together as an island state.

For all these reasons the navy became increasingly important. Moderate and constitutional monarchy depended for its survival on isolation from more totalitarian movements abroad, and this was achieved by the use of the navy. The army could be kept relatively small and was never large enough to enforce the arbitrary power of the monarch as in France. The growing empire, though still largely based on private enterprise, was often expanded by amphibious invasions, particularly in the West Indies and South Africa; it was invariably defended and kept under control by squadrons of warships. Trade in wartime was protected by the convoy system and by naval patrols, while the homeland itself was defended by strong fleets in the English Channel and elsewhere.

All this needed a navy far larger than Queen Elizabeth or Charles I could ever have dreamed of. In place of Elizabeth's navy of 42 ships, William of Orange inherited 173 when he took power in 1688. By the middle of the next century there were 282, and in 1783 there were 471. By 1806, at the height of the Napoleonic Wars, the fleet consisted of 949 ships, which if they could all have been fitted out at once would have employed nearly 200,000 men. Every year parliament voted a particular number of seamen to man the fleet (though this was often just a target figure rather than what was actually achieved). Under William of Orange the largest number voted was 40,000. By the 1760s, 60,000 was a common figure in wartime, and 100,000 was exceeded for the first time in 1783. By 1801, 135,000 men were supposed to be raised for naval service, and by 1812 the figure had risen to 145,000.[3]

In 127 years between the Glorious Revolution and the Battle of Waterloo, Britain was at war with France for 57 but at the same time with Spain alone for a further five. Counting the various mobilisations that took place on threat of war, and several years of conflict with the North American colonists before the major powers joined the war, the country was at war, and the press gang was in use, for more than half the period in question. Wars were also longer than had been common – the early Stuart mobilisations had usually been quite brief, and none of the Dutch Wars had lasted more than three years. Some kind of navy had been kept on active service throughout the 1640s and 1650s, but apart from the First Dutch War it was usually quite small; even so, it was enough to strain the resources of the government and contributed to the downfall of the Cromwellian state. The conflicts after 1688 outlasted any of these. Out of seven major wars, none was less than eight years long, and the longest lasted for eleven years.

During the seventeenth century wars it had been normal for seamen to be discharged after the summer season; after 1688 this become much less common, for several reasons. Assuming he survived the hardships of battle, disease and the sea, and did not desert His Majesty's service, it was possible for a seaman to spend eleven continuous years in the navy against his will. This put enormous strain on the seamen themselves, and on the maritime and trading community at large.

DYNASTIC AND CLASS WAR

The country was deeply divided by the overthrow of James I, and this added a new dimension to French strategy – over the next half century they would devote some effort to supporting revolts in Scotland and Ireland. British sea power always succeeded in reducing the level of this support, and the rebellions, though they seriously disrupted the British state in the short term, were never successful. There was always a substantial majority, in parliament and the country, in favour of the new king and queen. The very fact that the war was being fought to maintain the English constitution ensured a greater level of support from parliament than kings had enjoyed before. It allowed the fleet to be almost doubled in the course of the war and caused a higher degree of mobilisation of the people, for both land and sea service, than would have been possible before the Revolution. It set the pattern for much that was to follow, both militarily and politically.

There were a few mutinies immediately after the Revolution, largely because the seaman had not been paid for their service under James and were uncertain about their future. Discontent in *Ruby* at the Downs started with a shortage of slop clothing. Captain Frederick Froud complained,

> my men grumble mightily for the want of it in this cold weather, having had
> none since the *Ruby* was fitted out, which is now almost five months, and the

new pressed men are as bare of clothes as the servants, and those sent by Waterman's Hall, and the Free Fishermen, barer than the rest of the ship's company, being most of them servants, and badly fitted out by their masters, having no more clothes than backs.

Things took a more serious turn a few hours later when the crew was ordered to raise anchor to cruise between Dover and Calais. 'They immediately all came out of the hold, they, midshipmen and quartermasters and one and all on the forecastle would know where they were bound.' Froud applied for help from a neighbouring ship, but her captain sent a message by his servant to say that his men refused to leave their own ship.[4]

It is doubtful if this was political, at least in the way that the mutinies of 1642 and 1648 were. War with France had not yet started, the seamen did not know the purpose of the trip and might have feared being sent abroad without being paid. It seems that the seaman of 1689 was more concerned with material than political matters, and the new regime, combining king and parliament, was one their forefathers of the 1640s would have approved of.

This is confirmed by the affair at Portsmouth a few weeks later. Because of the crisis an unusually large number of ships had been kept in pay during the winter. As well as making the seamen highly discontented, it meant that fewer men were available for hire by the dockyards to fit out the ships for the spring. One obvious way around this was to order the crews of the ships in commission to help, but the men of *Bristol* and *Mary* refused to do this in March. Commissioner Richard Beach complained that 'if they gain their point in this particular, farewell the discipline of the navy, for for the time to come they will obey no commander's orders'. Beach left the yard to have dinner with a friend, and the house was attacked by some 80 seamen bearing cudgels. He promised that they would have their victuals tomorrow and called out the soldiers, which caused the seamen to disperse before they arrived.

Two days later the men of *Bristol* and *Mary* were ordered to leave their ships and be 'turned over' into *Rupert*. When the order was read, they 'swore and damned themselves they would not stir out of their ship till they had their money, nor would a man of them go on board the *Rupert* to help rig her'. Beach was calmer this time and wanted to humour them, while making an example of others by classing them as deserters, who would lose their pay, or mulcting them of money for the time they refused duty. Two weeks later the reduced crews of the flagships *Royal Charles* and *Royal James*, which were laid up 'in ordinary', or reserve, refused to do any work off their own ships. Even in their own ships they 'did little service' and were 'of far greater charge considering their pay and victuals than if they had borne a whole number of workers on board these royal ships'. Beach wanted to dispense with the crew of *Speedwell*, 'for there is no duty to be expected from them'.[5] It was not easy to get a fleet ready for the summer campaign of 1689. All this should have served as a warning to the authorities – that there were several things the seamen would not put up with: keeping them at sea during the winter, failing to provide adequate victuals and clothing, making them work in the dockyards and, above all, 'turning over' men from one ship to another.

It was perhaps the element of bitterness in this war that caused harsh treatment of prisoners of war. After their ship was taken off Brest in 1689, the crew of *Portsmouth* were marched handcuffed in pairs and joined together by chains in groups of 60, across France twice, 'under such miserable, harsh and severe usage, with hunger cold, travelling and beating, & c. That many of them died on the way, who were then knocked out of the irons, and left open in the fields without burial'. John Hutchins, the yeoman of the powder room, was one of those who tried to escape from prison – 'their guard when they took them, would chain them to a wall without shelter from weather, and there let them lie languishing for several days together.' Their captain, George St Lo, also visited the prison at Dinan in Brittany, where he found that 700 men had died.[6] Fortunately they were soon exchanged, before any more were lost.

DEFEAT OFF BEACHY HEAD

In 1689 the English had one immediate advantage – that a strong winter squadron was already mobilised with a theoretical strength of more than 12,000 men (though it is not likely that the ships were fully manned). At this stage in the war, the navy had several different commitments. As always in a war with France, the south coast of England had to be protected against invasion. The Scottish Jacobites rose against William and Mary, and a naval squadron was sent to help suppress them. Trade had to be protected, and this took many ships away from the main fleet. In the early years of war, however, the most urgent task was to put down the revolt in Ireland, and this produced the first fleet battle, at Bantry Bay, in 1689. The British squadron, though outnumbered, was not heavily defeated, as the French did not press their advantage home. The widespread commitments left the main fleet in the Channel rather weak, and in 1690 the combined Dutch and English fleets met a strong French force off Beachy Head. The Dutch fought hard and lost fourteen ships; the English were more cautious and lost only one. The crew of the 70-gun *Anne* fought well and behaved 'with great gallantry' according to their captain, John Tyrrell. The boatswain was killed by the first French broadside and his mate, Thomas Anderson, took over his duties 'with a great deal of courage and care of the stores'. More than a hundred men were killed and wounded, the masts were shot away and the ship received about 60 shot 'betwixt wind and water', close to the waterline. She had to be beached near Hastings and set on fire to prevent capture.[7]

The English and Dutch were driven from the Channel, leaving the French in control. In Ireland, King William won the Battle of the Boyne at almost the same time, but the English had lost their main line of defence, and the Revolution was in great peril. Fortunately for them, the French did not press their advantage home and contented themselves with burning Teignmouth in Devon, rather than a full-scale invasion. But it would be necessary to expand the fleet to beat the French, and Parliament voted money for 27 new ships of the line.

Meanwhile the crew of *Anne* were taken to Portsmouth under the same captain, who was now in command of the 90-gun *Ossory*, and they refused to board their new ship until they were paid for their service in *Anne* and the clothes they had lost in the wreck; they were also upset by the lack of bedding. Tyrrell had to write to the Admiralty again; the men were paid, and, even though only 100 sets of bedding were sent down instead of the 500 asked for, the ship was able to sail.[8]

PRESSING

To man its ships the navy used the old methods as far as possible, and the usual press warrants continued to be issued to the local authorities – in 1692 and subsequent years 8,100 men were supposed to be found by them. In 1690, especially after Beachy Head, other state officials were brought into the impressment effort, possibly against precedent. The Constable of the Tower of London was ordered to impress men, and the Lieutenant of Dover Castle was to raise 300. The customs officers of the various ports were also to help with the impressment, along with other officials such as the Surveyor of Navigation, the 'tide Surveyors' of London, and the 'Tide Waiters'. They were also to make out lists of mariners, with the help of the civil magistrates and Trinity House; there is no sign that this work was ever completed.[9]

The navy, however, knew from long experience that much of this effort was wasted and began to rely more and more on its own resources to raise men. From about 1691 it was normal to issue press warrants for the lieutenants every time a ship was commissioned, so it could raise men for itself. Ships of the third rate and upwards were allowed pressing tenders, hired merchant vessels that were used to board merchant ships, land gangs at small ports and to keep men who had been impressed. By 1693, each captain was given an allowance of imprest money, at the rate of £40 for a fourth rate and £80 for a first rate. At a shilling per man, this would have allowed a first rate to raise 1,600 men, compared with her full complement of 780, so it can be assumed that much of the money went on other expenses. Attempts were also made to raise volunteers. In 1690 men who offered to serve in third rates and above were to be allowed six weeks' extra wages. The amount varied over the years, reaching three months' wages in 1694.[10] By that time the navy had expanded to an unprecedented size, and seamen were more reluctant to serve than in the early years of the war because of the increased length of service.

Despite the French victory in 1690, they neither invaded nor sought battle in 1691. A large force under Admiral Tourville put to sea in June that year, before the British fleet was out of the Downs. Tourville successfully evaded his enemies all summer, but did them little damage.

SAILORS AND MARINES

The marine regiments were revived to help with the manning crisis and became known as Prince George's Maritime Regiment of Foot, after Princess Anne's husband, who became Lord High Admiral. Their status in relation to the ship's crew was made clearer: they were to be 'reckoned part of the complement' of a ship and were not just passengers, and as such they were to be 'exercised at the great guns'. They were to help prevent mutiny by their very presence, in that,

> the whole body of seamen on board the fleet, being a loose collection of undisciplined people, and (as experience shows) sufficiently inclined to mutiny, the Marine Regiments will be a powerful check to their disorders. And will be able to prevent the dangerous consequences that result to their Majesties' service.[11]

The marine regiments afloat were becoming recognised as a 'nursery for seamen', and it was ordered that 'no man shall be discharged out of the said regiment and turned before the mast as an able seaman without first being examined by the commander and officers of the ship ...' Six men were transferred in this way in May 1697, which was not unusual. A seaman, on the other hand, was not to be transferred to the marines. As soldiers they claimed the right to have wives with them, at the rate of three per company of 100 men. The marines (sometimes know as 'mariners' at this time) had their critics, and one pamphleteer wrote,

> this marine establishment is no nursery for seamen, but rather the contrary ... There is a natural antipathy between seaman and land soldiers, having different customs, manners, economy and officers ... Instead of making landmen sailors, they have made sailors landmen; more seamen having been inveigled to be mariners, than mariners made seamen.[12]

Sailors, it was claimed, were just as good as marines ashore,

> for they have been employed together but one upon land-service during the late war, which was at the siege of Cork; where a few seamen, under the conduct of the Duke of Grafton, did gallanter actions, and better service, than the whole body of mariners either performed at that time or ever since.[13]

And even in the traditional soldiers' role of musketry, it was claimed that the sailors were better:

> It has always been observed, that sailors have been better marksmen than land-soldiers, as having through the course of their lives been used to arms, not only in sea-service, but in their voyages, and the several ports they have come into, by exercising themselves to shoot wild-foul. But if this is not true, what hinders but it may be made part of sea-discipline, to exercise them by turns on board? Unless we think there is an intrinsic virtue in the word mariners.[14]

This was answered by a marine officer, who laughed at the wild fowl reference and stated:

> And as or being equally useful, I have often heard it owned by the flag officers, as well as private captains, they had rather have one fourth of their men marines, than be wholly manned with seamen, for they always found them more obedient to command in time of action, whether quartered at the great guns or small shot, or put sentries over the scuttles; whereas the seaman at such times are not so governable, being accustomed to greater liberties and disorders, and from their frequent variety of service, when the marines are kept to a constant and severer discipline.[15]

The marines did not always serve afloat: two thirds of them were expected to be ashore at any given moment. They proved very useful as guards in the dockyards, but attempts to make them into dockyard labourers were not successful. And in peacetime those who were not discharged served almost entirely on shore, so that the maximum number of seamen could be trained up in the few ships in commission.

A Victory at Last

In 1692 the fleet was even larger than in previous years, with a theoretical strength of more than 40,000 men. This was stretching the resources of the kingdom to the full, for contemporary estimates of the number of seamen in the merchant fleet usually put the number at about 50,000.[16] Even if only half the 40,000 aboard the fleet were actually ex-merchant seaman, and assuming that numbers of landsmen, boys and foreigners were taken on to fill the places in the merchant navy, it is clear that the naval mobilisation, kept up over a prolonged period, was seriously affecting the interests of trade. Moreover, it was not easy to raise such a large number. Many of the men who had been given leave over the winter had not returned, and others were reluctant to serve, despite the bounty.

In May 1692 the British and Dutch fleets fought a French force at Barfleur and by this time the Allies had a numerical advantage. Chaplain Richard Allyn of *Centurion* was ashore at the time but he got a credible account from the captain's and lieutenants' journals:

> In a trice we were so buried in fire and smoke, and had such a hot service our selves, that we could not see or mind what others did ... We lost in the engagement seven men, and had eighteen wounded; most of them having their legs shattered, or shot off above the knee. The cook, James Duell, was one of the first that fell. Soon after half of poor Webber's face was shot away; notwithstanding which he lived two days, and almost all the time kept singing. A shot came through my cabin, which killed one Kern, a Plymouth man. A gun on the quarterdeck split, which killed two and wounded three, one of which was Mr Raymond, whose leg was much shattered, and is since cut off. Our long boat was sunk at our stern. Most of the damage we received was from the Vice-Admiral of the White who, finding the Sovereign's side too warm, tacked astern and revenged himself upon us.[17]

The French were forced to retreat. A few days later part of their fleet was trapped near La Hogue, and fifteen ships were destroyed by fireships.

> As soon as the French saw our boats with a fireship coming near them, being afraid of being served as the poor fellows were at Cherbourg the day before ... Our boat was the first that got aboard any of the ships. Lieutenant Paul entered a three-deck ship, and found no creature aboard, so he ordered the boat's crew

to cut chips and lay them together in order to set her on fire, which was soon done … In the whole action (both overnight and this morning) we lost not ten men. They plainly saw King James's camp and standard near La Hogue from their boats.[18]

Indeed, ex-King James himself was watching and was said to have remarked tactlessly to his French hosts, 'Ah! None but my brave English could do so brave an action!' Out in the water Captain Danby of *Centurion* was hailed by Admiral Rooke and asked if he was ready to attack the transports in the harbor. 'Ay! It can be safely done,' he replied, ' for now I believe my men will do anything!'[19]

It was an overwhelming victory, with the destruction of a dozen French ships of the line, though it was not totally devastating – the French still had about 70 ships left, enough to pose a serious threat. But France was not primarily a maritime power in the same way as England or the Netherlands, and most of her resources had to be sent to the land war in Flanders. After 1692 the French navy began a decline that was to last for several decades. Ireland and Scotland had already been pacified, and now the Allies were in control of the English Channel. The war entered a new phase.

THE *GUERRE DE COURSE* AND THE MEDITERRANEAN

The victory at Barfleur was far from being the end of the sea war. The French turned to a new strategy, the *guerre de course*. Compared with the Dutch and the British, their trade was relatively small, but they had quite a large number of seamen, while the merchant ships were largely unemployed because of the lack of sea power. The solution was for the crown to encourage the fitting out of privateers to raid Allied shipping. This strategy was new to the British, for it had never been used in the Dutch Wars, both sides having large merchant fleets of their own, which were equally vulnerable to such an attack. Those most affected by the campaign, the merchant classes, were strongly represented in Parliament and demanded that something be done about it. While the British fleet of recent years had concentrated on building large ships, now small fast ones, able to stay at sea all year and chase the fast French privateers, were in demand, and many had to be bought or built. They too needed crews, which often had to be kept in service all year. A ship of the line could often earn her keep simply as a deterrent, at anchor in port, while an escort ship needed to be out there in all weathers. There was neither glory nor prize money to be earned in large quantities in convoy escort – only blame if things went wrong.

In 1694 the sea war was extended to the Mediterranean. Spain was being invading by land, and the British fleet was sent out in the summer to her support. As yet, Britain had no base of her own in the Mediterranean, and the fleet wintered at Cadiz. Again this increased the need to keep the men in service for longer periods. With the war in the Mediterranean and the *guerre de course*, the English fleet was now bigger than ever. From 1694 onwards, Parliament regularly voted for 40,000 men, but the actual fleet, if fully manned, would have needed up to 48,000 in 1695. This was equal to the size of the merchant navy before the war.

At Cadiz during the winter of 1694/5 the crews were sent to work ashore but were paid the same as dockyard workers. They seemed to enjoy the life and adapted to the Spanish cuisine, though in fact most of the supplies were sent from home. But they were cold-shouldered by the Spanish authorities, who had not forgotten what the sailors' ancestors had done under Drake, so shore leave was highly restricted, even for sick men. Even so, there were no signs of the mutinies and dissent that would have occurred in these circumstances in home waters.[20]

MORE PROBLEMS FOR THE SEAMEN

In the first years of the war it had been common to keep the men of the smaller ships in service throughout the winter. This had not proved very successful as it led to resentment and desertion, but it was decreed in September 1692 that the policy be extended to first and second rates. The Navy Board, which managed the dockyards, was cynical as well as sceptical and suggested a high level of desertion might even be turned to advantage: 'if those who should not return by the day appointed were made *Run*, and to lose their wages irrecoverably, as proposed, it was hoped those forfeitures would compensate the charge of procuring others in their rooms …'[21] When the policy was announced to the seamen at Chatham they were incensed: some of the proclamations put up announcing the new policy were ripped down, others were smeared with 'the filth of the kennel'. Seamen rioted in the streets, dockyard officials were 'grossly abused, robbed and injured', and a mob arrived at where the proclamation was posted, where they 'collared the porter and threatened to sacrifice us all'. When 183 of the men of *Royal William* and *Saint Andrew* at Sheerness were to be turned over to the new 80-gun *Boyne*, only 43 could be found. The Navy Board suggested removing some of the ships to Blackstakes, a remote spot on the

Medway where they were normally fitted with guns. Isolated in this way, they might 'among many other obvious advantages, in all probability have their people under better government and discipline'. Allowing the men leave did not always work in the atmosphere of mistrust. Some of the crew of *Dreadnought*, refitting at Portsmouth, 'went for London to visit their friends and relations, and returning not in time were made 'run' by the Clerk of the Cheque'. Some of them eventually turned up, and their captain begged for the 'R' to be removed, even though 'they ill enough deserve it'.[22]

The manning crisis was even worse during the spring of 1693, and increasingly desperate measures were adopted. In February, 'bad accounts' were received from officers pressing in the west – there were very few volunteers, and seamen were going into hiding. Two magistrates of Dartmouth did execute their duty and were being sued by another one. As a result, the seamen generally were beginning to dispute the authority of the press gangs, which the authorities feared would be of 'ill consequence'. By the end of April there was still no sign of the fleet being ready, and it was decided to take half the crew of every privateer, though normally they were protected. Early in May it was decided to put five army regiments on board ship at Portsmouth, to live on the same terms as seamen, as part of the complement and be distributed among the ships as the naval authorities saw fit. This left a gap in the defences of Portsmouth for a while, and new bedding was needed for them 'to prevent their falling sick, and infecting others', which took time. By 24 May, only a third of them had arrived.[23]

The policy of 'turning over' men from one ship to another was no help, and in February the admirals complained that they had not been consulted about an order to transfer 570 men out of smaller ships into the first and second rates.

> We think the turning over of men will be a general dissatisfaction and we fear, of ill consequence, having observed by experience that nothing can be more grievous to the seamen than turning them out of one ship into another; and admit you should think fit to continue this way of proceeding, we can have no prospect of that the great ships be manned in time, and consequently the whole line of battle will become insufficient.[24]

All this had serious consequences. In May, Sir George Rooke finally sailed with the main fleet, to escort a convoy of 400 merchant ships trading with Turkey. Since they had been waiting 22 months for a convoy, there were an unusually large number of ships, and they were richly loaded. Rooke left them off the coast of Portugal, and they were ambushed by the French – a national disaster that cost the nation almost as much as the Great Fire of London.

PAYMENT

The system of paying crews created problems in itself, which it would have required a substantial amount of government money to rectify. Ships were paid occasionally when the Clerk of the Cheque of the nearest dockyard came on board and issued the money to each man. There was no provision for paying ships in foreign waters, and each man was only paid for his service in the particular ship in which he was serving at the time. This created huge problems for men who had been turned over. They were issued with 'tickets' or certificates entitling them to money earned so far, but these were only to be cashed at the Navy Pay Office in Broad Street, London – in theory, each man would have to make the journey there. In practice, it meant that the tickets were sold on to friends, tradesmen, landladies and professional ticket brokers at a substantial discount. William Hodges satirised this practice in a pamphlet of 1695:

> *Poverty*. I have a small ticket to sell; I am in great distress. I was in such a ship, and fell sick, and was run out of my money but I crawled into the King's service again, and now I have a ticket of £6 or £8 and we have not a penny to buy a bit of bread for my family, neither a rag of clothes for myself and yet I have been in the service all this war; what will you give me for my ticket, Cruelty?

After much bargaining, Cruelty agrees, 'I will allow you 34s and abate you all the charges for writings, and all will be about 6s more, and that is 40s altogether, though *you* have but 34s *your self*.'[25] In fact, a discount of about 40 per cent was more normal, but it still took a huge proportion of the seaman's hard-earned and barely adequate wages.[26]

Another problem affected the men who had left a ship through sickness or other causes. Records were produced in the form of the muster books kept by the individual pursers and the pay-books that were drawn up in London, but with nearly 300 ships in commission the central administration was not able to process the movement of a man from one ship to another, far less his periods ashore in the chaotic hospital system. Initially men who disappeared from the records were marked as 'R' for 'Run', meaning deserted. As the Navy Board pointed out in 1700, men might be lost to the system because they had been pressed into other ships, left behind by the sudden sailing of their own ships or arrested for debt – which was quite common as they often had not been paid and had to find some of their own provisions.[27] Then it was up to the men to prove that they had in fact been available.

There was an attempt to moderate the system in 1691, when the admirals asked for a 'Q' or 'Query' to be put against the man's name in doubtful cases. But this was converted into an 'R' if he did not show up within a month, so plenty of men still found themselves without the wages due to them. All this was a source of constant complaint by pamphleteers as well as seamen throughout the 1690s, but little progress was made by a cash-strapped government. In 1700 a group of 'several thousands mariners belonging to His Majesty' petitioned the House of Commons:

> your Petitioners have served their Country in His Majesty's Navy for many years, and are kept out of their pay for the said Service upon pretence of 'Q's and 'R's being set upon their names in the Navy Books.
>
> And notwithstanding they have petitioned, solicited and tried all probable ways to recover their wages, they have met no redress. So that they altogether impoverished, their families ruined, and become burdensome to the Parishes where they live.
>
> Now, considering the Sailors of England are the chief security of this Kingdom, and how much just payment of their wages conduces to the Strength, Honour and Glory of the English Navy:–
>
> They humbly lay their case before this Honourable House, praying that your Honours, in consideration of the good services of your petitioners to their Country, and out of a tender regard to their distressed condition, to give them such relief in the premises as your Honours, in your great wisdom, shall think fit.[28]

As a result, the system was modified in the seamen's favour and the rules about Qs became less rigid.

MEDICINE AND HEALTH

John Moyle, a naval surgeon 'for not a few years' and since retired, wrote in 1702, 'wherever a ship goes you may expect wounds and disasters (especially if it is in time of war) ...'[29] The surgery in battle was now well established 'in the hold abaft the mast, between that and the bulkhead of the cockpit from side to side'.[30] According to Ned Ward, the surgeon operated in this 'infernal region of his, he calls the cock-pit; and well it may, for there he has slain many a game-cock in his time. 'Tis a bloody place, that's the truth on't, and dark enough to hide all his miscarriages.'[31]

Moyle described some of the injuries that men might suffer, presumably from his own experience of dealing with them.

> By this time I will suppose the fight is begun, and your ship is engaged, and the wounded men begin to be brought down, and first one who having the small of his leg and foot shot off, must have the rest of his leg amputated to save his life ...
>
> A man is brought down having the greatest part of the thick of his thigh carried away with a great shot, and the vessels laying extremely lacerated, producing great effusion of blood, and the bone grazed upon but not broken ...
>
> A man by boarding the enemy receives a wound with a cutlass athwart his wrist, and the wound goes slanting, so that the bone is not touched, but the vessel and nerves are most of them divided. This is a dangerous wound ... because the nerves and tendon are divided ...
>
> You have another man brought down, having a musket ball penetrated into the thick of his groin, and lodged there, the great vessels wounded, and bleeding lamentably ...
>
> A man in boarding the enemy has got a wound on the side of his face by a poleaxe, insomuch that the flesh of the cheek hangs down, and the weapon has glided along the cheek bone, but has not broke it ...
>
> Either a rapier, or pistol bullet, has passed through the throat, and out behind in the neck, has missed the aesophagus and aspera arteria, but wounded the internal jugular, and there is a large effusion of blood.[32]

In addition there was the risk of being 'lamentably burned by powder; a cartridge taking fire or the like'. Even commonplace injuries could be crippling, when men suffered from 'cricks in their backs that disable them ... grievous pain it puts them to when they do but stir ... by lifting forcibly the breech of a gun to raise the metal'.[33]

There were no naval hospitals at this time, and injured seamen were put ashore at convenient places near the naval ports. Those at Chatham were mostly taken to nearby Rochester, though the Admiralty complained that there was a 'long conveyance by water'. Once there, they were quartered in private homes and public houses, as Edward Barlow had been some years before. It was pointed out that, 'Most of the quarters being public houses, there is more attendance given to their guests than the circumstances would allow them to entertain, by which the sick are neglected the greatest part of the day, except when the Physician and surgeon call.' Furthermore, 'The noise and confusion in such houses (when multitudes of sailors sit up all night to be rid of their money) very much disorders the sick in preventing their rest ... Most of those lodged in alehouses often relapse into fevers more dangerous than the first (by their excessive use of the strongest liquors, as brandy, punch and flip), before the remaining discomposure and weakness after sickness can allow them to drink plain ale or beer.' The nursing staff were incompetent and untrained: 'by the poverty of these nurses, few of them can afford fit clothes for their beds, which occasions the deaths of many, by taking cold after necessary sweating, great weakness after fevers and frequent gangrenes.' And many of the carers were less than honest. 'These unthinking creatures [the seamen] being commonly wheedled in their sickness to leave all their wages and clothes to their landlady, seldom recover, and many of their families are turned over to the parish or constrained to increase the numerous tribe of beggars.'[34] The Navy Board refuted most of these charges; however, a small hospital had already been set up in the new naval base at Plymouth, and this was to prove a road for the future.

Hospital ships could also be used: there were two of these in 1689 and six by 1696. They could follow the fleet or remain moored in the main harbours, for the administration preferred to keep its men afloat as far as possible to avoid desertion or action in the civil courts. All were converted warships or merchantmen, with holes cut in the sides for better ventilation. By further orders of 1702, a hospital ship was to have a lower deck that could be reserved entirely for the accommodation of the sick, with no bulkheads, so that the space was uninterrupted except for canvas screens to isolate those with contagious diseases. Each had a medical staff of a surgeon, three mates and four attendants. It was recommended that two or three sets of sheets should be available for each patient and that there should be six nurses and four laundresses; all were to be over fifty years of age, presumably to make them less attractive to the seamen, and it was considered whether they should be the wives and widows of seamen.[35] But there was no suggestion of any training for them; nursing was not a respectable profession in those days.

GREENWICH HOSPITAL

The ancient Royal Palace beside the Thames at Greenwich was considered as a site for a naval hospital in the conventional, modern sense in 1691, but it was to develop in a different direction. When the idea of a hostel for disabled and retired sailors began to surface that year, it was considered in comparison with Carisbrooke Castle on the Isle of Wight. After the victory at La Hogue, Queen Mary took a personal interest, and it became 'the darling object of her life'. She granted the land at Greenwich to a trust. Sir Christopher Wren, the great architect of St Paul's cathedral, was taken on and produced a design for four grand blocks, one of which had already been built by King Charles. Mary's husband, William III, was not enthusiastic on his return from the war in the Netherlands, but when Mary died in 1694 he felt obliged to carry the project on. He issued a charter, backdated so that it could include Mary's name,

> to erect and found a Hospital within our manor of East Greenwich in our county of Kent for the relief and support of seaman serving on board the ships or vessels belonging to the Navy Royal ... who by reason of age, wounds or other disabilities shall be incapable of further service at sea and be unable to maintain themselves. And for the sustenance of the widows and the maintenance and education of the children of seamen happening to be slain or disabled ... Also for the further relief and encouragement of seamen and improvement of navigation.[36]

The foundation stone of the new hospital was laid on 31 December 1696, but it would be many years before the buildings were completed. It was difficult to raise the money, and there is a suspicion that the needs of the pensioners were subordinated by the desire to create a monument, particularly after Sir John Vanbrugh, the designer of Blenheim Palace for the Duke of Marlborough, was appointed in 1705. It became, in the words of the architect Sir Charles Reilly, 'the most stately procession of buildings we possess'.[37] But the masterpieces, the Chapel and the Painted Hall decorated by Sir James Thornhill, were rarely seen by the pensioners.

The first 42 pensioners moved in to the new hospital early in 1705, clad in dark grey coats, which were later changed to brown on the grounds that they 'appeared dirty on a little time'. By 1709 there were 450, each with single 'cabins' arranged in dormitories. Every cabin had room for a chest and a flock bed on a sacking bottom, with sheets changed every three weeks. Men were not allowed to bring their wives with them, but sailors' widows might find work as nurses in the hospital.

THE SYSTEM OF IMPRESSMENT

The system of recruitment was at its most anarchic and inefficient during this period. The old method of raising men with the help of the local authorities had fallen into decline; the ancient corporations such as those of the Fishermen and Watermen were still expected to send men, but the numbers were quite small in proportion to the size of a modern fleet, so the contribution was not of great significance. Volunteers were hard to come by, as always, so the majority of men were recruited by the press gangs from individual ships. It was now customary to issue a captain with press warrants for his lieutenants when the ship was commissioned, but apart from that the Admiralty and its subsidiary bodies paid remarkably little attention to how the men were raised. From 1696, near the end of that war, this slowly began to change, and a national system of recruitment eventually developed, though it would never replace the old method of sending out gangs from individual ships.

Obviously the most fertile ground for a press gang was London and its surroundings. It was the greatest port in the world, and by 1700 it was clearing 652,000 tons of shipping per year. On the other hand, the city contained dark alleys and dingy taverns where thousands of men might hide from the gangs, so recruitment there took some effort. London was close to the main naval bases in the Thames, Deptford and Woolwich, where many ships were first fitted out. It was not much farther from the Nore anchorage, outside the great dockyard at Chatham, which was still the largest in the country and the winter base for much of the main fleet. Tenders from the major warships could easily pass up-river, and their gangs could find men in the city and its environs, then take them down river with a suitable wind and tide. It is not surprising to find that most of the major ships kept a gang in London while the ship was having her winter refit. Nor is it surprising to learn that the gangs were not efficiently organised – that they competed for the same men, got in one another's way and made a nuisance of themselves to the respectable citizens. In this atmosphere of fierce competition, they often took up men who were unfit or who were not seamen – which caused inconvenience to the men taken up, ill feeling with the other citizens and caused the Admiralty expense in transporting useless men both to and from the fleet before they were discovered to be so. 'Frequent complaints' were 'daily made to this board that many persons are impressed to serve in His Majesty's fleet, and carried on board the tenders in the river, who either ought not to be impressed, or are not capable to do His Majesty's service at sea'.[38]

In an effort to reduce this difficulty, the Admiralty appointed the first Regulating Captains in March 1696. Two captains were to be detached in turn from the fleet at the Nore to inspect the men on the tenders every day and to reject 'any persons that are impressed that are either housekeepers, men of good condition either as to estates or to employment, apprentices, or others whose bodies have not been used to the sea'.[39] However, the war ended not long afterwards, and for the moment the experiment had little impact.

THE REGISTER

In 1696. Parliament passed an act for 'the increase and encouragement of seamen'.[40] Up to 30,000 of them were invited to register with a government agency in return for a payment of £2 a year and certain other privileges. If taken into the navy they would be given preference for petty officer posts, would be exempt from turning over and would enjoy all the privileges of Greenwich Hospital. If they were killed, their widows and families would be provided for. In return they had to be ready to serve in the navy as required, if they were not already in it. The seamen's sixpences, established in the days of Sir John Hawkins, were to be collected more effectively and used to finance Greenwich.

The register of seamen was supervised by a board of four members, two naval officers and two from the Navy Board. A house next to the Navy Board office in Tower Hill was acquired and a staff of a secretary, four clerks and a doorkeeper, housekeeper, porter and messenger were appointed, along with officers at the ports where seamen might be found. Many of them also doubled as customs officers. Posters were printed describing the advantages of the scheme to the seaman. The authorities apparently thought that they were doing the seaman a great favour – but were soon to be disillusioned. The men were more inclined to think of the short term rather than the distant prospect of retirement to the unfinished hospital at Greenwich, and in any case they, and the masters of merchant ships, had a deep distrust of the navy. It was soon found that many masters flatly refused to pay the sixpences, and the act did not make any effective provision for prosecuting them. It was quite difficult for a seaman who was not already in the navy to register because he had to do it before a justice of the peace in his home town. Not all the officers of the out-ports behaved well; Mr Bathurst was suspended from the post in the port of London for 'several irregular practices'. The seamen were unenthusiastic, to say the least. The captain of *Lyon* reported that none of his men had registered, not even the midshipmen and mates, and he asked if they should be 'turned before the mast'. Both in the ports and ships everything seemed to go wrong. Certificates were somehow lost in the post. One unfortunate man on board *Oxford* had his name mis-spelt on his registry certificate – David Hughes instead of David Hewitt – and his captain kept him in irons until the matter was cleared up. And Captain Lestock soon discovered signs of fraud among the men:

on the 21st inst. here came a town boat from Spithead onboard the *Captain*, she being rowed by two young men. I caused them to be examined if they belonged to any ship, they answered they belonged to the *Content*. I was desirous to see what they had to show, one pulled out this inclosed register certificate. I asked him why he did not repair to his ship, he said he was put sick on shore, and his month was not up. Then I ordered my lieutenant to carry him aboard the ship he belonged to, he saying that he would tell the truth (which was) that he did not belong to the *Content* nor had he registered himself but borrowed this certificate of Peter Moore now belonging to the *Content*, and put sick ashore at Gosport to ferry to and again to get money. So I have detained him, his name is James Britnell and he did belong to the *Lark* put sick ashore at Gosport and the *Lark* now gone used this course to get money. The other man belonged to the *Content*, and was a consort of his, whose month I suppose was up, but did not go on board as long as they could live idle.[41]

The Board had Moore struck off the register, but it had no power to punish Britnell.

The Board did its best to support those who had registered, but it was ineffective. Four men who had become detached from *Shrewsbury* at the Downs made their way to London and asked the Board to take up their case but were advised to apply to the Navy Board. When four registered men were turned over from *Mary* to *Weymouth*, the Board wrote several times to Captain Poulton about the situation but got no reply. John Horne, a registered man from *Berwick*, was pressed into *Namur*, and his wife alleged that it was only done so that the prestmaster could get hold of his belongings; the Board wrote to the prestmaster asking him to explain his actions. But none of this had much effect. The seamen remained sceptical, and the press gangs were still lawless. Certificates were found to be changing hands for cash sums, but ironically their real value was greatly reduced – gangs were still taking men despite their certificates of registry. Registered seamen proved no more trustworthy than the others: some registered men of *Warwick* were sent ashore to make purchases in October 1696, but deserted.

The actual registration of seamen proceeded extremely slowly – 426 names by September 1696, and 3,801 by November after an intensive drive. Even among these, nearly all were already in the navy. Early in 1698, it was found that only 137 men were registered 'which do not actually belong to the fleet', and 57 of these were mates or midshipmen, potential naval officers between appointments. It soon became clear that the act was 'defective in many particulars', and it was repealed in 1710.

CHARACTER OF THE SEAMAN

Though there are very few accounts by the seamen themselves in this period, we hear something of their character by those who observed them, whether on board ship or not. Captain George St Lo knew them well and challenged the view that merchant ships produced the best men:

> There are a great many people have entertained a notion that those bred up in merchantmen are better seamen than those bred up in men of war; but to undeceive them in this particular, it is evident that a cruising man of war in two months time ploughs more sea, and wanders further between heaven and earth, than a merchant ship does in a year, by reason he chases every sail he sees to discover what they are; whereas a merchant ship, like a carrier's horse, goes only the direct road, to come to port the nearest way he can.[42]

As chaplain of *Centurion*, Richard Allyn had the chance to see the men as they reacted to danger:

> But though the wind was boisterous, yet the running of shot, chests, and loose things about the ship, made almost as great noise as that. We had about sixteen or seventeen butts and pipes of wine in the steerage, all of which gave way together, and the head of one of them broke out. We shipped several great seas over our quarter, as well as waist. Sometimes for nigh the space of a minute the ship would seem to be all under water; and again, sometimes would seem to settle fairly on one side. The chests etc swimmed between decks; and we had several foot of water in the hold. In short the weather was so bad, that the whole ship's company declared they thought they had never seen the like, and that it was impossible for it to be worse. Notwithstanding all this, our ports were neither caulked nor lined, the want of doing which, was supposed to occasion the loss of the *Coronation*. During this dreadful season I kept my bed, though very wet by reason of the water that came into my scuttle.
>
> The behaviour of our pugs [*sic*] at this time was not a little remarkable: some few of them would pray but more of them cursed and swore louder than the wind and weather. I cannot forbear writing one instance of this nature, and that is in the story of George the caulker and old Robin Anderson. Poor George being very apprehensive of being a sinner, and now in great danger of his life, fell down upon his marrow bones, and began to pray, 'Lord, have mercy upon me', – Christ have mercy, etc, etc to the Lord's Prayer. All the while Robin was near him, and between every sentence cried out, 'Ah, you lubberly dog!' 'Ah you coward!' 'Z—ds, thou hast not got the heart of a flea'. Poor George, thus disturbed at his devotion, would look over his shoulder, and at the end of every petition would make the answer to old Robin, with a 'G—d d—mn you, you old dog, can't you let a body pray at quiet for you, ha! A plague rot you, let me alone, can't ye?' Thus one kept praying and cursing, and t'other railing for half an hour, when a great log of wood by the rolling of the ship tumbled upon George's legs and bruised him a little; which George taking up into his hands,

and thinking it had been thrown at him by old Robin, let fly at the old fellow, together with a whole broadside of oaths and curses.

Alyn thought that only showed, 'the incorrigible senselessness of such tarpaulin wretches in the greatest extremity of danger'; but it also illustrates the difference between a caulker, who had probably learned his trade ashore, and a true-bred seaman.[43]

In general the seaman was not ambitious, as a ship's cook explained:

> that my niggard stars never designed me a loftier mansion than a cook-room; so ... I conformed my ambition to my supposed destiny, and centred even my very wishes there: very, very seldom did my thoughts soar one inch higher than the steam of my burgoo-kettle ... but very happily melted away all my smoky days, in the downy embraces of a calm and thoughtful tranquillity; with now and then a small chirping can of flip, and pipe of tobacco.[44]

Ned Ward, a London tavern keeper and humorist, followed in the tradition of Richard Braithwaite with his *Wooden World* – indeed he updated some of Braithwaite's passages. Of the ordinary seaman he wrote:

> He looks then most formidable, when others would appear most drooping; for see him in bad weather, in his fur-cap and whapping large watch-coat, and you'd swear the Czar was returned from Muscovy; yet he's never in his true figure, but within a pitched jacket, and then he's as invulnerable to a cudgel, as a hog in armour.[45]

Wooden World was published in 1707 but apparently written earlier – he refers to 'His Majesty', though Queen Anne was now on the throne, and the Battle of La Hogue was in the current war,[46] which implies that it was written between the death of Queen Mary in 1694 and the end of the war in 1697. Since Ward produced a whole pamphlet rather than just a chapter in one, he was able to devote some time to each of the characters on board a ship – the captain, lieutenant, chaplain, master, purser, surgeon, gunner, carpenter, boatswain, cook, midshipman, captain's steward and the seaman. This also reflects the greater complexity and stratification of shipboard life, with more steps between the common mariner and the commissioned officer. Braithwaite's mariner was a possible future officer; Ward's seaman was not. Instead that role was taken over by the midshipman.

Ward's reliability has been questioned. For the 1750s at least, 'his work does not deserve to be used as evidence'.[47] Certainly there is no reason to believe that he had any personal experience of the sea – at worst he was an ill-informed satirist, and perhaps nothing he says is literally true. However, he did know something about the sailor ashore, and even more he reflects the contemporary attitudes to the seaman and what was believed about him. When he writes that a ship of war was, 'the New-Bridewell of the nation, where all the incorrigible rascals are sent …',[48] we can see that it was already common belief that ships were partly manned by criminals and miscreants.

Ward's seaman was apparently less able than Braithwaite's to cope with luxury:

> He can no more sleep in sheets than in a horse-pond; and put him in a feather-bed, he shall fancy he's sinking straight, and fall to swimming in all weathers; but sling him up in a hammock, and he shall lie a whole night as dormant as Mahomet hanging betwixt two lode-stones.[49]

For all his satire, Ward has great respect for the common seaman, less for his officers. He writes of the captain, 'Thus the wretched ship's crew, that sweat and fight for bread, get scarce the very husk, whilst he runs away with the flower of the cargo, and epicures his pocky carcass for ever after.' Moreover, 'Our ships of war are indisputably the best in the world, and so might the sailors be too; for all depends on the merit of the commander …'[50]

Of the other members of the crew of lower-deck origin, the boatswain, 'fancies himself the best sailor in the ship, and would have you believe, that she had perished a hundred times, had he been from her …'[51] The gunner, according to Ward, was often promoted through influence and favouritism. He was, 'commonly the spawn of the captain's own projection; he was originally his footboy, and from thence, step by step, mounted to be his steward; in which station, having acquitted himself with singular sharpness, his creator rewarded him with this lazy office of a gunner, which was the mark he always aimed at.'[52] The ship's cook was invariably a disabled seaman: 'Has been an able fellow in the last war, and had been so in this too, but for a scurvy bullet at La Hogue, that shot away one of his limbs, and so cut him out for a sea-cook.'[53] His culinary skills were not high, and he was not to be confused with the captain's cook, who cooked in a very different style:

> His knowledge extends not to half a dozen dishes; but he's so pretty a fellow at what he undertakes, that the bare sight of his cookery gives you a belly-full.

He cooks by the hour glass, as the parsons preach sermons ... All his science is contained within the cover of a sea-kettle. The composing of a minced-pie, is metaphysics to him; and the roasting of a pig as puzzling as the squaring of a circle.[54]

Much of his income came from the sale of grease, so, 'He has sent the fellow a thousand times to the devil that first invented lobscouse ...'[55] That traditional sailors' dish was made from it.

Ward's captain's steward is apparently a disreputable minor gentleman who has been saved from transportation to the colonies and elevated by the captain:

He is a great virtuoso, that's certain, for he has been many years a close student in both the universities of Newgate and Gatehouse; and having at last passed his probation at the Old Bailey, was, *nemine contradicente*, adjudged a qualified person for any of His Majesty's plantations; but considering the present juncture and the great need that Europe might have of him, he came to have the navy assigned him for his portion.[56]

DRESS

Detailed contracts for seamen's slop clothes, to be sold on board by the purser, were drawn up in 1706. There is no sign that blue had been established as the seaman's colour, grey faced with red being the most common. There were 'shrunk grey kersey jackets, lined with red cotton, with fifteen brass buttons and two pockets of linen, the button holes stitched with gold coloured thread, at three and fourpence each'. Waistcoats were in 'Welsh red'; there were red kersey breeches and 'red flowered shag breeches', as well as a striped version, 'lined with linen, with three leather pockets and fourteen white tinned buttons, the button holes stitched with white thread, at eight shillings each'. Shirts were made of blue and white chequered linen, and leather caps were available in two models, at ninepence and sixpence each. There were drawers of blue and white check, grey woollen stockings and grey woollen gloves. Shoes were double-soled and round-toed at $\frac{3}{4}d$ a pair, while brass buckles were extra at $2d$ a pair.[57] The contract was re-written twenty years later with some changes – 'striped ticking waistcoats of proper lengths' were added to the wardrobe, along with 'striped ticking breeches'.[58]

There is no reason, however, to assume that this led to uniformity of appearance among the seamen. Sailors continued to wear what they came on board with until it wore out, including the contents of their sea chests. Even if they were not allowed shore leave, they might well buy more from the 'bum boats' which came alongside in port. And even if he was forced to resort to the purser when all else failed, the sailor could also make or modify his own clothes, as well as washing them. Ned Ward points out: 'He has a wife, that's certain, though he had the least occasion of any man living for one, for he has every thing made and dressed to his hand; and he that cannot be his own laundress is no sailor.'[59]

There was a serious attempt at uniformity in at least one area. Each captain dressed his boats' crews as he saw fit and, according to Ned Ward, gave the matter a good deal of attention:

> He spends a great deal of puzzling thought upon his boat's crew, and racks his invention about their equipment; if he hits upon any new maggot in their caps or coats, he is prouder of his ingenuity than a first-rate tailor, when his new-span fashion takes at St James's. He had rather see his coxswain in a clean shirt than his lieutenant, and believes a kittisol a nobler piece of magnificence than a good table.[60]

PROMOTION PROSPECTS

The new system of promotion to lieutenant by examination was now in full force, and, despite a great deal of favouritism and corruption, it seemed to work quite well. But its effect on the lower deck's promotion prospects was rather ambiguous, and on balance it seems that the seaman's chances of rising to the quarterdeck were less than they had been in previous generations. Captains now tended to bring in whole layers of their own boys and men as potential officers. The midshipman was now firmly in this category, and Ned Ward observes, referring to his berth below decks: 'Though he be elevated in preferment, quarter-deck height above a foremast-man, yet to balance accounts ... he's one half his days depressed under the other's feet, being birthed in that infernal cell, the orlop ...'[61] But the midshipman's prospects were good, 'for all admirals, as well as captains, are obliged to begin their rise here'.[62] As a result, a large number of positions which had once been available to the common seamen were now spoken for, as one cook complained: 'How many opportunities of preferment offer to those hardy sons of industry, in becoming quarters, midshipmen, mates and so on, and how very few fill them up, according to their deserts ...' Furthermore, he asked, will these gentlemen put up with, 'rugged storms, and more rugged commanders; and to the inhospitable entertainment of greasy pork and burgoo: and to swing most vilely in some lousy berth, surrounded by noise and stink of rot-ye-dogs and blackguard boys?'[63] On the evidence of the next century or so, it seemed that they would.

Though promotion was not impossible, the common sailor no longer expected to rise high in the Royal Navy, partly because he knew nothing of navigation – 'for yard-arm, whip-staff, or stowing of an anchor, he is the best of sailors; but as to higher matters, he leaves them to deep-read scholars; for he has no more notion of navigation than an African of snow, or a blind man of colours.'[64] Robert Crosfield identified this as a reason why the embryonic middle class did not send their sons into the navy. The 'middle sort of people' were 'greatly averse to the bringing up their children sailors'.[65] In contrast, promotion was much freer in the merchant service for a boy without friends and influence: it was 'mainly the charming prospect of becoming in a short period, mate, or gunner, or the like officer aboard those vessels; by which they ever after stand fair in rising to be commander ...'[66]

LIFE AFLOAT AND ASHORE

Life on board was cramped, as one surgeon described:

> The air is very much confined between the decks of a ship; the ports that would carry off the bad, and bring us fresh air, being obliged for safety to be shut, and great numbers of men to lodge there. The effluvias from perspiration, and their breathing together, will load the air with corrupting particles, and, as it fills with such heat, weakens its spring and elasticity; and by that means renders it unfit for receiving again. Add to this the filth and nastiness bred from such a number, by neglect and idleness ...[67]

It is not surprising that sailors wanted to escape from this, even if only briefly, but their captains did not help them:

> While ships are at sea, as there is no ground for complaint, so is there no freedom then sought after, but when they are fast moored, and have nothing in hand, but what half, nay a quarter of the crew can mange by turns; in such a case, to keep them pent up for whole months together is what they hate like death; is smells so much of Newgate, has so much the show of a prison: that these poor pounded cattle, will leap over all considerations and in spite of everything, run, or swim on shore, even merely to convince their wives and children that they are not what they take them to be, slaves or gaol-birds.[68]

As a tavern keeper, Ned Ward was perhaps more familiar with the seamen's behaviour when he did get ashore, and his dealings with prostitutes:

> He's one that's the greatest prisoner, and the greatest rambler in Christendom; there is not a corner of the world but he visits, and yet the poor slave very rarely

makes one step beyond the sight of his old habitation; but when he does get ashore, he pays it off with a vengeance; for knowing his time to be but short, he crowds much in a little room, and lives as fast as possible.

His first care, is to truck some old cumbersome coat or other, for a good warm lining to his belly; and then to be sure his courage is up, and he must have a brush with some vessel of iniquity or other. He's sure to board the very first vessel he sees, and carries her straight, without expense of shot or powder; but unlucky fortune, that should favour the bold, leaves him in the lurch; for, instead of meeting with a purchase, he finds himself grappled to a fireship ...[69]

According to the *Dictionary of the Vulgar Tongue* a century later, a fireship was 'a wench who has the venereal disease'.[70]

Ward often saw the seamen in London after they had finally been paid off: 'and then he must go to London, though he lose his pay for his labour. Here he becomes the *Primum Mobile* of all hurly-burlies, and the terror of the Spitalfield weavers. No music-house but has his presence ... Thus he lives, till he can no longer live thus, and then he puts to sea again to fish for more silver.'[71]

PEACE AND WAR

The War of the League of Augsburg ended in 1697. The power of Louis XIV was checked, the Netherlands saved from invasion by France, and the English Revolution was secure for the moment, William III's right to the throne being recognised by the French King. It had been a massive effort, for, as well as a great navy, Britain had also raised an army of 40,000 men. It was to set many precedents for wars that were to follow, some of them unfortunate.

The Peace of Ryswick did not last long. In 1700 the King of Spain died childless, and two main claimants were put forward for the throne. The Bourbon one, Phillip V, would clearly form an alliance with his cousin in France. Britain and Holland were determined to prevent this and supported the Habsburg claimant, whom they called Charles III. The next year, ex-King James II died in France. Louis XIV immediately recognised his Catholic son, the 'Old Pretender', as King of England. William III began to prepare for war, but it had not yet begun when he too died early in 1702, to be succeeded by his sister-in-law Anne, Protestant daughter of James.

Even before the war began, preparations were being made to mobilise the fleet. On 2 January 1702, the Lord High Admiral gave orders to captains 'to imprest the seamen from such homeward bound merchant ships as they shall meet with in the Downs'.[72] An embargo was placed on shipping, though ships which had already cleared Gravesend in the Thames were allowed to proceed on delivering up a quarter of their crews, while those still upriver from Gravesend had to give up half.[73] Evidently this was not successful, as the crews merely hid themselves ashore. The usual orders were issued to the local authorities and the vice admirals of the counties, while the press gangs roamed the country. Bounties of 30/- were offered to able seamen who volunteered and 25/- to ordinary seamen. In addition to the squadron already sent to the West Indies, a fleet of 30 English and 20 Dutch ships of the line, plus transports and smaller warships, was ready to sail from Spithead in June.

REORGANISATION OF PRESSING

Regulating captains were appointed again. This time their instructions were a little more detailed, though their basic responsibilities were not greatly extended. They were 'to appoint a proper place near Tower Hill, where to meet and manage that affair, and publish what certain times of the day you shall think most proper for such persons to attend who shall have occasion to apply themselves to you'. They were to visit the tenders daily, to send them back to the ships to which they belonged when they were full, and to supervise the raising of watermen by their Company.[74] 'All persons aggrieved by the press' were entitled to apply to them for redress.[75] During the course of the War of the Spanish Succession, they began to take on responsibility for controlling the press gangs sent to London by particular ships. By an order of 1711, they were

> required and directed to give orders to the several lieutenants, which now are or may be employed with tenders in the River of Thames to procure men for Her Majesty's ships wherunto they belong, that they do use their best endeavours to impress for the service of the fleet all watermen that can be found on or about the said river.

They were also to 'direct the aforesaid lieutenants to be very diligent also in the impressing able seamen, or seafaring men, that are fit for Her Majesty's service, and no others'.[76] It was clear that they were beginning to direct the gangs, to plan their activities, collect information of seamen evading the press and allocate particular areas to each gang. The captains were allowed £5 per week pay and a boat rowed by two watermen from Deptford Dockyard.[77]

In the 1700s, Matthew Bishop was part of a gang landed from *Fox* – 'a pretty large body of us went.'[78] Bishop persuaded his companions (for apparently the gang was not led by officers as it should have been) to split into two, going himself with 'those that were liberal and facetious, and could make anything agreeable that we could meet with'. Later he landed with another gang at Dublin, made up of twenty men. Again he persuaded them to split up. 'I knowing that men had rather shun than meet a press gang, we divided into three companies, and I said to them, as they had approved of the division, I think we will go into the town, and two companies may go down to the [out]skirts; but we will go through the middle of the town, and by that means we shall sweep it clean, and then we shall meet together at the end.'[79]

New means were found for raising men. Debtors owing less than £30 were offered release from prison on condition that they would volunteer for the navy, while it was ordered that men serving with the fleet could not be arrested for a debt of less than £20. The marines were used to help prevent desertions and to prevent seamen travelling by land about the country. Guards were posted at strategic points, and in 1703, for example, cavalry were placed on the road between Portsmouth and London to catch stragglers.[80] At sea, the use of pressing tenders was further increased; even fourth rates were now given one each when completing with men, while a first rate serving as a flagship might have as many as four.[81] Ships were sent to patrol in key areas – between Scilly and Ushant, the Bristol Channel, the Nore, the Downs and between Dungeness and the French coast – to pick up men from homecoming ships.[82]

In the 1690s a small vessel was attached to each major ship to help with pressing seamen. There were 130 of these 'press-ketches' in 1694, though actually some of them were smacks, yachts or hoys. It was not very efficient as it was increasingly common for men to spend days on board the tender, one of the most unpleasant aspects of the whole experience. Robert Crosfield complained, 'It's the press-ketches which are guilty of all this; and it's by reason of their slowness and difficulty they meet with in getting men for His Majesty's service, which is the grand cause why our merchants have been so long detained in port and they and the coasters have been so much exposed to the violence of the enemy.'[83] The Admiralty tried to mitigate this in 1695, when it found out that men were 'obliged to lie, either on the cask or ballast, to the great endangering their health'. It issued orders to the Navy Board to

cause fitting accommodation to be made on board the tenders belonging to the [*Royal Katherine*] either by furnishing them with hammocks, board to make platforms, or in such other manner as you shall think most proper, for the greater encouragement and better preserving the healths of such men as are frequently put on board them for His Majesty's service.[84]

This did not have much effect. In 1728 in one tender, 'her hold was secured with strong iron bars, and gratings and hatches on deck, with only a small place left open, guarded with sentinels, who let down the prest men, one at a time, through a narrow scuttle or trap-door'. It was reported:

> A poor fellow, just turned into the hold, looking up at the iron gates over him, passionately broke out in these terms: 'I am in a dungeon! What have I done to be dragged from my wife and children in this manner? Why was I shut in here? I that am born to be free, are not I and the greatest duke in England equally born free?'[85]

THE WAR

The French fleet made no serious challenge to dominate the English Channel in this war and never threatened invasion, though in 1708 a squadron supported a Jacobite rising in Scotland. The *guerre de course* continued and caused the building of some small warships of the fifth and sixth rates. Otherwise there was no new building of ships, merely rebuilding of old ones and replacement of those lost. During the war the total number of ships increased only from 272 to 278. However, the range of the war was greater than ever before. The French claimant arrived in Spain early in the war and established himself upon the throne. This meant that the vast empire of Spain – in Latin America, the Caribbean and the Mediterranean – was available for attack by British forces.

The new war began with a débâcle in the West Indies. In August 1702, Admiral John Benbow chased a French squadron with his own force of seven ships but was let down by his captains, especially Richard Kirkby of the ill-named *Defiance*. When Kirkby sheared off from the action and ordered his crews to cease fire, there was fury on the gundecks, 'the men crying out that they should be knocked in the head at their guns, and that if some few guns were fired now and then 'twould prevent the enemy having so fair an object at them ...' John Hazlehurst, coxswain of the ship's barge, was brought down to the cockpit with a severed arm and railed against the captain. He 'exclaimed extremely against Colonel Kirkby his then captain for ill conduct, saying it was God's just judgment on him for sailing with a person he knew to be a coward ...' He was reproved by the dying second lieutenant of the ship but remained defiant – 'they were destroyed at their guns without making any resistance' and suffered 'barbarous usage for standing still to be dashed at the guns without making any resistance that commanding no gun should be fired ...'[86] Two days later *Defiance* was under the stern of one of the French ships, but still Kirkby would not fire. When Benbow called over with orders to engage, this was repeated by *Defiance*'s boatswain and the men on the forecastle, 'whereupon his Captain reproved him bid him hold his tongue and told him to mind his own business and not intermeddle in that affair which if he did not regard he would run his sword into him ...' The men in the gun crews 'cried out they had as good throw their guns overboard as stand by them ...'[87] The next day Captain Cooper Wade of *Greenwich* committed the opposite fault, firing his guns towards the enemy at about three times their effective range. Neither captain did anything to maintain his men's morale. The crew of *Defiance* asked to be fed and the captain replied with 'very hard language'. Moreover, according to that ship's boatswain, 'during the whole time of the engagement, he did not know of any encouragement his Captain gave to any of his men, but the contrary rather from his own pusillanimity by walking and dodging behind the mizzen mast and falling down upon the deck ...'[88] Kirkby and Wade were both tried and shot for cowardice. Benbow, seriously wounded during the action, died soon afterwards. He was to achieve posthumous fame as a hero of the people, a tarpaulin admiral let down by his aristocratic captains; in fact, his origins are obscure, and he may have been a son of a gentleman.[89]

Six years later, Sir Charles Wager led a squadron off the Spanish-American port of Cartagena. He captured one treasure ship and destroyed several others, to the detriment of the Spanish war effort, and to the enrichment of himself, his officers and crews. This was the kind of success that often made war with Spain seem attractive and gave even the common seaman some hope of personal enrichment.

War in the West Indies posed special problems. The area was rife with disease – it was described in Parliament as 'a sink where our seamen have perished'.[90] So men had to be replaced from time to time. Locally there were few means for doing this. The white population was small, and officers did not want to employ either slaves or free negroes. Privateering was common in the area and generally offered better rewards than naval service. Furthermore, an act of 1708, largely inspired by the American and privateering interests, abolished the use of the press gang in America, while impressment was not allowed in the West Indian islands without the authority of the governor. In general, the navy was forced to keep up its supply of men by sending out drafts from England.[91]

THE MEDITERRANEAN

In Europe, the main fleet operated mostly off the coast of Spain, in the Atlantic and the Mediterranean. The fleet of 1702 failed in an attack on Cadiz but went on to take a combined French and Spanish squadron, including a treasure fleet, sheltering in Vigo Bay. Two years later, Admiral Rooke took Gibraltar and gave England her longest-lasting base in the Mediterranean. This was followed by the Battle of Malaga, in which an Anglo-Dutch fleet fought a Franco-Spanish one. Matthew Bishop describes the action as seen from the decks:

> Next day Admiral Leake led the van with his blue flag at the fore topmast head. We were about fifty sail in the line of battle; it was a beautiful line, and would have cheered the heart of any who loved their Queen and country to have seen it. And the French were as beautiful. We sailed in the morning till within gun shot, looking at each other. When Admiral Leake got up to their van, Sir George Rooke fired a gun, and every man to be at his post. Then at it we went, loading and firing, as quick as possible. We were closely engaged, and for my part I loaded twelve times the eleventh gun, in steering [steerage?] on the starboard quarter. And would have loaded more, had I not been prevented, by a cannon ball which cut the powder boy almost in two, and I thought had taken my arm off. For it took a piece of my shirt sleeve, which caused my arm, in a moment, to swell as big as my thigh. I went down to the doctor and he put a red plaister to it, and would have had me to have staid below; but I said I would go up and see how my comrades sped, and do all I could as long as I had hand or leg to support myself. When I came up I found four of those I had left killed, and another wounded.[92]

Malaga, the only full fleet battle of the war, was tactically indecisive because both sides adhered rigidly to the line of battle and did not press home their attacks. Strategically, it allowed the English to retain their hold on Gibraltar.

In 1708 the British increased their Mediterranean position greatly by the capture of Menorca. This was regarded as a much better base than Gibraltar; it was closer to the French dockyard at Toulon, it included a large natural harbour at Mahon, and as an island it was immune to attack by land. Both these captures were to be retained at the end of the war, and the British presence in the Mediterranean became permanent.

By 1708 it was realised that the French did not intend to use their main fleet again. In August of that year they had only 19 ships of the first three rates in commission at home and 23 abroad. By 1712 there were no first rates in commission, only one second rate and 21 third rates. On the other hand, the war on British and Dutch commerce had been stepped up. By 1708 there was considerable dissatisfaction about the navy's efforts to protect trade, and Parliament passed the Convoys and Cruisers Act, which compelled the navy to supply a certain number of ships, regularly cleaned, 'for the better securing the trade of this kingdom'.[93] These ships were smaller than those needed for the main fleet but seem to have employed as many men. Parliament regularly voted for 40,000 seamen throughout the war, which was no more than in the mid 1690s, and it may have become easier to raise them. The merchant fleet continued to expand, though there are no reliable figures for the actual numbers employed. Estimates of the total number of seamen in the country, put forward in parliamentary debates in 1703, ranged from 65,000 to 80,000.[94] The proportion of seamen employed in the navy had probably been reduced by the end of the war.

THE SCOTTISH NAVY

Scotland and England had been ruled by the same king or queen since 1603 but had retained their separate parliaments and governments. During each of the Dutch Wars the English government had demanded a certain quota of seamen from Scotland, but, despite embargoes on trade and fines for ports, these quotas were never fulfilled. The wars were unpopular in Scotland, whose trade with Europe went through the staple at Veere in the Netherlands, and privateering was far more profitable. There was a small Scottish navy in the 1690s, never more than three ships, all of the sixth rate and all built on the Thames.

In 1707 the Scottish Parliament was united with that of England, and the tiny Scottish navy was integrated with the English one. Even this caused trouble. In October the men of *Glasgow* picked up a rumour at Leith that they were to be sent to the West Indies, and they mutinied. A hundred of them out of a crew of 145 deserted in boats from the shore.[95]

The union also raised the possibility that the press gang could be legally extended north of the border, though captains were advised to be circumspect at first, since the Scots were not used to such harsh methods and might resist them violently.[96] Captain James Hamilton, formerly of the Scottish Navy, advised his new masters that 'the method of impressing may not be used [in Scotland] except in cases of absolute necessity'. Instead he undertook to find 200 seamen himself in western Scotland by offering cash bounties.[97] The government apparently took his advice about impressment, and for the moment the British Navy showed little interest in forcible recruitment in Scotland.

THE NEW REGIME

The war ended in 1713 with the Treaty of Utrecht. Once Phillip V had been established as King of Spain it was clear no reasonable effort would dislodge him, and peace was made on that basis. It was agreed that the crown of France was never to be united with that of Spain, and the Spanish Netherlands (modern Belgium) were taken from her and given to Austria. The British were allowed to keep their conquests in Minorca and Gibraltar, and were given the 'asiento', the right to supply the Spanish colonies in America with black slaves. The war had begun as a campaign to maintain the balance of power in Europe, but it had done much to extend the British navy's role overseas, and in that respect it looked forward to the colonial wars that were to follow.

The Treaty of Utrecht was followed quite quickly by the deaths of Queen Anne of Britain and Louis XIV of France. In September 1714, King George I landed at Greenwich from Hanover in Germany. He was not an attractive man and, unlike most of his predecessors, had no connection with the navy. Indeed, his accession took the royal succession a further step away from the Stuart line, and there were many who questioned his legitimacy, including ministers who were dismissed as soon as he arrived. Many senior officers still kept in contact with the Jacobites and plotted with them even as they carried out their naval duties – among these was Admiral Byng, who had led the pursuit of an invasion force in 1708 and took command again in 1715 but also plotted with the Duke of Ormonde, a leading Jacobite. At a lower level, in 1715 Lieutenant George Weston of *Happy* was overheard praying for King James III and arrested. During a minor rebellion in 1719, William Bagnall, probably a relative of the first lieutenant of *Worcester*, was arrested for neglect of duty, which may have arisen from Jacobite sympathies.[98] But there was no sign of rebellion among the lower deck.

Since the new French king, Louis XV, was rather less ambitious than his predecessor, there developed a policy of alliance between Britain and France, continued when Sir Robert Walpole came to power as the first Prime Minister in the 1720s. One great source of conflict was removed, and the period after 1715 is sometimes known as the 'long peace' of the eighteenth century.

However France was not the only country that could threaten the balance of power. War continued in the Baltic between Sweden and Russia. The new British King wanted to protect his territory in Hanover, while the navy felt obliged to look after its supplies of timber, tar and other materials, which came from the Baltic. Strong British squadrons were sent there each summer from 1715 to 1720, though they did not engage in action and were not large enough to require impressment. According to Thomas Corbett, the Navy Board wrote in 1716: 'In time of peace it is not usual to allow conduct money, the men readily entering for want of employment.'[99] Presumably the thousands of men raised for wartime service were now trying to find jobs on merchant ships, in competition with the foreigners, landsmen and apprentices who had taken their place in wartime. Small ships were put into commission in peacetime, while a selection of the larger ones, known as guardships, were kept partially rigged and stored in the main dockyards, manned with about a third of their full crews. These men would take turns to row around the ships laid up 'in ordinary' to prevent sabotage or surprise attack, and they would provide a nucleus of men to begin a mobilisation when necessary.

The role of the regulating captains continued to expand during many minor mobilisations between 1714 and 1739. In 1718 four captains were appointed instead of two, and one was stationed at Gravesend to supervise the pressing of men from ships passing there. It was now recognised that 'all the officers employed in the press, and the tenders' were 'entirely under their direction'.[100] In 1738 the provision of gangs from ships was no longer left entirely to the discretion of their captains. By an order of 26 July, six ships at the Nore were each to send a lieutenant and a press gang to the yacht *William and Mary* at Greenwich. They were to go on board at dusk and to follow the orders of her captain for a surprise raid in London. On the following day, the Admiralty ordered that each ship at the Nore that was not under orders for sea was to send a gang up the river, 'to employ themselves diligently on shore or on float or both, as may be most proper for their impressing men for the fleet, and to dispose them as the regulating captain shall direct'.[101]

Spain was now seen as Britain's principal enemy. Some clauses of the Treaty of Utrecht caused many conflicts, particularly over trading with the Spanish colonies. The British commercial classes imagined that there were millons of pounds' worth of gold to be made by raiding Latin America, while those of more historical or religious bent remembered the Armada and the Inquisition. The Spanish lived up to their image when they adopted an expansionist foreign policy in 1718 and invaded Sicily. The British government responded by an embargo on Spanish shipping and raised a considerable fleet. This was sent to the Mediterranean, where it destroyed a Spanish fleet at Cape Passaro and forced them to make peace. In 1726 there was another brief war with Spain, and Admiral Hosier was sent with a fleet to the West Indies. Here his men were decimated by disease, a foretaste of things to come.

King George II succeeded to the throne in 1727, and prospects looked good for the seamen when he told Parliament:

> I should look on it as a great happiness if, at the beginning of my reign, I could see the foundation laid of so great and necessary a work, as the increase and encouragement of our seamen in general, that they may be invited rather than compelled by force and violence, to enter into the service of their country ... This leads me to mention to you the case of Greenwich Hospital, that care may be taken by some addition to the fund, to render comfortable and effectual that charitable provision for the support and maintenance of our seamen, worn out and become decrepit by age and infirmities in the service of their country.[102]

Even if the King's other hopes remained unrealised, this did indeed lead to a boost for Greenwich. The school for the son of disabled seamen, founded in 1715, expanded to take in 60 boys. The building of the hospital was transferred to the Treasury, which allowed it to progress much faster, while the king granted lands and funds in its support. Though it was not finished until near the end of the reign, in 1759, it had expanded by 1748 to take in 900 more men.

MEDICINE

As John Moyle had pointed out, accidents and illnesses at sea happened in peace as well as war, and in 1708 he described some of them. Toothache could be traumatic. 'Various things are used to stop an aching tooth, or assuage pained gums, but sometimes they take effect and sometimes not ... But if all these fail, and the rotten or hollow tooth still torment, you have no better way than to draw them out.'[103] Often accidents were quite ordinary in their causes:

> A young sailor running hastily in at the steerage door, and hitting his head violently against a cross beam, was struck down backward, and received a severe bruise on the sinciput, near the coronal suture, but no wound. However, by the greatness of the blow, and the astonishment of the man, it was reasonable to suspect all was not well within.

A man, aged about 30 years, happened by a fall off the forecastle, and his head hitting against the windlass; to receive a large depression of the skull, with a considerable fissure about an inch and half long through both tables.[104]

Often they arose from violence or carelessness:

Two of the gun-room crew falling out, the one happened to receive an unlucky blow on the head with an handspike; insomuch as there was great contusion and laniation by the claw of the handspike, which also bruised the skull.

Two men heaving in the ballast, the one gives the other a violent blow with his shovel on the side of the head and face, making a large contused and lacerated wound in the temporal muscle, the edge of the shovel bared the bone in one place, making an attrition thereto ...[105]

John Atkins, another medical officer, described the techniques of amputation, though only from the point of view of the surgeon:

Thus ready, your patient should be placed on a stool; both that he may be supported behind, and that the assistance about you may be more commodiously used.

We begin by fixing the tourniquet. And for this purpose, having drawn the muscles taut upwards, we enfold the thigh or arm with a thick linen compress.

As I remember it happened in an amputation I was present at, on board Mr C—. The tourniquet broke; and while everybody was surprised and confounded for another. I instantly interposed, and with a strong gripe supplied the room; when otherwise, the man must have expired with the flux in less than two minutes.

Besides these, we fasten two other tape ligatures at the very place we are to make amputation, leaving only room between them for the knife to go round. The use of these is to swell the flesh to the knife, and to guide it for a smooth circumcision which you are now to make, bringing it at once as near the bone as you can, and as far round. What is wanted of a complete circular incision, you are to supply with another stroke of the knife or catlin; with which also you are to separate the flesh from between the focils, and clear it for the saw.

The saw is to be set on both bones at once, (if two) and divided at as few strokes as possible, taking heed in the division that the nearer you come through, the easier to move, lest the bones should splinter.[106]

From a year's experience on the coast of Guinea, he was able to describe one of the fevers prevalent there:

The fever generally begins with a violent pain and dizziness of the head, nausea, vomiting, and restlessness. After the first day, the patient, that was dry and scorching, falls into excessive sweats; the consequence of which is faintness and sudden prostration of energy, in inextinguishable thirst, and involuntary ruining, the pulse neither high nor quick, but altering on light occasions. In the progress came on either delirium, convulsions and speechlessness, or sometimes a lethargy; under the former they commonly expired at four or five days end, with the latter continued a day or two longer.[107]

There were some improvements in health. The first naval hospital, in the conventional modern sense of a building for treating the sick and wounded rather than a merely a hostel, was built in Port Mahon harbour, Minorca, in 1712. It was situated on the Isla de Ray, for like later naval hospitals it was designed not just to cure them but to prevent their desertion. It was a single-storey building 310 feet long with wings on each end, containing fourteen wards to hold 336 men. It signalled the increased role of the fleet in the Mediterranean, in peace as well as in war.

Any credit the naval administration might have had for improving the health of the men overseas was wiped out in 1727 when Rear Admiral Francis Hosier was sent to the West Indies during a minor war with Spain. His men were already weakened by scurvy when yellow fever came on board, and more men died than the original complements of the ships (replacements having been found in Jamaica) – a total of around 4,000, including Hosier himself. It was commemorated in *Admiral Hosier's Ghost*, a melancholy song still popular with seamen three quarters of a century later:

> See these mournful spectres sweeping
> Ghastly o'er this hated wave
> Whose wan cheeks are stained with weeping;
> These were English captains brave.
> Mark those members pale and horrid
> Who were once my sailors bold;
> See, each hangs his drooping forehead,
> While his dismal fate is told.[108]

4
IMPERIAL WAR
1739 to 1783

In 1738, Robert Jenkins, former captain of the merchant ship *Rebecca*, was ordered to appear before a House of Commons committee investigating Spanish outrages in the Caribbean. In fact he never appeared, but he claimed that a *Guard Costa* officer had beaten and half-strangled him and cut off part of his ear. This soon captured the popular imagination and fuelled a war fever – the public believed that there was immense treasure in the decaying Spanish empire, with its legendary gold and silver mines. The Walpole government was reluctant to commit to an expensive operation it did not really believe in, while Parliament was keen to fight but less happy to pay. Parliament had its way. When war was declared in October 1739, Walpole commented, 'They now ring the bells, but soon they will wring their hands.'

Press warrants had been issued to ships from the middle of the year. There had been about a dozen minor mobilisations over the preceding 25 years, and many of these had involved the use of impressment, so the apparatus, ramshackle as it was, had not become rusty. Vernon's squadron was manned quite quickly with 3,670 men, of which 2,157 were volunteers and the rest pressed – though it is always possible that many volunteered only to avoid being pressed.[1] There was plenty of enthusiasm for the war, even among the seamen. Henry Roberts soon got over his dismay at being pressed:

My Dear Life,
When I left you, heven nose it was with an akin hart for I thout it very hard to be hauld from you by a gang of rufins but hover I soon overcome that when I found that we were about to go in earnest to rite my natif contry and against a parcel of impadent Spaniards by whom I have often been ill treted and god nows my heart I have longed this four years past to cut off some of their ears and was in hope I should haf sent you one for a sample ...[2]

At this stage there was no reason to believe that it would last longer than any of the crises of the preceding few years. Ships for the other squadrons fitted out in 1739 seem to have found plenty of volunteers, but the quality was poor, and it was complained that many were over or under age, diseased, or unskilled.[3]

Roberts thought highly of Vernon: 'Our dear cok of an Admiral has true English blood in his vains.' When Vernon captured Portobello in November 1739, Roberts was delighted: 'our good Admiral God bless him was to merciful we have taken Porto Belo with such coridge and bravery that I never saw before for my own part my heart was rased to the clouds and woud ha scaled the moon had a Spaniard been there to come at him as we did the Batry.'[4] Vernon became the hero of the hour, but the war dragged on far longer than anyone had intended, and the West Indies fleet became bogged down in a campaign against Cartagena. The Caribbean climate had its usual effect on the seamen, and early in 1741 Vernon wrote of 'the weak condition of your ships in point of seamen'. All the hospital ships and the accommodation on shore were already full.[5] In 1742, 3,000 men out of a total complement of 6,620 were unfit for duty.[6] Thousands of seamen and soldiers died, but it was impossible to recruit any substantial numbers locally, so again drafts had to be sent out from home.

There, the initial enthusiasm soon evaporated. There were epidemics aboard the ships of the fleet, causing 26,000 men to be hospitalised in the first eighteen months of war. Ten per cent of these died, and about eight per cent more deserted.[7] Admiral Norris had intended to cruise in the Bay of Biscay with a squadron of twenty ships. Because of shortage of men, he was forced to sail with only thirteen[8] The recruiting effort was at full power during 1740 but it was mid-1741 before the fleet reached an effective strength of just under 50,000, but this actually fell during 1742 because of disease and desertion. The supply of volunteers was drying up, and the offer of increased bounties in 1741 did nothing to compensate for this.[9] Lieutenant Campbell was sent by land to his native Scotland to organise recruitment there. He did not carry a press warrant but instead relied on the use of a cash bounty to attract men, as his poster, put up in Edinburgh and Leith, showed. He also toured the west, finding 52 men there out of a total of 222 during the whole trip.[10] But Scotland was still virgin territory for the press gangs; in 1742, Robert Spotswood, a young surgeon from Scotland, was amazed to be accosted by a press gang on his arrival in London, 'having never heard of impressing seamen on shore for the navy'.[11]

ANSON'S VOYAGE

Early in 1740, Commodore George Anson began to organise and man his ships at Portsmouth for a voyage with instructions to 'annoy and distress' the Spanish in the Pacific. It looked backward to Drake and forward to an idea of taking over large parts of the Spanish empire, but it was spectacularly mismanaged on many levels, as money and men were short, and priority was given to other operations, especially in the West Indies. Eventually he was allocated a force of six warships from 60 to eight guns, and two storeships. To man them, Lieutenant Phillip Saumarez found 39 volunteers from his native Jersey, while *Defiance* brought in 'a great number of supernumerary pressed men' from the Downs, where merchant shipping could be preyed upon. Meanwhile parties were sent out locally, including two midshipmen in a tender called *Happy Greeves* and another consisting of a lieutenant and 32 seaman.[12] Famously, the War Office tried to solve the manning problem by sending aged Chelsea Pensioners as marines – they seemed to have reasoned that marines were simply soldiers who did not have to march. Even worse, they were far from the pick of the bunch – Anson's chaplain regretted that 'the most crazy and infirm only should be culled out for so laborious a service ...' Not all of them appeared, as 'those who had limbs and strength to walk out of Portsmouth deserted, leaving behind them only such as were literally invalids ...'[13] All the rest would die during the voyage.

Departure was delayed until September, which meant that the ships had to round Cape Horn in very unfavourable conditions. In *Pearl*, the carpenter tried to repair the chain plates, which extended the sides of the rigging, but was driven underwater when the ship heeled and did not recover fully from the injuries he received.[14] The ship battled with terrible storms round the Cape, but the crew remained determined.

> Those poor men ... stood the deck with a resolution not to be met with in any but English seamen, though they were very thinly clad, having sold their clothes at St Catharines, and when chased by the Spaniards had thrown half ports, bulkheads and tarpaulins overboard, for want of which they were continually wet in their hammocks, the tarpaulins I made being of little service for want of sun to dry them. Yet under all these difficulties and discouragements they behaved beyond expectation ... being now quite jaded and fatigued with continual labour and watching, and pinched with the cold and want of water ...

But there was huge disappointment when land was sighted ahead and it was discovered that the ship had made less progress than expected against contrary winds and still had not rounded the Horn. The crew of *Pearl* fell apart and 'became so dejected as to lay themselves down in despair, bewailing their misfortunes wishing for death as the only relief to their miseries, and could not be induced by threats or entreaties to go aloft ...' After six more days, Captain Murray was obliged to turn back, along with *Severn*.[15]

Having got round the Horn, the weakened crews of the remaining ships were vulnerable to scurvy. *Centurion*'s chaplain describes the horrors of the disease:

> These common appearances are large coloured spots dispersed over the whole surface of the body, swelled legs, putrid gums, and above all, an extraordinary lassitude of the whole body, especially after any exercise, however inconsiderable; and this lassitude at last degenerates into a proneness to swoon on the least exertion of strength, or even on the least motion. This disease is likewise usually attended with a strange dejection of the spirits, with shiverings, tremblings, and a disposition to be seized with the most dreadful terrors on the slightest accident.[16]

Centurion arrived off Juan Fernandez in the Pacific, where Alexander Selkirk had once been marooned. 'Even those amongst the diseased, who were not in the very last stages of the distemper, though they had long been confined to their hammocks, exerted the small remains of their strength that was left to them, and crawled up to the deck to feast themselves with this reviving prospect.' *Gloucester* and the storeship *Anna* arrived later, with only 335 men surviving out of combined crews of 961. Even so they recovered their strength and raided the town of Paita in Chile but were too late in the season to intercept the treasure galleon to Acapulco as planned. They decided to sail across the Pacific, where scurvy struck again. *Gloucester* was in a very bad way, both ship and crew:

> she hath but seventy-seven men, eighteen boys, and two prisoners on board (including officers), out of which there were but sixteen men and eleven boys only to keep the deck, though very infirm, all the rest, being sixty-one men and seven boys, including all the carpenters, quite incapable of duty, being all violently afflicted with the scurvy.
>
> That both officers, men and boys have worked twenty-four hours at the pump without intermission, and are so fatigued that they cannot stand at it any longer. They left it with seven foot [of] water in the hold, the salt water then being over the casks that they could not come at fresh water to drink ...[17]

Anson decided to burn *Gloucester*, and for once the men did not object to being turned over from one ship to another. At last they found a small island where they could take on coconuts, to their great joy, but there was no anchorage or fresh water. 'This was a great damp to our spirits, for we well knew we were in too deplorable a condition to cruise long in search of other islands, or of a convenient place to anchor in; for we often buried eight or ten men of a day which, considering our most unhappy circumstances, we could very ill spare.'[18] At last they arrived at the island of Tinian, where they anchored, and the sick went ashore. They began to recover, thanks to the 'smell of the earth together with coconut milk, oranges, limes, bread-fruit and fresh meat ...'[19] But a small party was sent ashore with the ship's butcher to slaughter cattle and had an unfortunate incident with the natives, which meant they were 'obliged to keep constant guards to prevent their stealing any of our effects, or doing any damage to our sick'. Far worse was to come: a squall severed *Centurion*'s anchor cables, and she drifted off with very few men on board. 'It is almost impossible to describe the sorrow and anguish that possessed us (who were on shore) the next morning when we discovered she was gone. Grief, discontent, terror and despair seemed visible in the countenances of every one of us, nor could we tell what to hope, or what to fear. It was generally imagined she had sunk at her anchors ...'[20] The men worked to enlarge a boat to take them to China, until after twenty days *Centurion* reappeared, sailed back by her tiny crew. 'As our sorrow had been extravagant on her driving out, so was our joy for her return.' The men had drunk nothing but water, juice and coconut milk for three weeks, and Anson ordered an issue of spirits from his reserve stocks.

> This proved fatal to a couple of our men, John Cross and Thomas Stevens, who having made too free with the Commodore's bounty grew pot-valiant, quarreled, and fought on the brink of a well they were filling water at, where lay a long range of casks on a kind of declivity supported only by that which lay nighest the well. In their struggling they happened to move that cask, which with the weight of twenty others that were behind it, forced them both into the well and rolled in after them, by which means they were both drowned.[21]

They sailed to Portuguese Macao, where the ship was more fully repaired and Anson found a few extra men. On 20 June 1743, they finally found the Acapulco treasure galleon, *Nuestra Señora de Covadonga*, carrying more than a million pieces of eight and 35,000 ounces of silver. Essentially a converted merchant ship, she would normally have been no match for a major warship like *Centurion*, but the British ship was seriously undermanned. Anson had taken good care to exercise his men at the great guns and small arms. With a reduced crew, he adopted a unique organisation for them at quarters. Thirty of the best marksmen were to be stationed in the tops to fire down on the enemy at close range, while more muskets were placed on the gratings of the upper deck ready loaded so that the men could use them when they were not working on the guns – 'for when the great gun is loading there cannot well be more than two men employed. The rest then discharge the small arms, and lay them down again for others (who were appointed for that purpose) to load.' Anson also manned the lower-deck guns on that principle –

> he therefore on his lower tier, fixed only two men to each gun, who were to be solely employed in loading it, whilst the rest of his people were divided into different gangs of ten or twelve men each, which were continually moving about the decks, to run out and fire such guns as were loaded. By this management he was able to make use of all his guns; and instead of firing broad-sides with intervals between them, he kept up a constant fire without intermission ...

By these means *Covadonga* was taken. The officers, especially Anson, all became immensely rich, while the crew became quite wealthy by lower deck standards – each ordinary or able seaman would eventually receive £171 in prize money. The battered ship was sold at Canton and *Centurion* set sail for home, arriving in June 1744 after nearly four years' absence.

Having taken on men at various stops on the way, the crew of *Centurion* was one of the first multi-national ones in the navy, 'for besides these English there were men of eighteen other different nations, viz. Dutch, French, Spaniards, Italians, Germans, Swedes, Danes, Muscovites, Portuguese, Lascar Indians, Malays, Persians, Indians of Manila, Timor and Guam, Negroes of Guinea, Creoles of Mexico and Mozambique'.[22] However, only those who had been present during the taking of *Covadonga* would become rich.

The arrival home was a scene of national celebration, though a few pointed out that it had been achieved at great cost in lives and money. The men joined a procession from Portsmouth to the Tower of London, 'a sight more rare and not less agreeable than the secular games to a Roman'. Thirty-two wagons were drawn through the City of London carrying the treasure, 'preceded by a kettle-drum, trumpets, and French horns, guarded by the seamen, commanded by the officers richly dressed, and was lodged in the Tower'.[23] At the New Wells Theatre in Clerkenwell, more than a hundred of the crew attended, to hear a new verse in honour of the taking of *Covadonga*, the first of several performances in the celebrations. Having endured such hardships, the crew applied for release from the naval service, but were eventually granted three months leave.

The seamen from Anson's voyage seem to have suffered from 'media attention' as well as what the modern age might call post-traumatic stress, and certainly some of them found themselves in news reports that did not reflect credit on them. John Maddox did well and married the widow of a silver-wire drawer, said to have a fortune of £1,000 to add to the prize money. But there was a far less pleasant scene three weeks later:

> On Tuesday night about eleven o'clock some of the New Gentlemen belonging to the *Centurion*, having been thought the City upon a frolic, attended with a fiddle and a French horn, in their return by Aldgate watch-house, fell upon one of the watchmen, and beat him very much; but some of the other watchmen sallying out to his assistance, the foremost man gave the word *Centurion*, upon which several more of the gang appeared and attacked them with bludgeons and cutlasses, by which one man, whose name is Adam Parker, got his skull broke, James Sparke two desperate wounds in the head and – Dashley a deep and dangerous cut in the hand; several more were slightly wounded.[24]

A seaman named Fortune had already been found dead through drink; one Martin was discovered drowned at Lambeth with fifteen guineas and some silver in his pocket; while another called Burton was attacked by four men between Stratford and Bow and defended himself until he was seriously wounded and robbed of eleven *moidores* and some silver.[25] The citizens of London must have been relieved when the crew of *Centurion* eventually went back to sea.

THE LOSS OF THE *WAGER*

The 24-gun store-ship *Wager* had traumas of its own. Like all Anson's ships she was not well manned: 'Her crew consisted of men pressed from long voyages, to be sent on a distant and hazardous service. On the other hand, all her land forces were no more than a poor detachment of infirm and decrepit invalids from Chelsea Hospital, desponding under the apprehensions of a long voyage.'[26] Separated from the rest of the squadron during the passage around the Horn, the ship was soon in perilous circumstances off the coast of Chile. According to her gunner John Bulkeley,

> Thursday May the 14th, 1741, at half an hour past four this morning, the ship struck abaft on a sunken rock, founded fourteen fathom; but it being impossible to let go the anchor time enough to bring her up, being surrounded on every

side with rocks (a very dismal prospect to behold!), the ship struck a second time, which broke the head of the tiller; so that we were obliged to steer her with the main and foresheets, by easing off one, and hauling aft the other, as she came to, or fell off. In a short time, she struck, bilged, and grounded, between two small islands, where providence directed us to such a place as we could save our lives.[27]

John Young, the ship's cooper, was relieved: 'the gladsome shore was a cheering view, no small abatement of our calamity. It was a circumstance of mercy towards us, requiring the sincerest acknowledgements, that our vessel was not instantly dashed to pieces ... Some expressions [of thanksgiving] were uttered but oaths and execrations greatly prevailed.'[28] Their troubles were only just beginning. Many of the crew believed that their pay stopped when the ship was lost, so naval discipline ceased to exist. A hundred and forty men got on shore, but 'some few still remained still on board, detained either by drunkenness, or a view of pillaging the wreck, among whom was the boatswain'.[29] This soon descended into chaos –

> they fell to beating every thing to pieces that fell in the way, and, carrying their intemperance to the greatest excess, broke open chests and cabins for plunder that could be of no use to them; and so earnest were they in this wantonness of theft, that one men had evidently been murdered, on account of some division of the spoil, or for the sake of the share that fell to him, having all the marks of a strangled corpse.[30]

Captain David Cheap asserted his authority over the men and felled the boatswain with a blow from his cane. Midshipman Byron commented of his followers: 'It was scarce possible to refrain from laughter at the whimsical appearance these fellows made, who, having rifled the chests of the officers' best suits, had put them on over their greasy trousers and dirty checked shirts – They were soon stripped of their finery, as they had before been obliged to resign their arms.'[31]

But Captain Cheap had none of Anson's leadership qualities, and his decisions (or lack of them) were constantly questioned by both officers and men on shore. Carpenter John Cumins, on the other hand, proved to be a great asset, his ability being 'of great use to us at land, as well as on the ocean, for by his assistance, soon after coming ashore, we had erected several conveniences for out habitation ... One of the houses was a superb structure, with distinct apartments for almost twenty persons ...'[32] The men ashore soon split into factions, though as John Young put it, 'These disputes and civilities were equally insignificant; the contending parties were neither reciprocally convinced nor reconciled.'[33] The captain tried to maintain his authority, and in his desperation he fatally wounded Midshipman Henry Cozens. Young was outraged:

> it was said that though the deceased was a conceited busy fellow, that was not a sufficient reason for killing him: that he had never appeared in arms; and to shoot a man through the head, on a mere surmise, without any inquisition or process of law, was something worse than manslaughter, and the captain's commission could not bear him out of it.[34]

One group, led by Gunner Bulkeley and Carpenter Cumings, decided to extend the ship's longboat and take it south. They thought it 'the best, surest, and most safe way, for the preservation of the body of people on the spot, to proceed through the Straights of Magellan for England'. A paper to this effect was signed by the gunner, carpenter, master, boatswain, two master's mates, the surgeon's mate, three midshipmen, the cook, two boatswain's mates, the cooper, quarter gunner and 25 seamen.[35] On 9 October, after five months ashore, they disarmed the captain and tied has hands. Four days later the enlarged longboat, now named *Speedwell*, sailed from the bay in company with the ship's cutter and barge. Between them they carried 81 men. Their troubles were far from over, as John Young records.

> You may now fancy us embarked, entering on our important voyage, all of us stocked with eager desires, feeble hopes, and gloomy apprehensions. We were not out of Wager Bay, as we called the place of our embarkation, when the *Speedwell* split her topsail, and was at the brink of perishing on the rocks.[36]

But Midshipman Byron apparently remained loyal to the captain, and with Midshipman Alexander Campbell he persuaded the ten men in the barge to return, as 'if they did get home, which they could not reasonably hope to do the way they were going, they would be hanged for mutiny'.[37]

Speedwell and the cutter continued with their voyage, navigating by means of a pilot book that Bulkeley had 'borrowed' from Byron. When Lawrence Millechamp died, Bulkeley commented callously, 'This gentleman was probably the first purser belonging to His Majesty's Service, that ever perished with hunger.'[38] After many adventures, and leaving some men behind, thirty of them reached Rio Grande in Portuguese Brazil, still quarrelling among themselves. It was observed 'how scandalous it was, for so small a number of men, of the same nation, comrades a long time, companions in a series of misfortunes, and in a foreign land, at the courtesy of strangers, to be at mortal enmity amongst themselves'.[39] They separated, and Bulkeley's party went via Rio de Janeiro and Lisbon, to arrive off Portsmouth on New Year's Day 1743. Cheap also got home by a very different route, along with Byron and Campbell, to arrive in 1746. The men of *Speedwell* feared court martial for mutiny, but no charges were ever brought, perhaps because Cheap feared a counter-charge of murder.

War with France

In 1743, France threatened to join Spain in the war against Britain, and another experiment with organised recruitment was attempted. This time it did not involve impressment. Nineteen ships were to provide one lieutenant each, who was to be allocated an area within twenty miles of a particular market town in southern England. He was to tour that town and the surrounding villages and to utilise his 'best endeavours to enlist volunteers' for his ship. He was to advertise the offers of bounty by beat of the drum and any other means that might suggest themselves.[40] The experiment was not a great success: the men showed no interest, and the letters of the lieutenants are filled with apologies for their lack of recruits. One wrote from Southampton, 'I am sent here by Admiral Steuart to raise men for His Majesty's ship the *Shrewsbury*, and have proceeded according to their lordships orders, and with very ill success, not having raised one man as yet.' Another, in Chichester, wrote, 'Since my last, I have met with no success, so that I have procured in the whole no more than the three landsmen mentioned in my former letter, and as the people most of them find employment on shore during the time of the harvest, I hope their lordships will be so good as to make that allowance, on assurance, that I have spared no pains to carry on this service.' According to returns prepared in July, 44 seamen and 47 landsmen had signed up, including 63 at Plymouth alone, but only 37 men had actually appeared on board ship. George Seton, at Canterbury and Faversham, had recruited no men at all.[41] This experiment was not repeated, but it set a precedent for allocating recruiting areas to particular officers.

Early in 1744 the British Mediterranean fleet under Admiral Mathews fought an indecisive battle with a combined French and Spanish fleet off Toulon. War with France followed soon afterwards, and this altered the whole nature of the conflict. The West Indies was no longer the main area of operations, for the French fleet, though still small compared with the British one, was equipped with very powerful and well-designed ships. By 1745 Britain faced a serious threat of invasion, and a strong Channel fleet had to be mobilised under Norris. At the beginning of the year the ships in commission should have had a total strength of 60,000 men, but in fact they were about ten per cent short of complement, and it would be the end of 1746 before supply matched demand. Fortunately, the French fleet was dispersed, more by storms than anything else, and there was no large scale invasion. The Jacobite rebellion began in 1745, but it involved no landings of French forces, and was eventually defeated after causing very serious concern to the government.

THE WESTERN SQUADRON

In 1745, Anson was appointed to the Board of Admiralty for the first time, and this began a phase of his career in which he was to reform all aspects of the navy. In the short term, however, his most important effect was on naval tactics and strategy. The idea of keeping a strong squadron permanently off the main French naval base at Brest was not entirely new, for it had been adopted to some extent in the 1690s; but after Anson revived it in 1746 it became the core of British naval strategy. It imposed yet more difficulties in manning the fleet, for it demanded a large number of ships, able to be rotated for repairs, and the maintenance of sufficient strength to fight the French; moreover, ships needed to stay at sea for long periods, raising the problems of scurvy and bad victuals.

In May 1747, Anson encountered a French convoy, escorted by several major warships, off Finisterre. It was 'the French fleet with 35 sail of Marchant Men going to Canadee, with 10 Sail of Men of Warr, all ships of the Line'. Anson ordered a general chase, and a seaman on board his old ship, *Centurion*, now under Captain Dennis, described what he saw of the action in a letter to his brother:

> Our captane being the Devile of a man run in amongst the hole fleet; Wee fought the French Admiral and thre more men of war biger than ourselves, the halve of one hour before the fleet came up with us; we have so destroyed them and kild them so fast, their decks were flotted with blood. The Ingagement held from two o'clock till almost six, and then they all struck, and we have taken all their Marchant Men. Such a Battell never was nown in all the hole world; Shot and Ball flew like hail from the Heavens. I bless God I am still alive. In one of the ships was found thre Milyon of Money, an the other about 16 Milyon ... If wee have justice done us, we shall have a thousand pound a man.

He was disappointed in this, and in his belief that this would 'crush the French for ever',[42] but they had indeed captured all the warships and some of the merchantmen. A few months later Admiral Hawke fought a similar battle at almost the same place, and the French gave up all hope of winning the war at sea. Peace was made in 1748, but since the French were victorious on land, neither side made any great gains.

THE FAULTS OF IMPRESSMENT

The war of 1739–48 brought out many of the inadequacies of the system of naval recruitment and illustrated several features that were to become characteristic of all British wars under sail. Firstly, it took several years (usually three) to get the active fleet up to full strength. This is explained partly by the fact that many of the seamen were abroad on foreign service and took some time to return, partly by their reluctance to enter the service, and largely by the inefficiencies of the system. This was not as much of a problem as it might have been. Though the French could generally mobilise their fleet more quickly at the beginning of a war, all the wars started slowly, with one opponent after another joining the conflict. Secondly, the shortage of skilled men was the most important limiting factor in the total size of the naval effort. Time and again, the government had to modify its plans to take account of the manning situation and keep ships in port while men were found for them.

Thirdly, the full-scale mobilisation, when it was finally achieved in each war, strained the resources of the merchant marine almost to breaking point. As always, statistics on the number of merchant seamen are hard to come by, but it is estimated that in 1792 there were 118,000 seamen registered in the British dominions. Within five years of that, the government was attempting to set out a fleet of 120,000 men and had actually raised 118,000.[43] In other words, the navy at full strength was almost equal in size to the merchant marine in peacetime. Of course, only about half the men mustered in the royal fleet were actually experienced seamen out of the merchant service, but clearly the landsmen, apprentices and foreigners who supplemented the regular merchant seamen in wartime were really needed. Furthermore, the seamen who did not get hold of a protection or exemption by one means or another probably stood very little chance of staying out of the navy in the course of a war that might last ten years. Finally, the seamen were discharged at the end of the war. In the meantime, the merchant service had trained up thousands of men and boys to fill the vacancies left by the press gang. This created a glut of seamen, and it was feared that many of them would seek work under foreign flags and be lost to their native land.

Above: Cogs in combat in the early fourteenth century, with soldiers engaged in hand-to-hand combat, and archers. (British Library/The Bridgeman Art Library)

Below: The fight against the Spanish Armada showing vessels engaging from many different angles. (NMM BHC0262)

Right: The cover for the *Mariners Mirror*, a collection of charts, shows typical late sixteenth century seaman's dress along with many navigational instruments. (NMM A1730-1)

Below: The *Sovereign of the Seas* of 1637. As well as the elaborate decoration of the ship, Payne's print shows seamen at work on deck, climbing the rigging, and a man standing on the stock of the anchor. (NMM A6719)

Above left: The *Royal Charles* drawn by Edward Barlow, showing the flags she flew at the Restoration of Charles II. (NMM B1686-033)

Above right: The *Monck* in which Barlow served during the Second Anglo-Dutch War. (NMM B1686-061)

Left: A ghoulish view of naval medicine, with the words of *Admiral Hosier's Ghost*. (NMM PW3959)

Above: The *Resolution* and *Adventure* in Matavi Bay, Tahiti in 1773. (NMM BHC1932)

Below and right: A modern model of Cook's *Endeavour*, showing the decks and some of the officers, crew, marines and stores. (NMM D3358-1, 13)

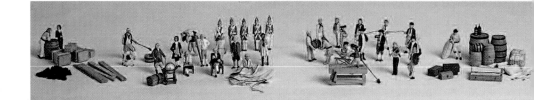

Left: A lively view of seamen soon after their discharge at Chatham at the end of the war in 1783. (The Trustees of the British Museum)

Below: A view of the Nore mutineers occupying the great cabin of a ship, with the picture of Britannia turned upside down and Parliamentary opposition, led by Charles James Fox, under the table. (NMM PW3899)

The DELEGATES in COUNSEL or BEGGARS on HORSEBACK

Above: A press gang meets resistance in a tavern, as drawn by Frederick Marryat. (The Trustees of the British Museum)

Below: Marryat's view of seamen washing decks early in the morning, supervised by a lieutenant sitting on the capstan. (The Trustees of the British Museum)

Above: Pressing men at Portsmouth. Although conventionally dated from 1798, this shows marines engaged in the activity, as happened in 1803. (Portsmouth City Museum)

Below: 'Nelson recreating with his brave tars'. There is no evidence that an event like this actually occurred, but it does represent the popular view that Nelson was far closer to his men than most admirals. (NMM PW3892)

Above: The death of Nelson by Denis Dighton. It is a reasonably accurate view of the *Victory's* decks, with gun crews and marines in action on both sides of the ship, including a black seaman to the right. (NMM BHC0552)

Below: The evolution of seamen's dress. In the 1820s (left) the collar is already quite large, but of more conventional shape. By 1849 (right) it is close to its distinctive shape, though worn with a short blue jacket. (NMM PW3734, PW4236)

Tentatively, Anson tried to reform this system at the end of the war, but unlike his reforms in shipbuilding and the dockyards, this would need legislation and therefore the support of Parliament. A bill 'for speedily manning the navy' was debated in the House of Commons in April 1749, proposing a reserve of 3,000 experienced men, to be paid £10 a year, about half a regular seaman's pay. They would be in shore jobs, and it was hoped that they would be ready for recall into the navy in the event of a sudden crisis, to ease the usual manning problem at the start of a war while at the same time avoiding disruption to the merchant service as had been common in the past. It was also hoped to expand the numbers over the years and perhaps introduce an element of training to create a true naval reserve. The opposition objected strongly on many levels. Men left ashore would soon lose their skills and would become useless both by land and by sea. Most important of all, the bill was 'a scheme for extending martial law over a great number of men, not before subject to it'.[44] This raised the hackles of the average backbencher, who feared any extension of state power even if it was intended to reduce the arbitrary tyranny of the press gang. The government had recently had to give up a clause in the Navy Bill which subjected half-pay officers to naval discipline, and this was a parallel for the lower deck. The bill was dropped. It might have proved the germ of a system that would eventually have reformed naval manning, for it was proposed at a time when relations between officers and the lower deck were better than they had been in the past, or would be in the future, of which William Spavens was able to write, 'His Majesty's service is, in many respects, preferable to any other.'[45]

After the war the navy was reduced, and in 1751 a very low level of 8,000 men was allowed by Parliament. Lord Barrington of the Admiralty argued that economy was 'absolutely necessary for this nation' and that previous levels of manning were excessive. In the first place, a possible rise in piracy, 'as has generally happened after a long war' had not materialised. Secondly, a number of ships had returned from Indian waters and could be paid off. Thirdly, some ships had been kept on in the Mediterranean because of continuing disputes there, but these had mostly been resolved. The opposition objected to this. 'Other gentlemen, Sir, may call this great reduction of seamen economy; but ... I always thought it the height of imprudence ... Let us consider, Sir, that in case of a war with France, we should lose our superiority at sea but for one summer, it would be gone for ever.' Nevertheless the navy sank to its lowest level since 1733.[46] Only a few ships were fitted out for sea in peacetime, mostly small ones of 40 guns or

The Number of Men Voted by Parliament, 1701–1813

Date	No. Voted
1701	30,000
Spanish Succession	
1702	40,000
1703	40,000
1704	40,000
1705	40,000
1706	40,000
1707	40,000
1708	40,000
1709	40,000
1710	40,000
1711–13	—
1714	10,000
1715	10,000
1716	10,000
1717	10,000
Spanish War	
1718	10,000
1719	13,500
1720	13,500
1721	10,000
1722	7,000
1723	10,000
1724	10,000
1725	10,000
1726	10,000
1727	20,000
1728	15,000
1729	15,000
1730	10,000
1731	10,000
1732	8,000
1733	8,000
1734–37	—
1738	20,000
Jenkins Ear / Austrian Succession	
1739	12,000
1740	35,000
1741	40,000
1742	40,000
1743	40,000
1744	40,000
1745	40,000
1746	40,000
1747	40,000
1748	40,000
1749–53	—
1754	10,000
1755	12,000
Seven Years War	
1756	50,000
1757	55,000
1758	60,000
1759	60,000
1760	70,000
1761	70,000
1762	70,000
1763	30,000
1764	16,000
1765	16,000
1766	16,000
1767	16,000
1768	16,000
1769	16,000
1770	16,000
1771	40,000
1772	25,000
1773	20,000
1774	20,000
War of American Independence	
1775	18,000
1776	28,000
1777	45,000
1778	60,000
1779	70,000
1780	85,000
1781	90,000
1782	100,000
1783	110,000
1784	26,000
1785	18,000
1786	18,000
1787	18,000
1788	18,000
1789	20,000
1790	20,000
1791	24,000
1792	16,000
French Revolutionary War	
1793	45,000
1794	85,000
1795	100,000
1796	110,000
1797	120,000
1798	120,000
1799	120,000
1800	120,000
1801	120,000
1802	130,000
Napoleonic Wars	
1803	50,000
1804	100,000
1805	120,000
1806	120,000
1807	130,000
1808	130,000
1809	130,000
1810	145,000
1811	145,000
1812	145,000
1813	145,000

Figures from Lloyd,
The British Seaman

less. One exception was the 74-gun *Invincible*, perhaps the finest of those captured by Anson at Finisterre. After the war she was reduced to a guard ship at Portsmouth, with a reduced crew but ready to put to sea quite quickly in an emergency. In 1752 she was fitted to carry a regiment of troops to Gibraltar, with her lower-deck guns removed. As such she carried 784 persons, but many of these were soldiers and their wives and children, so she sailed with a crew of 240 compared with the 625 she normally had in a wartime commission.[47] In these circumstances there was little or no need for the press gang, and it was quite easy to find enough seamen for the navy.

THE SEVEN YEARS WAR

The peace of 1748 did not last for long, and by 1755 British and French forces were already in conflict in India and North America. Naval mobilisation began early in 1755, and seventeen ships of the line were fitted out and put to sea without any great difficulty. They attempted to intercept French reinforcements for North America (though war had not yet been declared) and succeeded only in antagonising the French without making any real impact on their resources.

By 1755, as the two sides began to line up for what became the Seven Years War, Lord Anson was firmly in control of the Admiralty. Unable to replace the system of impressment, he carried out a substantial reform of the regulating system. In January, Regulating Captains were appointed for London and the Thames as usual, but their powers were extended a little further. They were instructed to 'take under your orders all lieutenants employed or who may be employed raising men in and about town, who are directed to obey all orders signified under your hands'. They were to appoint the lieutenants to local rendezvous and stations, and to ensure that the commissioned officers went with the gangs when on duty.[48] Other officers were soon appointed for areas outside London. Following the precedent of 1738, Captain Ferguson was sent to Edinburgh, where he was to organise the raising of men. In 1755 and 1756, several captains were sent to the major ports and towns of England, assisted by lieutenants, usually two each, and supported by press tenders. They were each given press warrants and detailed instructions on how to organise their officers and control the gangs under them.

This new system was to fill up several gaps in the old. Firstly, it would extend it well beyond the traditional areas of southern and eastern England; among the ports covered were Liverpool and Whitehaven in the north-west; Newcastle in the north-east, Pembroke in Wales, and the inland towns of Reading and Leeds. These were merely headquarters for the gangs; the lieutenants were to open offices at smaller towns in the areas and to search the surrounding countryside, so that the Admiralty was no longer dependent on the local officials for finding seamen who had fled inland. Finally, the new system placed much less emphasis on the officers of the individual ships, and the country could be scoured in a planned and rational way. Combined with the more systematic employment of pressing tenders, the reorganisation of the second half of the eighteenth century tried to ensure that all the gaps were covered; nevertheless, there remained a few, especially in Scotland.

Liverpool remained a tough nut for the press gang. Having been pressed himself, William Spavens was not unusual in forming part of a gang a few weeks later:

Pressing on shore at Liverpool had been deemed impracticable, and some gentlemen told our Captain that they were certain he durst not attempt to do it; but soon after he came to the dock head, and stepping into the barge, ordered us to put off, and go on board; and when it was dark, sent us and the cutter's crew, with come officers and a suitable reinforcement of men, to try if it were possible to succeed or not. We accordingly began our business, and soon picked up 16 men, but only one of them being a seaman, him we detained, and the rest we set at liberty. The next day, July 25th, being their fair day, mustering a gang of 80 men, we went ashore; and after picking up several stragglers, we surprised the *Lion*'s crew in the Custom House just as they were renewing their protections. We secured 17 of them, and guarding them along the streets, several hundreds of old men, women, and boys, flocked after us, well provided with stones and brickbats, and commenced a general attack; but not wishing to hurt them, we fired our pistols over their heads, in order to deter them from further outrage; but the women proved very daring, and followed us down to low water mark, being almost up [to the] the knees in mud.

The word 'gang', like the term 'impressment', had rather innocent origins. To a landsman, it was in use by the early seventeenth century to mean a group of workmen. According to Falconer's *Marine Dictionary* of 1769, a gang was simply 'a select number of a ship's crew appointed on any particular service, and commanded by an officer suitable to the occasion'.[49] A press gang, then, was just another group of men assembled for a 'particular service'. In modern times, of course, the term has strong associations with violence and criminality, and the press gang may have played its part in bringing about this change – the landsman was not aware of the work of the boatswain's gang or the cable-stowing gang aboard ship, but he certainly saw the work of the press gang in the streets of his town, and despite the legality of the proceeding, the violence of the press gang's work did not fail to make an impression on him.

In modern times, the press gang is always seen as a collection of ruffians, 'sub-human' in morals, appearance and intelligence. To contemporaries, the picture was not very different. Cartoonists invariably showed the gang with gorilla-like features, harassing innocent members of the public or dragging a seamen away from his wedding or his family. Matthew Bishop, who went ashore with a large press gang at Cork in the 1700s, believed that 'the greatest part of us were licentious men'.[50] To a seaman like William Robertson, the gang was 'a nest of vipers'. Tobias Smollet, the novelist, who had some naval experience, describes a fictional encounter with the gang:

> As I crossed Tower wharf, a squat tawny fellow, with a hanger by his side and a cudgel in his hand, came up to me, calling, 'Yo, ho, brother, you must come along with me.' As I did not like his appearance, instead of answering his salutation, I quickened my pace, in the hope of ridding myself of his company; upon which he whistled aloud, and immediately another sailor appeared before me, who laid hold of me by the collar and began to drag me along.[51]

Robert Spotswood encountered another London gang after his arrival from Scotland in the 1740s. He was 'gripped by the fist by a gentile fellow, who commanded me to go along with him. I refused. He insisted with hideous oaths.' He 'threatened he would drive my teeth down my throat', and had the appearance of 'a blackguard and robber'. Spotswood was convinced he was to be 'robbed, perhaps murdered'. Another man appeared, 'not in a sailors habit', and dragged him to a rendezvous, where he was able to convince the lieutenant that he was not a seaman.[52]

William Spavens had become a seaman in 1754 because he 'thought sailors must be happy men to have such opportunities of visiting foreign countries, and beholding the wonderful works of the Creator in the remote regions of the earth'. He had made merchant voyages to Russia and Sweden and was returning from Le Havre when he was pressed at Hull and taken on board the tender *John and Joyce*. Some of the pressed men plotted to take over the ship, but the lieutenant got wind of it and sent for reinforcements:

> He doubled the guards, giving them positive orders to fire amongst us if we attempted to mutiny. After this we were all confined below every day and

night, and in the day-time only two of us were suffered to come on deck at once. Our confinement in this floating prison lasted thirty-two days; after which we were happily released and put on board His Majesty's Ship *Buckingham* of 70 guns ...[53]

In addition, more ways were found to recruit landsmen and boys. The Marine Society, founded in 1756, recruited young waifs and orphans and gave them a minimum of naval training. Foreigners were occasionally allowed to volunteer, and even prisoners-of-war could be taken on in certain circumstances. Some towns were persuaded to offer extra inducements for men who volunteered, while debtors and smugglers were offered the navy instead of prison if they were in reasonably good health.

THE LOSS OF MENORCA

Late in 1755, war had still not been declared, but it became known that the French were fitting out a strong force. British manpower resources were limited, and the 168 ships in commission were manned by only 36,000 men instead of 49,000. The problems of naval manning contributed directly to the first great crisis of the war. The government decided to strengthen the defences at home and send a comparatively small force to reinforce the garrison of Menorca against French attack. Admiral Byng, in command of it, found that his ships were seriously undermanned – he was short of 722 men, who had been lent to other ships, were sick in hospital or who had never been recruited. His flagship alone, *Ramillies*, was missing 222 men, lent to *Ludlow Castle*, which was at sea.[54] It was particularly frustrating because the Admiralty had given priority to the western squadron off Brest and the war in America. Arguably there were good strategic reasons for doing this, but Byng's intemperate friend Captain Augustus Hervey thought it was a typical example of Anson's favouritism. Byng sailed late and there was further confusion at Gibraltar when the governor claimed some of the troops on board, which Byng had intended to use as marines.

Byng arrived off the island of Menorca late in May to find that the French had already landed and were besieging Fort St Phillip, while a fleet roughly equal to Byng's own was off Port Mahon. Captain Hervey joined him, and on board the flagship he was told about the dire manning situation. 'He told me 'twas worse than I saw, for his ships being almost all the worst of the fleet, that even they were not manned, and that troops of Lord Bertie's regiment, which were to be landed at Mahon, made up the complement now of the fleet ...'[55] Nevertheless Byng engaged, but his plan of attack was too difficult for the signalling system of the day, and he broke off the action. Hervey was transferred to *Defiance*, which had lost her captain, which he 'accepted of, altho' a perfect rack and the worst manned ship in the service now'. His men were 'the very scum of the fleet', and he could only muster 226 out of 400. 'I was obliged to borrow men to fit her, but had her in order that evening.'[56] Byng called a council of war, which decided to retreat and protect Gibraltar. News of this travelled though France – that a British admiral had retreated from a battle – and reached London before Byng's own dispatch. The London mob came to believe that there was treason or cowardice in high places. Byng was subsequently tried and acquitted of cowardice but found guilty of failing to do his utmost against the enemy. The Articles of War, redrafted in 1749, allowed only the death penalty for this, and the government was too afraid of the mob to reprieve him. In Portsmouth Harbour, in front of boats sent out from every ship in the port, he was executed by a marine firing squad.

MARY LACY – A SERVANT'S LIFE

Mary Lacy disguised herself as a man, took the name of William Chandler and became servant to the carpenter of *Sandwich* in 1759. She provides a few glimpses of the life of a servant to various warrant officers. When the carpenter showed her how to make his bed, she had to bite her tongue:

> So we went to his cabin, in which there was a bed that was turned up, and he began to take the bed clothes off one by one. Now, said he, you must shake them one by one, you must tumble and shake the bed about, then you must lay the sheets on one at a time, and lastly the blankets. I replied, Yes, Sir. Well, said he, you will soon learn to make a bed, that I see already. But he little knew who he had got to make a bed ...[57]

Some servants were more efficient than others – 'of all the officers' boys in the ship, the boatswain's was the least serviceable of any, inasmuch as he could not even boil the kettle for his master's breakfast.' 'William Chandler' also had difficulties with that meal, or at least her master's reaction to it:

> Notwithstanding this agreeableness of his temper at intervals, it was in general a difficult matter to please him; for sometimes, after providing one thing for his breakfast, he would require another; for instance, when I had made sage tea, he would have gruel; and, after green, he would order bohea to be made, with biscuit split, toasted and buttered; and if either of these things were prepared in any respect displeasing to him, he would fling it at me, though not with any real intention of hurting me; nay, the very cups and saucers would not escape his violent passion...[58]

She was not the only servant to be persecuted: the facetious *Advice to Sea Lieutenants* suggests, 'If, when first lieutenant, you have a dispute with one of your mess-mates, you must revenge the quarrel upon the posteriors of his servant, which, as boys are always in mischief, you will soon find an opportunity of doing.'[59] But Mary Lacy at least found of her master that 'if he beat me himself, he would not suffer any body else to do so', and he would even dispute with a lieutenant who issued orders to her. As well as her domestic duties, she was expected to act as a powder boy in action.

> My master asked me how I liked the sea? I replied, I liked it very well, But, said he, should you not be afraid if you were to come to an engagement? I answered, No; for I should have work enough to fetch powder to the gun I was quartered at, therefore should not have time to think of that. He then told me, I should not be able to bring the powder fast enough. I replied, I'll take it from the little boys, and cause them to fetch more, before the gun shall want powder; at which he laughed heartily, to hear me talk so, as well he might.[60]

QUIBERON BAY

The main fleet was sent to blockade Brest, as in the previous war, though in 1756 the French were still inactive in that area. British naval strength was gradually built up over the years, reaching 55,000 men in 1756, 65,000 in 1757 and exceeding 80,000 in 1759. *Sandwich* was one of the ships of the line deployed off Brest, for Lord Anson had decided that a strong Western Squadron was the best way to contain French sea power. Mary Lacy was on board when Admiral Hawke decided to make a demonstration in front of the port:

> And on the 10th of November 1759, being his majesty's birthday, the admiral made a signal for all the ships to fire the same number of guns as in England on this occasion. We ran in as near the French coast as we could; after which, the admiral began to fire; and having fired all round, we all tack'd about, and stood off from the land; yet did not stand so far off, but lay to, to see if the enemy would venture out. It seemed as if they thought we were going to land at Brest, or some other place; for in the night they made bonfires all round the country, to alarm and give notice to their people, that we were about to land.[61]

A few days later she just missed a battle as *Sandwich* was sent to Plymouth for repairs. William Spavens was in the frigate *Vengeance* off Brest when the French fleet under Admiral Conflans came out, and she was sent to warn Commodore Duff's squadron in Quiberon Bay.

Our captain returning, we hoisted in our boat, and applied ourselves to the dangerous task assigned to us, carrying a press of sail, all the night and the next day; and in the night of the 17th, we discovered ourselves in the midst of the enemy's fleet consisting of twenty-one sail of the line, and four frigates; but the wind blowing hard, and being very dark, we soon cleared them undiscovered, as they were on the contrary tack. The next day we saw them to leeward of us, but at such a distance that we thought ourselves in no danger; and on Monday the 19th, bringing the bay open we made the signal to the squadron to cut or slip their cables, and come out with all possible speed, by which we effected the service we were sent upon …[62]

On the way out they sighted the enemy fleet again, and *Vengeance* was chased by one of them – 'the *Thesée* of 74 guns was once within point blank musket shot of our ship, but did not fire at us, and by our superior alertness in setting and hauling down our steering sails, & c. repeatedly it blew very strong, and was squally, we got away from her …' Later in the day,

the man at the fore-topmast head descried the English fleet, which the *Juno* had spoken with, coming to our relief under a press of sail … The day now cleared up, and exhibited a grand and awful sight – a powerful French fleet drawn up in fighting position, ready for action; and a British fleet with well-appointed officers, and properly manned, bearing down on it with crowded sail, and each breast glowing with ardor to decide the grand dispute betwixt the two nations which should have the sovereignty of the seas. We now hoisted our colours, gave three cheers, took a reef in our top-sails, and hauling our wind, stood for the fleet, which we joined with gladness.[63]

Frigates were not expected to take part in fleet battles, so *Vengeance* was largely a spectator as Sir Edward Hawke's force of 23 ships of the line chased the French into Quiberon Bay, braving all the navigational hazards. *Vengeance*'s old adversary, *Thesée*, was sunk and four of her crew were rescued. They revealed that their captain had been determined to sink *Vengeance,* for he was particularly incensed that she was a French prize; and also that the French fleet had been planning a landing in Ireland before it was intercepted. That night the crew of *Vengeance* heard signals of distress but could not be sure whether it was a British or French ship. They discovered it was one of their own, *Resolution*, which had hit the rocks. *Vengeance* was ordered to fit out some of her boats for a fire raid on several French ships that had jettisoned their guns and got into the River Vilaine, but the idea was abandoned when the French moored two frigates across the entrance.

Nevertheless, Quiberon Bay was the greatest naval victory of the century so far, with much of the French battle fleet sunk, burnt, stranded or captured. *Vengeance* was chosen to take the news to Plymouth, and on the way she passed close to another British force: 'Off Ushant, we fell in with Admiral Geary's fleet, and we were hailed by the *Foudroyant*, the captain ordering us to bring to under the lee of the *Sandwich*, as the Admiral wanted to speak with us; but our captain replied, that being charged with an express, he must not bring to; being asked what news, he answered Good.'[64] At Plymouth they were warned not to say anything to the locals except that the news was good, but they found 'the intelligent west-country men knew almost as much of the affair as we did'.

VICTORIES

1759 became known as 'the Year of Victories', in which it was said that Englishmen became tired of hearing church bells ringing to celebrate yet more triumphs. It is perhaps no coincidence that it was the third year of war and the year in which the navy reached its full strength. Admiral Saunders led the fleet that took Wolfe to capture Quebec. Admiral Boscawen won a fleet battle at Lagos, off Portugal, which was followed by Hawke's victory at Quiberon Bay. Britain was safe from invasion and was in control of North America and India.

When the British invaded Martinique early in 1762, Admiral Rodney landed his men some distance from the main town of Fort Royal, and the seamen had the job of moving guns and heavy equipment across difficult country. Sailors always enjoyed working ashore, and the soldiers were impressed with their ingenuity and spirit – 'A hundred or two of them, with ropes and pulleys, will do more than all your drayhorses in London.'[65] Rodney himself wrote of, 'the eager and cheerful activity of the officers and seamen who contributed every thing in their power towards the reduction of the place; and made no difficulties in transporting numbers of the heaviest mortars and ships' cannon, up the steepest mountains at a very considerable distance from the sea, and across the enemy's line of fire.'[66]

Spain joined the war against Britain in 1761, but since the French were already immobilised and the Spanish fleet was relatively weak, this merely afforded further opportunities for the British triumph. Havana and Manilla were taken, together with many warships. Britain made enormous gains when the peace treaty was signed in 1763 to end the Seven Years War. She had taken Canada and gained the upper hand in India, while Menorca was restored to her.

On being paid off, a crew might find ways of taking revenge for ill treatment, as the men of the frigate *Coventry* did in 1763:

Being soon unrigged, the ship's company was paid off, and everyone was at liberty to go where they pleased. The world was all before them, where to choose a place of rest, and Providence their guide. The first lieutenant, a severe disciplinarian, had been threatened, so wisely set out for London two days before; but this did not avail, for [a] party of the men, headed by a gunner's mate, hunted him in town, and meeting him in Cheapside gave him a severe drubbing ...[67]

THE NEW SHIPS

When Anson died in 1762, he left behind a far more streamlined and efficient naval administration than the one that had let him down so badly in 1740, though he failed to solve the central problem of manning. In 1755 the marines, which had been disbanded as usual after the end of the war in 1748, were taken directly under Admiralty control for recruitment and

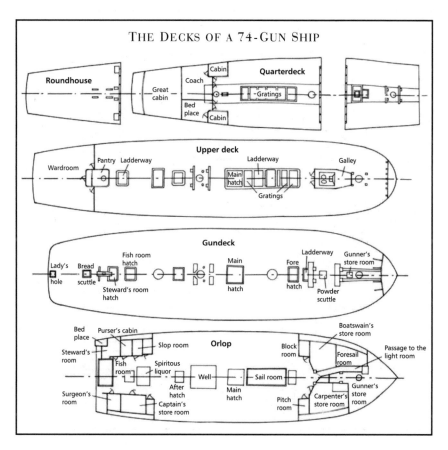

THE DECKS OF A 74-GUN SHIP

training as well as operations, and from that point they remained a permanent and efficient force. Anson did much to improve the spirit of the officer corps, and oversaw the introduction of uniforms for them in 1748, more than a century before the seamen. One of his greatest reforms was in shipbuilding, where outdated practices and designs were abandoned in favour of new ships, inspired by, but not slavishly copied from, French practices.

The 100-gun ship of this time, descended from *Sovereign of the Seas,* was unchanged in principle, though bigger than her predecessors. The largest ship of the era was the famous *Victory*, which was launched in 1756 but did not put to sea until 1778. She was of 2,141 tons, compared with the *Sovereign*'s 1,141. The 90-gun ship of the 1677 programme grew into the 98, though with lighter guns than the 100-gun ship. The old 80, misconceived after the defeat at Beachy Head, was abandoned and the 70 was expanded into the 74, able to carry a powerful and effective battery of

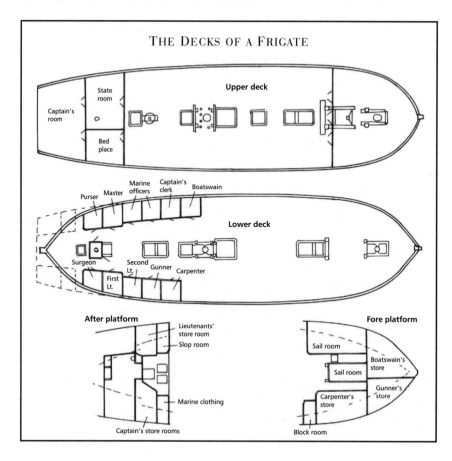

THE DECKS OF A FRIGATE

32-pounder guns on her lower deck. There were already 37 74s in service or on order by 1762, and 57 by 1775, forming the majority of the effective line of battle. The 64 was a smaller two-decker, with only 24-pounders on the lower deck and only just strong enough for the line. The intermediate 40- and 50-gun ships survived in smaller numbers largely because they were useful as peacetime flagships. Apart from the 74, the classic ship of the age was the frigate, with an unarmed lower deck and a row of 12- or 18-pounders on the upper deck. It had excellent sailing qualities with a moderate amount of firepower and soon became the most useful general-purpose ship outside the line of battle. In total there were 32 32-gun frigates by 1762.

Generally, although the new ships were larger than the ones they replaced, this did not necessarily make them less crowded, as complements were increased. An old 70 had 480 men in 1742, a new 74 had 650 in 1762; a 'common class' 32-gun frigate had 220 men, 80 more than the 20-gun ship she replaced. The increasing complements led to new problems of discipline and organisation. In 1730 there were only 60 ships with crews of more than 400 men in the fleet; by 1762 there were 134 such ships, and the number increased to 177 by 1803. The figures for ships with more than 600 men are even more dramatic – seven in 1730, 65 in 1762 and 132 in 1803.[68]

OFFICERS

Every ship, however large, had a single captain, and life on board depended very much on his character. Seamen tended to remember those of strong will and iron discipline more than the others. William Spavens served under Captain Penhallow Cumming in *Blandford*:

> He was an excellent seamen, but extremely rigid in his discipline, and would frequently withhold the men's allowance of grog on the most trifling occasions. I have known him call all hands to sway up the main topgallant yard, which ten men would have effected with ease; and if we were not all upon deck in five minutes, he would place a petty officer at each hatchway to stop those who remained below, and would order each man a dozen lashes at the gangway for his tardiness. He would on the least provocation given by him by any of the quartermasters, boatswains' mates, midshipmen, or other petty officers, break them and turn them before the mast, disrate them of their wages, and sometimes flog them.[69]

Cumming's men once produced a round robin complaining about his cruelty, but it was mostly charges brought by his officers and warrant

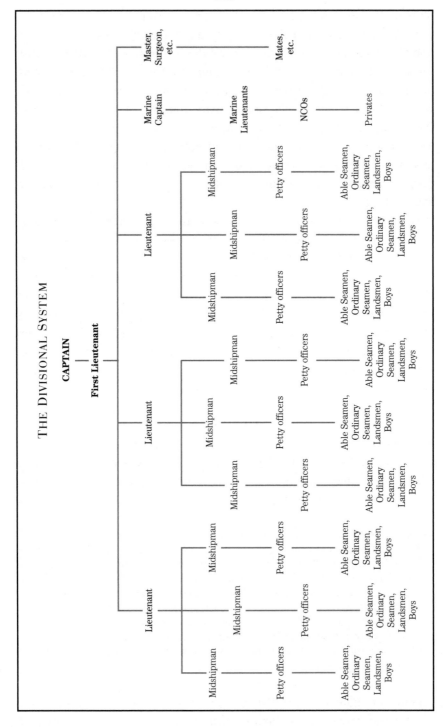

THE DIVISIONAL SYSTEM

CAPTAIN

First Lieutenant

Master, Surgeon, etc. ——————————— Mates, etc.

Marine Captain
Marine Lieutenants
NCOs
Privates

Lieutenant — Midshipman — Petty officers — Able Seamen, Ordinary Seamen, Landsmen, Boys

Lieutenant — Midshipman — Petty officers — Able Seamen, Ordinary Seamen, Landsmen, Boys

Lieutenant — Midshipman — Petty officers — Able Seamen, Ordinary Seamen, Landsmen, Boys officers that eventually led to his dismissal by court martial. John Nicol found that Captain Reeves could also be taut: when *Surprise* was in port he allowed a degree of license to his men, but he was a strict disciplinarian at sea, 'punishing the smallest fault'.[70]

Larger ships demanded more officers, particularly lieutenants. Half a century earlier, Ned Ward could write of the second lieutenant as 'a kind of spare topmast, that lies idle while the first is standing'.[71] By the 1750s a ship had up to eight lieutenants, and plenty of work was found for them, in watch-keeping and divisional duties. The term had obviously changed in meaning, now indicating not just an officer ready to take over if the captain was absent or killed, but as one who took a full share in the running of the ship. In effect, he did some of the work that the masters' mates had done in earlier years, so the task of leading a watch moved further away from the lower deck.

The first lieutenant was the second in command of the ship and in charge of administration, so he did not normally keep a watch. When posted to *Flora*, Spavens found that 'Mr Hawker ... being now first lieutenant, and having gained an ascendancy over the captain's temper, seemed more haughty in his station than formerly ...' and thus he decided to desert.[72] A junior lieutenant spent a good deal of his time in charge of a watch in full view of the crew, and, rather like a schoolteacher, his irritating habits might be exaggerated out of proportion. In *Royal George* in 1782, Lieutenant Monins Hollingbery became known as 'Jib and Foresail Jack', 'for if he had the watch in the night he would always be bothering the men to alter the sails, and it was "up jib" and "down jib" and "up foresail" and "down foresail" every minute'. He was considered 'more of a troublesome officer than a good one', and the seamen surmised correctly that his habit of moving his fingers showed that he was musician.[73]

The master's mate had once been close to the lower deck, and in the 1690s they were often 'registered men' and supported lower-deck protests. But the post was comparatively well paid and became increasingly attractive to midshipmen of some experience who were not yet able to take up commissions as lieutenants. By the 1750s the midshipman was long-established as an officer under training, mostly recruited from the upper and middle classes. Falconer warned naïve young midshipmen how to deal with seamen, perhaps from his personal experience:

No character, in their opinion, is more excellent than that of the common sailor, whom they generally suppose to be treated with great severity by his officers

... Blinded by these prepossessions, he is thrown off his guard, and very soon surprised to find, amongst those honest sailors, a crew of abandoned miscreants, ripe for any mischief or villainy. Perhaps, after a little observation, many of them will appear to be equally destitute of gratitude, shame, or justice, and only to be deterred from the commission of any crimes by the terror of severe punishment. He will discover, that the pernicious example of a few of the vilest in a ship of war is too often apt to poison the principles of the greatest number, especially if the reins of discipline are too much relaxed, so as to foster that idleness and dissipation, which engender sloth, diseases, and an utter profligacy of manners.

But he should persevere to find the hidden virtues in each man:

He will probably find a virtue in almost every private sailor, which is entirely unknown to many of his officers: that virtue is emulation ... There is hardly a common tar who is not envious of superior skill in his fellows, and jealous on all occasions not to be out-done in what he considers as a branch of his duty![74]

Theoretically a young man could not become a midshipman until he had served at least three years at sea. Though rules were often broken, most potential officers spent some time in the rating of 'captain's servant'. 'Servant' was an ambiguous term in those days, for it could mean a domestic, an apprentice or just an employee. The captain of a 74-gun ship was allowed 16 servants, and two or three of these were probably domestics; the rest were young men of ambition, usually under the age of fifteen.

Senior warrant officers, including the master, purser and surgeon, shared the wardroom with the commissioned sea officers and the marine officers. The purser was a hate figure on most ships, and according to facetious but well-informed 'advice', 'Whenever a man deserts, you may safely charge against his wages a few pounds of tobacco, and a few articles of slop clothing; particularly shoes, for it is natural to suppose that when he is prepared to march off he provided himself with a stock for his journey.'[75]

Though chaplains were provided for they were not always appointed. Neither officers nor seamen were particularly religious, and Gunner Bulkeley of the *Wager* wrote:

The duty of public prayer had been entirely neglected on board, though every seaman pays fourpence per month towards the support of a minister; yet devotion, in so solemn a manner, is so rarely performed that I know but one instance of it during the many years I have belonged to the navy.[76]

Each ship still had its three 'standing officers', the boatswain, gunner and carpenter, so called because they stayed with the ship even when she was out of commission. Excluded from the society of the wardroom, each had risen from the lower deck – the gunner and boatswain from the generality of seamen, the carpenter from skilled men who had probably trained ashore in the Royal Dockyards or private shipyards. Each lived in a cabin forward on the upper deck, perhaps with his wife and even his children on board. They were mostly held in great respect by the crew, and they provided a role model for their own advancement. In fact, however, they were not really part of the lower deck – they had a permanent career and were considered trustworthy enough to be given shore leave and other privileges.

ORDER BOOKS

Larger ships needed larger crews, which demanded better regulation. It was no longer adequate for the captain to delegate the organisation of the crew to the boatswain or to assume that the ship's routine would simply follow the established practices that had grown up over the centuries. Captains also became more concerned about their crews' health, while some tried to improve their men's conduct for disciplinary or religious reasons. In any case, from the 1750s onwards, captains and admirals began to issue detailed order books on how a ship should be run. Most were addressed to the officers, and only selected passages might be read out to the crew, but they invariably had an effect on the life of the lower deck.

The first known order book was issued by Admiral Thomas Smith at the Downs in 1755. He was aware that larger crews meant officers had less direct contact with the men – they did not keep the same watches as them, and a lieutenant might have a different group every time he was on duty with others in battle or for manoeuvres such as tacking or raising anchor. Therefore Smith ordered his captains:

> Divide the rest of your ship's company ... into as many parties as you have lieutenants, and put one of these parties under the charge of each lieutenant. Each lieutenant to take an account of the clothing and bedding of each man in his party, and report the same to you, keeping an account of the same himself.
>
> Each lieutenant to subdivide his party of men into as many smaller parties as there are midshipmen allotted to him, giving an inventory to each midshipman of the clothes and bedding belonging to each man whom he has put in the said midshipman's party.[77]

Smith made it clear that each division was to be a cross-section of the crew:

> Let each midshipman's party consist as near as possible of proportional
> numbers of Able Seamen, Ordinary Seamen and Landsmen, to the intent that
> if men are wanted to be detached on any service from the ship, the detachment
> may be made by one or more parties, by which means the men who are not
> seamen will sooner become so ...[78]

This was the origin of a system that would become the basis of the navy's
welfare policy in centuries to come, but it was not universal by 1782 when
Admiral Thomas Kempenfelt wrote of 'a defect in discipline' in the fleet –
'if six, seven or eight hundred men are left in a mass together, without
divisions, and the officers assigned no particular charge over any part of
them, who only give orders from the quarterdeck or gangways – such a
crew must remain a disorderly mob.'[79]

Smith was quite liberal in his attitudes to the crew. Midshipmen were to
patrol the decks at mealtimes but were 'not to interrupt the men in mirth
and good fellowship while they keep within the bounds of moderation; the
intention of it being to prevent excessive drinking, which is not only a
crime in itself but draws men into others which when sober they would
most abhor.'[80]

Captain Richard Howe issued his own orders for the 74-gun *Magnanime*
in 1759, and he tended to trust the seamen less. Though a man was always
stationed at the masthead during the hours of daylight, a midshipman was
to be sent up every half hour to check he had not missed anything. If a
lookout was first to spot something, he was relieved; if it was spotted from
the deck first, he was given double duty.[81]

The hammock was now well established, after more than a century and
a half, as almost the only kind of sleeping arrangement for the lower deck.
According to Falconer they were

> crowded together as close as possible between the decks, each of them being
> limited to the breadth of fourteen inches. They are hung parallel to each other,
> in rows stretching from one side of the ship to the other, nearly throughout her
> whole length, so as to admit no passage but by stooping under them.[82]

GUNNERY

Howe's gunnery orders for *Magnanime* in 1759 were detailed and complex.
It was assumed that a gun was already loaded when an exercise began, but
it needed seven orders to cast it loose and prepare it, seven more to get it

ready to fire and six for aiming and firing. It took three movements to sponge the gun to remove any danger of a spark remaining after firing, eight to insert and ram home the cartridge, and finally seven to insert the shot: 'Shot the Gun; Wad to your shot; Ram home wad and shot; Draw the rammer; Stop the touch hole; Lay on the apron; Run out the gun.'[83]

In 1769 Falconer published a new system 'introduced by an officer of distinguished abilities'. The men would take up positions around the gun. If the guns on only one side were in use, the man in charge of the powder would stand on the opposite side of the ship; if both were being used, he would stand amidships. The first command was for silence, so that orders could be heard. Then the men were ordered to cast loose the guns, taking off the muzzle lashing that held it up against the ship's side and releasing the lashings on the gun tackles on each side. Then the gun was levelled by inserting a wedge or 'quoin' under its breech, and a man took out the tompion, which blocked the breech against sea water. The fifth order was to run out the guns, by hauling on the tackles on each side, the most labour-intensive part of the process. The cartridge, already inside the breech, was then primed by pricking it through the touch-hole and filling the hole with powder. If it were not to be fired immediately, a lead 'apron' was placed over the hole. If it was to be fired, the order 'point your guns' was given. The wedge was adjusted to alter the height of the muzzle, while men operated levers known as handspikes to train it in a lateral direction. One man was holding the match, and he passed it to the gun captain, who applied it to the touch-hole on the order 'fire', covering the hole so that no sparks escaped. The gun was allowed to recoil inboard, bringing it well inboard until halted by a stout breeching rope. Then the interior of the gun was sponged down to remove any spark that might remain there, while the loader went to a cartridge box towards the rear to get the next powder charge. On the order 'load with cartridge', this was thrust into the gun and pushed home with the rammer, which required considerable force. A wad of old rope was usually put in after that, then the shot – roundshot, grape or chain according to the type of action – with another wad to stop it dropping out with the roll of the ship.At the end of the exercise the tompions were put in again, and the crew were ordered to 'house the guns' by taking out the quoin, running the gun forward with its muzzle against the side of the ship just above the gunport. Finally, in order number 14, the men were to 'secure your guns' by attaching the muzzle lashing and putting all the implements – rammers handspikes and so on – in their proper places.[84]

There was an important experiment during the Seven Years War when gun locks were fitted to some ships to replace the old system of lighting the touch hole by match. At first they were not successful, and at Quiberon Bay the tin tubes associated with them tended to fly out in action, endangering the crew. They were modified in time for the Battle of the Saintes in 1782, where they proved a great success. Other techniques, such as wetting the wads, allowed a greater rate of fire, while Sir Charles Douglas developed ways of aiming the guns farther fore and aft. He claimed, 'Such ships as have their guns fitted accordingly derived unspeakable advantage from some improvements lately made in the use of naval artillery, their fire having been so quick and so very well-directed, and extending so far to the right and left, that the French cannot comprehend how they came to lose so many men, and we so few on the late bloody day; for they were generally so mauled by the guns alluded to as to be most part driven from their quarters before they could bring their guns to bear upon us.'[85]

COOK'S VOYAGES

Now that America and India were largely under British control, the French sought new places to colonise in the rest of the world and the British followed suit. The hydrographer Alexander Dalrymple believed that the South Pacific contained a great southern continent to balance the land in the northern hemisphere, much larger and more fertile than Australia, which was already partly known to Europeans, and much less cold than Antarctica. Philosophers believed they might find the 'noble savage' in the Pacific, and reports from Tahiti raised their hopes. Naturalists expected many new species of plant and animal, while astronomers would discover much more about the universe, which would be of great benefit to navigation.

The British started with Captain John Byron, the survivor of the *Wager* mutiny, but his voyage was rather desultory: he set a record for the fastest circumnavigation but found little of value. Captain Wallis turned back from his voyage, while Lieutenant Carteret sailed farther south than anyone else and proved that the southern continent did not exist in the areas he covered. Louis-Antoine de Bougainville was the most formidable French competitor. He spread the myths about Tahiti and proved that Espiritu Santo in the New Hebrides was not part of the great continent. It was in this atmosphere that an obscure warrant officer named James Cook was promoted to lieutenant and given command of a new British expedition.

On 26 August 1768, a 100-foot-long converted collier, now known as His Majesty's Bark *Endeavour*, set sail from Plymouth Sound, 'having on board 94 persons including the officers seamen gentlemen and their servants, near 18 months provisions, 10 carriage guns 12 swivels with good store of ammunition and stores of all kinds'.[86] As well as officers and gentleman scientists, there were about 75 seamen on her very cramped lower deck, with just four feet of headroom. The purposes of her voyage were to observe the transit of Venus across the moon from the island of Tahiti, to look for a 'great southern continent' in the vicinity of the land already known as New Zealand and to carry out all kinds of scientific observations.

Her commander, James Cook, was the son of a farm labourer; he had begun his career in colliers from Whitby, just like the *Endeavour* he was now commanding. He had spent most of his time in the navy in the warrant rank of master, from which it was quite rare to be commissioned. Though he was always known by the courtesy title of 'captain', he was in fact only a lieutenant during his first voyage. In many ways he was closer to the lower deck than the great majority of naval officers, hard-headed, practical and resolute. He worked his men hard, though sometimes he allowed them to be in three watches during longer periods at sea. He kept his crew under strict control on board ship, but during the whole voyage there were only fourteen floggings, and it is no coincidence that more than half of these were for offences ashore and dealings with the natives – discipline always tended to weaken when the men were not at sea. Few of the men were incorrigible, and only Robert Thompson of Inverness and Henry Stephens of Falmouth were punished more than once.[87] Since this was peacetime, it was not difficult to recruit men for the navy, and none of the adults was rated less than 'able seaman'. Five of them had followed Cook from his previous ship. The crew of *Endeavour* was quite young, mostly under 30. Cook must have seemed quite old at the age of 40, though not alongside the sailmaker John Ravenill, who according to Cook was an 'old man about 70 or 80 years' but was recorded as 49 in the ship's books.[88] The seamen seem to have respected Cook, apart from the sea-lawyer Matthew Cox of Dorset, who tried to bring an action against him after the return.[89] Cook was generally satisfied with his men, who gave less trouble than the midshipmen, one of whom was 'good for nothing', while another eventually deserted because he was suspected of cutting off part of the ears of the ship's clerk. However, 'the only useless person on board the ship', according to

Cook, was the drunken gunner Stephen Forwood.[90] Of the crew Cook commented, 'They have gone through the fatigues and dangers of the whole voyage with that cheerfulness and alertness that will always do honour to British seamen.'[91] Joseph Banks, the eminent and wealthy naturalist who accompanied the voyage, was less happy: he accused them of stealing his wine and filling up the casks with salt water, and he occasionally questioned their seamanship.[92]

During several years at sea in a very small ship there was a chance for each man to get to know each other's character – perhaps a little too well. The captain had originally objected to the appointment of John Thompson as ship's cook because he had only one hand, but he gave good service. Boatswain's Mate John Reading of Kinsale, Ireland, was apparently efficient enough except in the matter of punishment – he himself was once flogged for not flogging others. Nevertheless he retained his rating as petty officer.[93] Able Seaman Thomas Flower had already served with Cook, who described him as 'a good hardy seaman' who had 'sailed with me above five years'.[94] Boy Nicholas Young gained everlasting fame when Cook offered a reward for the first to sight land, and 'Young Nick's Head' in New Zealand was named after him. It is not known what he did with the gallon of rum that was also part of the prize, but it must have made him popular with his shipmates (though not Midshipman John Bootie, who described him as 'a son of a bitch').[95]

Crossing the Equator was celebrated in traditional fashion, when 22 men who had not done it before, and were unable or unwilling to pay forfeits in rum, wine or brandy, were ducked.[96] A visit to Rio de Janeiro was very unhappy. There was a dispute with the Portuguese governor, so the men were not allowed ashore except in carefully controlled conditions. Three of them were flogged, and the worthy Thomas Flower was accidentally drowned on the way out. On Christmas Day, according to Banks, 'all good Christians that is to say all hands get abominably drunk so that night there was scarce a sober man in the ship, wind thank God very moderate or the lord knows what would have become of us.' The passage around Cape Horn was achieved 'with as little danger as the North Foreland on the Kentish coast'.[97]

On reaching the first destination, Tahiti, the men were delighted to be allowed ashore and enjoy the company of the native women, for according to one of the crew, 'The women of Otahitee have agreeable features, are well proportioned, sprightly, and lascivious; neither do they esteem continence as a virtue, since almost every one of our crew procured temporary wives among them, who were easily retained during our stay.'[98] Cook reported they were 'so very liberal with their favours, or else nails, shirts etc were temptations that they could not withstand'.[99] This led Archibald Wolf to break into a store room to steal nails, and Cook took this threat to the ship's safety very seriously – he had Wolf flogged with two dozen lashes. But the men of *Endeavour* did not go so far as those of Wallis's *Dolphin*, who pulled nails from the ship's timbers.[100] Unfortunately venereal disease had recently taken hold on the island, attributed to a visit by a Spanish ship. Cook ordered his men to be examined, but only one was found to be ill in any way, and he had not 'had connection with one woman in the island'.[101] The men were intrigued by the native custom of having 'tattows' applied to their body, and Able Seaman Robert Stainsby had his arm 'marked' in this way.[102]

In New Zealand they found the Maoris much less accommodating than the Tahitans but could not help admiring their warlike rituals: 'in martial courage the New Zealanders are much superior; and indeed it is impossible to see, without astonishment, the degree of madness to which they will elevate themselves even in their harangues, that are preparatory to a feigned battle.'[103] They remained there several months while Cook completed a remarkably accurate survey of the islands.

Cook's voyage was pioneering in many ways, not least in the feeding of the crew. Following the advice of Dr McBride, 'well-dried malt' was loaded on board 'for treatment against scurvy'. More effective were 'portable' (condensed) soup and sauerkraut. The former was to be issued on 'banyan', or meatless, days, 'when fresh provisions are not to be had to the well men as well as to the sick and convalescents, it having been found extremely beneficial in long voyages'.[104] After the voyage Cook wrote that, 'sauerkraut together with the many other anti-scorbutics my Lords Commissioners of the Admiralty were pleased to order to be put on board did so effectually preserve the people from a scorbutic taint that not one dangerous case happened in that disorder during the whole voyage.'[105] All the same, the traditional issue of ship's biscuit continued, harbouring five different kinds of vermin, and Joseph Banks wrote, 'I have often seen hundreds, nay thousands shaken out of a single biscuit.'[106] Other improvements included twenty cork jackets, presumably for life-saving, and the issue of 'a Fearnought jacket and a pair of trousers' to each man for cold weather. After that Cook 'never heard one man complain of cold [though] the weather was cold enough'.[107]

Off the coast of Australia, the ship had its greatest moment of danger when it struck the Great Barrier Reef. A huge hole was knocked in the side, and the ship was only saved because a large piece of coral had lodged itself in it. The crew remained calm until a new man took over sounding the water in the hold and misunderstood how the water level was being measured: he immediately announced an increase of sixteen or eighteen inches, 'which for the first time caused fear to operate upon every man in the ship'. The mistake was soon corrected, and the crew worked even harder at the pumps and sails until the ship was grounded on the coast. It was very different from the loss of *Wager*, and Cook commented, 'No men ever behaved better than they have done on this occasion, animated by the behavior of every gentleman on board, every man seemed to have a just sense of the danger we were in and exerted himself to the very utmost.'[108]

The ship was patched up and sailed to the Dutch colony of Batavia for more extensive repairs, where another disaster struck. So far there had been very few deaths, and none from scurvy, but the men soon picked up malaria and dysentery. When the ship sailed again, 40 of them were seriously ill. Cook took the precaution of recruiting nineteen 'supernumeraries' at Batavia, and these became full crew members as the others died. On one of the worst days, 31 January 1771, Cook John Thompson, Carpenter's Mate Benjamin Jordan and Seamen James Nicholson and Archibald Wolf all died. Cook recorded that it was 'a melancholy proof of the calamitous situation we are at present in, having hardly well men enough to tend the sails and look after the sick, many of the latter are so ill that we have not the least hopes of their recovery'.[109] One man, who 'had long tended the sick and enjoyed a tolerable good state of health' came on deck one morning and 'found himself a little griped and immediately began to stamp with his feet and exclaim I have got the gripes, I have got the gripes, I shall die! – In this manner he continued until he threw himself in a fit and was carried off the deck in a manner dead, but soon recovered and did very well.'[110] The aged sailmaker, John Ravenhill, was hardened by his long experience and constant drunkenness and never succumbed. At last, on 27 February, three men died, including one who had joined the crew at Batavia, and Cook hoped that the outbreak was finally over. In all, 24 had died.

The ship reached Cape Town on 14 March and stayed for a month, recruiting ten more men of mixed nationality to make up the numbers. They arrived back in Britain in 1771, having surveyed New Zealand and discovered a way through the Great Barrier Reef to the fertile east coast of Australia, but having largely disproved the existence of the southern continent. The rewards of the crew were less tangible, for there was no prize money. Some of them prospered. Quartermaster Samuel Evans became a boatswain, despite the fact that he was unable to sign his name, while several became warrant officers in Cook's later voyages. Others fell on hard times, such as Able Seaman John Goodjohn, who petitioned Banks for a place as a watchman, paradoxically because his sight was failing. Banks, now a grandee of natural history, wrote, 'Give him a guinea.'[111]

THE LATER VOYAGES

In 1772, Cook set sail again with two larger ships, *Resolution* and *Adventure*, to finally disprove the existence of the southern continent by sailing well into Antarctic waters. Banks did not come this time, for the Admiralty had refused his demand to take charge of the voyage over the head of Cook. Among the seamen of *Resolution* were several interesting characters. William Peckover was unusually ambitious for the lower deck and later tried to have himself appointed midshipman. John Frazer was a diver and inventor, but as a ships' corporal he was not considered experienced enough as a seaman to become a boatswain.[112] John (or Jack) Marra was by far the most colourful. He had first joined Cook in *Endeavour* at Batavia, an Irishman from Cork, 'a good seamen and had sailed in both the English and Dutch and service'. According to Cook, he was a citizen of the globe – 'I never learned that he had either friends or connections to confine him to any particular part of the world, all nations were alike to him ...'[113] He was one of thirteen seamen and one marine who rejoined Cook for the second voyage. Rated as a gunner's mate, he was the only member of the lower deck to publish a journal of the voyage, heavily edited by his publisher and deplored by his officers but containing a few insights into lower deck life and attitudes.[114]

The two ships left Plymouth in July 1772, and in the following January they became the first to cross the Antarctic Circle, where Marra was soon engaged in work among the icebergs:

> Saw some loose ice near an ice island which was likely to answer our purpose, shortened sail and hauled out wind. Employed getting ready the boats [2 am]. Could not find the island so bore away [6 am]. Saw another, stood for it, hauled close and shortened sail and hoisted out all the boats and took up, the decks full of loose pieces of ice, which we found to yield excellent water, as everybody was employed it afforded a very humorous sight, thus to see people busied, some

hacking away at a large piece of ice, others drawing it up out of the sea in baskets, and I believe it is the first instance of drawing fresh water out of the ocean in hand baskets.[115]

Later Marra recorded that, despite the cold and hard work among the ice, 'yet under all these hardships, the men cheerful over their grog; and not a man sick but of old scars.'[116] They spent the southern winter in more northern climes and during a second trip south in February 1774 they were struck by a storm, where Cook earned Marra's respect: 'The service bearing hard upon the mariners, the captain to ease them as much as possible, very humanely ordered the officers' mates before the mast.'[117] And when Cook was taken ill a few days later, it was 'to the grief of all the ship's company'. When he recovered, the crew's delight was to be seen 'which each might read in the countenance of the other form the highest officer to the meanest boy on board the ship'.[118]

But Marra was rootless and looking out for an opportunity. Off Tahiti in May 1774, he was allegedly promised 'a house, land and a pretty wife' by the local chiefs. An excellent swimmer, he attempted to desert but was caught by the ship's cutter. He jumped overboard but was caught again and clapped in irons when he got back to the ship. But Cook was kind to him, and young John Elliot agreed that 'he would have been a great loss to us' so he was soon released. Later Marra, or perhaps his editor, made an ingenious defence of his conduct:

And pity it was that he happened to be discovered, as from him a more copious and accurate account of the religion and civil government of the people might have been expected after a few years stay among them, than could possibly be collected from a few short visits, by gentlemen who had the language to learn, and whose first business was to procure necessaries, in order to enable them to pursue more important discoveries.[119]

Resolution, having been separated from *Adventure,* arrived home at the end of July 1775. Only four men had died during the voyage, none of them from scurvy.

On 14 July 1776, Cook set off on his third voyage with *Resolution* and *Discovery*, this time to seek the fabled North-West Passage from the west. On the face of it, he had a good crew, including 44-year-old William Watman, the old man of the lower deck, beloved of his fellows for his 'good and benevolent disposition'. 'There was never such a collection of fine lads,' according to the surgeon's mate.[120] But Cook was past his best, tired and ill, and relations with the crew got steadily worse. Watman died during the voyage, and the crew began to object to Cook's experiments with local food and drink. When he issued a new concoction every second day instead of grog, the men refused to drink it, and Cook accused them of 'a very mutinous proceeding'.[121] Relations with native peoples were also bad, particularly at Hawaii, where Cook was at first treated as a god, then with great suspicion when he was forced to return. When a fight broke out, Cook and four marines were killed – the crew were devastated, despite all the problems. 'Greif was visible in every countenance, some expressing it by tears, others by a kind of gloomy dejection.' They took their revenge by firing rather indiscriminately into native villages and eventually sailed home.

THE AMERICAN WAR

The British victory in the Seven Years War had seemed complete, and one magazine claimed,

> The trade of the whole world centred on this island; she was the mart of all nations: the merchants engrossed the riches of the universe, and lived like princes: and the manufacturers were enabled to live in credit and reputation, being supplied with many things necessary for their sue from our conquests, at an easy rate for which they had been obliged to pay dear before.[122]

But Britain had deserted her allies in Europe and had no friends there, while the American colonists no longer had to fear the French, who were determined on revenge. Meanwhile, King George III was determined to impose taxes on the colonists – which led to revolt.

Difficulties began quite soon after the peace, but the build-up to major war was even slower than usual. In late 1763 a squadron of 21 ships was stationed in North America, largely to enforce the new taxes and to prevent smuggling. This was an unusually large force for peacetime, and the usual desertions and deaths caused a manning problem. As early as 1764 the commanders on the spot were asking permission to impress men from the colonies.[123] Though it was reluctant to start pressing at home, the government tried to use the press in a different way. An act of 1708 had made pressing illegal in America, but that was repealed, and it was used in punitive fashion against ports that opposed British authority. It was a risky strategy: if successful it might fill His Majesty's ships with disaffected men; if it failed it would strengthen resistance among the colonists. Thus in February 1775 the frigate *Lively* was stationed off Marblehead, allegedly to 'harass and impress the seafaring population of that town', while the population 'determined on rescuing any impressed men'.[124] Three months later Vice Admiral Samuel Graves 'wrote to the collector of customs at Salem to let the town know that he would not press their sailors if they did not stop the supplies for the squadron'.[125]

Some Americans hoped that British naval power might be undermined and even destroyed by lower deck discontent. Christopher Gadsen, Congressman for South Carolina, claimed some naval experience and wrote to John Adams:

> He has several times taken pains to convince me that this fleet is not so formidable to America, as we fear. – He says, we can easily take their sloops, schooners and cutters, on board whom are all their best seamen, and with these we can easily take their large ships, on board whom are all their impressed and discontented men. He thinks, the men would not fight on board the large ships with their fellow subjects, but would certainly kill their own officers – He says it is a different thing, to fight the French or Spaniards from what it is to fight British Americans – in one case if taken prisoners they must lie in prison for years, in the other to obtain their liberty and happiness.[126]

Certainly there were plenty of discontented seamen, and British sailors had long had a tendency to desert in American waters, either to join well-paid American ships or to settle ashore. Admiral Graves admitted, 'When seamen are bent upon leaving a ship no consideration stops them.'[127] But there is no sign of revolt on anything like that scale. Indeed Captain Edward Medows of the *Tartar* wrote in June 1775 that though he was short of men, 'from the number of men we have, Sir, I have the satisfaction to think we should do as much as could be expected from us with great cheerfulness and good will'.[128]

The American war began seriously in 1775, with the revolt largely led by New England. Apart from a few strongholds, the British were no longer in control of the thirteen colonies, and they needed a large army to attempt to reconquer them. They also needed an enormous fleet of transports to carry and supply the army, as well as warships to patrol the coasts and rivers of America, cutting rebel supply lines and destroying their commerce. As yet there was no need for ships of the line, as the Americans had no navy; but frigates and small two-deckers were employed to the full. By this time there were 110 ships and 16,000 men in pay. They had mostly been raised without impressment, for this war, unlike the previous ones, was dividing the country to such an extent that the Lord Mayor of London would later refuse to back press warrants in the City, while William Pitt, 'organiser of victory' in the Seven Years War, was opposed to the new conflict and suggested placating the Americans. In the circumstances, the government had to tread warily.

Even after the Americans declared independence in 1776, the government was not ready to resort to large-scale impressing at home. A few weeks before the Declaration of Independence, the cabinet decided 'to go on with the raising of volunteer seamen for the use of the fleet'. It also decided 'to prepare measures for a press with secrecy that it may be carried suddenly and effectually into execution if necessary', but that was not done.[129] Instead, the navy relied on bounties to attract volunteers. This seems to have had some success: it managed to raise 21,565 men during that year, by paying bounties of £42,846.[130] But it became necessary to raise an even larger fleet for the next year. Late in 1776 an embargo was placed on shipping, and press warrants were issued for use by the local authorities and regulating officers. Such was Admiralty sensitivity about public opinion that not until May 1777 were officers from ships allowed to press men on their own account.

DISCIPLINE

Eighteenth century legislators and judges tended to prefer savage deterrents to effective policing, and the Royal Navy was no exception. The punishment of 'flogging around the fleet' was not unknown before then, but it seems to have increased in frequency and severity during the century. William Spavens attended many courts martial as one of the crew of the captain's barge. When a man was sentenced to 600 lashes,

> on hearing his sentence pronounced by the judge advocate, addressed himself to the court, and in the most humble and pathetic manner requested he might be hanged! Being asked the reason for such request, he replied, I cannot endure the punishment. On which Sir William Burnaby answered with a degree of severity in his looks, the sentence contains no more than what the court thought fit to impose, and dead or alive it must be carried into execution. The punishment was to be inflicted three times on three fortnight days ...[131]

John Nicol describes the effects:

> One of the men was whipped through the fleet for stealing some dollars from a merchant ship he was assisting to bring into port. It was a dreadful sight; the unfortunate sufferer tied down on the boat, and rowed from ship to ship, getting an equal number of lashes at the side of each vessel from a fresh man.

The poor wretch, to deaden his sufferings, had drunk a whole bottle of rum a little before the tie of the punishment. When he had only two portions to get of his punishment, the captain of the ship perceived he was tipsy, and immediately ordered the rest of the punishment to be delayed until he was sober. He was rowed back to the *Surprise*, his back swelled like a pillow, black and blue; some sheets of thick blue paper were steeped in vinegar and laid to his back. Before he seemed insensible, now his shrieks rent the air. When he was better he was sent to his ship, where his tortures were stopped, and again renewed.[132]

Captain Phillip Patton had to deal with a mutiny of the crew when he was in temporary command of *Prince George* in 1779, though it had nothing to do with politics. The seamen were already discontented at being ordered to leave port to patrol in the Western Approaches, and a revolt flared up on 16 January when the captain ordered the men to bring their hammocks up on deck, as the lower and middle gunports had been closed for several days due to bad weather, and the decks needed to be aired. The men refused and threatened death to the boatswain who was sent below to order them. Patton called the men on deck and explained why the order was necessary, but he added that 'this explanation was not necessary, because it was sufficient for them that such were his orders'. He called the officers to the quarterdeck and in the hearing of the men instructed them to take parties of men below according to the hammock list and order each individually to bring his hammock on deck. Eventually it was done, and the leader of the mutiny was soon identified and punished. Quite typically, the mutiny was barely mentioned in the ship's logs. It was unusual in that it took place in a ship at sea, but in some ways it was a taste of things to come.

THE EXPANDING WAR

In 1778 the war took a new turn. France, still resentful about her defeat in the Seven Years War, was encouraged by the American victory at Saratoga in 1777 and decided to send help to the American rebels. Of course, this was opposed by the British, and war broke out in the spring of 1778. France had a fleet of 73 ships of the line, compared with Britain's 125. Clearly the British main fleet could not lie dormant much longer. All sorts of efforts were made to raise seamen. The bounty was increased by 30/-, and numerous towns raised money for extra bounties. An embargo was placed in May, and a hot press was organised, in which even men with protections from the Admiralty were not safe. By the middle of June, Admiral Keppel, in command of the main fleet, wrote that the fleet was 'totally equipped', though no allowance had been made for replacements of deserters and sick.[133] By 1 July, Britain had 66 ships of the line in service, against France's 52. However, the British force was more dispersed, and the French had a slight advantage in European waters.[134] The Battle of Ushant followed soon afterwards; it was indecisive but led to recriminations, which demoralised the British officers.

In 1779 the situation became yet more serious when Spain declared war in alliance with France, hoping to regain her lost possessions of Gibraltar, Menorca and Florida. She brought a fleet of about 60 ships of the line – and the British navy was outnumbered for the first time in the century. The navy had to allow enough seamen to man the transports that supplied the army in America as well as providing the ships protecting the convoys to take them there; it had to guard widespread possessions all over the world, especially in the West Indies; and it had to help in attacking the American ports, such as Charleston. The fleet that year reached a record total of more than 87,000 men. 42,000 of these were raised in 1779. Late in the previous year a contract had been signed with a Mr. Nathaniel Bland, who undertook to raise seamen at a price of 10/- each, and he produced 1,878. The rest were raised by the more conventional means, and in April permission was given to press men from outward bound ships. There was a 'concerted attack'[135] to impress fishermen, and yet more bounties were offered from various towns. Nearly 2,500 men were employed on the impress service ashore and afloat, at a cost of £83,000. Despite these efforts, the home fleet was heavily outnumbered in 1779, and in July it could muster only 31 ships in home waters against a Franco-Spanish force of about 60. The threat of invasion was greater than ever. In August there was panic in Britain as the enemy fleet took control of the Channel and appeared off Plymouth. But the Franco-Spanish plans were not well prepared, and no invasion was launched.

Contrary to popular myth, the Admiralty did not routinely resort to taking on criminals as seamen, but smugglers were one class who might prove useful – they were good seamen and fighters, and their crimes were not 'anti-social' in the sense of robbery or murder. However, they were crafty and had their own group loyalty, as John Nicol discovered when serving in a pressing tender which with another ship surprised a smuggling vessel in St Andrews Bay, Fife:

> The smuggler fought them both until all her ammunition was spent, and resisted their boarding her until the very last by every means in their power. A

good many of the King's men were wounded, and not a few of the smugglers. When taken possession of, they declared their captain had been killed in the action, and thrown overboard.

After a spell in Edinburgh Castle they were locked in the press room of the tender, where they attempted to murder an alleged informer from Leith. Arriving at the Nore, a writ for debt was sent on board for one of the smugglers in the hope that it would gain his release. Nicol was transferred to the 20-gun *Proteus* along with most of the smugglers, who made an impression on the captain as 'stout, active and experienced seamen', and he manned his barge with them, appointing one as coxswain. But when he went ashore in the West Indies, all except one deserted, including the coxswain. The man who remained was shunned by the rest of the ship's company, as a coward.[136]

As always, the efforts at raising seamen were often wasted because large numbers died or deserted. In general, the number of desertions per year was approximately half the number raised. Thus, in 1780, 28,000 men were raised, but 14,000 deserted. Over the years from 1778 to 1780, nearly 20,000 men died from sickness or battle, while 42,000 deserted. However, the number of desertions was smaller than in the Seven Years War: in that conflict, 1,512 men died in action and 132,196 were listed as missing, presumably having deserted.

By 1780 it had become clear that the French and Spanish were not going to invade the British homeland, and the main fleets moved to the West Indies, with all the manning difficulties that involved. In 1781, for example, out of 10,600 men that should have been borne aboard Sir Samuel Hood's squadron, 1,300 were sick, and the ships were a further 691 short of complement.[137] By the end of that year more than 400 ships were in commission, employing nearly 97,000 men.[138] In 1782 there were 38 British ships of the line in the Caribbean. By this time any hope of keeping America under British control had been abandoned, and the navy was fighting to save the remaining parts of the empire. The War of American Independence extended both the range and the size of the fleet, and the West Indies, which had become a theatre of war for the first time in the 1700s, became the main area of naval conflict for a while.

Though they started with no navy at all, the Americans soon began to fit out privateers to raid British shipping. John Nicol was the cooper in the 28-gun *Surprise* when she took on the American privateer *Jason* in 1779:

I was serving powder as busy as I could, the shot and splinters flying in all directions, when I heard the Irishmen call from one of the guns (they fought like devils, and the captain was fond of them on that account), 'Halloo, Bungs where are you?' I looked to their gun, and saw the two horns of my *study* [anvil] across its mouth; the next moment it was through the Jason's side ... 'Bungs for ever!' they shouted, when the saw the dreadful hole it made in the *Jason's* side.[139]

Among his other duties, Nicol was detailed as a boarder:

We were all armed, when required, with a pike, to defend our own vessel, should any enemy attempt to board; a tomahawk, cutlass and a brace of pistols, to use in boarding them. I never had occasion to try their use on board the *Proteus*, as the privateers used to strike after a broadside or two.[140]

THE BATTLE OF THE SAINTES

The large British fleet in the West Indies and North America experienced a sequence of frustrations. In an indecisive battle off Martinique in March 1781, neither British nor French lost a ship. In September off the Chesapeake, the British failed to relieve the siege of Yorktown and in effect lost their control of the American colonies. In January 1782 a plan to take the French by surprise at St Kitts misfired, and the British fleet needed a brilliant defensive action to save its position. But finally, in April, the two fleets met on equal terms off the islands of the Saintes between Guadeloupe and Dominica. Sir Gilbert Blane, the senior medical officer in the fleet, was proud of his achievement in keeping up its health:

Nothing had been wanting to equip this fleet for the great and decisive exertion it was to make. Every ship, except two, might be said to be healthy, most of them were complete in men, well appointed with officers and well found in stores and provision. Conformable to this was their eagerness, the confidence and resolution, which led them to success and victory.[141]

If the American hopes of a revolt by the British navy had ever been realistic, there were eliminated by the inclusion of France and Spain in the war. Blane had heard that the anticipation of battle with the forces of France and Spain had improved the health of Admiral Mathew's fleet off Toulon in 1744:

But if the mere expectation and ardour of a battle, without any happy event, could have such a sensible effect, what must have been the effect of exultation of victory, a victory in which the naval glory of our country was revived and retrieved, after a series of misfortunes and disgraces which had well nigh extinguished the national pride in every department of service! The plain and honest, though unthinking seaman, is not less affected by this than the more enlightened lover of his country. Even the invalids at the hospital demonstrated their joy, upon hearing of the victory, by hoisting shreds of coloured cloth on their crutches.[142]

Blane had the chance to watch the seamen at close hand during the battle and even helped at a 9-pounder gun at one point.[143] He observed,

> When the mind is interested and agitated by active and generous affections, the body forgets its wants and feelings, and is capable of a degree of labour and exertion, which it could not undergo in cold blood. The quantity of muscular action employed in fighting at a great gun for a few hours is perhaps more than what is commonly employed in a week in the ordinary course of life, though performed in the midst of heat and smoke, and generally with the want of food and drink, yet the powers of nature are not exhausted nor overstrained; even the smart of wounds is not felt ...[144]

For one reason or another, the British seamen were found to be far more effective than their French counterparts. Blane commented,

> The only cause therefore that can be assigned for British superiority, in this and many other naval encounters, can be no other than the closeness of an action, an advantage, however, which being mutual and equal, can be available only to that part which possesses the moral pre-eminence of undaunted courage, and consequent physical superiority of a better sustained fire; and this was never more fully exemplified and proved than in the present instance. In breaking the line, the *Formidable* passed so near the *Glorieux,* that I could see the cannoniers throwing away their sponges and hand-spikes, in order to save themselves by running below, while our guns were served with the utmost animation.[145]

The British captured the French flagship *Ville de Paris* and several other ships. The victory came too late to affect the American colonies, but the rest of the British Empire was now secure as peace negotiations began.

THE LOSS OF THE *ROYAL GEORGE*

James Ingram was a seaman in the great flagship *Royal George* anchored off Spithead in August 1782 as the ship was heeled slightly to one side to repair some piping. When a tender arrived with stores, he overheard an argument between the carpenter and the lieutenant of the watch, in which the latter exclaimed, 'D—e, Sir, if you can manage the ship better than I can you had better take command!' The lieutenant had apparently agreed to allow the tender to use tackles to unload at the same time, greatly increasing the angle of heel. As a result of this basic error, the ship began to capsize.

> The water then rushed in at nearly all the ports of the larboard side of the lower gun-deck, and I said directly to Carroll 'Ned, lay hold of the ring-bolt and jump out at the port. The ship is sinking and we shall all be drowned.' He laid hold of the ring-bolt and jumped out at the port into the sea. I believe he was drowned, for I never saw him afterwards. I immediately got out at the same port, which was the third from the head of the ship, on the starboard side of the lower gun-deck, and when I had done so I saw the port was a full of heads as it could cram, all trying to get out. I caught hold of the best bower anchor, which was just above me, to prevent falling back into the port, and seized hold of a woman who was trying to get out of the same port. I dragged her out.

Ingram could not swim well, but he was lifted by an updraught after the ship hit the bottom.

> When I was about half way up to the top of the water I put my right hand on a man that was nearly exhausted ... He tried to grapple me, and put his four fingers in my right shoe, alongside the outer edge of my foot. I succeeded in kicking my shoe off, and putting my hand on his shoulder I shoved him away. I then rose to the surface of the water ... I got the tar about my hand and face, but I struck it away as well as I could, and when my head came above water I heard the cannon ashore firing for distress ... I swam to the main-topsail halyard-block and sat upon it, and there I rode. [146]

The losses are unknown because no register was kept of the women and children on board, but around a thousand people perished, including hundreds of seamen.

THE END OF THE WAR

With the cessation of hostilities in 1783, the seamen were discharged as usual. Samuel Kelly was in a merchant ship that was given the job of ferrying 127 men, formerly part of the crews of the ships of the line *Elizabeth* and *Edgar*, to their homes in Scotland. He found them an unruly bunch who 'being now free from restraint took the management of our ship in a great measure on themselves; that is, in taking in and making sail at their pleasure ...' Their officers knew to keep out of the way and even join in their dances, but it all got out of hand, and one man was asphyxiated when his comrades piled beds on top of him 'in their mirth'. Kelly was relieved as various shore boats arrived along the way so that men could be dropped off at their own ports, and only a few of them were left when they arrived at Leith.[147]

A seaman from *Magnificent*, rich from prize money, hired a whole stagecoach for himself and his friends. An officer tried to get 'a berth' inside the coach:

> 'I'll be damned if he shall, though,' replied Jack. He never axed me into his cabin aboard the *Magnificent*. Howsomever, tell him he may go on deck if he likes; and I hope he'll look after you and see that you are steady at the helm, and don't sarve us the same as one of you land-lubbers did about three years ago, when he ran foul of one of the land-marks, and pitched us all overboard.
>
> The lieutenant heard Jack's reply, and taking it all in good part, mounted the coach and rolled away to London.[148]

5

The CRISIS
1783 to 1803

The years after the American war were a 'time of profound peace' according to one official of the Navy Board.[1] He exaggerated a little – there were several major mobilisations against other naval powers on the threat of war, which caused embargoes to be placed on shipping, press warrants to be issued and men impressed to man quite large squadrons – but the differences were settled by diplomatic means, and no wars followed. The machinery apparently worked well, and Admiral Byam Martin later wrote,

> In the armaments of 1787, 1790, and 1791, the guardships, by means of impressments, completed their full complements almost in an instant of time, and were speedily joined by other ships of the line, fitted and manned by impressment with incredible despatch.
>
> Those who can recollect these several armaments, can well testify that it was impressment which enabled us, on each occasion, to make so gigantic a display of our naval strength; and though we regard with abhorrence the principle of impressment, it is notorious that it was solely the cause of the pacific outcome of those rapid armaments. It gave to the country the blessing of continued peace; and by preventing war, saved thousands of lives and millions of money.[2]

It was less impressive to William Richardson, returning from a slave-trading voyage in March 1791. 'Off Beachy Head we were brought to by the *Nemesis* frigate (Capt. Ball), who pressed all our men except four Germans ... Some of the poor fellows shed tears on being pressed after so long a voyage and so near home.' Richardson was not taken, as he was chief mate, until someone informed the press that he was only acting in that rank. The gang came back for him and he found himself in the 98-gun *London*: 'I went on board, and was stationed in the maintop. Her lofty masts and square yards appeared wonderful to me, and I wondered how they were able to manage them; but I soon got accustomed to that, for we had plenty of exercise with them and the great guns almost daily.' He was less happy with the discipline, 'for soon after I got on board we had to cat the anchor, and in running along with the foul, boatswains' mates were placed on each side, who kept thrashing away with their rattans on our backs, making no difference between those who pulled hard and those who did not.' Like the other crises of the period, the 'Russian Armament' did not last long, and Richardson was paid off after four months.[3]

THE *BOUNTY*

'On the 9th of September 1787,' wrote Boatswain's Mate James Morrison, 'I entered on board His Majesty's Armed Vessel *Bounty*, Lieutenant Bligh, Commander, then lying at Deptford.' Morrison probably knew already that she was fitting out for a long voyage to the Pacific, but of course he had no idea how the name of the ship and her captain would resound throughout the world for centuries afterwards. A native of the Hebridean island of Lewis, Morrison was 25 years old and highly educated for a seaman. He had served as a midshipman on board *Termagant* in 1782–3, and it might be argued that he was not a true member of the lower deck but a young man who had dropped in status to serve on a voyage of exploration, as the young Nelson had done in *Racehorse* in 1773. But there is no sign that Morrison had the patronage necessary to become an officer in that way, and throughout the voyage he identified with the lower deck rather than the officers. It seems more likely that he was a promising and intelligent young seaman who had once been given a chance to try for quarterdeck status.

In any case, he would soon find out that the main division on board the *Bounty* was not between officers and ratings, but in attitudes to Captain Bligh. He was not the tyrant often portrayed in story and film, but his capriciousness, his fastidiousness and sarcasm could become very wearing in a small ship – and *Bounty* was very small, with a crew of only 45 men. It was not Bligh's fault that the voyage started very late in the season, but it was soon dogged by bad luck, and the ship had to turn back several times. After replenishing at Tenerife, Bligh assembled the crew and outlined his plans for the voyage. They were on the way to Tahiti to pick up breadfruit, which was to be fed to the slaves in the West Indies. The well-educated but inexperienced master's mate, Fletcher Christian, was to be made acting lieutenant over the head of the master, John Fryer.

> Mr. Bligh then informed them that as the length of the voyage was uncertain till he should get into the South Sea, he was not certain whether he should be

able to get round Cape Horn, as the season was so far spent; but at all events, he was determined to try. It became necessary to be careful of the provisions (particularly bread) to make them hold out. For this reason he ordered the allowance of bread to be reduced to two-thirds, but let everything else remain at full. This was cheerfully received, and the beer being gone, grog was served.[4]

After that the supply of food came to dominate the thoughts of the men, in Morrison's view at least. When two cheeses were found to be missing, 'Mr. Bligh, without making any further enquiry into the matter, ordered the allowance of cheese to be stopped from the officers and men till the deficiency should be made good, and told the cooper he would give him a damned good flogging if he said any more about it.' As the bread began to run out, the men were issued with pumpkins instead – but queried the rate of exchange of one pound of pumpkin to two of bread. When they refused to eat it, Bligh raged, 'You damned infernal scoundrels, I'll make you eat grass or anything you catch before I have done with you.' The men, unlike the officers, were used to such behaviour from a captain: 'The seamen, seeing that no redress could be had before the end of the voyage, determined to bear it with patience and neither murmured nor complained afterwards. However, the officers were not so easily satisfied, and made frequent murmuring amongst themselves about the smallness of their allowance, and could not reconcile themselves to such unfair proceedings.' The structural problem on board *Bounty* was that she had no commissioned officers apart from the captain, and the warrant officers soon fell out with him, in particular the master, carpenter and surgeon.

There was a much greater trial in March and April as the ship tried to round Cape Horn out of season, against unfavourable winds and possible storms. Bligh paid tribute to the efforts of his men:

> The sails and ropes were worked with much difficulty, and the few men who were obliged to be aloft felt the snow squalls so severe as to render them almost incapable of getting below, and some of them sometimes for a while lost their speech; but I took care to nurse them when off duty with every comfort in my power. The invalids I made attend and dry their clothes and keep a good fire in every night. They were at three watches, and when lying to, I would suffer two men on deck at a time. I gave them all additional slop clothes, and I made their meal pleasant and wholesome ...[5]

But at last Bligh gave up, as Morrison records:

> On the 18th of April Mr. Bligh ordered all hands aft and, after giving them his thanks for their unremitted attention to their duty, informed them of his intention to bear away for the Cape of Good Hope, as it appeared to him an impossibility to get round Cape Horn. This was received with universal joy and returned according to custom with three cheers. The ship was instantly put before the wind ...[6]

A hog was slaughtered, 'though scarce anything but skin and bone was greedily devoured'. Then Bligh spotted that the wind had shifted to the northward and decided to try again. *Bounty* turned westwards but had to give up again after four more days. The ship then sailed to the Cape of Good Hope and replenished with food and drink. Eventually in October, after ten months of voyaging, they reached Tahiti to receive a tremendous welcome – 'We were presently surrounded by the natives in their canoes, who brought off hogs, breadfruit and coconuts in abundance.' The sailors were soon seduced by the lifestyle, the fine weather, abundant food and easy sex. During a long stay, Bligh kept his men busy repairing the ship and loading more than a thousand breadfruit plants, and suffered the usual problems of theft by the natives and neglect by his officers and crew. Three men deserted, including the ship's corporal, Charles Churchill, whose duty was to prevent such actions. They were brought back, put in irons and flogged.

It was only after sailing from Tahiti that dissent boiled over. Fletcher Christian had ceased to be a protégé of Bligh, and in his own words he was 'in Hell' with his captain's abuse and sarcasm. He had originally planned to desert the ship using a makeshift raft until one of the midshipmen told him ambiguously that the crew were 'ready for anything'. It was not clear whether this meant that they could be induced to mutiny now, or would do so anyway if Christian left. In any case, he took control of the ship during one night with the aid of four men, including Churchill. Morrison claimed he was not involved: 'In the morning of the 28th, the boatswain came to me in my hammock and waked me, telling me to my great surprise that the ship was taken by Mr. Christian. I hurried on deck and found it true – seeing Mr. Bligh in his nightshirt with his hands tied behind him and Mr. Christian standing by him with a drawn bayonet in his hand and his eyes flaming with revenge.' After some negotiation, nineteen men, including most of the officers who had opposed Bligh, were put into the longboat with some food and navigational equipment. Three midshipmen remained with Christian along with most of the petty officers and seamen, but, as Bligh always acknowledged, at least four of these were kept against their will to avoid overcrowding the boat. The party in the boat did not dare to land at a nearby island, which was believed to be hostile, but instead made an epic voyage to Batavia.

The 25 men on board *Bounty* were divided and undecided. Some wanted to go back to the delights of Tahiti, but others knew that this would be suicidal – that sooner or later the navy would come looking for them. Some had always opposed the mutiny; some, like Morrison, claimed they were only waiting for a chance to re-take the ship. After much wandering they did eventually go back to Tahiti, where the party split. Christian sailed off with *Bounty*, and Morrison was not entirely happy with the manner of doing it: 'We were all much surprised to find the ship gone as Mr. Christian had proposed staying a day or two to give us time to get on shore what thing we might want or had forgot to take on shore; this gave us reason to suppose that he was afraid of a surprise or had done it to prevent his companions from changing their mind.' He sailed with eight seamen, six male Tahitans and nineteen men, six of whom were dumped on a nearby island as being 'rather ancient'. The mutineers landed to found a new colony on the remote Pitcairn Island, *Bounty* was destroyed and Christian was one of several to be murdered. The leadership of the group was taken over by former Able Seaman John Adams, also known as Alexander Adams and Alexander Smith. The settlement remained undiscovered for nineteen years, by which time Adams was the only one of the originals alive. He was probably the only member of the navy's lower deck to found a colony.

Morrison stayed behind with the others and attempted to build a boat in which to get home. His work seems to have been highly skilled but was interrupted in March 1791, when HMS *Pandora* arrived seeking them out. They surrendered and soon found that Captain Edward Edwards was a far worse seaman and a far greater tyrant than Captain Bligh had ever been. He imprisoned all the *Bounty* men, whether mutineers or not, in appalling conditions:

> The poop, or roundhouse, being finished, we were conveyed into it and put in irons as before. This place we styled '*Pandora*'s Box,' the entrance being a scuttle on the top, eighteen or twenty inches square, secured by a bolt on the top through the coamings; two scuttles of nine inches square in the bulkhead for air with iron grates; and the stern ports barred inside and out with iron. The sentries were placed on the top while a midshipman walked across by the bulkhead. The length of this box was eleven feet on deck and eighteen wide at the bulkhead, and here no person was suffered to speak to us but the master at arms. His orders were not to speak to us on any occasion but that of our provisions.

The heat of the place when it was calm was so intense that the sweat frequently ran in streams to the scuppers and produced maggots in a short time. The hammocks, being dirty when we got them, we found stored with vermin of another kind, which we had no method of eradicating but by lying on the plank.[7]

When *Pandora* was wrecked on the Great Barrier Reef, the prisoners were in great danger:

> Burkett and Hillbrant were yet handcuffed, and the ship under water as far as the main mast. It was beginning to flow in upon us when the Divine Providence directed William Moulter (boatswain's mate) to the place. He was scrambling up on the box and, hearing our cries, took out the bolt and threw it and the scuttle overboard. Such was his presence of mind, though, that he was forced to follow instantly himself. On this, we all got out, except Hillbrant, and were rejoiced even in this trying scene to think that we had escaped from our prison – though it was full as much as I could do to clear myself of the driver boom before the ship sunk.[8]

Eventually they were brought back to Portsmouth and ten men were tried for mutiny. Morrison was eloquent in his own defence. He had not gone on board *Bounty*'s launch with the loyal men for good reasons:

> A boat alongside already crowded, those who were in her crying out she would sink, and Captain Bligh desiring no more might go in, with a slender stock of provisions; what hope old there be to reach any friendly shore, or withstand the boisterous attacks of hostile elements? ... by staying in the ship an opportunity might offer of escaping, but by going in the boat nothing but death appeared ...[9]

Nevertheless he was convicted along with four more seamen and the feckless midshipman Peter Heywood. Heywood's friends had enough influence to have him pardoned, and Morrison was included in this. Another seaman, William Musprat, was acquitted on appeal. Three men, Thomas Ellison, John Milward and Thomas Burkitt, were the only ones hanged for the affair, in HMS *Brunswick* in October 1792.

Despite its later fame, the mutiny on *Bounty* was an odd affair, essentially a dispute among officers on a very small ship on an unusual voyage, though underneath it might reflect a mood of revolt that would affect all parts of European society over the next two decades.

THE WAR WITH FRANCE

When the French Revolution broke out in 1789 (just a few weeks after the *Bounty* mutiny), it was at first welcomed by many in the British political classes, cautiously by the conservatives as tending towards the sort of constitutional monarchy that Britain herself enjoyed, and enthusiastically by the radicals. As power in France passed to more extreme hands, the British government became more wary. The execution of the King and Queen in 1792 caused considerable revulsion in Europe, as had the death of Charles I some century and a half earlier. In 1793, Britain joined in the war against Revolutionary France, in alliance with Austria, Prussia, Spain, Sardinia and Naples. She was to provide the finance and the naval power, while the others were to supply the armies. In normal circumstances, such a powerful alliance should have been decisive. The French navy was largely torn apart by the after effects of the Revolution, while the British were able, with the support of French Royalists, to take the main French Mediterranean base of Toulon, hold it for a time and capture or destroy many of the ships there.

The full resources of the British fleet were not needed in the circumstances, and in 1794 Parliament voted for only 85,000 men, quite small by the standards of the last war. So far there was no real threat to the British homeland, or her colonies; indeed, several West Indian Islands were captured from the French in 1794, albeit at heavy cost in deaths from disease.

By the late spring of 1794, the French population was in danger of starvation, and a huge grain convoy from America was expected to relieve their suffering and save the revolutionary regime. The French fleet set out from Brest to escort it in, while a British fleet under Lord Howe was sent to intercept it. The two fleets met 400 miles out into the ocean. A seaman in *Queen*, the flagship of Rear Admiral Gardiner, records, 'On the 28th, at eight o'clock in the morning, we saw, to the great joy of us all, the French fleet to windward of us, all sails set.'[10] There was some action the next day. 'I was quartered on the poop, to observe signals; but owing to the smoke, could not see our bowsprit end; and in fact I had nothing to do, but to stand like a crow to be shot at; there were several poor fellows shot close to me.' *Queen*'s rigging was damaged in the exchanges, as the French followed their usual tactic of firing high. 'About four o'clock we had got through their line; we lay a complete wreck; we had not a single stay left standing in the ship; our shrouds were all shot and cut to pieces; we had not a single cloth left in our sails, but what was shot and shattered in such a manner as to oblige us to unbend and bend new ones.'[11] The ships repaired themselves during the night, and finally on 1 June they were ready for a further engagement. The Admiral addressed the men:

> When we were in sight of the French fleet, before the last action, Admiral Gardiner called all the seamen and officers on the quarter-deck and said, 'he had been in many actions, but none of ever saw anything, to equal the last; that their coolness and determination exceeded anything of the kind he ever saw, and if they went on in the same manner, he was sure the French could not stand us half-an-hour.' One of the sailors said, 'Never fear, admiral, only lay us close enough.' 'That I will,' says he, 'and will be bound we will singe their beards.' He could hardly get an opportunity of speaking for the great and repeated huzzas and symptoms of joy and determination that seemed to glow in each breast of every jolly lad.[12]

Not everyone was as brave as that. In *Defence* a Swedish seaman serving under the name of John West was captain of one of the guns and showed some 'backwardness' in action. The second captain, John Lee, saw him about to desert his quarters and knocked him down with a handspike. This was rather counter-productive, for West was able to go down below to the surgeon and claim to be injured. Nevertheless, as a quarter gunner he was allowed a petty officer's share of the prize money afterwards. Lee refused his seaman's share of £2 in protest.[13]

One officer in *Defence* was unhappy about the fighting qualities of the crew generally. He spotted a gun crew apparently slacking and threatened them with his sword:

> The tars were rather astonished at this proceeding of their officer as, hitherto, he had approved of their conduct. They had been fighting upwards of two hours, and naturally were fatigued. They explained their anxiety to do their best. This pacified the heroic lieutenant. He sheathed his sword, and the men went to the guns as before.[14]

This battle was the only one of the age of sail to be fought well away from land, and as a result the British called it 'The Glorious First of June'. Six French ships of the line were captured and one sunk – a great boost to British morale – but the vital grain convoy escaped.

The land war meanwhile turned against Britain and her allies. The campaign in Flanders went very badly, while General Bonaparte conquered Italy. Prussia made peace with France in 1795, and Holland changed sides to fight with the French. Spain declared war on Britain in 1796, and Austria withdrew from the war in 1797. As in 1780, Britain found herself opposed by three major sea powers and had no ally in Europe to create a diversion. The new French armies were more powerful and enthusiastic than anything the old monarchy had produced, and they dominated continental Europe. All this would make the lower deck of the Royal Navy more important than ever.

THE BATTLE OF ST VINCENT

Early in 1797 Admiral Sir John Jervis meet a Spanish fleet of 27 ships off Cape St Vincent. John Nicol was below decks in *Goliath* as they approached them:

> We were only eighteen; but we were English, and gave them their Valentines in style. As soon as we came in sight, a bustle commenced, not to be conceived or described. To do it justice, while every man was as busy as he could be, the greatest order prevailed. A serious cast was to be perceived on every face; but not a shade of doubt or fear. We rejoiced in a general action; not that we loved fighting; but we all wished to be free to return to our own pursuits. We knew there was no other way of obtaining this than by defeating the enemy. 'The hotter the war the sooner peace,' was a saying with us. When everything was cleared, the ports open, the matches lighted, and guns run out, then we gave three such cheers as are only to be heard in a British man-of-war.[15]

He was down below as the ship engaged, and had limited knowledge of what was going on.

> I was stationed in the after magazine, serving powder from the screen, and could see nothing; but I could feel every shot that struck the *Goliath*; and the cries and groans of the wounded were most distressing, as there was only the thickness of the blankets of the screen between me and them. Busy as I was, time hung upon me with a dreary weight. Not a soul spoke to me but the master-at-arms, as he went his rounds to inquire if all was safe. No sick person ever longed more for his physician than I for the voice of the master-at-arms.[16]

The day was won by the young Commodore Nelson, who used his initiative and attacked directly with his ship, *Captain*. Four Spanish ships of the line were taken, and Nelson became a public figure for the first time.

THE MANNING CRISIS

With no allies in Europe, the fleet had to be increased in size. In 1795, in response to a Parliamentary vote for 100,000 men, 90,000 were mustered. In the following year Parliament demanded 110,000, and the navy exceeded this and had 114,000 on its pay books, though only 106,000 of these were actually mustered. In 1797 the Parliamentary vote was raised again to 120,000, and nearly 119,000 of these were mustered.[17]

In 1795, Admiral MacBride wrote, 'The operation of the impress service is limited to within 10 miles of Edinburgh, the effect of it is confined to a very small compass; and the more distant parts of the Firth of Forth, as well as the whole North East coast of Scotland, may be considered as nearly exempted from contributing to man the navy, except by the few who come voluntarily from thence.'[18]

There was still no regular head of the recruiting effort, but in 1795 the Admiralty began to employ half-pay admirals to tour the country making reports on individual areas. They visited the local rendezvous, assessed the performance of the officers and made reports, which occasionally caused the end of an officer's career. In general, one retired admiral was employed each year after that, to make a report. He had no executive authority but merely reported to the Admiralty, who decided on what action to take. The service continued to expand over the years and in 1797 it employed one admiral, 47 captains and commanders, and 80 lieutenants.[19]

The orders to a regulating captain in the outports of the kingdom instructed him to go to the named town to 'superintend and regulate the service of procuring men for His Majesty's fleet'. He was to 'apply to the chief magistrate and let him know [he was] ordered by us upon this service, and desire his assistance in providing the same'. (Captains who did not get the cooperation of the local officials, for one reason or another, often found themselves in trouble.) He was to take under his command several lieutenants, and 'to employ them in such manner as may be likely to meet with most success in raising men', by keeping them at his headquarters port or sending them to smaller towns nearby. Each lieutenant was to take charge of his own gang and was to carry proclamations of the bounty for seamen to post in suitable places. The captain was to examine all the men raised to assess their suitability, to send them on board tenders, or else to have them kept securely by the local authority, and to send full accounts of his work to the Admiralty.[20]

One recruit of the 1790s describes his encounter with the regulating captain aboard a tender off the Tower of London: 'Some time before noon the regulating captains came on board and took their seats in the cabin at a large table where the books were spread out which were to receive such particulars of each person as he might think fit to communicate – such as his name – his birthplace – his age – his trade – his attitude – the reason for his appearing there – his object, if he be a volunteer – and such other matters.'[21]

In contrast to the permanent press gangs ashore, a ship's gang had to be made up of men who were not likely to desert. At the beginning of a mobilisation they were usually recruited from the crews of the guard ships, who were the nearest thing to regular navy men. At other times, captains had to choose carefully. According to Samuel Leech's experience in the Napoleonic Wars, a press gang was 'made up of our most loyal men, armed to the teeth'.[22] It was well known that recently pressed men could become enthusiastic members of the gang. George Jackson was a midshipman with *Carysfoot* in 1803, helping to press men at Shields and Shetland. He wrote later, 'One fact deserves notice: I frequently captured men who, though inclined to be violent at first, soon resigned themselves to their fate, and became voluntary members of the press gang, to which they became very valuable auxiliaries.'[23] Captain Cochrane fitted out *Pallas* in 1803: 'Having, however, succeeded in impressing some good men, to whom the matter was explained, they turned to with great alacrity to impress others; so that in a short time we had an excellent crew.'[24] But Cochrane was an exceptional captain whose success with prize money made him popular with the seamen; this was the only time had to use impressment, and only because his last cruise had been unsuccessful.

Local men could obviously be useful members of the gang, as they would know the seamen and their haunts. It is recorded that at Hull in 1811 the gang included three or four natives of the town, including one called Jem White, who had been well known to the local seamen before he joined the gang and used his knowledge to help find men. This made him very unpopular, and his lodgings were attacked 'by a crowd, principally women, vowing his destruction'. He was obliged to defend himself with a cutlass until rescued by a party of soldiers and taken to the pressing tender for his own safety.[25] Such incidents were common enough throughout the country, and the wages of the press gang were often hard earned. It was not a job that everyone would find attractive.

A captain or lieutenant could gain wealth or glory in the sea service, but the rewards of work in the impress service were rather less dramatic. He had a relatively safe berth, away from the hazards of the sea, though he would have many enemies among the local seamen and merchants – physical violence was part of the normal life of an impress officer. A regulating captain had his half pay plus £5 per week; a lieutenant on the impress service had 5/- per day and 10/- for every man raised. The impress service was not likely to attract the cream of the officers, though some were quite pleased to be appointed to it if nothing else was on offer. When William Dillon was appointed to the impress service in 1803 he was shattered: 'This news was so astounding that I was completely taken aback, as I thought it a degrading appointment. None, generally speaking, but worn out lieutenants were employed on that service.' He was persuaded to accept the appointment as it might lead to something better and because he was told that 'Lord St. Vincent [then First Lord of the Admiralty] had changed the whole system relating to the Impress Service by nominating young and active officers to do it instead of old ones'.[26] There is no real evidence for this. But Dillon did, according to his own account, bring some zeal to the service before he was offered a seagoing post.[27] There is some evidence that success at recruiting could get an officer promoted to a post at sea. George Peard was given command of a sloop for raising 150 men during the Seven Years War.[28] On the other hand, older officers became set in their ways and unsuitable for anything else – 'Some officers, from being so many years at a rendezvous, lose sight of the service in every other point of view.'[29]

A surgeon of the impress service was responsible for examining men, both pressed and volunteers, and rejecting those who were unfit. 'There was also a surgeon appointed to inspect the men, as to their being sound in health, wind and limb. The examination took place in the apartments of my rendezvous every morning about 9 o'clock.'[30] In view of the large numbers later rejected by the captains of the ships they were sent to, it seems that his examination was not very thorough, and indeed the surgeon had no incentive for rejecting men – thereby denying the lieutenants of the gangs their pay. Usually there was one surgeon for each regulating captain.

The regulating captain generally remained at his headquarters, examining men as they were brought in, directing the gangs and receiving intelligence of the movements of seamen. This was crucial to the operation, and rewards were offered to those who gave information leading to the discovery of seamen. On the other hand, Dillon reports that his gang was often diverted by false information, deliberately planted to keep him away from the men's real hideouts. A lieutenant of the impress service was usually expected to spend his time on the streets at the head of his gang, for the press warrant was directed to him alone and was not valid without the presence of a commissioned officer. In a country district he would perhaps form a rendezvous of his own in a village or small town, while in a city he would be more under the eye of the captain. In either case, the service was dangerous, thankless and unpleasant.

THE QUOTA ACTS

The expansion of the fleet was carried out at great cost, both materially and psychologically, the biggest innovation being the Quota Acts of 1795.

According to these an embargo was imposed on shipping until specified numbers of men were raised for the fleet. Each local authority was ordered to provide its 'quota' of men with skilled seamen counting as double. Parliament appointed four men to assess the different ports and districts, including Admiral Lord Hood from the navy and Henry Dundas from Scotland. The maritime county of Devon, for example, was to send 393 men, and the inland county of Hereford was to provide 102. There was some controversy over the assessment in Dundas's native Scotland. While the whole of the Clyde was to provide 683 men, Rothesay alone had to find 162. This was disproportionate even for a centre of the herring fishery, and the Duke of Atholl complained to Dundas: 'The Isle of Bute is assessed to the number of 162 men. I did not know that the island was to be brought within the act, nor do I know on what grounds such an assessment was made.'[31]

To find the men, the local authorities adopted various tactics. Usually they provided bounties – sums of up to £70 were not unknown, an enormous amount when an able seaman was still paid about £15 per annum. The local magistrates were also given power 'to raise and levy under certain regulations such able bodied men and idle persons as shall be found within the said counties to serve in His Majesty's navy'. They were allowed to take up vagabonds, idlers and certain categories of criminal, and sent them to the regulating captains to be enlisted in the navy. Dr Thomas Trotter gave specific examples of gross over-payment:

> The landmen received from their respective parishes, very high bounties; 20, 30, and 40£ were common sums; and in one instance 64£. The person who received the last sum, was the only man in his parish; he was small in size, had a sickly look, was a taylor by trade, and when he was drafted from the guard-ship to another ship, was, with some others, brought forward for survey as an invalid, unfit for service. I asked him what he had done with his large bounty? To which he answered, that it was kept for his return home, to set him up in business. Although a poor subject, yet as he might be useful in his employment as a taylor, he was retained.[32]

In London skilled seamen were slow in coming forward, but eventually 623 able and 748 ordinary were found, attracted by bounties of £25.5s and £21 respectively. The 2,522 landsmen showed great variety. Some were from occupations that might be useful on board ship, such as George Salter, who was a ship-breaker and so perhaps could apply his skills in reverse in the carpenter's crew. Some, such as labourers Humphrey Salomon and Richard Wall and coal porter John Forbes, could at least offer physical strength. Many, for example Abraham Wool of Shoreditch, were from occupations such as weaving, which were suffering from technological change. Even in London displaced farm workers such as William Hill of Somerset and William Willis of Berkshire might be found looking for work. Hawkridge Rough of West Chester was presumably not short of business in his occupation of 'regimental cap maker', and perhaps he was seeking adventure. Saul Kobi, a 29-year-old sugar baker of Strasbourg, and Samuel Aronto, a picture-frame maker from Milan, would probably find it very difficult to adjust or find a role. But H. Robert of Genoa would no doubt find a role in his profession of dentist, though he seems rather young at eighteen. London had fulfilled its quota by October, sending 2,522 landsmen as well as 220 pressed seamen, to a total of 5,704.[33]

On the Isle of Wight, 25 men were recruited by bounties varying from £20 to £30. All were apparently able or ordinary and most were local, though Matthew Elliot, 40 years old, 5 feet 3¼ inches tall and with 'grizzled hair', was from Falmouth in Cornwall. John Henry Schuldt from Lubeck in Germany was an inch taller, 30 years old with dark hair and pitted from smallpox. Samuel Hines came from Boston in New England and was the same age, 5 feet 8½ inches tall, with 'dark brown hair tied, several little scars on the right side of his neck'.[34]

Altogether the acts raised around 31,000 men and were considered a success by the standards of the time, even a model for future army recruiting.[35] The naval physician Thomas Trotter was in favour of them for the future, even if the execution had been faulty:

We have at last found an alternative for pressing; the requisition of seamen and landmen for the navy, which was made in the spring of 1795 … has formed a precedent that ought to be imitated on every future emergency. I am only sorry that the act was not made permanent, so as to enable ministers to call upon the counties and towns whenever a levy of men was found necessary. There is not an objection of force to be offered against a repetition of this kind: and had the officers, who regulated the volunteers, been somewhat more attentive in examining them, there remains no doubt but it would have affected all that wished for the good of the public service. At some places, very high bounties were given, even to forty guineas [£42], which was the cause of much fraud and imposition; men utterly unfit for duty, but with no apparent disease, entered for the sake of this sum, and after a few months or weeks on board, discovered their complaints to get invalided. It was particularly hard to press an able seaman after such bounties had been given to landmen; for the King's bounty and these bear no comparison.[36]

DISCONTENT IN THE FLEET

One result of the Quota Acts and the general drive towards greater recruitment was the considerable lowering of standards and an increase in the proportion of unskilled men in the service. Some have suggested that the mutinies of 1797 were due mainly to the system of naval recruitment – that criminals and failed businessmen recruited from the prisons provided a core of discontent the old-fashioned seamen would never have developed by themselves, and the smooth-talking landsmen persuaded the simple hard-working seamen into taking drastic action. One captain, writing a novel some years afterwards, has retired seamen saying that mutinies were never started by true seamen, but by 'your King's benchers, your jail birds, and them there jaw-breaking chaps as are reg'larly brought up to the law'.[37] There is a kernel of truth in this, but there were plenty of good reasons for the mutiny, and many factors were present to contribute to it. The detailed grievances of the seamen about pay, victualling and discipline are well known and were well enough founded. Taken in context, the demands of even the Nore mutineers were moderate by any reasonable standards, except to a government and an officer corps which were inured to watching such hardship, were terrified of the effects of revolution as seen in France, and were desperately afraid of the effects of a breakdown of naval discipline on the navy itself, and upon the strategic situation.

Indeed, the great expansion of the navy over the preceding fifty years had probably had some effect on the character of the officer corps as well as on the seamen. In the 1750s the aristocratic structure of the navy had to a large extent reflected the situation on shore, and this had tended towards stability. Many of the new officers were of a more middle-class background, less confident of their authority and less respected by the seamen, who could be won over by social rank as much as anyone else. Society itself was changing, and it would be rash to assume that the true seaman would be immune to this. Even the common seaman had higher expectations of life than at the beginning of the century, and the ideas of the French Revolution would have reached him one way or another, even without the Quota men. However, he was not a revolutionary in 1797, and there is no doubt that he accepted the authority of his officers, provided it was exercised reasonably and with consideration.

Trotter had a rather different explanation of the effects of the Quota man, based on the huge bounties paid to them:

211

> The true bred seaman is a high-minded being. In his lounge or forecastle walk he views the landmen in the Waist as an inferior animal, and the latter soon learns to know the depression of his species. The seaman, therefore, looks with a jealous eye at every favour conferred on the clod-hopper as done at the expense of his own acquirements. Such as the rankling effects of these exorbitant premiums to the landed volunteers; and great was their influence in exciting the general mutiny of 1797.[38]

In fact there were many causes for the seamen's discontent. One was that the fleets most concerned were largely static. The Channel Fleet had a adopted a policy of 'open blockade' of Brest. Instead of staying permanently off the port in all weathers, the main body was anchored at Spithead or Torbay, while frigates kept watch and reported the movements of the enemy. In many ways it was kinder on both ships and men, but it tended to emphasise the overcrowding on board, as watches were not set. It allowed both seamen and officers to become lazy and disgruntled – indeed, it was well known that crews were far more likely to mutiny in harbor than at sea. It also left the seamen tantalisingly close to their homeland, and in some cases their home towns, but with no provision for shore leave. Among their principal demands was the 'opportunity to taste the sweets of liberty on shore, when in any harbor, and when we have completed the duty of our ship, after our return from sea'.[39]

As always, the men served under a combination of good and bad officers, sometimes co-existing in the same ship:

> Our captain is a very worthy commander, but Mr Colvile our First Lieutenant and Mr McCloud, master's mate, are beyond description, and so tyrannical that such officers are a disgrace to the service. We only request, as your lordships have remedied such grievances before now, we wish to have them either discharged from the ship or better usage for us on board another ship, as we have experienced the service this many years past, and willing to fight for King and country. We wish to have the same usage as other ships have done to us, so we require an answer from your lordships, and most compassionably require redress.[40]

In addition, the seamen began to feel increasingly controlled, with their few liberties curtailed. Officers were usually motivated by the need to maintain health when they ordered their men to wash ships, persons and clothes, but they did not take into account the lack of equipment, or the cutting into the men's private time. As the crew of *Reunion* put it in 1795,

Captain B also obliges us to wash our linen twice a week in salt water, and put two shirts on every week, and if they do not look as clean as if they was washed in fresh water he stops the person's grog for three or four days. Which has the misfortune to displease him in the above and if our hair is not tied to please him he orders it to be cut off.[41]

A petition from *Blanche* in 1795 highlighted a different aspect of the problem:

In the first place, we are employed from morning to two or three of clock in the afternoon washing and scrubbing the decks, and every day our chest and bags is ordered on deck, and not down till night; nor ourselves neither even so particular as to wash the decks with fresh water, and if we get wet at any time and hang or spread our clothes to dry, our captain throws them overboard ...[42]

The seaman could not choose whether he would be in the navy or not, which ship to serve in, how long it would last or his duties on board. His greatest and most jealously guarded privilege was the right to change messes almost at will, so that each man could pick his companions, especially for mealtimes, when he was relaxing off duty. There are signs that this was under attack at the time of the great mutinies. Captain Griffiths wrote,

Till within these few years, the privilege the seamen and marines had of changing their messes the first of the month if they thought fit was their Magna Carta and I confess I am inclined to attach much benefit to it. The original interference therewith I trace to the complaints of the pursers and the little squabbles about double days and single days where there was an odd man. To obviate this it became common to order all messes to be even numbers, and afterwards they were in many ships obliged to be not less than four or more than eight. In some others the number was decided by the size of the berths, each being one mess. Some little probable advantage might be gained by these arrangements, but as the pursuit of man is to obtain the largest possible portion of happiness his situation is capable of affording and as there are infinite varieties of opinion wherein it consists, mine is that few things are more annoying than an unpleasant or quarrelsome messmate. Few but have experienced this in their passage through a midshipmen's berth, or a wardroom mess.[43]

Pay was perhaps the most important issue of all. Prices had been reasonably stable for more than a century – in 1792,consumer goods cost about 122 per cent of what they had done in 1700. But in 1795 they rose to 147 per cent, and in 1796 to 154 per cent. Wheat rose from 43*s* in 1792, to 78*s* 7*d* in 1796, and the price of bread, the basic food of the poor, soared with it.[44] As Thomas Trotter put it, those affected

were men about middle age, married and had children. Their families were daily claiming relief for them; provisions for the two preceding years, 1795 and

1796, had been enormously high, and they found themselves starving. These families contrasted their situation with that of more fortunate seamen who escaped impressment, and were receiving from the merchants £4 and £5 a month, while seamen in the King's ships got only 22/6 [£1.12½p]. How was it possible for men placed in such circumstances to be insensible of their wives and children, and how were they to be redressed? [45]

SPITHEAD

One of the best officers was Admiral 'Black Dick' Howe, victor of the Glorious First of June and seen as 'the seaman's friend'. Discontented sailors placed great hopes on his support, though he was now 71 years old, almost retired and recovering from gout at Bath. In February 1797 a petition to him was drawn up on board his old flagship, *Queen Charlotte*, and circulated around the fleet, probably by means of ships' boats, bum boats and private letters between seamen. Each ship was requested to produce its own version, which most of them did. The men of *London* commented that it might be better to ask Howe to pass it on to the House of Commons, who controlled the money that would be needed for an increase in wages, rather than the Admiralty. The Charlottes replied that 'the Board of Admiralty were all professional men, and might take umbrage at not having the compliment paid them first'.[46]

The petition pointed out that soldiers, including those serving on board ship as marines, had received a significant pay rise two years earlier, while the seamen's pay had not been increased since the time of Charles II. Prices of necessities ashore had almost doubled, and even naval slops now cost 30 per cent more. Howe was implored to use his influence at the Admiralty to have the situation rectified, but he flatly refused to answer anonymous letters, and the men were disappointed. One of their number wrote that 'we flattered ourselves with the hopes that his Lordship would have been an advocate for us, as we have repeatedly, under his command, made the British flag triumph over that of our enemies:– but, to our great surprise, find ourselves unprotected by him, who has seen so many instances of our intrepidity, in carrying the British flag in to every part of the seas with victory and success.'[47] Other methods would be necessary.

When the doubtful crew of *Defence* was recruited to the petitioners' cause, the leaders in *Royal Sovereign* outlined something of their plans:

We are carrying on the business with the greatest expedition. We flatter ourselves with the hopes that we shall obtain our wishes, for they had better go to war with the whole Globe, than with their own subjects. We mean the day the petitions go to London, to take charge of the ships until we have a proper answer from government. The signal will be first made by the *Queen Charlotte*. The first signal is the Union Jack at the main with two guns fired; this is for taking charge, and sending the officers and women out of every ship. The second signal is a red flag at the mizzen topmast head, and two guns.[48]

Captain Phillip Patton of the Transport Office got wind that something was happening. He told the port admiral, who went to Lord Bridport, Hood's successor as commander-in-chief. Bridport wrote to the Admiralty, and decided on conciliation. He promised to consider the ship's petitions and not to sail until he had done so. He warned the Admiralty, 'I therefore conclude their Lordships will not direct the squadron to proceed to sea before some answer is given to these petitions, as I am afraid it could not be put in execution without the appearance of serious consequences,

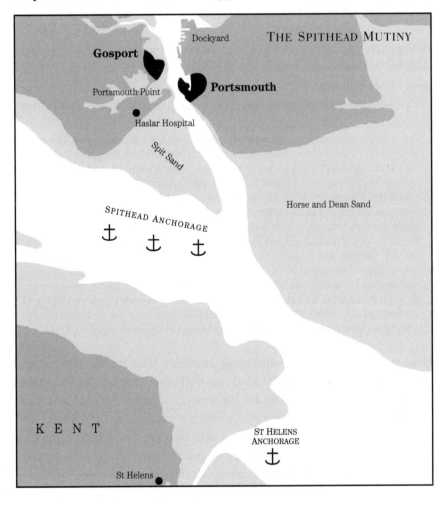

which the complexion of the Fleet manifestly indicates.'[49] But the Admiralty had decided otherwise, believing that mutiny was far less likely once the ships were at sea. An order was sent down to sail at once, and on Easter Monday the signal was raised. The seamen, now well organised in their different ships, were ready for it. An 'old sailor' describes the events of the day from his retirement in Greenwich Hospital:

> The signal was made by old Bridport in the *Royal George* to prepare for sailing … Up went number 154 to the masthead, and up went the ships' crews into the rigging and along the gangways to give 'em three cheers. The *Queen Charlotte's* began first, indeed they were always first in the fray … and the rest of them soon followed the example. There wasn't so many let into the secret of the mutiny as was at first imagined; but then they were chiefly Petty Officers and able seamen who possessed a strong influence over all hands. Many of the men, when they first heard the cheering came running on deck and asked what was the matter.[50]

Repression was impossible in the circumstances, and despite the more bellicose attitudes of admirals like Sir John Colpoys, Bridport stuck to his policy of conciliation.

The seamen soon began to feel elation and fear in different proportions:

> Some of the men would stand with their arms folded, rummaging what they had done, with countenances 'more in sorrow than in anger', seeming to think their fate was sealed, yet feeling more for their messmates than themselves. Others, with bold frounts, would brave the consequences and dare the worst, though you might frequently catch their eye taking a broadside glance at the yard-rope, with the hangman's noose at the end. On the main deck might be seen two or three eyeing a group of talkers with the utmost suspicion and stealing by degrees to catch hold of their discourse. But the forecastle was the principal resort, and all the various workings of the mind might be traced – from undaunted recklessness to sickness of heart and here the hardy boatswain's mate vociferated his oaths, insensible to danger; there, the more placid, yet not less firm quarter-master leaned over the nettings, looking towards the shore in all the distraction of thought. Thus it continued for several days, till all hands found they were tarred with the same brush and sure to live or die together.[51]

Most of the ships had already found their own leaders. Valentine Joyce, who emerged as the overall leader, was born in Jersey, but his family had apparently moved to Portsmouth. He wrote, 'I am now twenty-eight years old, and have been seventeen in his Majesty's Navy – am a Seaman, who from his soul, wishes well to his King and Country, and whose conduct, I flatter myself, has and will free his character from the effects of malice and misrepresentation.'[52] He was a quartermaster's mate, which implies he was a good seaman and had the trust of his officers. He was obviously quite well educated, though he had gone to sea at the age of eleven.

A list of the other delegates makes it clear that it was not the landsmen raised by the quota who were running the mutiny. Sixteen ships sent two delegates each, twelve of them rated able seaman, fifteen petty officers such as quartermasters, gunner's mates and yeomen of the sheets. Five were midshipman, with ages ranging from 28 to 39, suggesting that they were promoted from the lower deck rather than young men with influence. Half of the 32 were over the age of 30, suggesting that it was the older men who felt the economic pinch the most. Only three were Irish, suggesting that the political problems of that country were not a major factor in this mutiny at least. Three came from Scotland, Joyce was from Jersey, and there was one delegate each from Wales and America.[53]

The delegates kept good order on their ships, occasionally even flogging men for offences like stealing drink. They insisted that their grievances were with the Admiralty and not the British nation, so they remained as patriotic as ever. The mutiny was mainly based in the ships of the line; frigates continued to do duties, such as convoy escort, with the encouragement of the mutineers, for they did not intend to harm British trade. When the mutineers hoisted the red flag it was the naval signal to prepare for battle. It meant that mutiny had started on board that ship, or was felt to be under threat. It was not a symbol of revolution, and the mutineers were not necessarily aware that it had recently been adopted by the Jacobins in France – but there were some on shore who chose to see it that way.

By now the situation was so serious that the Admiralty had to take notice, and on the 18th a delegation headed by the First Lord, Earl Spencer, arrived in Portsmouth. The men soon had a detailed petition ready to present to them. They drew attention to 'the many hardships and oppressions we have labored under for many years, and which, we hope, your lordships will redress as soon as possible'. The 'first grievance' they drew attention to was of course pay – 'our wages are too low, and ought to be raised, that we might be the better able to support our wives and families in a manner comfortable ...' Next they wanted to change the rule by which a purser's pound consisted of 14 ounces instead of the normal 16, and the food to be 'of a better quality'. They wanted vegetables instead of flour when in port (and naval opinion would soon come round to the view that this was essential to prevent scurvy). They complained about 'the state of the sick on board his majesty's ships', though Dr Thomas Trotter was outraged by this and insisted on showing some of the delegates good conditions on board the hospital ship *Medusa*.[54] They wanted clear rules for shore leave,

> that we may be looked upon as a number of men standing on defence of the country; and that we may in somewise have grant and opportunity to taste the sweet fruits of liberty on shore, when in any harbour, and when we have completed the duty of our ship, after our return from sea. And that no man may encroach upon his liberty, there shall be a boundary limited, and those trespassing any further, without a written order from the commanding order, shall be punished according to the rules of the navy.

Finally, the men wanted the wounded to continue in pay until discharged or returned to duty.[55]

Lord Spencer was a political lightweight and resisted a wage increase as being too costly for a state that was already stretched for money, but he soon heard from Prime Minister William Pitt, who saw that the 'amount of the expense' was 'comparatively of no consequence'. The Admiralty was determined to introduce formally a new rating of landsman below ordinary seaman, but the seamen resisted this as a possible trick to reduce overall payments. Nevertheless the captains of the individual ships made good progress in persuading the men to return to duty, for example on *Duke*, where Captain Holloway was eloquent about the advantages. But as in other ships, the men remained cautious – 'Wait and see what the *Queen Charlotte* does!' Admirals Gardner, Pole and Colpoys therefore repaired on board the flagship and addressed some of the delegates. Again they had some success until four missing delegates, including Valentine Joyce, arrived from the shore. They persuaded the men that a promise of amnesty for the mutiny was valueless and that the only thing that would be valid was be a king's pardon. Gardner switched from conciliation to rage, called the men 'a damned mutinous blackguard set' who were 'skulking fellows' and monstrously accused them of refusing to go out to meet the French because they were afraid. Scuffles developed in the normally quiet setting of the great cabin, and the admirals were bundled out and sent ashore.

The men began to turn their attention to 'the grievances of private ships' – in other words the conduct of individual officers. The treatment of unpopular officers was a key element in the men's position. According to the 'old sailor' at Greenwich, 'After it broke out, it was a curious sight to watch the looks of the seamen and notice the conduct of the officers. Yet those who had exercised mercy, were mercifully and generously treated.'[56]

Back in London, the Admiralty issued a proclamation increasing seamen's pay and began to put a bill through Parliament. On 23 April it was read on board the ships at Spithead. There were cheers, and most of the ships apparently returned to normal discipline, though there were many reservations.

But in the meantime the mutiny was spreading to other ports. A squadron under Admiral Sir Roger Curtis mutinied quietly and efficiently at Plymouth in support of Spithead and demanded the use of a cutter to take delegates to communicate with them. At Yarmouth, the men on Admiral Duncan's flagship *Adamant* presented their demands to him. The Admiral, 6 feet 4 inches in height and of 'manly and athletic form', seized one of the leaders and held him over the side. 'My lads, look at this fellow, he who dares to deprive me of the command of my fleet!' That mutiny soon ended. But back at Spithead the Admiralty issued ill-timed orders to the officers on how to restore discipline, and in the House of Lords an intervention by the Duke of Bedford reached the seamen through garbled reports, and they began to doubt whether the bill would pass. On 5 May the crew of *Duke* burst into Captain Holloway's cabin and demanded to see the repressive orders, and the leaders on *Queen Charlotte* issued a proclamation warning that the mutiny could be renewed:

> This is the sole agreement of the fleet, that our matters is not fulfilled. We are still to a man on our lawful cause as formal. We have come to an understanding of Parliament, finding there is no likelihood of redress to our former grievance. Therefore we think it prudent to obtain the same liberty as before. [57]

By 3 May, Admiral Bridport wanted to take the fleet out – he believed that the French were at sea – but he did not dare raise the flag for sailing, and on the 7th the men demonstrated their power by cheering from ship to ship. The delegates sent boats around the fleet to secure their agreement. Admiral Colpoys spoke to the crew in his flagship, *London,* but he misunderstood their answers to his loaded questions. He had the ship's boats hauled in and closed her hatchways and lower gunports to prevent communication with the other ships, but the men resisted this. When the delegates' boats arrived, scuffles broke out and some of the men began to loose a gun to fire at the officers. Lieutenant Peter Bover fired at one of them and wounded him mortally. Several men were killed on both sides, but the marines joined the crew, and the officers had to surrender. The crew were ready to hang Bover when Valentine Joyce arrived, a powerful voice of moderation, as always:

Several minutes elapsed when Joyce of the *Royal George* called the delicates aft into the cabin and begged them to suppress their passions. Shipmates, said he, this has gone too far; what can we promise ourselves by the destruction of an old man? What advantage can we obtain by it? Believe me, it will be mark of disgrace upon a blue jacket as long as it shall continue to be worn. No, let us rather send 'em ashore and wash our hands from blood. He obeyed his instructions and has only done his duty. Accordingly they proceeded to the forecastle, and communicated their decision … He dropped down like a stone; but he recovered in an instant, and shortly afterwards went ashore.[58]

With the mutiny renewed, the men began to extend their activities against unpopular officers. In the frigate *Hind*, Lieutenant James Anthony Gardner was one of several named by the crew and handed a note:

Gentlemen, it is the request of the ship's company that you leave the ship precisely at eight o'clock. As it is unanimously agreed that you should leave the ship we would wish you to leave it peaceable or desperate methods will be taken.[59]

More than a hundred officers were put on shore, some treated with respect, some roughly handled. From one ship, for example, the captain told Bridport of

the mutinous conduct of the crew of H.M.S. *Mars* by turning me and the officers named on the other side out of the ship yesterday morning after having taken possession of all the arms and placed additional sentinels over us all Sunday night, and prevented my having any communication with any person except the First Lieutenant and Master, and with those a very short time, and upon going out of my cabin this morning I was stopped by a sentry, and told it was the ship's company's orders that I was not to go on the Quarter Deck. I am sorry to say that the marines have taken a very active part in the mutiny.[60]

There was still a serious risk of extreme violence against the officer who remained on board, and one newspaper reported inaccurately that Colpoys had been tried and condemned for murder. That might still have happened to Bover, as he was threatened by a seamen's court martial, but for the intervention of John Fleming, a 25-year-old Glaswegian seaman who was appointed an extra delegate after the *London* affair. He wrote to the court:

In the first place they had followed the momentary impulse of passion, and wreaked their vengeance on that unfortunate gentlemen, a few minutes would have brought to their recollection the amiable character he always bore amongst them, and I am confident would have embittered the latest moments of their lives, Now, my brethren, your general cry is 'Blood for blood.' Do you mean that as a compliment to us to assist us in following error after error? If so, it is a poor compliment indeed; or do you, let me ask you, think it justice? I hope not; if you do, pray, from whence do you have the authority to sit as a court over the life of even the meanest subject?[61]

Bover was released and eventually resumed good relations with the men under his command.

Meanwhile a resolution was put before Parliament on 8 May to increase the £12 million defence budget by £372,000 to pay the seamen more. The opposition made some capital out of the government's mismanagement of the affair, but it was passed through all the stages in a day. Notice of this was sent post-haste to Portsmouth, where it was received with joy and relief by the seamen. But there remained the matter of the royal pardon. Admiral Howe himself was at last persuaded to go to Spithead. He went from ship to ship, talking to the men, and was well received, though they insisted that the needed to see the King's Pardon before the affair was over. When eight of the mutinous ships from Plymouth sailed in, the exhausted septuagenarian also visited their flagship, *Prince*. At last the Pardon arrived on the 15th, and Howe took it to *Royal George*, where it was read out to the crew and then passed round so that the literate seamen could read it, while the others could at least examine the Royal seal. That evening ashore in Portsmouth, Howe was carried ashore by the delegates and paraded through to town in front of great crowds, while the settlement was celebrated by local army regiments firing a *feu de joie*. Next morning, after a month of mutiny, the Channel Fleet was ready to sail again. The French had heard nothing of the affair until it was too late and had not taken advantage of the navy's paralysis.

THE NORE

Among those who had approached Valentine Joyce in Portsmouth on the last days of the mutiny were four men sent from the ships anchored at the Nore, at the mouth of the Thames. They too had mutinied in support of the Spithead men and their demands, but of course they were too late to make any difference. The Nore mutiny, however, had already taken on a life of its own.

The ships at the Nore were not a coherent fleet, just a collection of ships passing through to other commands after fitting out on the Thames or awaiting a wind to take them up to the dockyards at Chatham, Deptford or

Woolwich. The nearest to a permanent resident was the old depot ship *Sandwich*, once a powerful 98-gun ship but now grossly overcrowded with men awaiting draft to other ships and with very little to occupy their minds in the meantime. As her surgeon wrote to the captain in March,

> Sir, it is my professional opinion, that there is no effective remedy, but by considerably reducing the number that have been usually kept for months in the *Sandwich*, for sickness and contagion cannot be prevented by any physical means where fifteen or sixteen hundred men are confined in the small compass of a ship, many of who are vitiated in their habits (as well as filthy in their dispositions. The circumambient air is so impregnated with human effluvia that contagious fevers must inevitably be the consequence.[62]

On 12 May many of the officers were absent from the ships to attend a court martial, these including Vice Admiral Charles Buckner, the port admiral, and Captain Mosse of *Sandwich*. At half-past nine, the men climbed into the rigging and gave three cheers, the usual sign of mutiny. Justice, the First Lieutenant, was ordered out of the ship and went to *Inflexible*, where the court martial was taking place. Proceedings were quickly suspended, and the crew of *Inflexible* joined the revolt. Other ships soon came over and indicated their support by cheering. The frigate *San Fiorenzo* arrived from Spithead later in the day, and her crew were fully

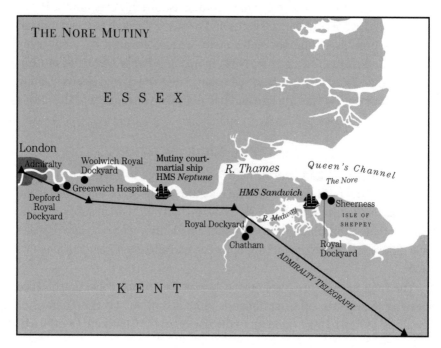

THE NORE MUTINY

ESSEX

London

Admiralty

Woolwich Royal Dockyard

Mutiny court-martial ship HMS *Neptune*

R. Thames

Queen's Channel

The Nore

Greenwich Hospital

HMS Sandwich

Depford Royal Dockyard

Sheerness

ISLE OF SHEPPEY

Royal Dockyard

R. Medway

Chatham

Royal Dockyard

ADMIRALTY TELEGRAPH

KENT

aware how well things were progressing at Spithead, so they obeyed their officers' orders not to return the cheers of other ships. *Inflexible* sailed out towards her under the command of the captain of the foretop and fired a shot at close range, which did minor damage to the rigging. The crew of *San Fiorenzo* succumbed. But the stakes were already higher than at Spithead – the mutineers had fired on a king's ship.

The delegates had found £20 to send four of their number to make links with Spithead, but on the 19th two of them returned with the bitter-sweet news that the affair had been settled. This posed a dilemma: there was no guarantee that the King's Pardon would extend to the men at the Nore, and they were already 'in very deep' after the *San Fiorenzo* affair.

Probably the Nore mutiny was unfortunate to fall under the leadership of Richard Parker. Valentine Joyce of Spithead was a true member of the lower deck, a man of humble background who was 'on the way up' – despite the mutiny he was promoted to midshipman and might have gone further had he not been lost at sea in 1800. Parker, on the other hand, had a roller-coaster of a career, but generally he was 'on the way down'. He came from a solid middle-class background in Devon and was well educated and joined HMS *Mediator* as a volunteer in 1782 at the age of nearly fifteen. He was clearly intended for a commission but left the navy due to ill health after two years. Naval appointments were difficult to find in peacetime, and like Nelson before him he served for a time in the merchant marine. He was about to re-enter the Royal Navy in 1793 when he was imprisoned for debt. After his release, he joined *Assurance* and became a midshipman, but he disobeyed an order to take up his hammock, claiming it was beneath his dignity as an officer. Disrated by court martial, he was ordered to serve before the mast. Then he was invalided out again and moved to Scotland, where his finances did not improve, and he was arrested for a debt of £23. He used the bounty as a volunteer to get his release and came on board the pressing tender at Leith on 31 March 1797. A month later he was in *Sandwich* to await drafting to an active ship, just in time for the outbreak of mutiny. He was then

about thirty years of age; wears his own hair, which is black, untied, though not cropt; about five feet nine or ten inches high; has rather a prominent nose, dark eyes and complexion, and thin visage; is generally slovenly dressed in a plain half-worn coat, and a whitish or light-coloured waistcoat, and half-boots.[63]

Parker always maintained that he had no part in the instigation of the mutiny, and there is no reason to disbelieve him. Like most of the delegates, he claimed that he had merely been led along by the feelings of the seaman and had indeed moderated them:

> I was compelled to accept these situations much against my inclinations by those who pushed me into them ... It is well known the authority the seamen had over their Delegates, and in what a ferocious manner the Delegates were frequently treated for not according every wild scheme which the sailors proposed to carry into practice. I further declare that from the aggregate body originated every plan, and that during the time the Delegates held their perilous situations, they always acted pursuant to, and obeyed the instructions of their constituents ... The only instances in which the Delegates acted of themselves were in those of checking the violence and turpitude of their masters, and this God knows we had hard work to do ...[64]

The Nore men were not the battle-hardened heroes of Spithead but a miscellaneous collection – recent recruits, quota men and rejects who were only on *Sandwich* because no captain wanted them. In contrast to the noble behaviour at Spithead, Parker came to see only fecklessness in the Nore mutineers: 'Remember, never to make yourself the busy body of the lower classes, for they are cowardly, selfish, and ungrateful; the least trifle will intimidate them, and him whom they have exalted one moment as their Demagogue, the next they will not scruple to exalt upon the gallows.'[65]

As at Spithead, the leaders of the mutiny were mostly experienced seamen and petty officers. Edward Thompson, for example, was captain of the maintop in *Repulse*. Hockless, one of the extremists, was quartermaster of *Sandwich*. John Davis, who took charge of *Sandwich*, was regarded as 'one of the best seamen in the ship exceedingly active a regular well disposed man and much repected by every officer in the ship'. James Jones produced evidence that he was 'a very good ship's corporal' before taking over as master-at-arms of *Sandwich*.[66] The leading activists on board *Saturn* were said to include petty officers – a yeoman of the powder room and quartermaster, plus a corporal and sergeant of marines. They also included two able seaman, one ordinary and four more of unspecified grade; one of them 'came on the forecastle and cheered first' at the outbreak, another 'steered the ship in'. There were also two marine privates and a drummer, one of whom wrote down the mutineers' oath as dictated by the sergeant.[67]

The Nore mutineers had a serious tactical problem in that refusing to weigh anchor would carry no threat to the authorities. *Sandwich* herself was permanently moored at the Nore, the other ships were passing

Above: Seamen landing stores and wounded on the island of Juan Fernandez during Anson's voyage. (British Library)

Below: A satirical print after the loss of Menorca, showing Byng and his captains with halters round their necks, earning the contempt of a stereotypical sailor with a parrot on his shoulder, and cobwebs in the rigging of the ships. (The Trustees of the British Museum)

Following pages: A double page from the muster book of the *Surprise* of 1796. For details of the interpretation of the columns, see the appendix. (National Archives, ADM 36/14942)

Bounty paid	Nº.	Entry	Year	Appearance	Whence and whether Prest or not.	Place and County where born	Age at Time of Entry in this Ship	Nº. and Letter of Tickets	MENS NAMES.	Qualities	D. D.D. or R.	Time of Disch.
⚫	303	27 May 1798		June 12	Zealand Prest	Wexford	34	10870	Martin Buttle	Lm	DD	25
⚫		„	„	„	„	Norwich	19		Robt Buttle	Lm	D	9
⚫	5	„	„	„	„	Carnarvon	21	BT933	Henry Parry to 30 June 98	Lm Ord	DD	7
⚫		„	„	„	„	Honiton	22		Jonas Staples	Lm	DD	6
⚫		„	„	„	„	Blythe	18		Willm Potts to 1st Augt 98	Lm Ord	DD	28
⚫	29	„	„	„	„	Dundee	18	BN824	Geo Smith	Lm	DD	20
⚫		„	„	„	„	Berwick	30		Jas Johnson to 30 June 98	Lm ab	R	9
⚫	10	„	„	„	„	Dartmouth	18		Robert Morgan	Lm		
⚫		„	„	„	„	London	23	BT949	Josh Brown	Lm	DD	9
⚫		„	„	„	„	Fifeshire	18		John Smith	Lm	Dy	3 a
⚫		„	„	„	„	Berwick	16		John Lilley to 30 June 98	Lm Ord	R	4
⚫	26	„	„	„	„	Norfolk	18	BN829	Willm Mason to 30 June 98 to 6th Oct	Lm Ord mis	DD	22
⚫	5	„	„	„	„	Milford	20		Isaac Owens	Lm	DD	12
⚫		28 Feby	-	- 19	„ „	Boston	26		Geo Atkinson to 1st July 98	ab 2d Gunr		
⚫		18 June	-	„ 20	Per Acting Order			BN856	John Job	Carpr	D	8
⚫		30 „	-	„ 30	Overyssel from Dol Hosp	Cork	33		Joseh Russell	Ord		
⚫		25 „	-	July 7	Per Louisana Cape Mclangon	London	34		Willm Cooper	ab	DD	3 a
Absent 20		11 July	-	„ 11	Per Men Paylists	Dublin	20		Jas Greeson to 5 March 99	Mid wrmo		
5 a	322	28 May	-	16	Per Vol	Edinburgh	21	BH987	George Tyrrie	Mrs Mate	DD	5 W
	322	19 Apl	-	21	S L W No 9	Liverpool	33		Richd Edward	2d Master		

Whither or for what Reason.	Straggling.	Necessaries supplied Marines on Shore	Venereals.	Cloaths in Sick Quarters.	Dead Mens Cloaths	Wages remitted from Abroad	Date of the Parties Order for allotting Monthly Pay.	Two Months Advance	Slops supplied by Navy Board.	Beds.	Tobacco.	To whom the Tickets were delivered.	When Mustered. Month Oct.r & Nov.r Days 1749 3 6 15 20 7 14 24 30
Killed in action with the Enemy				0.2.0			8 July 48 1/0/6		1.11.9	13/	12/	NC	
Unic in H.l their theurney													
Drowned									2.16.4	13/	23/6	NC	
Port R.e Haspl									0.3.6	Zealand			
									1.1.2	13/	—		
D.o d.o									1.7.7	13/	6/		
On board				0.8.0					0.10.0	Zealand		NC	
									2.3.9	13/	8/		
Pad R.e from Duty									1.13.7		2/3		
				0.15.0					0.3.7	Zealand		aberdghi	
									2.5.2	13/	23/10		
Port R.e Haspl									0.4.0	13 Scotland		NC	
									2.9.11		7/		
Haslar									0.4.7	Zealand			
									0.3.0	13/			
Port Royal				0.9.0					0.12.2	Zealand			
									1.16.8	13/	8/		
On board				13.0.3					2.16.2	13/		NC	
Port R.e Haspl									0.3.0	Zealand			
									1.8.2	13/			
									1.4.0	13/	6/	aberdghi	
S.t R.e Yard in lieu of N.o 384				10.16.0					1.4.0		5/	Duty	
									1.4.9		5/6	aberdghi	
Falmouth									1.12.2				
				6.12.0								aberdghi	
On board				15.4.9					0.8.7		5/	NC	
									0.4.0		8/8	aberdghi	

Above: William Bligh and the *Bounty* loyalists are put in a boat, as the mutineers menace them from the stern of the ship. (NMM PAH9205)

Below: Seamen attaching tags to their hammocks, as drawn by Lieutenant Gabriel Bray in 1775. (NMM PT1992)

Above left: Richard Parker presents the demands of the seamen to Admiral Buckner. (NMM PAG6424)

Above right: A popular print of Jack Crawford at the masthead at Camperdown. (NMM PU3446)

Right: A seaman of around 1800. Men only shaved about twice a week, but beards were still very rare. (NMM PU8576)

Above: The storm after Trafalgar, showing ships trying desperately to clear the rocks off the Spanish coast. (NMM PW5883)

Right: A boatswain's mate as drawn by Chaplain Edward Mangin. He is holding a rope's end to punish crew members, and he has the name of the ship painted elaborately on his hat. (NMM D7689-4)

Above: A cockpit scene from an anonymous book of drawings, showing the surgeon just about to amputate a leg and other wounded spread around. (NMM PU8484)

Below: Another drawing from the anonymous notebook showing a gun crew in action, stationed on the quarterdeck where casualties from enemy small shot were most likely. (NMM PU8487)

Above: A 'Milling Match between decks', with the men lashed to the ends of a sea chest while settling a disute, and plenty of women on board the ship. (NMM PX8578)

Below: Sailors in irons below decks, guarded by a marine sentry, with midshipmen studying and the ship's tailor in the background. (NMM PU0157)

through in ones or twos, and none of them would be seriously missed, whereas the immobilisation of the Channel Fleet left a huge hole in British defences. The authorities in London do not seem to have been very concerned at this stage, assuming that it was an offshoot of the Spithead affair that would soon be settled. It took the mutineers eight days even to articulate their demands, which were presented to Admiral Buckner on the 20th. They demanded that 'every indulgence' granted at Spithead was to be extended to the Nore. That went without saying as far as the improvements in conditions were concerned, but it may also have meant an extension of the Royal Pardon. Secondly, they wanted a right to 'liberty ... to go and see their friends and families', an issue that was never resolved at Spithead. Thirdly, they wanted all wages to be paid before the ships went to sea, 'according to the old rules'. Also in the matter of pay, they wanted pressed men to have two months advance of wages to cover their costs. They also demanded: 'That no officer that has been turned out of any of his Majesty's ships shall be employed in the same ship again, without the consent of the ship's company' – an element of democracy that would never be acceptable to the Admiralty. They wanted a virtual amnesty for deserters who had rejoined the fleet in one way or another and, most controversially of all, a reorganisation of the prize money system to give a greater share to the men. Finally, they wanted the harsher Articles of War to be moderated, to be 'the means of taking off that terror and prejudice against his Majesty's service, on that account too frequently imbibed by seamen, from entering voluntarily into the service'.[68] In short, there were three types of demand: some had already been granted; some, like the reform of the Articles of War or the prize system, would have to be the subject of long-term reform including legislation; and some would be impossible for any naval administration to grant. The delegates had not put themselves in a good negotiating position.

Nevertheless, the government was now beginning to take the matter seriously, and on the 27th the cabinet met to discuss it. On the same day, members of the Board of Admiralty arrived at Sheerness to negotiate, despite Lord Spencer's disgust at having to go to such a desolate place. No firm agreement was reached, but the royal proclamation issued at Spithead was read out on several ships, whose crews then began to question the need for the mutiny. Three remained solidly loyal to the mutiny and in *Iris*, *Pylades* and *Firm* there were struggles that were won by the mutineers. The frigates *Clyde* and *San Fiorenzo* had never been enthusiastic about the revolt. They took down the red flag and hoisted the white, but were then threatened by the guns of the others. Their captains agreed to cut their cables and head for Sheerness, but there was confusion early in the morning of the 30th when *Clyde* cut hers at the wrong moment. She drifted for some time before the delegates on the other ships noticed her, and her crew kept very quiet. Eventually she set a foresail to allow her to tack towards Garrison Point, at the entrance to the Medway, and the crew of the mutinous ships became alarmed. Guns were fired at long range but to no effect. A boat took a pilot out secretly to *San Fiorenzo* on pretence of sending out dockyard riggers, and the frigate cut her cable about noon as the men were having their dinner. Again there was confusion, and she drifted in the wrong direction, to be fired on yet again by many of the ships in the fleet. She made her way out of the estuary to the Goodwin Sands.

YARMOUTH

Elsewhere, events were taking a very different turn. On the 29th Admiral Duncan's fleet off Great Yarmouth raised their anchors reluctantly to put to sea. Lieutenant Edward Brenton describes what happened in his ship:

> On board the *Agamemnon* little suspicion was entertained of an intention to mutiny till the people had dined, when they were called by the boatswain's mate, but none appearing, a petty officer came, and gave information that the ship's company had retreated to the fore part of the lower deck, and refused to come up. I was at that time officer of the watch, and fourth lieutenant. I acquainted the captain, who desired me to accompany him down to speak to them. We went forward on the lower deck, and found the men had made a barricade of hammocks from one side of the ship to the other, just before the fore hatchway, and had left an embrasure on each side, through which they had pointed two 24-pounders; these they had loaded, and threatened to fire in case of resistance on the part of the officers. The captain spoke to them, but, being treated with much contempt, returned to the quarter-deck. A few minutes after a number of the people came up. Some seized the wheel, while others rounded in the weather braces and wore the ship.

When Duncan's flagship signaled to come back on to course, *Agamemnon* replied with the signal of inability. The ship headed back for Yarmouth, the captain retired to dinner with his officers, and Brenton was left in charge of the deck.

> About half-past 3, Axle, the master-at-arms, came to me, and openly, in the presence of others, said, 'Mr. Brenton, you have given the ship away; the best part of the men and all the marines are in your favour.' I replied that I could not act by myself; that the captain had decided, and I feared there was no remedy.

Brenton told Captain Fancourt about this and he replied, 'Mr. Brenton, if we call out the marines some of the men will be shot, and I could not bear to see them lying in convulsions on the deck; no, no, a little patience, and we shall all hail magnanimity again.' *Agamemnon* arrived in Yarmouth Roads next morning to find three ships already there, flying the red flag the mutineers called 'the flag of defiance'. Delegates were sent from each ship to a meeting at which it was decided that some of the ships should go to the Nore to support the mutiny there. At this point, 'the officers of the Agamemnon declined doing duty, and retired to their cabins, or to the ward-room, where they remained unmolested, and were even treated with respect.' As on other ships, the mutineers demanded the keys to the arms chests and magazine, which the captain eventually gave them. As the ships prepared to sail, Vice Admiral Sir Thomas Pasley came on board to speak to the men:

> no argument could prevail with men who had so recently thrown off the ties of discipline and obedience. Having set forth the inevitable consequences to themselves, and to their country of the conduct they were pursuing, the vice-admiral demanded of what they had to complain? A man named Patrick Shea, a delegate of the *Leopard*, replied, That they were not allowed to keep the Sabbath-day holy, and that the fiddler had been ordered or allowed to play to them on Sunday.

Such, according to Brenton, 'were their grievances'.[69]

This was a mutiny in a real fleet. Potentially it had far greater strategic consequences than the revolt at the Nore. Admiral Duncan was left with only two ships to blockade the Dutch coast. He took them to sea and misled the enemy by signalling as if there were more over the horizon.

The crew of the fireship *Comet* took a rather passive role, as logged by one of the mutineers: 'PM. Hoisted a red flag at the Fore topgnt Masthead seeing His Majesty's ships laying there had done the same – viz, the *Standard*, *Lion*, *Nassau*, *Inspector*, etc, etc, etc.'

On 31 May the mutineers' log recorded:

> AM light airs at 5 the Delegates from HMS *Standard* came on board & desired to know if we did not mean to go to the Nore in company with the rest of His Majesty's Ships that were going there with an expectation of being paid their Wages, etc. They told us if we wanted hands, they would send a gang to assist us round – gave charge of the ship to the Pilot Mr Williams. Weighed at 7 Captain Duncan desired the hands to come aft and after addressing some time told them if they liked that he Capt. Duncan with the assistance of the rest of the officers would take charge of the ship and carry her round to the Nore, the

ships Company answered him they hoped he & his Officers would not conceive that they had ever meant to take any charges from them ...[70]

Naturally the arrival of more ships caused jubilation at the Nore and revived the flagging cause, much to Brenton's distress:

> The insolence of the leaders was raised to such a height that it was difficult to say where their excesses might end; and it was intimated by some of the delegates who came to *visit* the *Agamemnon* that violence might be offered to the officers and their adherents ... the officers prepared for the worst, went to their cabins, put their pistols by their sides, and lay down in their clothes. A seaman was placed as a sentinel at the wardroom-door with *three* loaded pistols ... but no incivility was offered to any one ... At sunrise I was awoke by the reports of the great guns and musketry, and saw what I supposed to be officers and men hanging at the yardarms of some of the ships. ... While hanging, volleys of musketry were fired at them; and we concluded that we should very soon share the same fate; not was it till two or three hours afterwards that we were undeceived and informed that the figures suspended were only effigies meant to represent the Right Honourable William Pitt, whom they familiarly termed 'Billy Pitt,' and considered as their greatest enemy.[71]

The government was taking increasingly strong action to isolate the mutineers, whose supplies were running out. The loyalty of the soldiers was secured, and defences were built up at Sheerness and around the estuary. Parliament was meanwhile considering bills to punish the support of mutineers by death. The delegates themselves took increasingly harsh action against those on board seen to be opposing them, as Midshipman Samuel Tomlinson of *Monmouth* described:

> On or about the 30th May about 10 o'clock at night ... he and others being in their berth on the larboard side of the cock-pit were taken out by Smith, late Corporal now styled Master at Arms, were taken into the Gun Room, and there confined in irons until this day the from 5th from 10 o'clock until 12 of this day, when we were taken up with a guard to the forecastle by order of the Committee, and there I received two dozen lashes on the bare back with a cat of nine tails in consequence of a pretended sentence of certain mutineers styling themselves Delegates ... Between the hours of 12 and 2 o'clock we were put in a boat with a halter round our necks ... and were then towed round the fleet alongside each ship and grossly abused. We were then put in a fishing vessel and sent on shore.[72]

On 2 June the delegates decided to take the most decisive action they could and issued orders to the ships they controlled:

You are hereby desired by the Delegates of the Whole Fleet to detain all vessels to and from the Port of London, those excepted whose cargoes are perishable, taking an account of the name of the ship.

This was an escalation – not far off declaring war on the government and risking any support they might get from the people. Parker was feeling the strain by this time. According to Snipe, the surgeon of *Sandwich*, 'He is constantly haranguing the people from morning to night, till he is absolutely hoarse and is now obliged to take medicines for his hoarseness, which he says was occasioned by his constantly talking to the people to keep them in good humour.'[73] The government began to remove buoys for the channels to prevent the mutinous ships from sailing, while on the 9th the delegates attempted a show of solidarity, as described in the log of *Comet*:

PM Moderate Breezes & fair Wr. At 4 o'clock came on board the President of the Committee of Delegates of the Fleet attended by a numerous procession of Boats with Colours flying the Band playing Martial & Loyal tunes the time he remained on board – Regaled him & the Boats Crews with Bread & Cheese & small grog – having no small Beer on board – Mr Parker after reading several Papers & Instructions to the Ships Company left the Ship – forming a regular Procession of Boats, Drums Beating &c. as also a band of Music. – Final determination of the whole fleet this day is to Cruiz of the Texel in pursuit of the Dutch Fleet.[74]

Parker asked the men of *Repulse*, 'Is there a rebel among you?' to receive the resounding answer 'No!', but they were becoming increasingly isolated. At three that afternoon Lieutenant Robb of *Leopard* organised the officers and loyal seamen in the wardroom while the delegates were away, loading the guns there and pointing them forward. The wardroom door was opened to reveal the battery, while another party put out of action the forward guns set up by the seamen, and a third loosed the sails so that the ship began to sail up the Thames. There was another attempted coup in *Repulse*, but by this time the mutineers were alert and fired on her after she went aground. Parker organised the fire himself on board *Monmouth*, putting excessive loads of shot in a gun and pushing aside a seaman who tried to restrain him. Vance, the seaman in charge of the ship, was doubtful about the possibility of getting out a cable to turn her round to make her guns bear, and Parker replied, 'Why, damn it, slip your bowers and go alongside the *Repulse*, and send her to hell where she belongs, and show her no quarter in the least.' In *Repulse*, the crew had to endure a sporadic fire for more than an hour until they were able to throw enough overboard to float the ship off.

On the 10th the mutineers made a final attempt to negotiate by sending Captain Knight to London with much more moderate demands, mostly to do with unpopular officers. But the authority of Parker and the delegates was visibly collapsing a battle for control took place in each ship. The Admiralty offered no concessions, and the mutineers sent most of the remaining officers ashore, offering each ship the chance to decide whether to surrender or make for a foreign port. In *Inflexible*, one of the leaders early in the mutiny, the men were offered the chance to step to one side or the other to show whether they supported continuation: more than half the crew voted against and were ejected from the ship. Even on *Sandwich*, the flagship of the mutiny, the delegates were undecided about whether to release the officers. As they debated during 13 June, some petty officers got hold of a royal proclamation offering pardons to everyone except the ringleaders and showed it to the crew. 'Black Jack' Campbell, as disreputable as his name suggests, called out, 'To the officers', and the flagship was back under government control. Ignoring the possibility of fire from the hard-liners remaining in *Inflexible,* the officers took the ship into Sheerness while Parker was arrested peacefully on board. Only *Inflexible*, *Montague* and *Belliqueux* held out, and their leaders tried to negotiate an amnesty. When that failed some of them took boats to Faversham and seized a small merchant ship, which they took to Calais. The others surrendered on the 16th, and the mutiny was over after a month.

Parker was quickly put on trial and sentenced to death – and, to make an example of him, his body was to be displayed in chains. He was hanged on board *Sandwich* on the 30th. Of the 412 other men to be tried by court martial, 25 were from *Sandwich* alone. In the end the majority were pardoned, but 59 were sentenced to death, including 15 from *Sandwich;* only 29 of these were actually executed; 9 men were flogged, with 40–380 lashes, and 29 were imprisoned for between one and eight years.[75]

THE POLITICAL ANGLE

For the politicians of the day, and for subsequent historians, the great question about the mutinies has always been how far they were *politically* motivated. Clearly it was in the interest of the government to prove that they were. It would deflect any suspicion that the had been caused by incompetence. It would fit in with a picture of simple and ignorant seamen who were heroes when led by their officers but were highly dangerous once that control was lost. And it would label the Corresponding Societies and other reforming bodies as unpatriotic, ready to put the country in danger to pursue their ends.

The charge of French influence is easiest to disprove. Nothing was ever found in the French records to suggest any involvement at all, and clearly their government would have taken action sooner if they had even known about the mutinies. The British government went to some lengths to prove that native radicals had somehow been involved. At Spithead the background of Valentine Joyce was thoroughly investigated by the government agent Aaron Graham, who made contact with his family in Portsmouth but found no evidence at all against him. He concluded, 'I am persuaded from the conversation I have had with so many of the sailors that if any man on earth had dared openly to avow his intention of using them as instruments to distress his country his life would have paid forfeit. Nothing like want of loyalty to the King or attachment to the government can be traced in the business.'[76]

Dr Thomas Trotter was on the spot, and he dismissed any idea of political influence:

> The original cause of this mutiny was a seaman's grievance, not to be charged to the leveling doctrines of the times. It was thought by many that disaffected persons had tampered with the credulity of the men and excited them to violent measures. This was not apparent in the early proceedings, and it was well known they had no communication with suspected people on shore.[77]

The position at the Nore was slightly more complex. The aims were more extreme, though that in itself does not suggest a conspiracy – if there had been one, the demands would have been produced sooner and worked out more clearly. There were occasional hints of a greater political awareness, for example in a document that surfaced at one of the courts martial.

Aaron Graham was employed again to investigate the matter with his associate Daniel Williams, and again they found nothing: 'They have unremittingly endeavoured to trace if there was any connexion or correspondence carried on between the mutineers and any private person or any society on shore, and they think that they may with the greatest safety pronounce that no such connexion or correspondence ever did exist.' They did not deny the possibility that there were 'wicked and designing men' among the mutineers and that professional revolutionaries 'whose mischievous dispositions would lead them to the farthest corners of the kingdom in hopes of continuing a disturbance once begun' had met delegates on shore and had even visited the ships; but they had no effect.

> Neither do they believe that any club or society in the kingdom or any of those persons who many have found means of introducing themselves to the delegates have in the smallest degree been able to influence the proceedings of the mutineers, whose conduct from the beginning seems to have been of a wild and extravagant nature not reducible to any sort of form or order …

Even this was going beyond the evidence. In 1913, Conrad Gill, writing in an age of paranoia about suffragettes, Irish rebels, syndicalists and German spies, failed to find any real evidence, though he was convinced that political plotting played a large part in the mutinies. He explained: 'The work was done partly by such agents on shore, and partly by those who had enlisted in order to spread sedition, and in a considerable measure by pamphlets and handbills that were distributed among the soldiers and sailors. Very little direct evidence of the work can be discovered because it was carried on in secret; and the seditious papers were either carefully concealed, or were destroyed as soon as they had been read.'[78]

The other ground for suspicion was that the petitions were too well written and sophisticated to have been penned by common seamen. Graham and Williams answered this:

> The systematic appearance with which the delegates and the sub-committees on board the different ships conducted the business of the mutiny may be supposed a good ground of suspecting that better informed men than sailors in general must have been employed in regulating it for them. This Mr. Graham and Mr. Williams at first were inclined to believe in too; but in the course of their examinations of people belonging to the fleet they were perfectly convinced that without such a combination and with the assistance of newspapers only (independent of the many cheap publications to be had upon the subjects relating to clubs and societies of all descriptions) the advantage of so many good writers as must have been found among the quota-men, they were capable of conducting themselves.[79]

Again, they are a little unfair. It was not necessary to assume that quota men were needed even as scribes, and many seamen were quite literate – James Morrison on *Bounty* and Valentine Joyce at Spithead, for example. A few years later, Captain Anselm Griffiths would write, 'Seamen nowadays are the thinking set of people and a large portion of them possess no inconsiderable share of common sense …'[80]

Probably the most political tract to emerge from the mutiny was one produced by the delegate William Gregory of *Sandwich* and left on board an American ship with a view to printing it, though that was never done. It was a confused document, using an absurd analogy about British seaman being like the lion which was 'gentle, generous and humane – no-one certainly would wish to hurt such an animal'. It has high flights of rhetoric, such as, 'Shall we, who amid the rage of the tempest and war of the jarring elements, undaunted climb the unsteady cordage and totter on the topmast's dreadful height, suffer ourselves to be treated worse than the dregs of London streets?' This in itself does not sound like the plain-speaking voice of the seaman, who would tend to take 'the topmast's dreadful height' in his stride. The document went on to give hints of class war. The seamen were 'victims of tyranny and oppression' from 'vile, gilded, pampered knaves wallowing in the lap of luxury'. Though the seamen had no wish to 'adapt the plan of a neigbouring nation', nor did they wish to be 'the footballs and shuttlecocks of a set of tyrants who derive from us alone their honours, their titles and fortunes'. There were references to the Roman villains, Nero and Caligula, and to the Age of Reason, all of which were more familiar to an educated man than even a literate seamen.[81] Yet the origin and authority of the document are unknown, and there is no evidence that it was ever adopted by the delegates in general.

Despite his higher standard of education, it is reasonable to conclude that the seamen of 1797 was far less overtly political than he had been a century and a half earlier in 1642. There is no real evidence that the mutineers at either Spithead or the Nore were seriously influenced by outside politics, and the problems of the navy alone were enough to explain the outbreaks.

THE IRISH

The case of the Irish is slightly more complicated. There was already a good deal of dissent in Ireland at the time of the great mutinies, led by Wolfe Tone, who did not realise the opportunity they afforded until they were over. He wrote in his diary:

> Five weeks, I believe six weeks, the English fleet was paralysed by the mutinies at Portsmouth, Plymouth and the Nore. The sea was open, and nothing to prevent both the Dutch and French fleets to put to sea. Well, nothing was ready; that precious opportunity, which we can never expect to return, was lost; and now that we are ready here, the wind is against us, the mutiny is quelled, and we are sure to be attacked by a superior force.[82]

Open rebellion broke out in Ireland in January 1798 and was not defeated until June. This caused a great deal of dissension on the decks of the 80-gun *Caesar*, attached to the Channel Fleet. According to one Protestant seaman,

> I came into the berth and my messmates were saying among each other that no Frenchman should govern us. Alexander Mathews replied well behaved my Briton. [John Dunne] was unlashing his hammock at the same time and made reply that he was no Briton but a true Irishman and that he was a true catholic and repeated I am no heretic. I replied I am no heretic but a true protestant. Dunne then said by the Holy Ghost I never will lie easy until I washed my hands in their blood.

Such dissension could not last long within an individual mess. The Protestant Ambrose Ellison and the Catholic Michael Butler were constantly in conflict over the table, disputing about religion, 'a subject far above either of our capacities to dispute', according to Butler. He admitted, 'When I have had or taken more liquor than was needful I might be guilty of some extravagance in my expression that would make me perfectly ashamed when sober.' According to Ellison, Butler could be far more political than was usually accepted in a mess:

> I heard him at different times say that the government of England had no right to take possession of Ireland for they ought to have a Roman Catholic government of their own, and expel all the Protestants from thence, which he hoped they would accomplish before the present rebellion was over.

But it was Ellison who was forced to leave the mess, and he continued to hold Butler 'in the greatest contempt'.

The divisions on board *Caesar* began to spread, and the Protestant seamen found that the Catholics dominated the galley, where they tended to congregate when off duty. It was physically dangerous 'for the English part of the ship's company passing to and fro from the galley on account of bodies of the Irish Catholics being there and insulting them'. Quartermaster John Symons was 'seized by the man Dempsey and Bryan O'Connor as I was going to the head caught hold of me and said now my boy we will have our will of you. You've had the will of us long enough so they both began a shaking me as hard as they were able with their fists.'

This led the Irish seamen to form a conspiracy under the leadership of Bartholomew Duff, 'not only to take away the lives of the Protestants, but to seize the ship, murder the officers, and carry the *Caesar* into France or

Ireland'. But they were betrayed by one of their countrymen, Marine Edward Brophy, and 22 men were put on trial. Eight, including Bartholomew Duff and Michael Butler, were identified as ringleaders and sentenced to hang; two more were awarded 500 lashes, and the remaining 14 were acquitted due to lack of evidence.[83]

All this tends to highlight the difficulties in a purely Irish mutiny. Though Irishmen were prominent on the lower deck, they did not constitute a majority on any individual ship. The English, Scottish and Welsh seamen were generally strongly Protestant and hated the Catholics almost as much as they did the French, so an Irish revolt would have to be staged by subterfuge and coup, in which the mass of the lower deck was not involved. It would have to be very different from the Spithead and even the Nore mutinies. Moreover, the Irish themselves were not united, as the conduct of Marine Brophy shows. This did not prevent further attempted Irish mutinies, for example in *Defiance* in 1798, when 25 men were accused of swearing 'to be true to the free and United Irishmen who are now fighting our cause against tyrants and oppressors, and to defend their rights to the last drop of my blood, and to keep all secret'. There were further incidents in *St George* and *Marlborough* in the next year or so, but all were detected and severely punished.

THE HEROES OF CAMPERDOWN

The formerly mutinous ships of the North Sea Fleet were at their anchorage off Yarmouth in October when a cutter arrived to alert them that the Dutch fleet was out. They met them sailing along their own coast near Kamperduin or 'Camperdown' as the British would soon call it. Admiral Duncan attacked in two columns, a dangerous tactic if the enemy gunnery was up to scratch, and on the approach he ordered his men to lie down to minimise the risk from enemy cannonballs. Seaman James Covey objected to this. He was 'a good seaman, and noticed among his shipmates for his intrepidity; but he was pre-eminent in sin as well as in courageous actions.'

> This stout-hearted and wicked Covey ... heaped in rapid succession the most dreadful imprecations on the eyes, and limbs, and souls, of what he called his cowardly ship-mates, for lying down to avoid the balls of the Dutch. He refused to obey the order, till fearing the authority of an officer not far from him, he in part complied, by leaning over a cask which stood near, till the word of command was given to fire. At the moment of rising, a bar-shot carried away one of his legs, and the greater part of the other; but so instantaneous was the

stroke, though he was sensible of something like a jar in his limbs, he knew not that he had lost a leg till his stump came to the deck, and he fell.[84]

He was taken down to the cockpit where he was helped by Dr Duncan, a chaplain and relative of the admiral:

A mariner (says the Doctor) of the name of Covey, was brought down to the surgery, deprived of both his legs; and it was, necessary some hours after, to amputate still higher. 'I suppose, (Said Covey with an oath,) those scissors will finish the business of the ball, master mate?' 'Indeed, my brave fellow, (cried the surgeon) there is some fear of it.' 'Well, never mind, (said Covey,) I have lost my legs, to be sure, and mayhap may lose my life; but, (continued he with a dreadful oath,) – We have beat the Dutch! – We have beat the Dutch! – So I'll even have another cheer for it – Huzza! Huzza!'

The navy was chronically short of surgeons at the time, and the scenes in the cockpits were even more horrific than usual. In *Ardent*, Surgeon Robert Young had no mate to assist him:

Ninety wounded were brought down during the action. The whole cockpit deck, cabins, wing berths and part of the cable tier, together with my platform and preparations for dressing were covered with them. So that for a time they were laid on each other at the foot of the ladder where they were brought down ... Joseph Bonheur had his right thigh taken off by a cannon shot close to the pelvis, so that it was impossible to apply a tourniquet; his right arm was also shot to pieces. The stump of his thigh, which was very fleshy, presented a large and dreadful surface of mangled flesh. In this state he lived nearly two hours, perfectly sensible and calling out in a strong voice to me to assist him. The bleeding from the femoral artery, although so high up, must have been inconsiderable, and I observed he did not bleed as he lay. All the service I could render this unfortunate man was to put dressings over the part and give him drink ...

Melancholy cries for assistance were addressed to me from every side by wounded and dying, and piteous moans and bewailing from pain and despair ... Some with wounds, bad indeed and painful, but slight in comparison with the dreadful condition of others, were most vociferous for my assistance. These I was obliged to reprimand with severity, as their voices disturbed the last moments of the dying. I cheered and commended the patient fortitude of others, and sometimes extorted a smile of satisfaction from the mangled sufferers, and succeeded to throw momentary gleams of cheerfulness among so many horrors ... The man whose leg I first amputated, Richard Traverse, had not uttered [a] groan or complaint from the time he was brought down and several, bathing in the news of the victory, declared they regretted not the loss of their limbs.[85]

John Crawford was born in Sunderland in 1775 and took up his father's trade of keelman on the River Tyne. He later joined the brig *Peggy* and volunteered for the Royal Navy on the outbreak of war. He was a seaman in *Venerable* during the battle, when the ship's mainmast was hit and the admiral's flag came down, which might be interpreted as a sign of surrender at a crucial point in the battle and affect the morale of other ships. Whether on his own initiative or not, Crawford climbed the mast and nailed a flag to its remaining portion, being wounded in the process. It was an act that looked back to the broom Admiral Tromp had hoisted at his masthead in the 1650s to show he had swept the English from the seas, and indeed some saw it as the moment when Dutch sea power finally collapsed. It also looked forward to the United States Marines hoisting the flag on Iwo Jima almost a century and a half later. Crawford became the first lower deck hero, celebrated in pictures and commemorated in the name of a public house. He was awarded a medal, presented to the King, given a pension of £30 per annum and eventually promoted to gunner. But, like his predecessors in Anson's voyage, he found it difficult to cope with celebrity.

Duncan succeeded in capturing eleven ships of the Dutch fleet, a step towards the principle, usually attributed to Nelson, of annihilating the enemy. His victory was a highly significant one when the war was going badly elsewhere, and it showed that the former mutineers could fight as well as ever.

THE *HERMIONE*

Captain Hugh Pigot of the frigate *Hermione* was probably one of the most tyrannical captains in the navy. He was quite successful in taking prizes in the West Indies, despite being accident prone. A collision with a British merchant ship led him to insult her master with 'most insolent, Provoking and Abusive Language', and he had an American captain flogged for allegedly running into his ship. When his own ship ran aground he blamed a lieutenant for not keeping a proper lookout and had him replaced. As to his relations with the crew of *Hermione*, he showed favouritism to the men who had transferred with him out of his previous ships, while relations with the others were very bad. He flogged nearly 90 men during less than a year from October 1794, among a crew of 220. He also had a midshipman flogged for not apologising on his knees for a relatively minor fault. Matters came to a head on 20 September 1797 when Pigot became impatient with the men for slackness in reefing the topsails and ordered that the last two men down from the yards should be flogged. This was clearly unjust and caused a panic during which three seamen fell to their deaths. Pigot ordered, 'Throw their bodies overboard', and commanded the flogging of fourteen maintopmen when they murmured dissent. That night the crew revolted and took control of the ship. Consumed by a savage bloodlust, they brutally massacred Pigot and nine of his officers. They then added high treason to their other crimes by taking the ship into a Spanish port and surrendering it to the enemy.

This was far worse than any of the numerous small-scale mutinies, or Spithead, or even the Nore. It had something in common with the *Bounty* mutiny in that the officers were overthrown and the mutineers took possession of the ship, but that was done without violence. Even the most discontented seaman in the fleet was unable to defend the crew's actions, which terrified the ruling classes, both afloat and ashore. They were told of a 14-year-old servant in *Hermione* who had urged the murder of his master, the ship's surgeon – enough to horrify every lady or gentleman who could afford a servant. An Irish surgeon's mate stood up and added a political element to the mutiny when he declared his republicanism to cheers from the crew. Radical politicians urged naval reform, but very few would go so far as to advocate mutiny, and none could condone the extreme violence in *Hermione*. The lower deck itself, despite many legitimate grievances, was embarrassed by an episode that did its members no credit – though John Wetherhell looked to it as an example against his own officers in 1803.[86] And every naval officer could see his profession insulted, his authority potentially destroyed, his comrades sacrificed and his own life in danger. The Royal Navy was determined to avenge this mutiny, and in 1799 HMS *Surprise*, under Captain Edward Hamilton, recaptured the frigate in the Spanish Caribbean port of La Guaira. The navy hunted for every man connected with the ship, and eventually 33 of them were found. Some turned King's Evidence against the others, some were acquitted, 24 were hanged and one transported.

OTHER MUTINIES

That was not the end of the wave of mutinies. Many more were to appear before courts martial in following five years, often far beyond the usual cases of individual drunkenness and disobedience. In an atmosphere of paranoia, even petitions were now suspect – in 1799, for example, three men of *Agamemnon* were convicted of organising a petition that gained 132 signatures. Sometimes the crew tried to release a prisoner, as in

Trompe in September 1797, when a marine sentry was put in irons for being drunk on duty. The crew called out, 'No irons, no irons', and released him to replace him with the purser's steward. One of the crew harangued the officer of the watch: they had 'released a good man and put a damned rascal in [his place]'; and, 'Times were changed, what right had I to put any man in irons?'[87] Crews might demonstrate to prevent flogging, as in the sloop *Dart* in 1799, when the crew were assembled for punishment and chanted, 'We will not be flogged.' Then there was the case of *Saturn* in 1797, when the crew took charge, as described by Seaman John Cole:

> On the 30th of June a little to the north-east of the Eddystone, the people mustered on the forecastle and gave three cheers, and a few minutes afterwards pushed aft on the quarterdeck – the jib was runned up in the meantime by the waisters. I was on the poop at the time when Robert Trumbull Quartermaster, James Dixon, John Farrell and Uriah Pugh directed their discourse to Captain Douglas about some grievances – something about letters, tobacco, and complaints against the purser which he had promised should be redressed.

The crew took over the ship and anchored it in Plymouth Sound 'against every advice of Captain Douglas and his officers'. Subsequently eleven men were sentenced to be hanged for the affair, and two of the bodies were to be displayed in chains.[88]

It was even more serious when elements of the crew plotted to hand the ship over to the enemy, as with *Haughty* in July 1797 and *Volage* shortly afterwards. Such a plot was successful in the schooner *Goza* in 1801, when the crew rushed into the cabin of the lieutenant in command and stabbed him in the face with a cutlass; after some debate it was decided not to throw him overboard, and he was landed at Naples. Even more serious were the plots to murder the officers, as in *Glory* in 1798. These were only the incidents that reached the stage of a court martial – there must have been many that were settled locally by concession or floggings. Mutiny was never far from the surface in most ships for the remainder of the war.

NELSON AND THE LOWER DECK

The years 1797–8 saw the rise of Horatio Nelson as a naval commander and hero beyond compare anywhere in the world. He entered the navy in 1770 as a typical candidate for the quarterdeck, the son of a large middle-class family with a naval captain as uncle and patron, but early on he had more direct experience of the lower deck than most potential officers. There was little to do in peacetime, so he joined a merchant ship for a voyage to the West Indies under a former naval officer. Living among the seamen, he soon learned how much they had 'a horror of the Royal Navy', and he picked up the saying, 'Aft the most honour, forward the better man', illustrating the lower deck attitude to its officers and their code. Back in the Royal Navy, 'It was many weeks before I got in the least reconciled to Man-of-War, so deep was the prejudice rooted.' Still anxious to learn seamanship, he applied to go with Captain Skeffington Lutwidge in *Carcass* on a voyage to the polar regions. When told that midshipmen were not to be taken, he served as captain's coxswain. Then he joined *Seahorse* for a voyage to India and served as a foretopman before being promoted to the quarterdeck.[89]

His rise was rapid, and he became a captain by the age of 20. As such he always had good relations with his crews, though there is no sign that he issued order books on the running of the ship, for he had no interest in organising them obsessively as some of his colleagues did. In the West Indies in the mid-1780s, he had Prince William, the future King William IV, under his command as captain of *Pegasus*. The Prince tried to organise his men in military manner. Most of his conflicts were with the midshipmen, but he alienated his petty officers when they were accused of 'shameful and infamous neglect' over the distribution of liquor, so that their rum was watered down along with that of the rest of the crew, while the master-at-arms was tried by court martial and dismissed the service.[90] Nelson tried to cover for some of the Prince's faults, which was one of the reasons why he became out of favour at the Admiralty and was denied a command for more than five years.

His rise began again with his appointment to the 64-gun *Agamemnon* on the outbreak of war in 1793, and then he commanded the 74-gun *Captain*. By May 1797 he was a rear admiral and shifted his flag to the 74-gun *Theseus*, whose crew was then close to mutiny. After a month of his command a letter was found on the quarterdeck:

> Success attend Admiral Nelson! God bless Captain Miller! We thank them for the Officers they have placed over us. We are happy and comfortable, and will shed every drop of blood in our veins to support them, and the name of the *Theseus* shall be immortalized as high as the Captain's Ship's Company.[91]

Despite his reputation for vanity, Nelson did not have a large entourage. His main servant was his valet, Tom Allen, from his home village in Norfolk. Physically, he was not ideal as a companion to the great man that Nelson would become. According to one report he was, 'clumsy, ill-formed, illiterate and vulgar, his very appearance created laughter at the situation he held; but his affectionate, bold heart made up for all his deficiencies; and … Tom Allen possessed the greatest influence with his heroic master.'[92] In the early part of the 1790s, Nelson was well served by his coxswain John Sykes, who did far more than his formal duty of taking charge of the captain's boat; according to Captain Miller, 'His manners and conduct are so entirely above his station, that nature certainly intended him for a gentleman.' But Sykes was promoted gunner and left Nelson's service in 1797.[93]

THE NILE

The battles of The Glorious First of June, St Vincent and Camperdown were decisive enough in normal terms, but soon Nelson would demonstrate far greater possibilities. In 1798 he was given command of his first independent squadron. After three months of fruitlessly searching for Bonaparte's forces around the Mediterranean, he found the French anchored in a line in Aboukir Bay, near Alexandria, supporting Bonaparte's invasion of Egypt. Two seamen were overheard in conversation on the approach to battle:

> *Jack.* There are thirteen sail of the line, and a whacking lot of frigates and small craft. I think we'll hammer the rust of them, if not the whole boiling.
> *Tom.* We took but four of them on the first of June, and I got seven pounds prize-money. Now, if we knock up a dozen of those fellows (and why should not we?) d—n my eyes, messmate, we'll have a bread-bag full of money to receive.
> *Jack.* Aye, I'm glad we have twigged 'em at last. I want some new rigging d— bly for Sundays and mustering days.
> *Tom.* So do I. I hope we'll touch enough for that, and a d—d good cruise among the girls besides.
> *Jack.* Well, mind your eye, we'll be at it 'hammer and tongs' directly. I have rammed three shot besides a round of grape into my gun; damme, but I'll play hell, and turn up Jack amongst them.[94]

Nelson wrote later, 'I knew what stuff I had under me', acknowledging that the quality of the lower deck seaman was a key factor in his successes.

John Nicol was in the magazine of *Goliath* again, so his description of the early stages of the battle is probably based on observations before he went to his station, or on hearsay.

> We had our anchors out our stern port, with a spring upon them, and the cable carried along the ship's side, so that the anchors were at our bows, as if there was no change in the arrangement. This was to prevent the ships swinging

round, as every ship was brought to by the stern. We ran in between the French fleet and the shore, to prevent any communication between the enemy and the shore. Soon as they were in sight, a signal was made from the Admiral's ship for every vessel, as she came up, to make the best of her way, firing upon the French ships as she passed, and 'every man to take his bird,' as we joking called it. The *Goliath* led the van. There was a French frigate right in the way. Captain Foley cried, 'Sink that brute, what does he there?' In a moment she went to the bottom, and her crew were seen running into her rigging.[95]

In *Swiftsure,* Captain Hallowell forbade his men firing the guns until the ship was anchored in position, for he was 'aware of the difficulty of breaking the men off their guns once they have begun to use them'.[96] The climax of the battle came when the French flagship *L'Orient* blew up; John Nicol was still in the dark at first: 'When the French Admiral's ship blew up, the *Goliath* got such a shake, we thought the after part of her had blown up until the boys told us what it was.'[97]

Nelson destroyed a French fleet of thirteen of the line, the few ships that escaped being captured later. The Battle of the Nile was the most decisive battle ever fought under sail, far more decisive than the Glorious First of June, and the only time the British had fought the French in a fleet battle in this war. It clearly showed the fighting superiority of British crews and ended any attempt by the French to revive their naval prestige and self-confidence after the Revolution. It re-established British control of the Mediterranean, isolated Bonaparte and his army in Egypt and led to the formation of a new coalition against the French.

In 1800 the British under Lord Keith landed troops in Aboukir Bay to fight the French in Egypt (Bonaparte himself having left by that time). It was strongly opposed on the beaches, as described by John Nicol:

I belonged to one of the boats; Captain A F Cochrane was beach-master, and we had the ordering of the troops in the landing. We began to leave the ships about twelve o'clock, and reached the shore about sunrise in the morning. We rowed very slow with our oars muffled. It was a pleasant night; the water was very still; and all was silent as death. No-one spoke; but each cast an anxious look to the shore; then at each other, impatient to land. Each boat carried about one hundred men, and did not draw nine inches of water. The French cavalry were ready to receive us; but we soon forced them back, and landed eight thousand men the first morning. We had good sport at landing the troops, as the Frenchmen made a stout resistance. We brought back the wounded men to the ships.[98]

Nelson led the British fleet into battle again at Copenhagen in 1801, though unfortunately no lower-deck account of the affair is known. Famously he ignored the signal of his superior by the gesture of putting his telescope to his blind eye. After a hard struggle, the Danish fleet gave up the fight. Nelson's prestige was added to, though it had been the closest of his great battles.

THE TREATY OF AMIENS

By 1801, as in 1748, the British were all-conquering at sea, the French on land. After a change of government in Britain it was decided to make peace with France, and the war ceased. Some members of the government appear to have believed that this was the end of the matter, and St Vincent, now First Lord of the Admiralty, set about reforming the dockyards and administration instead of civil affairs. However, Britain remained suspicious of French intentions, and neither side carried out all the clauses of the peace treaty. Napoleon Bonaparte was rising to power in France, and it seemed that he, like Louis XIV before him, would want to expand his power in Europe.

Parliament voted to keep 50,000 seamen in service, about twice the size of a normal peacetime force. This meant that not all the pressed and quota men were released, and it was largely a matter of luck where their ship happened to be at the time, and whether the ship was needed for service. Among the ships kept in service was the 74-gun *Bellerophon,* a veteran of the Glorious First of June and the Nile. She was anchored in Torbay by the beginning of November while most of the other ships were being paid off, but the government wanted to keep a strong squadron in the West Indies to match the French. Early in March 1802 she sailed for Jamaica with five other ships of the line. There is no evidence that the crew protested about being sent away like this; there was no court martial for mutiny and no petition can be found in the Admiralty records; but it is not likely that they were happy, and for them the war was not really over.

6

A LARGE FLEET in a LONG WAR
1803 to 1815

THE HOT PRESS

On 8 March 1803, King George III sent a message to Parliament on the
advice of his Prime Minister, Addington:

> As very considerable military preparations are carrying on in the ports of France
> and Holland, he has judged it expedient to adopt additional measures for
> precaution for the security of his dominions [1]

The French claimed that they were fitting out ships to regain their West
Indian colonies, which had been lost to slave revolts during the Revolution,
but King George and his government did not believe it. Napoleon
Bonaparte, now all-powerful as the 'First Consul' of France, was not to be
trusted.

On the evening of the 8th, before the King's message was known about,
more than 600 men left the ships in Portsmouth, organised into press gangs
each led by an officer. They boarded the coal ships awaiting unloading and
took away every man they found, including visiting landsmen and captains,
chief mates and carpenters, who were protected from impressment. They
would be released later, but in the meantime the victims were held on
board ship or in a marine guardhouse near the dockyard. For days the town
was paralysed.

The Admiralty messenger arrived at Plymouth, at 4 o'clock in the
morning of the 9th. The gates of the marine barracks at Stonehouse were
quickly closed, and communication with the outside world was stopped.
At 7 that evening the gates opened again and parties of twelve or fourteen
marines left the barracks, each headed by a naval and marine officer.
Some went to the colliers at the New Quay and boarded them. It was
only then that the marines learned what they were to do – to seize every
man on board. They took them towards the flagship, HMS *Culloden*.

Other gangs went by boat to merchant ships anchored at Cattewater and Sutton Pool. Some toured the gin shops of the port, taking landsmen as well as seamen. One gang went to the Dock Theatre and cleared out all the men in the gallery. The town, as the *Naval Chronicle* reported, 'looked as if in a state of siege', but more than 400 useful men were found for the navy.

John Wetherell was a merchant seaman at Shields when he heard an early rumour of a frigate pressing men in the Thames estuary. He was anxious to get to London, so he got a forged protection for a ship's carpenter and set sail in a collier. On 19 March the ship was boarded by naval, boats and an officer said to the master, 'Where is your carpenter?' The master pointed him out at the helm, and the officer ordered, 'Relieve him and put his things in the boat.' 'WHY SIR HE IS PROTECTED.' 'That is the reason we want him in our carpenter's crew. Come, make haste. Coxswain, bundle his things in the boat.' Wetherell became a seaman in the frigate *Hussar*.

He was soon part of a press gang himself. On 1 April boats from *Hussar* and two other ships landed men at Harwich to begin a 'man plunder'. 'The Market house was to be their prison, where a lieutenant was station'd with a guard of Marines and before daylight next morning their prison was full of all denominations, from the Parish Priest to the farmer in his frock and wooden Shoes. Even the poor Blacksmith cobler taylor barber baker fisherman and doctor were all dragg'd from their homes that night ...' The people of Harwich gathered outside: 'their business was quickly made known. Wives demanded their husbands, children their Fathers, and aged parents their Son perhaps their only support.' A lieutenant was obviously nervous as he tried to pacify them:

> My good people, you no doubt feel alarmed at this unexpected visit we have paid your town and its vicinity, a visit to you very rare and to us very unpleasant but as our orders are from the Admiralty we dare not refuse to obey their command. However, good people, I give you my word and honour that by this day noon your husbands, Fathers and Children shall be restored to your arms again, only such as are entitled to serve their king owing to being able Seamen or gain their living by the Salt water such as Fishermen &c. Every other will be liberated as soon as my brother Officers can all meet here, which I know must be shortly.

The men who were considered to be seamen were marched down to boats in parties of twelve or fifteen, guarded by the marines. A fishermen leapt from his boat as it left the shore and ran up the beach, dodging the marines' fire. The rest were taken to the ships.[2]

Lieutenant Frederick Hoffman was appointed to the 74-gun *Minotaur*, laid up in the Medway without masts, stores or guns. He had no crew and relied on the services of the dockyard riggers and Greenwich pensioners from Greenwich Hospital. When the captain finally arrived he lobbied the port admiral, who sent more officers and a company of marines under their officers as well as fifteen prisoners sent by the magistrates of Maidstone, including smugglers, who were always welcome as skilled seamen. Two hundred more recruits came from the Chatham press gangs but, a month after commissioning, the ship had only half her crew of 640 men, and only about 40 of these were experienced seamen. The ship headed for Plymouth, hoping to find men there. On arrival, Hoffman and the captain went on board the port flagship, *Salvador Del Mundo*, where pressed men were held awaiting allocation to ships. There were very few left, but the remaining ones were lined up with their toes on the 'seam' of tar between two planks. The captain told Hoffman,

> You help me look at these fellow's phizes ... I am to take thirty of them; they are queer-looking chaps, and I do not much like the cut of their jib ... But mind, don't take any one that has not a large quid of tobacco in his cheek.
> I went up to the second man, who had a double allowance of Virginia or some other weed in his gill, the captain following me. 'Well, my man,' said I, 'How long have you been to sea?' 'Four months,' was the reply. 'Why, you d— d rascal,' said our skipper – for observe, reader, he never swore – 'what the devil business have you with such a quantity of tobacco in your mouth? I thought you were an old sailor.' 'No sir,' answered the man, my trade is a tailor, but I have chawed bacca from my infancy.' 'Question another,' was my order. I interrogated the next, who was a short, slight, pale-faced man. 'And pray,' said I, 'what part of the play have you been performing: were you ever at sea?' 'No, sir,' said he; 'I am a hairdresser, and was pressed a week ago.' 'D—n these fellows!' said my captain, 'they are all tailors, barbers or grass-combers. I want seamen.'[3]

Eventually he settled for 21 men, including the tailor, though they were 'bad enough, as they were the worst set I ever saw grouped. Their appearance and dress were wretched in the extreme.'

There was another hot press in Plymouth on 17 April when some of the 'holiday folks' in the area were found liable to serve in the navy. Later in the month gangs were landed from ships at sea in the Devon ports of Dartmouth, Paignton, Brixham, Torquay and Teignmouth, with orders to ignore protections unless they were guaranteed by Act of Parliament, or for ships on voyages of immediate use to the navy. It was not particularly successful. Shipwrights, a sailmaker, fishmonger, coal-factor, grocer, cooper, watchmaker, ostler, waggoner, labourer, shoemaker, constable and a basket maker had to be let go, as well as a man who appeared to be dumb. Only ten eligible men were found.[4]

The Channel Fleet under Admiral Cornwallis was concentrating in Torbay. By 6 May there were ten ships of the line in the bay, or on the way there, but many of them were poorly manned. *Thunderer* was short of 46 seamen and ten marines out of 590. Moreover, 'her men of all descriptions appear to be weak, and a very moderate crew, she having ten more ordinary and fifty-one more landmen than the scheme allows, and only 101 petty [officers] and able [seamen].'

This mobilisation carried out with unique ruthlessness, became known ad the 'hot press' of 1803. It was successful in that the 10,000 men voted by Parliament were soon raised, but in the long term it was chiefly remembered for the ruthlessness with which it was carried out. Many legends of the press gang were created by the 'man plunder' at Harwich, the clearing of the gallery of a theatre at Plymouth, and the ignoring of legitimate protections.

Occasionally impressed landsmen were kept on out of spite. On being pressed into HMS *Hero* later in 1803, John Parr tried to swim ashore and was flogged for it. He tried to conceal this from his mother and wrote to tell her that he was 'very Happy at my Situation at present' and asked her to send on 'my Box and Dixionary and some wrigthing Papper.' But he revealed the true extent of his misery in a letter to his brother in January 1804 – he was still kept under confinement and had not been able to take off his clothes more than half as dozen times since he was impressed. 'Brother,' he wrote, 'I Ham sorry to Hear of my Mother Taken it so Much to Heart a Bou it but Make her as Comfortabel as Posibel and I Hope I shal injoy her Once a gain Brother I shal by Much a Oblige to you if you will send me a few Nessereys for have got Nothin but What I stand huprite in for I have had but One Shirt on since that Fatal Job Happined.'[5]

Even seamen who were pressed legitimately were not always happy. Benjamin Stevenson, alias Thomson, was taken in the spring of 1803 and put on board *Victory*. In August he wrote to his brother at Gateshead, explaining that some men had secured their release by finding substitutes: two men would have to be found at £2 each. However, 'I think if you can get two for twice as much I would not begrudge the money for to be got clear of this prison.' But Stevenson was still unhappy in May 1804 and wrote, 'I shall live in hope of God to set me clear of this wicked wooden world. This one long twelvemonths I have lived in this wicked state of life.'[6]

THE LONG BLOCKADES

Having declared war, the Addington government had very little idea about how to prosecute it. There were no offensive plans, and the navy settled down to blockade all the main French ports, while preparing to resist Napoleon's planned invasion of England. In *Hussar*, attached to the Channel Fleet off Brest, John Wetherell might have expected an exciting time in a fast frigate, and indeed he did describe some adventures, but he cannot conceal the longueurs and disappointments between them:

> We made sail and left the fleet with a smart breeze from the N.E. and cruised several days. Nothing particular took place; we fell in with all Nations on the entrance of the channel. One day a sail was reported; we made sail and with a fresh gale ran under all we could crowd nearly 12 hours before we got alongside. We found her to be the Swallow packet from Jamaica to Falmouth.[7]

The seaman's life differed according to which of the main fleets his ship was allocated to. The faraway fleets in the West Indies and India were less important at this stage, but the North Sea Fleet under Admiral Keith was the first line of defence against Napoleon's invasion force. Many of the ships were based in the Downs and spent a good deal of time off the French and Belgian coasts, raiding invasion barges heading for the concentration at Boulogne. It was exciting but dangerous work, and Keith warned his captains not to take too many chances against coastal defences. Other parts of the North Sea Fleet were based at the Nore and Yarmouth, from where they blockaded the Dutch coast – because of the tidal pattern, they only needed to spend a few days at sea every fortnight.

The Channel Fleet, based at Spithead, Plymouth and Torbay, was equally important. In many ways it was the most difficult service in the navy, with long weeks spent in strong currents in the rocky and stormy waters off Brest, and only short breaks in harbour. The commander-in-chief, 'Billy Blue' Cornwallis, was well regarded by the seamen.

Seaman John Powell was in the 74-gun *Revenge* as she prepared to join the fleet in 1805. He was a volunteer, which meant that he was treated better than pressed men, who arrived in tenders when he was in the depot ship *Zealand*. He was grateful not to be in a relatively defenceless merchant ship. Moreover, naval ships had larger crews:

We keep watch the same here as at sea, ie four hours up and the same down. I am in the starboard watch so that when the larboard watch is on in a morning we can sleep till 7 or 8 o'clock and sometimes longer, which I could not do in an Indiaman. We have very little work to do and plenty of men to assist when any work is to be done. Some days we have but little to do but on others nobody would believe that is unused to the sea what a hurry we are all in. As a proof of it, last Monday I ate one part of my breakfast upon deck, another in the mizzen top and finished it on the mizzen topsail yard.

Powell did not paint an optimistic picture to reassure his mother, and some of his phrases must have made her heart sink. The young man accepted she was 'so much concerned for my safety', but he also wrote, 'a man of war is much better in war time than an Indiaman for we laugh at and seek the danger they have so much reason to dread and avoid'. Later he was keen to get to sea again, because 'French hunting ... is a glorious sport'. He was rated as a mizzen topman, young yet experienced enough to work aloft on the smallest of the ship's masts. In battle he was quartered at one of the lower-deck 32-pounder guns and was proud that his ship was 'of great force'. He had 'the most agreeable shipmates that can be' and no enemies on board – 'they either love me or fear me.'

He was still interested in his lady friends ashore and was both surprised and pleased to hear that a certain Miss Page was married, as it would be 'the means of preventing her pursuing the road to ruin'. His mother wanted him to keep up his hopes with 'Miss Y', but he answered,

I have long since renounced them in favour of a gentleman 'worth thousands', nevertheless it would be some consolation to a (real) lover to hear that his mistress was not engaged for life to such an old and superannuated figure as he is I am much incensed against him but I will not say any more on the subject lest if I do you should suspect me of being more enraged than I really am.

Powell also declared his interest in a Miss Springwell, but warned his mother:

I must stop to reproach you for writing her name so obscurely, which I dare say you did intentionally for it was almost half an hour before I could find it out, which greatly perplexed me. I mounted my stilts and did not get down for a good while. Present my love to her and tell her I sincerely hope she and her father are well but as for her mother it is vain to hope she has not got some indisposition.

When *Revenge* anchored at the Downs for a week, vendors were allowed on board, and Powell found a great deal of dishonesty:

Any inexperienced person may be taken in by a set of abominable wretches like them when the men received their money they were ready to tear themselves to pieces to buy them new things. One man belonging to another ship had received one hundred pounds and getting drunk the next morning he lost it all every farthing. On the day appointed for payment about two hundred jews came on board bringing with them all sorts of slop, watches, hats, rings, lockets, telescopes etc. It was exactly like a fair. There was also provisions of all sorts to be sold together with gingerbread and cakes which many of the men were fools enough to buy. One man gave eight guineas for a watch and the next morning he found it was good for nothing. Another gave thirty shillings for a hat that was not worth 12, so that's the way that they are always so poor or the usually are. One man got his pocket picked out of twenty six pounds and marine got a flogging for robbing his messmate of six and twenty shilling, but that is only a specimen of their tricks. As for me, as soon as I got mine I locked it up.

But he did go so far as to buy a cake and some soap for four shillings. 'I have got the character of a miser and credit of having plenty of money for they are all very sure I did not spend it and must have it.'

The Mediterranean Fleet, under Nelson, was crucial in preventing a French breakout from Toulon. He believed in keeping his fleet together, with the whole force withdrawing at once to replenish, leaving frigates on watch. Nelson's relatively informal relations with his crews were illustrated one evening in May 1804 while *Victory* was off Toulon. He spotted something under the foresail and went to the side to investigate just as the Boatswain piped 'down hammocks'. 'One of the main topmen who had hauled his hammock out of the netting swinging it over his shoulder came in contact with his lordship's head and laid him prostrate on the deck.' The seaman lifted Nelson to his feet with great dexterity and apologised profusely, explaining that was not aware of anyone behind him. With some officers this would have led to a flogging, but Nelson merely replied, 'My man, it was not your fault, it was my own. I ought to have known better than to stand in your way.'[8]

In the spring of 1805, after two years of blockade, the French fleet under Admiral Villeneuve did escape as part of a plan to lure the British fleets away from European waters then invade England. As he chased them across the Atlantic, Nelson took care to inform the crew of *Victory* personally. He sat on the pump near the mainmast on the lower deck and made a short speech to the men, telling them that he expected and hoped to fall in with the French fleet before they reached Barbados. 'I have it from good authority that they have 15 sail of the line and we have only 13. I am very sure every ship will easily manage one each when there will be two left for us, and it be very harsh indeed if we are not able to give a very good account of them.' It was a 'pretty and laconic speech' and the men gave him three cheers.[9] But he just missed the French in the West Indies and chased them back across the Atlantic. He was given a well-earned rest, but the French and Spanish were now assembling a huge fleet in Cadiz, and a new British force under Nelson's command was set up to counter that.

TRAFALGAR FROM THE LOWER DECK

Nelson rejoined the fleet off Cadiz, and the seamen were delighted. James Martin of *Neptune* wrote that it was 'Imposeable to Discribe the Hearfelt Satisfaction upon the whole fleet on this Occasion and the Confidence of Success with which we were Inspired'.[10] A Spanish admiral commented on the British sailor's attitude to battle, reflecting comments by one of his predecessors 217 years earlier at the time of the Armada:

> An Englishman enters a naval action with a firm conviction that it is his duty to hurt his enemies, and help his friends and allies, without looking out for directions in the midst of the fight; and while he thus clears his mind of all subsidiary distractions, he rests in confidence of the certainty that his comrades, actuated by the same principles as himself, will be bound by the sacred and priceless law of mutual support. Accordingly both he and his fellows fix their minds on acting with zeal and judgement upon the spur of the moment, with the certainty that they will not be deserted.[11]

This applied to the sailor in a gun crew or a boarding party as much as to a captain or admiral.

Nelson's fleet could have waited for years off Cadiz in demanding conditions, but instead Villeneuve was goaded into coming out. Nelson was ready for a battle. Seaman John Brown of *Victory* wrote, 'At daylight the French and Spanish fleets were like a great wood on our lee bow which cheered the hearts of every British tar in the *Victory* like lions Anxious to be at it.'[12] But there was time for dinner as the light winds carried the ships towards the enemy in two columns. In *Tonnant*, according to Able Seaman John Cash,

> Our good captain called all hands and said, 'My lads, this will be a glorious day for us and the groundwork of a speedy return to our homes.' He then ordered bread and cheese and butter and beer for every man at the guns. I was one of them, and, believe me, we ate and drank, and were as cheerful as we had been over a pot of beer.[13]

At this point Nelson sent his famous signal, 'England Expects that Every Man will do his duty', which was 'answered with three hearty cheers from each ship, which must have shaken the nerve of the enemy'.[14] It was agreed that it 'produced the most animating and inspiriting effect on the whole fleet'.[15] Even the cynical pen of William Robinson took pride as the leading ships approached the ragged enemy line:

> Could England have seen her sons about to attack the enemy on his own coast, within sight of the inhabitants of Spain, with an inferior force, our number of men being not quite twenty thousand, whilst theirs was upwards of thirty thousand; from the zeal which animated every man in the fleet, the bosom of every inhabitant of England would have glowed with indescribable patriotic pride; for such a number of line-of-battle ships have never met together and engaged, either before or since.[16]

Nelson's plan was to cut off part of the enemy line and overwhelm it, but in the event the battle descended into a series of engagements between single ships and small groups, in which the gunnery skills of the lower deck became the decisive factor. Lieutenant Senhouse of *Conqueror* noted:

> Our seamen, it is generally observed, fought not in their usual style, firing as fast as their guns could be wadded, and trusting to chance for the result, but with the determined coolness and skilful management of artillery-men regularly bred to the exercise of great guns. Such valour nothing could withstand, and if our fleet had been six sail less than they were the victory would still have been ours.[17]

As usual the seamen were fired up and totally absorbed in the task of loading and firing. Lieutenant Lewis Rotely of the Royal Marines described how difficult it was to get marines away from the guns and later told a naval audience, 'I need not inform a seaman of the difficulty of separating a man from his gun.'[18]

Each ship had its own story to tell. According to Robinson in *Revenge*,

A Spanish three-decker ran her bowsprit over our poop, with a number of her crew on it, and in her fore rigging, two or three hundred men were ready to follow; but they caught a Tartar, for their design was discovered, and our marines with their small arms, and the carronades on the poop, loaded with canister shot, swept them off so fast, some of them into the water, that they were glad to sheer off.

In the same ship, John Powell was calm when enemy fire came close to him: 'A shot came in at the Porthole of the Gun to which I belong killed a midshipman & 5 other men besides cutting the foremast but I nor any of the men at my Quarters were hurt.' One of his fellow members of the gun's crew was the ship's cobbler, 'a very merry little fellow, the very life of the ship's company, for he was ever the mirth of his mess, and on whatever duty he might be ordered, his spirits made light the labour'. He was knocked out and taken for dead. His comrades were about to throw him out of a gunport, as often happened with men killed in action, when his legs began to kick, and he was saved. 'It was well that I learned to dance; for if I had not shown you some of my steps, when you were about to throw me overboard, I should not be here now, but safe enough in *Davy Jones's Locker.*'

Belleisle was the most damaged of the British ships and the only one to lose all of its masts:

> At every moment the smoke accumulated more and more thickly, stagnating on board between decks at times so densely as to blur out the nearest objects and blot out the men at the guns from those close at hand on each side. The guns had to be trained as it were mechanically by means of orders passed down from above, and on objects that the men fighting the guns hardly ever got a glimpse of … You frequently heard the order … to level the guns 'two points abaft the beam', 'point blank' and so on. In fact the men were as much in the dark as if they had been blindfolded and the only comfort to be derived from this was that every man was isolated from his neighbor that he was not put in mind of the danger by seeing his messmates go down all round. All he knew was that he heard the crash of shot smashing through the rending timbers, and then followed at once the hoarse bellowing of the captain of the guns, as men were missed at their posts, calling out to the survivors, 'Close up there! Close up!'[19]

For others, the noise was more dominant:

> A man should witness a battle in a three-decker from the middle deck, for it beggars all description. It bewilders the senses of sight and hearing. There was fire from above, fire from below, besides the fire from the deck I was upon, the guns recoiling with violence reports louder than thunder, the deck heaving and the side straining. I fancied myself in the infernal regions, where every man appeared a devil. Lips might move, but orders and hearing were out of the question: everything was done by signs.

A seaman in the *Royal Sovereign* summarised the action in a letter to his family:

This comes to tell you I am alive and hearty except three fingers; but that's not much, it might have been my head. I told brother Tom I should like to see a great battle, and I have seen one, and we have peppered the Combined Navy; and for matter of that, they fought us pretty tightish for French and Spanish. Three of our mess were killed, and four of us winged ... How my fingers got knocked overboard I don't know; but off they are, and I never missed them till I wanted them.[20]

Throughout the afternoon of 21 October the French and Spanish ships surrendered one by one, but word spread slowly that Admiral Nelson had been shot and fatally wounded. The seamen were deeply affected by this.

Our dear Admiral Nelson is killed! so we have paid pretty sharply for licking 'em ... all the men in our ship who have seen him are such soft toads, they have done nothing but blast their eyes, and cry, ever since he was killed – God bless you! chaps that fought like the Devil, sit down and cry like a wench.[21]

But for many seamen the three-day storm that followed the battle was even worse than the fight itself. Most of the ships were towing captured French and Spanish prizes, but this soon proved impossible, as the British ships were already damaged in the rigging. *Revenge* had released her tow at 10 o'clock on the morning of the 24th, but there were not enough boats to take all the Spaniards off.

On the last boat's load leaving the ship, the Spaniards who were left on board, appeared at the gangway and ship's side, displaying their bags of dollars and doubloons, and eagerly offering them as a reward for saving them from the expected and unavoidable wreck; but, however well inclined we were, it was not in our power to rescue them or it would have been affected without the proffered bribe.[22]

Robinson wrote, 'It was a mortifying sight to witness the ships we had fought so hard for, and had taken as prizes, driven by the elements from our possession, with some of our own men on board as prize masters, and it was a great blight to our victorious success.'[23]

Back at Chatham, Seaman Brown of the *Victory* wrote to a friend, 'There is three hundred of us pickt out to go to Lord Nelson's Funral. We are to wear blue Jackets white Trowsers and a black scarf round our arms and hats, besides gold medal for the battle of Trafalgar Valued £7-1 round our necks. That I shall take care of until I take it home and Shew it to you.'[24] The funeral was one of the most emotive events in British history, as the body was carried up the Thames from Greenwich in a procession of naval barges rowed by seamen, and then to St Paul's Cathedral, in a parade that included 'Forty-eight Seamen and Marines of His Majesty's Ship the *Victory*, two and two, in their ordinary dress, with black neck handkerchiefs and stockings, and crape in their hats'. But even then the lower deck was able to introduce an element of farce as the body was lowered:

> The Comptroller, Treasurer, and Steward of his Lordship's household then broke their staves, and gave the pieces to Garter, who threw them into the grave, in which also the flags of the *Victory*, furled up by the sailors, were deposited. – These brave fellows, however, desirous of retaining some memorials of their great and favourite Commander, had torn off a considerable part of the largest flag, of which most of them retained a portion.[25]

A LONG WAR

The seamen's hopes were not realised – Trafalgar was far from being the end of the war. The French armies continued to go from strength to strength, and once again Britain lost all her European allies. Unable to invade Britain, Napoleon, now Emperor of France, imposed the 'Continental System': the ports of Europe were forbidden to trade with Britain. In retaliation, the British navy was ordered to blockade all the ports operating the system, including all those of any importance in western Europe. France's navy, though defeated, was not extinct, and with so much of Europe under French control, it was possible for it to revive.

> When the ample and almost boundless resources of the extended empire of France are considered, it becomes evident that no relaxation could be allowed to our naval energies; that the blow which had been given must be followed up, or its effects would be lost on the power of our gigantic enemy. France, in possession of the Texel, the Scheldt, Cherbourg, Brest, L'Orient, Rochefort, Toulon, Port Espezia, Genoa, Venice and Corsica, with the extensive forests of ship timber either contiguous to or within water carriage of these places, still possessed the means of building ships ... Another navy, as if by magic, sprang forth from the forests to the sea shore.[26]

The British fleet continued to expand. After 1806, Parliament voted for 130,000 men, and more than 140,000 were actually on board the ships in 1809. From 1810, 145,000 men were regularly voted, though that figure was never attained; at its maximum strength in 1810 the navy had 142,000 men, with 1,048 ships and vessels in commission. Nearly two centuries earlier, the Stuart kings had virtually destroyed themselves in attempting to raise a thirtieth of that number – so much had British resources expanded over the years.

The Georgian regime did not destroy itself in the effort, but both society and the navy were put under considerable strain. Support for the French Revolution had died out by this time, and there were no mutinies on the scale of Spithead and the Nore, but unrest continued among the men; mutiny remained a constant threat, and desertions were perhaps more common than ever. The idea of the Quota Acts was not revived, so the proportion of real seamen aboard ship remained quite high. One estimate suggests 75 per cent, though this excludes all the non-seamen categories such as officers, servants, artisans and marines.[27]

An actual 74-gun ship of this period had a crew of nearly 600. Apart from the officers and marines, it had 227 men who had come to sea from other occupations, and only 212 men, just over a third of the complement, were professional sailors.[28] The proportions must have varied considerably from time to time, and after a long commission most of the former landsmen would have been able to qualify for seamen.

GOOD AND BAD OFFICERS

The seaman's life depended very much on the quality of the officers and petty officers set over him, especially during a long campaign. As always, there were good officers and bad. Robert Hay served under Admiral Collingwood, a great friend of Nelson, who succeeded him after his death. He wrote of him: 'A better seaman – a better friend to seamen – a greater lover and more zealous defender of his country's rights and honour, never trod a quarterdeck.'[29]

Collingwood, in short, take him all in all, will perhaps stand second to none that ever hoisted a flag. He was as careful of the ship and her stores as if he had been sole owner. Scarcely could she be put about at any hour of the night but he would be on deck. There, accompanied by his favourite dog, Bounce, he would stand on the weather gangway snuffing up the midnight air, with his eye either glancing through his long night glass all round the horizon, or fixed on the light carried by Cornwallis in the *Ville de Paris*, the van ship of the weather line. When the ship was round and the bowlines hauled, he would exchange a few kindly words with the lieutenant of the watch, and then retire to his cot. Duties of every kind were carried on with that calmness and order and regularity and promptness, which afford a strong evidence of the directing hand of a master spirit. No swearing, no threatening or bullying, no startings were to be seen or heard. Boatswain's mates, or ship's corporals, dared not to be seen with a rattan, or rope's end in hand; nor do I recollect a single instance of a man being flogged while he remained aboard. Was discipline neglected then? By no means. There was not a better disciplined crew in the fleet.[30]

When an officer in *Culloden* called a man by shouting, 'You, Sir', Collingwood answered this by example:

> Going aft when he found the Lieutenant near the break of the poop, he addressed himself to the steersman, but loud enough to be heard by the Lieutenant.
>
> 'Jenkins, what is that man's name in the weather-rigging?'
>
> 'Dan Swain, your honour.'
>
> Forward the Admiral goes, and putting his hand instead of a speaking trumpet to his lips looked up and called out,
>
> 'Dan Swain.'
>
> 'Sir'
>
> 'The after end of that ratline is too high; let it down a handbreadth.'
>
> 'Aye, aye, Sir'
>
> The Lieutenant knew right well for whom this hint was intended and forthwith expunged You-Sir from his vocabulary.[31]

At a more junior level, Hay sang the praises of his master, Edward Hawke Locker, son of Nelson's old patron and secretary to Admiral Pellew:

> His person, which was always dressed in a plain manner but with great neatness, was below the middle size, and remarkably agile. His countenance was mild, affable and engaging. He possessed such presence and firmness of mind, such coolness in the midst of action, that under those various crosses, vexations and disappointments which so readily irritate other men, his features remained unchanged and serene. Though a certain suavity of air, and condescension of deportment, invited the approach of all, yet their appeared in his countenance that kind of dignity which repels improper levity of low familiarity.[32]

A bad captain could make the lives of his crew a misery, as John Wetherell found in *Hussar* in 1803. His hatred of Captain Wilkinson was obsessive:

> This evening our Captain returned on board and the verry planks appeard oerladen with his wretched frame; his weight of abominations were enough to Sink him Ship and crew in all the boundless deep. Sodom and Gomoro were destroy'd for their wickedness and Wilkinson ought to have been in the midst of them ...[33]

The men became so exasperated at his capricious and unjust floggings that they conspired to overthrow him, constantly reminding themselves of the *Hermione* affair. But even the cynical Wetherell recognized that officers like Wilkinson were not the whole story, and the crew referred to Admiral Sir Robert Calder for relief. The Admiral told the captain,

You well know my principles Wilkinson. When I commanded a single Ship it was my chief delight to have the goodwill of my men, and I can safely assert ev'ry man under my orders would freely lay down their life to obey me or my commands, and by such means I have made my crew both love and fear me. They loved me for my humanity and fear'd to cause my displeasure, and this I found the best school for Seamen … I have been advised by the honourable William Cornwallis to have a watchful eye on the *Hussar* while in port. He also informed me of the barbarous methods you practised daily on your crew, and now I am satisfied with the truth of the complaint and will use my interest to put an end to such base and unchristianly proceedings.[34]

Captain Robert Corbett had distinguished himself at the taking of Ile Bourbon in 1810 but had a very bad relationship with his crew, which led to a mutiny. One of them gave a typical example of his cruelty:

I was beat by Captain Corbett's order when setting a fore topmast studding sail. I was putting the tack block on the main rigging, and happened to take the hitch above the tail instead of under. The captain asked me who did it. I said it was me. He then sent for John Allen, boatswain's mate, and told him to beat me, which he did. The weight of the stick was so heavy that I could not stand. Captain Corbett said, 'If you don't stand I'll make you', and then sent the boatswain's mate to seize me up to the Jacob's ladder, which he did, and then beat me as long as Captain Corbett thought proper. I was then cast off. My flesh was terribly bruised, but I was not incapable of doing my duty.[35]

In his defence before a court martial, Corbett saw a spirit of resistance among his seamen and claimed, 'When necessary to inflict punishment of a lighter nature, some men stood as if seeking an increase of it. Some turned their faces to it and seemed to wish an unlucky blow on the face or head. On such occasions, seizing up the Jacob's ladder was resorted to … It requires little penetration to observe a cabal forming in the main top, where Slade and Wilkinson have both done duty; where all the instances of punishment have proceed from.'[36] This did not impress the court, who reprimanded him. Later his ship was engaged with two French frigates and Corbett was killed – it was never quite clear which side fired the fatal shot.

One of the worst types of junior officer was in *Revenge* in 1805, as described by William Robinson. 'He was a youth of not more than twelve or thirteen years of age: but I have often seen him get on the carriage of a gun, call a man to him, and kick him about the thighs and body, and with his fist would beat him about the head; and these, though prime seamen, at the same time dared not murmur.' This was Edward F. Brook, who was thirteen years old according to the muster book. There is no way of knowing how often this happened during the four and a half months in which Brook and Robinson served together in *Revenge*, and certainly Robinson was inclined to seek sensation. During such a rapid expansion of the navy, many unsuitable officers must have been appointed.

Occasionally midshipmen were 'turned before the mast' as a punishment for crime or negligence; an example was William H. Hamilton in 1805:

> One of our men ran away from the boat of which I was an officer – in consequence of which I was confined, turned before the mast and discharged as a seaman into His Majesty's sloop of war the *Oriquixo* (where I now am) with a strange captain and no recommendation. For about two months I did my duty before the mast but my good conduct so recommended me to my captain's favour that I am reinstated and still an officer.[37]

Even young gentlemen of more influence sometimes had a surprising affinity with the lower deck. According to Basil Hall, 'some young fellows set out in their professional life by making themselves, as they suppose, thorough-bred sailors, merely by aping the broadest external features of the character of the foremast men. These "kiddy blades" or "tarpaulin men", as they are called in the cockpit slang, have their hands constantly in the tar-bucket ...'[38]

It was not unusual for officers to be commissioned from the lower deck, though there were many who tried to put obstacles in their way. Robert Hay tried to learn navigation, the skill that divided the lower deck from the sea officers:

> The appearance of a servant-boy on the upper deck of a war-ship with a quadrant in his hand would have been a flagrant breach of discipline that four or five dozen at the breech of a gun would scarcely have atoned for. But to a willing mind many expedients will occur. A lighted candle placed on the dressing table, elevated or depressed as circumstances required, was made to represent the sun; and on my knees before this minor luminary, I endeavoured to find out how the instrument worked.[39]

Men of humble origin might well encounter resentment at their promotion. In the frigate *Pearl*,

> the Captain had taken his coxswain from the boat, and placed him on the quarter-deck, with orders for his being messed in one of the midshipmen's berths, against which the young gentlemen remonstrated, on the ground that the coxswain, in his capacity as coxswain, had been employed in menial services, such as taking the Captain's foul linen, to wash, and other low officers; these remonstrances availed them nothing, and upon some little difference with

this ci-devant coxswain, shortly after, two or three of the midshipmen were under the necessity of leaving the ship.[40]

Sometimes it was the seamen themselves who resented officers of humble origin. John Wetherell complained about Captain Wilkinson of *Hussar* that, 'His Father kept a small Barbar's Shop in the town known by [*sic*] old Wilkinson the Barber.'[41]

Officers of lower deck origin formed a useful stratum in the naval hierarchy. One was John Quillam, who had apparently left the Isle of Man due to some family disgrace to sign on as a seaman in 1791. He enjoyed support from his fellow islander Peter Heywood of *Bounty* fame and was promoted to masters' mate, then commissioned. He was First Lieutenant of *Victory* at Trafalgar, and as an officer with very little influence he was not likely to be promoted quickly, so he stayed on to bring experience, stability and maturity to the job.[42]

In short, the boundaries between the quarterdeck and lower deck were far more fluid than they were to become in Victorian times.

PETTY OFFICERS

As often happened in the aftermath of mutiny, officers paid greater attention to the selection of petty officers, though there was no serious attempt to train them for the role. According to Basil Hall,

> The higher ratings of quarter-master, gunner's mate, captain of the forecastle and of the tops, and so on, are given chiefly to men who may not, in fact, know more than every Able Seaman is supposed to be acquainted with, but who have recommended themselves by their superior activity and vigilance, and have not only shown themselves fit to command others by their decision of character, but evinced a sincere anxiety to see the work of the department well performed. It is of great consequence to assist in every way the authority of these leading hands over the other men stationed in the same part of the ship; and judicious officers will generally be able to avail themselves to great purpose, in moments of trial, of the energetic co-operation of these persons.[43]

But the essential problem was that most of the petty officers had begun as pressed men.

> The great difficulty in manning the Navy lies in procuring a sufficient number of these thorough-bred seamen, and from among them all the seamen petty officers are and must be selected. The consequence is that all the boatswains', gunners' and carpenters' mates and all the quartermasters are almost all pressed men throughout the Navy in time of war. Besides the great and evident

disadvantage of the most confidential class being the most discontented men, the service constantly suffers by want of real complete seamen and ships are wrecked and taken which might easily have been saved by the alert management of true British sailors.[44]

It was felt that he would be able to train the men in small arms and apply military style discipline far better.[45] He was often known as 'Douse that Glim' because his duties included seeing that no candle or lanterns were kept burning overnight. Robert Hay found that Mr Young of *Culloden* was 'a cruel, tyrannical knave, and a base time-serving sycophant'.[46]

The boatswain's mates' duties included flogging, which gave them a strained relationship with the rest of the ship's company. They ought to be

> very select men as the leaders of the ship's company. They should be very perfect seamen, and as having an irksome, unpopular part to perform, they ought to be circumspect and determined in their conduct ... The situation must be countenanced and supported, as no man otherwise would feel spirit sufficient to enforce the orders he delivers, and obedience to his commands.[47]

The principal job of the quartermaster was to supervise the steering of the ship under the officer of the watch. In the frigate *Amazon*, 'the quartermasters ...whilst at the conn ... are to take care the man at the helm is attentive and steers properly, and if the quartermaster observes that the man cannot steer as well as is expected, he is to report accordingly to the officer of the watch. But the quartermaster ought to be ashamed ... of obliging the officer to dictate in the least to the man at the helm.'[48] The quartermaster also helped the master and his mates in other areas. They were 'appointed by the captain to assist in the several duties of the ship, as stowing the ballast and provisions in the hold, coiling the cables on their platforms, overlooking the steerage of the ship, keeping the time by the watch glasses, and, in turn, over-looking the purser's steward in his delivery of provisions, &c'.[49] The work was 'not so laborious as other situations, which makes it frequently a retreat for old seamen ...'[50]

Quarter gunners were rated as petty officers and were assistants to the gunner; there were many of them, one to every four guns, which meant eighteen in a 74-gun ship. In practice they seem to have been used as an elite division of seamen. In *San Domingo* in 1812, for example, they were stationed on the gangways during setting sail or tacking to 'see the booms unclamped and tricing lines rove and clear', work which required a certain amount of skill and initiative but not the athleticism of the topmen. Captain

Davie deplored the use made of them in most ships: 'The gunner's crew in a ship appears to be a class much neglected. For instead of making them skilful artillery men, and retaining them principally for that service, they are too often suffered to remain totally ignorant of it, and only perform that part of the duty of seamen which is attached to their station.'[51]

Coxswains were appointed to all the boats, sometimes one for each watch, which might mean up to twelve in a large ship. Even the storeship *Dromedary* had 24 men in her boats' crews out of a total complement of 120. It was not easy to find suitable men: *Dromedary* only had 30 'fit for boats', which presumably meant they could be trusted not to desert. Though he received no extra pay, a boat's coxswain had to be a good seaman, able to handle his craft under both oars and sail. He would usually be under the command of a midshipman when making shore trips, but even so the coxswain's experience would be relied upon very much. The captain's coxswain, the petty officer in charge of his barge, was a special case, as much a servant as a seaman, and paid extra for his duty. Unlike captains' and admirals' servants, the coxswains could not be isolated from the rest of the crew, so they were a fertile source of gossip. According to John Wetherell, 'We learnt all this afterwards from Sir Robt's Coxswain who heard the whole story', for 'boats crews will talk and repeat over old stories'.[52]

Captains of the tops and other stations had been appointed for many years, but until 1806 they were unpaid and enjoyed no formal authority. When Captain Riou wrote the orders for *Amazon* in 1799, he had to direct that, 'The men who are appointed as captains of the different stations will ever be protected for the directions they may give in the execution of their duty, and any complaint of disobedience, neglect or drunkenness made by them of any man whose duty it is to serve under him will be attended with punishment.'[53]

Normally the captain of the top was a good leader, but this could be compromised if he was seen to be the officers' toady. John Wetherell wrote of one, 'We were now left to the mercy of this Judas Iscariot as we used afterwards to term him in our discourse, he being a Captain of the Top and we all station'd in the tops left us under his eyes or ears continually, caused us to be constantly on our guard ...'[54]

Other petty officers had duties that had little to do with leadership or discipline and were perhaps relics of the days when the term meant the holder of a particular office. These included the yeomen of the sheets, who had to ensure that these vital ropes were free to run during tacking and wearing and were properly belayed at other times. The yeomen of the boatswain's, carpenter's and gunner's store rooms were essentially storekeepers, who had to be literate and trustworthy.

CHARACTER

After many years of naval experience, Dr Thomas Trotter provides one of the most detailed descriptions of the seaman of the age of Nelson:

> That courage which distinguishes our seamen, though in some degree inherent in their natural constitutions, is yet increased by their habits of life, and by associating with men who are familiarized to danger, and who, from natural prowess, consider themselves as rulers by birth-right. By these means, in all actions, there is a general impulse among the crew of an English man of war either to grapple the enemy, or lay him close aboard; French men shudder at the attempt, and whenever it has been boldly executed on our part, they run from their quarters and are never to be rallied afterwards. Nor does this courage ever forsake them; we have seen them cheering their shipmates, and answering the shouts of the enemy, under the most dreadful wounds.

This came from long experience at sea.

> It is only men of such description, that could undergo the fatigues and perils of a sea-life; and there seems a necessity for being inured to it from an early age. The mind, by custom and example, is thus trained to brave the fury of the elements in their different forms, with degrees of contempt at danger and death that is to be met with nowhere else, and that has become proverbial. Excluded by the employment which they have chosen from all society but people of similar dispositions, the deficiencies of education are not felt, and information on general affairs is seldom courted. Their pride consists in being reputed a thorough bred seaman; and they look upon all landmen, as beings of an inferior order.

The seaman loved to apply his own vocabulary on land, 'sometimes with pedantic ostentation'. A seaman, *'cunns* a horse when he rides; *heaves the lead* from the top of a stage coach, and *wings* his enemy when he shoots away his stunsail halyards'. But ashore the seamen was seen, as always, as a holy fool and indifferent to money:

> Having little intercourse with the world, they are easily defrauded, and dupes to the deceitful, wherever they go; their money is lavished with the most thoughtless profusion; fine clothes for his girl, a silver watch, and silver buckles for himself, are often the sole return for years of labour and hardship. When his officer happens to refuse him leave to go on shore, his purse is sometimes consigned to the deep, that it may no longer remind him of pleasures he cannot command.

All this was caused by his rootless and insecure existence.

> If such are the follies and vices of the sailor, his virtues are of the finest cast. In the hour of battle he has never left his officer to fight alone; and it remains a solitary fact in the history of war. If, in his amours, he is fickle, it is because he has no settled home to fix domestic attachments; in his friendships he is warm, sincere and untinctured with selfish views … his charity makes no preliminary conditions to its object, but yields to the faithful impulse of an honest heart … Was I ever reduced to the utmost poverty, I would shun the cold threshold of fashionable society, to beg among seamen; where my afflictions would never be insulted by being asked through what follies or misfortunes I had been reduced to penury.[55]

One ship's boy from the merchant service had a brief experience of naval life, after being freed from imprisonment in Denmark, when he and his fellows were put on board a warship. They saw something of the seaman's generosity of spirit:

> One of my fellow apprentices and I were put into a mess with twelve of the ship's company; one of whom, attended to conduct us to their berth. It was now too late to get any provisions served out to us for that night; and the lieutenant recommended to our messmates to give us a share of any thing they had remaining … This was most cheerfully complied with; but the poor fellows had but little to spare. They had been on short allowance of everything – six-upon-four, (that is, six men on the ordinary allowance for four) for some time before we joined the ship. The mess I was attached to had their berth at the armourer's table, a midships, and close by the main-hatchway; and when we had seated ourselves here, we learned that we were on board his Majesty's ship *Brunswick*, a seventy-four, commanded by Captain Graves. Some salt pork and biscuit were instantly produced; and they were in every respect most acceptable.[56]

But there was a less positive side. 'The crew of the *Brunswick* were a most mischievous set. Every night there were robberies among them; and all stole water and provisions when it was in their power.'[57]

Phillip Patton, who served on the Board of Admiralty during the Trafalgar Campaign, wrote,

> Although seamen may have been regarded (by certain characters who have unfortunately had power and who were ignorant of their dispositions) as a species of mankind deficient in the nicer feelings of humanity, whose attachments might be sacrificed, their friendships disregarded and even their healths ruined or destroyed upon the most frivolous occasions; yet they are very far from being inferior to other men, either in generous or in elevated sentiments.[58]

One writer accepted the difference between lower deck and quarterdeck in terms of the status of a gentleman, an important distinction of the age:

> Habits and education create essential differences in the minds and manners of men. To dismiss an officer from His Majesty's Service would be esteemed a heavy punishment; whereas a common sailor would look upon it, in many cases, as a favour conferred upon him. Corporal punishment, which seldom operates on the feelings of common seaman or soldier, must affect a petty officer (such as a midshipman) so sensibly, if he has the sentiments of a gentleman, to render his future life a burden to him.[59]

This is perhaps a little confused if essentially true. The term 'petty officer' was rarely used to describe midshipmen by this time, and moreover it was quite common to subject them to corporal punishment, though in private rather than in public. This was in accordance with the standards of the day, when the beating of boys was considered necessary and even laudable in all classes. A more important difference, according to Captain Griffiths, was that the officers wanted to be there: 'by far the larger portion of a ship's company are there against their will. Many are impressed and forcibly brought. Others enter because if they do not, they will be impressed and although they are cheerful and apparently contented, there is still that difference between them and the officers; the latter are there by choice.'[60]

RATINGS

Of course, there were many divisions among the seamen themselves, by skill and experience as much as anything else. Robert Wilson describes the procedure in rating men on board ship:

> On your first appearance on board, you are summoned before the First Lieutenant, who interrogates you concerning your profession, your abilities as a seaman, place of nativity, and dwelling; name and age, length of time you have been at sea, whether in ships-of-war or merchantmen, etc; to which questions you are looked to for prompt answers. You are then rated on the ship's books according to your abilities, as the First Lieutenant may think fit – the same without prejudice or favour being shewn to any one. Should it so happen that you are found not competent to the rating you at first had, you are disrated.[61]

Naturally most landsmen and ordinary seamen would expect to learn more and be rated higher, but it was often difficult for landsmen who had started at the age of about 25 or more and had not been 'bred to the sea'. Bartholomew Hughes of Dublin served in *Bellerophon* from 1803 to 1815 and was aged 49 by the end of the period, but he never rose above landsman. Captain Davie believed that before being rated up a man should know the names of all the ropes, the exercise of great guns and small arms, and 'be able to row, make sennet and knot yarns', but he implies that not all captains were so demanding. To make the next step to able seaman, a man should be able to:

> Steer, heave the lead, knot, splice, secure a gun, make points, robands and gaskets, set studding sails, make up sails, serve rigging, strop blocks, turn in a deadeye, and clap on a seizing.[62]

For day to day work the men were employed in the 'parts of ship', principles, which dated from ancient times but were much more clearly described during this period. According to Davie, 'The afterguard and waisters are generally composed of indifferent seamen and landsmen and are the largest part of the crew, on whom the whole drudgery of the ship devolves. These men have not only the burden, but every dirty and inferior duty to execute.' The forecastle men, on the other hand, did skilled work with the anchors and were 'generally chosen from their abilities as seamen, and from some peculiar distinctions attached to the station feel pride in their department'. There were three groups of topmen, one for each mast. 'Topmen are mostly composed of young active men who have been at sea three or four years and understand the rudiments of seamanship. They have the largest share of duty to perform, and are the most useful class of people on board.'[63] Ships' boys were usually employed as servants until they were big and strong. After that they were often attached to the mizzen, the smallest of the three masts, to learn the skills of topmen.

TYPICAL SEAMEN

Some captains made a habit of keeping 'description books' of the men under their command, for they might be useful in tracking them if they deserted. They often depict the seaman as a rather un-military figure. Captain Rotherham's book for *Bellerophon*, begun just after the Battle of Trafalgar, shows a great deal of diversity. Some of the men would not have been recruited by any modern navy – John Millikan was an 'amaciated thing'; Thomas Jewell had lost his right eye, and Henry McGee was blind in one; Michael Carvel was 'not a good character but very strong'; James Robinson was a 'stupid fellow', and John Sullivan was 'very old looking'.

Not all were young – more than a fifth of 264 men on *Bellerophon* who were not officers, marines or boys, were over 40. James Marshall was oldest at 56, followed by James Gill, aged 51, who had served since the age of 11 with 27 years in merchant ships and 13 in the Royal Navy. He was a quartermaster and a 'good old seaman'. Eighty-seven men were in their thirties, 57 in their late twenties and 64 were aged from 20 to 25. Jack Allen, a Negro from Grenada, was the tallest at 5 feet 11 inches. Some were very short, including Edward Ford of Sunderland, who was less than 5 feet tall but made up for his lack of height by being 'thick set, strong made'. John Cook, a watch motion maker from Cripplegate in London, was only 4 feet 11 inches and worked in the cramped conditions of the hold, where small stature might be an advantage.

The crew of the first gun on *Bellerophon's* forecastle were mostly old salts, often scarred from earlier campaigns. Samuel King was a 40-year-old American from Philadelphia who had served fourteen years in the Royal Navy. He had a scar on his upper lip. Joseph McCrea of Aberdeen was 'much scarred in the throat from scrofula'. He had been at sea since he was 14, with eight years in the Baltic trades before entering the Royal Navy. His companions were three other Scots, two of them merchant service veterans. Thomas Jones was a 34-year-old Welshman with a broken nose. His countryman Owen Roberts was missing the third finger on his left hand. Peter Johnson of Karlscrona in Sweden was 39 years old and had spent 15 of these at sea. William Taylor had spent less than three years in the king's service after almost twenty years in the West India trade. He was born in Banff in the north of Scotland, but his wife was in Plymouth. Robert Dowey, a 28-year-old former weaver from Newburgh in Fife, was 'well made' and 'good looking'. John White from London was the tallest man on this particular gun at 5 feet 10 inches and also the oldest at 41. Richard Schofield of Yorkshire had served five years in the Jamaica trade and 12 in the Royal Navy.

Tattoos had become increasingly common in the navy since they were discovered by Captain's Cook's men, and officers tended to encourage them since it might help to identify deserters. That was evident among the crew of *Bellerophon*. Peter Johnson had a flowerpot on his right arm; Richard Schofield had a pierced heart on his left arm and signal flags on his right; John White had the letters 'SBMM' on the back of his left hand, while John Stewart recorded most of his family history on his arm – in 1792 he had married Helen Hunter of Plymouth, and two of their children were alive.

NATIONAL AND RACIAL ORIGINS

Though it was often still referred to as the 'English' navy, probably only about half the crews were literally English (the Scots, in particular, were far less sensitive about being included in the term than they later became). Fewer than half of the 439 seamen in *San Domingo* were English, and they served alongside 117 Irish, 34 Scots and 14 Welsh. Just over half the 585 men in *Caledonia* were English in 1810, with 154 Irish, 45 Scots and 21 Welsh.[64]

One source of seamen that was more fully exploited than in the past was foreigners. Again, these had not been unknown in the past, but it is notable that many ships of the 1800s had quite high proportions: *Victory* at Trafalgar had 71, of 12 different nationalities; *San Domingo* had 62 out of 439 seamen. Many were Americans, and this was an issue that was to become important in 1812; but they also included men from traditionally seafaring nations such as Denmark, Holland and Portugal, and even several Frenchman. Such men were there for various reasons, not least because the war against Napoleon was to a certain extent ideological and could sometimes cut across national boundaries. In the circumstances, the British navy was only too glad to accept them.

Black seamen were quite common on board ships. In addition to 'Black Tom', who died of 'former excesses', Samuel Leech describes 'a colored man whose name was Nugent, who possessed a remarkably fine person, was very polite in his manners, and easy in his address'.[65] Captains did not always record racial origins, but *Caledonia* had six West Indians and three from the Spanish West Indies, along with one African; *San Domingo* had ten West Indians. The Description Book of HMS *Blake* in 1808 described Able Seaman George Lavicourt of Antigua as 23 years old, of black complexion, stout made and married.[66] Captain Rotherham of *Bellerophon* was meticulous in recording the grades of coloration produced by racial mixing in the West Indies: Samuel Marlow of Jamaica was a 'Sambo', one quarter white, and worked as a wardroom steward; David Young and Evans Lyon were both 'mustees', one eighth black, from Antigua; Jack Allen from Grenada was 'very infirm' at 43, and 'good for nothing'. But not all West Indians were black or of mixed race. Ordinary Seaman James Mills of Nevis was 37 years old, 'stout made', of fair complexion and had light brown hair.[67] Black American seamen were also not unknown. John Hachett, a Negro from Maryland, served on board *Bellerophon* at Trafalgar. He had spent eight years at sea since the age of fourteen and had not been in

America for ten years; it is quite likely that he was a runaway slave. Quarter Gunner Perry Stacey of Baltimore had a 'yellow' complexion with 'black short woolly hair', which suggests he might have been of mixed race.[68]

There was no particular bar on black men becoming able seamen and petty officers: Perry Stacey, for example, became a quarter gunner. But there was a tendency for them to be employed on domestic duties, such as the stereotyped cook's assistant described by Basil Hall: 'Behind him stands his mate, generally a tall, glossy, powerful Negro, who, unlike his chief, has always a full allowance of limbs, with a round and shining face.'[69] Black seamen are often seen in prints of the period, and again domestic duties predominate. The well known picture of 'Ben Blockhead' being introduced to the midshipmen's berth has a tall negro, apparently a servant. Later, when Ben takes over the watch on a rainy night, a black man appears in a flimsy nightshirt, apparently serving refreshments. Denis Dighton's famous painting of Nelson being wounded has a black man serving in one of the gun crews without comment; and 'The Sailor's Description of a Chase and Capture' shows a black man in of a mess of six, who are presumably all experienced seamen – to be a member of such a group was a sure sign of acceptance.

THE ROLE OF THE MARINES

In the aftermath of the great mutinies, St Vincent began to develop a new role for the marines, to intimidate the crew while in port when they were most likely to revolt.

> When at anchor in this position, the whole party of marines in the respective ships in the fleet is to be kept constantly at drill or parade under the direction of the commanding officer of the marines, and not to be diverted therefrom by any of the ordinary duties of the ships. Sighting the anchors or getting under sail are the only exceptions which occur to the commander in chief.[70]

They were also to parade during punishment:

> Whenever there is occasion to inflict punishment on board any of His Majesty's ships under my command, the respective captains are hereby required and directed to cause an officer's guard of marines to attend the punishment, with loaded arms and bayonets ...[71]

While at sea, apart from sentries on such vital points as the captain's cabin and the spirit room, most of the marines were employed among the seamen, though only on deck – 'The marines are not to be forced to go aloft, nor on the other hand are they to be retrained from learning the duty of seamen ...'[72] As well as cleaning decks and other unskilled duties, they often provided most of the muscle at the capstan when raising anchor and had other stations for different manoeuvres. In *San Domingo* in 1812 they helped to haul on the fore and braces while tacking, and when swaying up the topmasts they pulled on the foretop tackle falls. In action they either formed small arms parties if the enemy ship was close enough, or assisted at the great guns.

But the status of the marines was low among the seamen, and Admiral Phillip Patton was concerned about St Vincent's policy:

> When ships seldom go to sea, during peace, marines are drawn into a degree of consideration by no means suitable to their real value in ships, by the parade and show common in harbour duty. But ... it will be perceived that under the present circumstances the effect of connecting *landmen* with the officers of ships as the confidential class is completely overturning the natural order of things. One consequence of this measure is certain; the seamen will be disgusted in a very high degree and much animosity may be expected to arise between the seamen and the landmen in every ship where violence is necessary. This state of hostility is not doubtful; it is an effect which will follow the cause as certainly as that *landmen* stand in no kind of comparison with seamen as to their value afloat. The duty of a sailor requires a habit of agility and skill which cannot be acquired but by an early service in handling the sails in tempestuous seas, whereas marines are landmen of all professions embarked in ships, who can load and fire a musket, which is an effort of skill by no means confined to them in the Navy ...
>
> Let us now suppose the ship to have such a degree of motion as discomposes landmen and let us suppose the officers of this ship depending on the marines for protection from the irritated seamen; where is the security? In such a case, it is well known that three seamen are absolutely superior in force to ten landmen, whatever the colour of their coats or their state of discipline.[73]

As First Lord of the Admiralty from 1801, St Vincent did boost the status of the marines by giving them the title of 'Royal', but there is little evidence that they were successful in preventing revolt – marines were as prominent as seamen in mutinies, and in many ships they were flogged more often than seaman for such offences as drunkenness.

Certainly there was animosity between seamen and marines in many ships, perhaps encouraged by officers of the St Vincent stamp. Sometimes it spilled over into violence, as John Nicol records:

> We got some marines from the Rock, to reinforce the *Goliath*'s complement – one of them a tall stout Englishman, who had been cock of the Rock. He was

very overbearing. There are often quarrels at the ship's fires, when the men are boiling their kettles. We had a stout little fellow of an Irishman, who had been long in the *Goliath*; the marine pushed his kettle aside. Paddy demanded why he did so? 'Because I choose to do it.' – 'I won't allow you while life is in me,' was the reply. 'Do you wish to fight?' said the Englishman. 'Yes, and I do,' said Paddy; 'I will take the Gibraltar rust out of you, or you shall beat the life out of my body before we are done.' A fight was made up in a minute; and they went well forward on the deck, to be out of sight of the officers. They went with it, and fought it out; we forming a ring, and screening them from observation. Paddy was as good as his word; for he took the rust off the marine so well, he was forced to give in, and we were all happy to see the lobster's-back pride taken out of him.[74]

WOMEN ON BOARD

According to William Dillon, in the early 1790s, 'It was the custom on board the ships of war to allow the seamen to take their wives as passengers when sailing from one port to another, but they did not go to sea. A few of the seamen were married; the others had nominal wives – an indulgence winked at generally in the Navy.' This was disrupted by the evangelical Captain Gambier, who insisted that the couples really had to be married, and some were hastily wed by the ship's chaplain.[75]

But Gambier was an exception, and the general trend was towards greater liberality. Perhaps this was encouraged by the practice of using soldiers as marines on board ship during that decade. Six men in every hundred were allowed to have wives 'on the strength', to go with them anywhere, even on board ship. In 1796 even a martinet like Sir John Jervis did not object to the presence of women in principle:

> There being reason to apprehend that a number of women have been clandestinely brought from England in several ships, more particularly those which have arrived in the Mediterranean in the last and present year, the respective captains are required by the admiral to admonish these ladies upon the waste of water committed by them and other disorders committed by them and be made know to all that on the first proof of water being obtained for washing from the scuttle-butt or otherwise under false pretences in any ship, every woman in the fleet who has not been admitted under the authority of the Admiralty or the commander in chief will be sent to St Fiorenze to be shipped to England by the first convoy ...[76]

By 1798 the policy varied from ship to ship even within a squadron. In Nelson's flagship *Vanguard*, Captain Berry noted that there were 300 women on board in port but decreed that, '*All* the females go on shore tomorrow – I have set my face against taking *one* to sea.' In any case,

Captain Foley's *Goliath* went to the opposite extreme, with large numbers on board during the Mediterranean campaign. John Nicol records their actions during the Battle of the Nile.

> The women behaved as well as the men ... I was much indebted to the gunner's wife, who gave her husband and me a drink of wine every now and then, which lessened our fatigue much. There were some of the women wounded, and one woman belonging to Leith died of her wounds. One woman bore a son in the heat of the action; she belonged to Edinburgh.[77]

After the battle Foley took the unique step of entering four of the women's names in the ship's muster book as supernumeraries to be allowed two thirds of the men's allowance of victuals, but no wages. All were wives of sailors or marines who had been killed in the battle, during which they gave 'assistance in dressing and tending the wounded'. If these women and their husbands were representative of the ship's company, then there might have been around a hundred women on board the *Goliath* for a crew of 570 men. Many years later, Ann Hopping and Mary Ann Riley claimed the Naval General Service Medal for the battle, but were declined solely on the grounds of sex; the Admiralty was worried that it would be followed by 'innumerable applications' from others.[78]

This had all changed by the time of Trafalgar in 1805, and there is no evidence of the presence of women in large numbers. On the contrary, the seamen of *Victory* were amazed when a French woman known as Jeanette was rescued from the water. They dressed her in clothes used for amateur dramatics, while officers gave their watch chains to tie up her hair.[79] Robinson confirmed the lack of women on board during the campaign when he wrote, 'Our crew, consisting of six hundred and upwards, nearly all young men, had seen one woman on board for eighteen months, and that was the daughter of one of the Spanish chiefs ...'[80] None of this affected the right of the seaman to have a 'wife' on board when in port.

As a literate seaman, John Powell often wrote letters for his messmates, which increased his popularity but gave him a dilemma:

> I have been requested by one of the women on board to write out a certificate of marriage between her and one of the men, she telling me she had forgot to bring the right one with her on board and that she might perhaps have occasion for it she should be glad if I would make one out and she would direct me how to draw it up but this I absolutely refused to do well knowing the consequence of forgery.

As everyone knew, the great majority of female visitors on board were prostitutes:

> On the arrival of any man of war in port, these girls flock down to the shore, where boats are always ready; and here may be witnessed a scene, somewhat similar to the trafficking for slaves in the West Indies. As they approached a boat, old Charon ... surveys them from stem to stern, with the eyes of a bargaining jew; and carefully culls out the best looking, and the most dashingly dressed ...
>
> After having moored out ship, swarms of boats came round us ... a great many were freighted with cargoes of ladies, a sight that was most gratifying, and a great treat ... So soon as these boats were allowed to come alongside, the seamen flocked down pretty quick, one after the other, and brought their choice up, so that in the course of the afternoon, we had four hundred and fifty on board.[81]

According to a pamphlet on 'Certain Immoral Practices',

> They then descend to the lower deck with their husbands, as they call them. Hundreds come off to a large ship. The whole of the shocking, disgraceful transactions of the lower deck it is impossible to describe – the dirt, the filth, and stench; the disgusting conversation; the indecent, beastly conduct and horrible scenes; the blasphemy and swearing; the riots, quarrels and fighting, which often takes place, where hundreds of men and women are huddled together in one room, as it were, in bed (each man being allowed only fourteen inches breadth for his hammock), they are squeezed between the next hammocks, and must be witnesses of each other's actions; can only be imagined by those who have seen all of this.[82]

OTHER SEXUAL PRACTICES

Since women were rarely present at sea, the seaman had to resort to other means of relief. The 1811 *Dictionary of the Vulgar Tongue* had the phrase, 'To box the Jesuit and get cockroaches', apparently 'a sea term for masturbation; a crime, it is said, much practiced by the reverend fathers of that society'.[83] The dictionary did into say how much the seamen themselves practised it, but they needed a descriptive phrase, so presumably it was not unknown.

Other sexual practices really were crimes in the Articles of War, and of course there is no way of knowing how common they were, but the court martial records give a few examples. In 1796, Seaman Thomas Hall testified, 'I heard Peter Rich my messmate say something was carried on that was not right.' The men went to look under the cable bitts. 'I saw two men under the cable, one lying down on his belly and his trousers down. I saw another man towards his feet and came close to them. I could plainly perceive that one of them had his privates out and his two hands hold of Savage's Jacket ...' William Savage was acquitted of homosexual acts, but John Morris was sentenced to death, having been reported by his own shipmates.[84] In *St George* in 1800, it was the master at arms who made such a discovery after being informed by a marine:

> I immediately fastened Thomas Hubbard by the neck. I called for assistance immediately; he tried to get away and I then found that George Hynes was under him, naked on his belly. On his trying to slue himself on one side in his hammock, I saw Thomas Hubbard's yard come from between the backside of George Hynes. I held him fast by the neck and got him out and made him button his trousers up.[85]

Others were found in more exotic sex. Isaac Wilson of the sloop *Orestes* was overheard by a marine corporal. 'I was standing at the main hatchway and, hearing a goat making a noise, I thought that she was dying. I went up on deck on the starboard side and opened the goat house door, where I found a man lying down all his length in the goat house and with his trousers unbuttoned and his shirt out before and behind.' But Isaac Wilson managed to convince a court that he had merely laid down in the goat house when he was drunk and the goat had trampled on him. John Sherwood of *Milford* was less fortunate when found with a sheep in 1812 and was sentenced to a hundred lashes.[86] Paedophilia was also a problem with a number of ships' boys on board, though it was mainly warrant officers who were detected in it, perhaps because they could use the privacy of their cabins.

DAILY ROUTINE

For most ships on most days there were no battles to be fought or ships to be chased, and life settled down to a routine while patrolling, escorting, blockading or making a passage. The ship's day began early, when the men off watch were called from their hammocks 'in a voice designedly of the most alarming loudness'. As a clergyman, William Mangin was rather coy about the language used: 'the Chaplain had better spare both his lungs and ears ...'[87] After that the seamen scrubbed the decks:

> They then come on deck again, pull off their shoes and stockings, turn up their trowsers to above their knees and commence *holy-stoning* the deck, as it is termed ... here the men suffer from being obliged to kneel down on the wetted deck, and a gravelly sort of sand [is] strewed over it. To perform this work they

kneel with their bare knees, rubbing the deck with a stone and the sand, the grit of which is often very injurious. In this manner the watch continues till about four bells, or six o'clock; they then begin to wash and swab the decks till seven bells, and at eight bells the boatswain's mate pipes to breakfast.[88]

Then it was time for breakfast:

The meal consists of burgoo, made of coarse oatmeal and water; others will have Scotch coffee, which is burnt bread boiled in some water, and sweetened with sugar. This is generally cooked in a hook-pot near the galley, where there is a range. Nearly all the crew have one of these pots, a spoon, and a knife; for these are things indispensable: there are also basons, plates &c. which are kept in each mess, which generally consists of eight persons, whose berth is between two of the guns on the lower deck, where there is a board placed, which swings with the rolling of the ship, and answers for a table.[89]

Breakfast was taken by the men in their messes and was a key part of their social life. According to Captain A. J. Griffiths, 'The privilege the seamen and marines had of changing their messes the first of the month if they thought fit was their Magna Carta.'

While in command, my crew ever messed as they liked. The berth was allotted to the number it was calculated to hold and if one, two or three messes were in it, that rested with themselves ... So satisfied was I with the misery of obliging men to mess together that among my punishments was a drunken, dirty, a blackguard and a thieves mess. Instead of being numbered, they were called by these names at the grog tub, the cook's coppers, etc. Experience showed me that a decree placing a man in one of these messes for a given time on account of misconduct had more effect than corporal punishment.[90]

For the rest of the morning, both watches and the idlers would probably be on duty, exercising as groups, as a ship or as part of a fleet.

In a little while we joined the Commodore in the bay and made sail to the eastward, passed outside of the sands into the North Sea where we passed away two days Exerciseing. This was Exerciseing Officers, Men, Ships, Sails, Guns, Yards Washing, Holystoning, Small arms, Mustering bags. Reefing in two minutes, punishment, Up and down hammocks, Stow them, Scrub hammocks. Up all chests and bags, Sprinkle and Scrub, Serve out pursers Slops and tobacco, Serve grog, Turn all hands up to skylarking, Set the watch. All those little changes were transacted in the course of two days cruise in the North Sea.[91]

There was always plenty of work to do in the rigging, which could sometimes be dangerous if carried out by enthusiastic and competitive boys:

After inspection the words 'away aloft' had scarcely left the lips of the master at arms, when Dennis and I found ourselves alongside each other in the fore-rigging. Up we went, side by side, and the ratlines scarcely bent beneath our tread. Not one ratline did we gain on each other till we reached the mast-head. I passed abaft the mast, Dennis before it, and down went still together. When within a fathom or two of the dead-eyes, a ratline gave way with me, and I was precipitated into the top. I was stunned for a moment.[92]

Late in the morning, any offenders were brought before the captain for punishment, perhaps after being held bound by their legs in irons overnight. This was deplored by Captain Griffiths:

> The practice of putting men in irons is a very bad one for many reasons. In itself it is a severe and degrading punishment. Yet a man complained of is ordered into irons. From weather, from Sunday intervening, chasing, etc, he may be kept there three or four days and then perhaps be found innocent, or that his punishment has already exceeded his error. Is there no wrong done to an innocent man, robbing him of his exercise, degrading him, obliging him to sleep on deck with his leg in irons, the worry of his feelings (for seamen have feelings) and the loss of his grog?

But the great majority of officers preferred to use the irons. The alleged offenders were brought before the captain, as described rather optimistically by Robert Wilson:

> The Ship's Corporal brings forward the prisoners. A grating is fixed for them to be seized on. They are called before the Captain one by one to make their defence; they are allowed a fair trial. If any officer speaks in their favour, they are acquitted or their punishment is mitigated; if they can clear themselves, well and good. In short, it's like a court of judicature.[93]

William Robinson described the punishment of those found guilty:

> About eleven o'clock, or six bells, when any of the men are in irons, or on the black list, the boatswain or mate are ordered to call all hands; the culprits are then brought forward by the master at arms ... All hands now being mustered, the captain orders the man to strip; he is then seized to a grating by the wrists and knees; his crime is then mentioned, and the prisoner may plead, but, in nineteen cases out of twenty, he is flogged for the most trifling offence or neglect.[94]

Thomas Bladen Capel, captain of the frigate *Phoebe*, was taking no chances of sparking a revolt during punishment:

In time of punishment the Marine Guard to be under arms on the quarterdeck, the marines paraded on the gangways, the officers to be in uniform, the mates and warrant officers in the waist to mix with the people and a lieutenant to attend in the outer rank to see no irregularity committed and every person … attentive during punishment and any irregular behaviour among the people to be immediately reported.[95]

To a man who was not used to it, the blows were painful enough:

I felt them so keenly, being the first and last time they scratched my back, that I thought I would rather let the rogue that caused what I endured kick me overboard another time, than have those unnatural devil cats at my shoulders.[96]

When John Wetherell was flogged, he was as concerned about the injustice as about the actual pain. 'In this manner they gave me four dozen and punished me for a thing that was done three days after I was in irons for what they term'd a crime …'[97] But he felt the after-effects for some considerable time – 'believe me the shirt on my back was like a butcher's apron, and so still that every time I had to stoop down, it would tear off the bladders of blood and water that were on my poor mangled body …'[98]

Robinson describes running the gauntlet, a punishment for theft:

The criminal is placed with his naked back in a large tub, wherein a seat has been fixed, and his hands lashed down his sides: this tub is secured on a grating, and is drawn round the decks by the boys, the master-at-arms with his drawn sword pointing to the prisoner's breast. The cavalcade starts from the break of the quarter-deck, after the boatswain has given the prisoner a dozen lashes, and the ship's crew are ranged round the decks in two rows, so that the prisoner passes between them, and each man is provided with a three yarn knettle; that is, three rope yarns tightly laid together and knotted. With this, each man must cut him, or be thought implicated in the theft.

Around midday the hands were piped to dinner, the main meal of the day. It was a happy occasion, partly because it came with the first issue of alcoholic drink – beer in home waters, brandy or wine in the Mediterranean and a very powerful rum in the West Indies. The meal was sacrosanct, only a few helmsmen and lookouts remaining on duty. Captain Riou was typical in ordering,

The ship's company are never to be interrupted at their meals but on the most pressing occasions and the commanding officer should be very punctual as to their hours of dinner and breakfast; and if the duty will admit they should never have less time allowed for their breakfast than three quarters of an hour and an hour and a half for dinner.[99]

After dinner, one watch was off duty until four o'clock and was usually allowed to relax. Sailors often indulged in clothes-making, or private work for one another:

> Here in one place many be seen a tailor, in another a shoemaker, a tinker, a brazier, a glazier, a plumber, a painter, a seamster, a draftsman, a twine-maker, stocking and glove makers, hat makers, hat coverers, button makers, knife makers, book binders, coopers; nay, almost every trade that you could mention, even to a watch maker, and all at their different occupations ... on the other hand, every sailor knows a little about his needle, though, and he can cut clothes, particularly trousers ... Those who are not employed sewing or mending, you'll see them either learning to read or write, or ciphering, or instructing others. Some are playing the violin, flute or fife, while others sing or dance thereto. Others are relating awful stories of what happened in awful times while their hearers are listening with respectful silence, especially the young sailors.[100]

However happy the men might seem at times like this, Samuel Leech claimed it merely hid their grief at separation and confinement:

> A casual visitor in a man of war, beholding the song, the dance, the revelry of the crew, might judge them to be happy. But I know that these things are often resorted to, because they feel miserable, to drive away dull care. They do it on the same principle as the slave population in the South, to drown in sensual gratification the voice of misery that groans in the inner man ...[101]

At four in the afternoon the men were called to supper, which consisted of 'a half pint of wine, or a pint of grog to each man, with biscuit and cheese, or butter.' By this time the ship was into the dog watches of two hours each, so that the routine would be varied and the watches would be on duty at a different time on alternate days. Robinson describes the ship's night:

> Our crew were divided into two watches, starboard and larboard. When one was on deck the other was below; for instance the starboard watch would come on at eight o'clock at night, which is called eight bells; at half-past is called one bell, and so on; every half hour is a bell, as the hour glass is turned, and the messenger sent to strike the bell, which is generally affixed near the fore-hatchway. It now becomes the duty of the officer on the deck to see that the log-line is run out, to ascertain how many knots the ship goes an hour, which is

entered in the log-book, with any other occurrence which may take place during the watch. At twelve o'clock, or eight bells in the first watch, the boatswain's mate calls out lustily, '*Larboard watch, a-hoy.*' This is called the middle watch, and when on deck, the other watch go below to their hammocks, till eight bells, which is four o'clock in the morning.

Usually there was not much for most of the men to do during a night watch, and most of them were resting. The fact that some captains expressly forbade the men to sleep suggests that others allowed them. According to Captain Riou of *Amazon*, the first lieutenant was to 'keep the watch awake and in motion, that they are not lying about the decks asleep, the cause of colds and fevers, and the increase of the sick list. Any amusement such as fiddle, etc, to pass away the time in exercise, when disengaged from duty, is to be encouraged.'[102] Captain Davie suggested that it was desirable 'to prevent them lying down on the damp deck or in wet places; a practice that does more injury to the constitution of seamen than at the moment can be imagined; which, when a ship's company is at two watches, it is scarce possible to prevent.'

There was considerable debate among officers about whether it was better to put the crew on a three-watch system. The obvious advantage was that they were allowed eight hours off for every four hours on and were much better rested. In St Vincent's fleet in 1797 it was found that the majority of ships used three watches, but the system seems to have declined in the 1800s. When Captain Willoughby took over the sloop *Otter* in 1809 he restored the two-watch system: 'Agreeably to the general line of discipline and arrangement [he] placed the men at watch and watch' because he found they were slovenly. Captain Davie discovered that there were 'various opinions respecting the propriety of a ship's company being at three watches'. Some captains believed there was 'an insufficient number of men'. Others believed that, 'A ship's crew, being at three watches, acquire a habit of laziness which disqualifies them for active pursuits when required, and that by inaction a restlessness of disposition is created, which degenerates either into gambling or a spirit of politics, two of the most baneful tendencies of a ship's company.' Davie considered that a crew should be put in three watches after some time at sea and the men were experienced, and the privilege should be withdrawn if short of complement for any reason, including desertion.[103] But the majority of ships seem to have used the two-watch system for most of the time.

DESERTION

Mutiny was rather less common by 1803–15 than in the previous period (though far from unknown), and there was nothing on the scale of Spithead and the Nore, or as violent as the *Hermione* incident. If the seaman had an outlet from naval discipline, it was now by means of desertion. That had been common enough in the last war, and Nelson estimated that 42,000 men had run during those years. In the thirteen months from May 1804 to June 1805, more than 15,000 men were lost to the service, and only 3,000 of these were invalided out. A total of 5,662 able seamen deserted, along with 3,903 ordinary and 2,737 landsmen.[104] As Thomas Trotter put it, the seaman might seem reconciled to his lot but often preserved 'a determination to watch every opportunity for effecting his escape'.[105]

Robert Hay deserted the service no less than three times. On the first occasion, soon after joining, he simply walked ashore, but found it inhospitable and went back before he was missed. The second time was when the frigate *Amethyst* was wrecked and he struggled ashore and hid from the press gang. Finally, in October 1811 he plotted hard with a fellow seaman to acquire some bladders and float ashore from *Ceres* off the coast of Essex. After many vicissitudes, they went ashore near Maldon.[106] William Robinson also deserted the service, though he makes no mention of it in his memoir. Deserters were usually obliged to make their living by sea, and they often found themselves pressed into the service again, where they were terrified that an officer might recognise them – if found, they might go before a court martial and be sentenced to flogging round the fleet, especially if the offence was compounded by other factors such as theft or assault.

WARTIME SERVICE

The great battles were only the tip of the iceberg of the British naval effort. Often the battle was the culmination of months and years spent blockading the main ports of Brest, Rochefort, Corunna, Cadiz and the Texel. Even after the battles were won, blockade service remained the bread and butter work of the Royal Navy.

> After refitting, we sailed to join the blockading squadron, off Cadiz, and remained there about eighteen months, during which time we were tacking and wearing ship continually, as the blockading service required us to keep as near the harbour's mouth as possible, and consequently, when the wind was

blowing on the land, we were obliged to beat off; and when it was blowing off the land, then to beat up to the harbour's mouth as near as we could, to prevent the escape of the enemy. [107]

In the Channel Fleet, Robinson got no satisfaction:

> We soon found that we had become *Channel gropers*, a term given to the Channel Fleet in war time, which is destined to hover about Brest when the wind is fair for the French fleet to come out, as we were blockading them; and when the wind blows strong into the harbour, so that they could not well get out; in those cases, our fleet would sometimes put in at Cawsand or Torbay, and might be what sailors call a *fresh beef station*, but it is such as few seamen like, for they say it is neither being abroad nor at home. One reason why they have a dislike to it is, that they are open to the ridicule of seamen who may be coming home from foreign stations, as well as by the girls and people in the sea-port towns, by cantingly telling them they would never have the scurvy, or that they might as well be by their mother's fire-side, and tied to the apron-strings, as merely running in and out of harbor; and nothing hurts Jack's feelings more than being taunted of anything unmanly or inferior.[108]

Convoy escort was another vital duty, but no seaman is known to have left a detailed record of it. Cruising for prizes was much more popular, and a successful captain like Thomas Cochrane could pick and choose his seamen without the use of the press gang.

In addition to the battlefleet actions, dozens of frigate actions were fought, and it was reckoned that a British ship could normally be expected to defeat an enemy ship of fifty per cent greater force. Thirty-seven ships of the line were captured during these years, plus dozens of smaller ships. Colonies were captured from the enemy, including St Lucia in the West Indies and the Cape in South Africa. It was an immensely complex war, both politically and strategically, and of much greater scope than anything that had gone before. It is one of the great paradoxes of history that the British seaman, worse treated and more discontented than ever before, and recruited by methods that had been outdated two centuries earlier, fought better than ever and outclassed his enemies, whose conditions (of recruitment at least) were in theory much better.

AMPHIBIOUS WARFARE

The colonial war continued as in the past, though enemy-held colonies were becoming harder than ever to find. The Cape of Good Hope, given back to the Dutch at the peace of 1802, was retaken in 1806. The same squadron then attempted to capture Buenos Aires from Spain, but that was abortive. From 1810, it was possible to reduce the fleet in the West Indies because there were no more enemy colonies to attack. The British fleet continued to range over European seas, and in 1807, at the second Battle of Copenhagen, the Danish capital was bombarded and her fleet interned. An ingenious attack with the use of rockets was made on Rochefort, the third most important of the French bases. In the ten years that followed Trafalgar, Britain found herself, at one time or another, at war with almost every country with any kind of navy, from Turkey in the east to the United States in the west, from Russia in the north to Spain in the south. All in all, the navy found more to do after Trafalgar than ever before.

To break the land/sea stalemate and win the war, the British had to find a way on to the continent of Europe, and an attempt was made on the Dutch island of Walcheren in 1809. Seamen were landed, and as usual they resisted any attempt to impose military discipline:

> The scenes which their eccentricities every hour presented were worthy [of] the pencil of Hogarth. Amongst the most humorous of these were the drills, musters, and marchings, or as they generally called such proceedings, 'playing at soldiers.' All that their officers did had no effect in preserving wither silence or regularity ... the object was not to subject them to that precision of movement by which soldiers are governed, but simply to keep them together when marching from one place to another ...
>
> 'Heads up, you beggar of a corporal there,' a little slang-going Jack would cry out from the rear-rank, well knowing that his diminutive size prevented his being seen by his officers. Then perhaps the man immediately before the wit, in order to show his sense of decorum, would turn round and remark, 'I say, who made you fugleman, Master Billy? Can't you behave like a sodger afore the commander, eh?' Then from another part of the squad would be heard a stentorian roar, and, 'I'll not stand this, if I do — me. Here's this — Murphy sticken a sword in my starn.'

Although unconventional, they were to be a formidable force in action:

> These extraordinary fellows delighted in hunting the *Munseers,* as they called the French, and a more formidable pack was never unkenneled. Armed with a long pole, a pike, a cutlass, and a pistol, they annoyed the French skirmishers in all directions, by their irregular and unexpected attacks. They usually went out in parties, as if they were going to hunt a wild beast, and no huntsman ever followed the chase with more delight. Regularly every day after breakfast ... they would start off to their hunt. They might be seen leaping the dykes by the aid of their poles, or swimming across others, like Newfoundland dogs; and if a few French riflemen appeared in sight, they ran at them helter-skelter, with pistol, cutlass, or pike [and] went to work in good earnest.[109]

From 1808 the navy took on a new commitment. The Spanish and Portuguese revolted against Napoleon's imposition of the Continental System, and British troops were landed in their support. Sir Arthur Wellesley's army was refused permission to land at Corunna by the Spanish, but found a barely adequate landing place at Figuera in Portugal, and reinforcements were later landed by boats in the surf farther south. The role of the seamen is described by Augutus Schaumann, a German staff officer who took part of the landing:

> With beating hearts we approached the first line of surf, and were lifted high up in the air. We clung frantically to our seats, and all of us had to crouch quite low. Not a few closed their eyes and prayed, but I did not close mine before we were actually in the foam of the roaring breakers on the beach. There were twenty to thirty British sailors on the shore, all quite naked, who, at the moment the foremost breakers withdrew, dashed like lightning into the surf, and after many vain efforts, during which they were often caught up and thrown back by the waves, at last succeeded in casting a long rope to us, which we were able to seize. Then with a loud hurrah, they ran at top speed through the advancing breakers up the beach, dragging us with them, until the boat stuck fast and there was only a little spray from the surf to wet us. Finally, seizing a favourable opportunity, when a retreating wave had withdrawn sufficiently far, each of them took a soldier on his back and carried him thus on to the dry shore.[110]

The army, now commanded by Sir John Moore, eventually had to retreat to Corunna, and there Schaumann found himself, quite literally, in the hands of the lower deck yet again:

> We therefore marched out towards the Citadel to the opposite shore, which was very rocky, and over which the breakers were beating furiously. The sloops from the men-o-war could not come up close, but were kept at a safe distance from the rocky boulders by means of their oars, while we had to go to the edge of the rocks which were being washed by the surf, and then, with the water splashing over our heads, take hold of one of the oars. Then we were grabbed by the mighty fists of the sailors, who were leaning overboard, and seized and dragged in like sheep ... At last my turn came, and closing my eyes, I plunged into the breakers. The water rose above my head, sealing both my ears and my eyes, and I felt myself being seized ... We started off immediately, and were flung head over heels on board the first transport, which was already under sail.[111]

Despite the retreat, the British still held the base at Lisbon, and the navy was able to keep the army there supplied over several years of war with food, ammunition, military stores and reinforcements. The Peninsular War, fought brilliantly by Wellington over the next five years, took place against a background of naval supremacy, which allowed British armies and Spanish guerrillas to operate without inland lines of communication. The seaman found plenty of use for his skills in landing artillery and raising it to great heights with the use of ropes, often in cooperation with local guerrillas. On a raid on the north coast of Spain in 1812,

> The sea was at this moment breaking with such violence against the rocks at the foot of the hill that it was doubtful if a boat could be got near enough to land a gun, but an opportunity offered of which Lieut. Groves availed himself with great activity and got the gun up a short distance by a crab, which was so tedious that all the draft bullocks of the army were sent for and 400 men. Captain Bouverie, who was directed to cover this party, landed with some seamen and the gun was dragged to the summit of the hill by 36 pairs of bullocks, 400 guerillas and 100 seamen. It was immediately mounted and fired its first shot at four. This gun was so admirably served that at sunset a practicable breach was made in the wall of the fort ...[112]

Another type of operation which became increasingly common was the 'cutting out' expedition, in which ship's boats were used to raid a small harbor or take a ship moored close inshore. Samuel Stokes of the 98-gun *Dreadnought* was involved in one against a small Spanish ship:

> At three o'clock in the morning, September 9th 1810, we manned nine boat loads to cut the ship out, commanded by the first lieutenant, and pulled directly into Ushant Harbour. I was one of the large cutter's crew this morning, and we was the third boat alongside the ship. The officer of our boat was kill'd about five minutes before we boarded the ship, and the Coxton was wounded with two musket balls in his breast.[113]

They boarded and soon captured the ship, most of the soldiers on board having fled, but as they sailed her out they came under heavy fire from a high promontory on shore. It took two hours to clear the harbour, and after that Stokes went into the cabin to sample the captain's drink, when a hidden Spanish mate crawled out. They took him on deck, where he was amazed at the carnage – 'The sight that was before his eyes struck him with wonder and surprise. Forty five men on the deck killed and wounded and the gangways cover'd with human blood, and that getting cold and congeal'd, was slippery as grease, so that a great many tript up and was stained with blood.'[114]

GREENWICH HOSPITAL

Greenwich Hospital flourished during the war years. Its estates and investments turned in a healthy profit, and the wars naturally created a supply of injured or aged seamen. Benjamin Silliman visited in 1805:

> Our guide was a venerable old pensioner, and wore something like a uniform. I enquired whether it was the badge of his office, as guide through the chapel. The old man's heart was not yet cold to naval pride and the dignity of rank, and while he informed me that this dress was worn by all who had been boatswains, I could read in his face some displeasure at my ignorance of his former consequence.
>
> We walked at leisure under the lofty colonnades and through the extensive courts of the hospital. Every where we met those veterans, who, after encountering the dangers of the ocean and of battle, uninjured, and facing death in its most dreadful forms, are now quietly counting their last sands of life as they run. A comfortable provision for their old age, is an act of common justice, due to them from their country, but, small is this in compensation for a life mercilessly cut off from all the charities of home, and for mutilated limbs, and broken constitutions. Their minds seemed to be very vacant; they were lounging, walking, or playing at cards, or sitting in listless silence. Some of them had but one leg; others none. They were dressed in coarse blue cloth, and appeared to be well provided for.[115]

The hospital gained national prominence in 1806, when Nelson's body lay in state there before his funeral. Meanwhile King George proposed a royal foundation, a school for 700 naval children that would take over the Palladian Queen's House opposite the Hospital. It was extended by adding wings connected by colonnades.

WAR WITH AMERICA

In 1812 there was another break in the Continental System, when Napoleon was obliged to launch his disastrous invasion of Russia; but for the British navy, the most important issue was the war with America, brought on directly by the system of naval recruitment, by the British claim of the right to search neutral ships for deserters and British merchant seamen. The conflict between Britain and America, known generally as the War of 1812, was the only war to result directly from naval manning policy.

Of course it was not easy to tell the difference between a British subject and an American in the days before birth certificates and passports. Certificates could be obtained from American consuls, but these could be forged, and in any case naval officers did not always pay attention to them.

According to Samuel Leech in *Macedonian*:

> Being in want of men, we resorted to the press-gang, which was made up of our most loyal men, armed to the teeth; by their aid we obtained our full number. Among them were a few Americans; they were taken without respect to their protections, which were often taken from them and destroyed. Some were released through the influence of the American consul; others, less fortunate, were carried to sea, to their no small chagrin ... To prevent the recovery of these men by their consul, the press-gang usually went ashore on the night previous to our going to sea; so that before they were missed they were beyond his protection.[116]

Pressing on shore in a British port was one thing, but it was far worse when American ships were stopped at sea to search for British subjects. The most celebrated case involved HMS *Leopard* and USS *Chesapeake* in June 1807, as described in the log of the American ship:

> At _ past 3 the Ship came up with us, back'd the Main Top Sail and Spoke her. was boarded by her. She proved to be the British ship *Leopard* of 50 guns. She came on board to demand some Men who had deserted from the English Navy. The Commodore refusing to give them up, the Boat return'd. they ranged along side of us and Commenc'd a heavy fire. We being unprepared and the Ship much lumber'd – it was impossible to Clear Ship for Action in proper time, though every possible exertion was made, and not suspecting an enemy so near did not begin to clear the Deck untill the enemy had commenc'd firing. In about thirty minutes after receiving much Damage in our Hull, Rigging and Spars, and having three Men killed ... and 16 wounded ... And having one Gun ready fired and haul'd down our Colours, the *Leopard* ceased firing and sent her Boat on board. Muster'd the Ships Company. At Sun down, they left the Ship taking with them 4 men Vizt John Strawn, Daniel Martin, Wm Ware and John Wilson, who had deserted from their Service ...[117]

Attacking an American warship in commission was escalating the dispute between the two countries yet further, and President Jefferson complained, 'A Frigate of the U.S. trusting to a state of peace, and leaving her Harbour on a distant service, has been surprised and attacked by a British Vessel of superior force.' As one American journal put it,

> When vessels are met with on the oceans by British vessels of war; on being boarded, a demand is made of the *roll*, or articles, and the men being mustered, the officer interrogates them, who (if it is bad weather) is generally the sailing-master, or one of his mates, or perhaps a lieutenant; with very little knowledge of mankind, or of national *dialects*, he undertakes to be sole judge, to decide and determine the place of birth of every man on board, their legal testimonials (the place where they embarked being strong *prima facie* evidence) to the

contrary of his opinion notwithstanding; the fate of the men being thus summarily decided, *the condemned* are taken on board the man of war, and turned before the mast. Melancholy prospect, the worst of slavery, *to fight for their oppressors!* [118]

War finally broke out in 1812. Things could go very badly for British seamen caught on the wrong side. John Erving was a 23-year-old sailmaker, apparently born in Newcastle upon Tyne but resident in the United States since 1800 and serving in the American frigate *Essex*. According to his account,

> All hands were pipe'd to muster when Capt Porter (Capt of said Frigate) told the hands they were called up to take the oath of allegiance to the Unites States, and gave them to understand that any men who did not chuse to take the oath should be discharged, that when the deponent's name was called, he told Capt Porter that he, the deponent, could not take the oath as required, being a British subject, on which Capt Porter called the Petty Officers and said to them, that they must pass sentence on him, the deponent, on which the said Petty Officers put him in the Launch which was along side the Frigate and there put a bucket of tar on him, and after which laid on him a quantity of feathers. They then rowe'd the said Launch stern formost on shore on New York island and put him on shore, but whereabouts deponent does not know as he was never here before. That deponent went from Street to Street naked from the waist up, smear'd with Tar & feathers, not knowing where to go …

Eventually he was taken into protective custody by the local magistrates, and shipped to Halifax. [119]

The British were complacent after years of defeating the French, and perhaps the easy success against the unprepared *Chesapeake* had given them false confidence. There was a series of defeats of British frigates against superior American ships. In October the 38-gun *Macedonian* accepted battle with the 44-gun *United States,* though Samuel Leech was aware that the American ship was 'larger in size, heavier in metal, more numerous in men, and stronger built than the *Macedonian*'. He describes his feelings in the action:

> I felt pretty much as I suppose everyone does at such a time. That men are without thought when they stand among the dying and the dead, is too absurd an idea to be entertained a moment. We all appeared cheerful, and I know that many a serious thought ran through my mind; still, what could we do but keep up a semblance, at least, of animation? To run from our quarters would have been certain death from the hands of our officers; to give way to gloom, or to show fear, would do no good, and might brand us with the name of cowards, and ensure certain defeat. Our only true philosophy, therefore, was to make

The Point of Honor.

Above: A flogging, showing the marines parading on the poop to intimidate the seamen, who are arranged in far less formal fashion on the quarterdeck. The intended victim is lashed to a grating and the boatswain's mate is about to start when another man pulls off his shirt and confesses to the offence. (NMM PU0177)

Right: 'The Sailor's description of a sea fight', showing a typical form of recreation round a mess table. (The Trustees of the British Museum)

Above: Marryat's view of the early evening as the watch is set. The seaman at the helm and the others on deck wear heavy coats, but the young midshipman is underdressed in the rain, as is the black servant arriving with a flask. (NMM PU4723)

Below: Ships in the harbour at Corunna, with boats carrying troops from the shore. (NMM PZ0007)

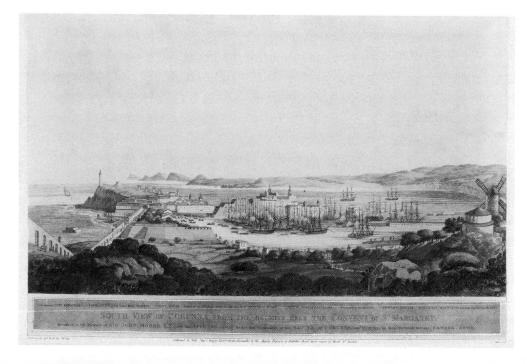

Above: Seamen landing guns. This is on Corsica in 1794, but it might represent many actions of the period. (NMM PY2355)

Right: John Rosedale, a guide or 'exhibitor', shows unappreciative visitors round the Painted Hall at Greenwich. (NMM PY3321)

JOHN ROSEDALE, MARINER.
Exhibitor of the Hall of
GREENWICH HOSPITAL.

Entered according to act of Congress.

A. Bowen, del. et sc.

THE UNITED STATES AND MACEDONIAN.

Above: The *Macedonian* is
dismasted and is about to be
taken by the *United States*.
(NMM PU5825)

Right: The Algiers
centrepiece, showing
seamen fighting natives, and
liberated slaves. (NMM
B9054-4)

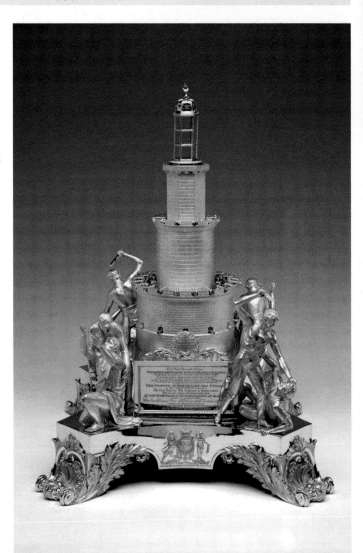

REEFING TOPSAILS.

Above: Seamen reefing a topsail with the studding sail boom lashed up out of the way and a man's hat blowing away. (NMM PW3760)

Right : The Prince of Wales's sailor's suit of 1846 was already close to the pattern that would become familiar. (F4848-001)

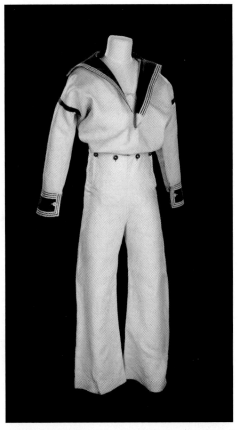

Above: The Battle of Navarino, with the *Genoa* engaging Turkish ships. (NMM PW4813)

Above: The gundeck of the *Excellent* around 1840 showing men at gun drill, and a stage in the evolution of the seaman's dress. (Royal Naval Museum)

Below: The boilers of HMS *Retribution* launched in 1844, with stokers at work. (Science Museum Archive)

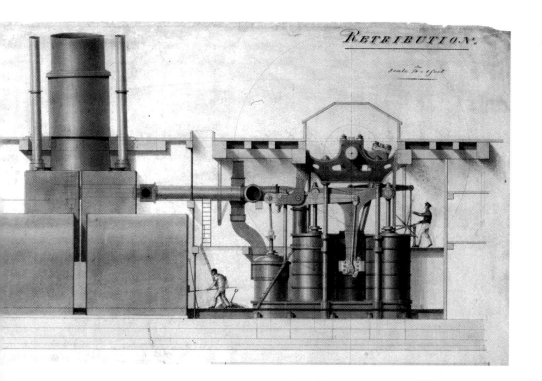

1ˢᵗ Class of Petty Officers.
Master at Arms, or Quarter Master.

London: Printed & Published by Engelmann Graf Coindet & Co. 9? Dean St Soho. Nov 1828

Above: A first class petty officer in 1828, wearing the crown and anchor badge on his left sleeve. (NMM PW4195)

the best of our situation, by fighting bravely and cheerfully. I thought a great deal, however, of the other world; every groan, every falling man, told me that the next instant I might be before the Judge of all the earth.[120]

He was soon involved in an intense fight:

Grape and canister shot were pouring through our portholes like leaden rain, carrying death in their trail. The large shot came against the ship's side like iron hail, shaking her to the very keel, or passing through her timbers and scattering terrific splinters, which did a more appalling work than even their own death-giving blows ...

Suddenly the rattling of the iron hail ceased. We were ordered to cease firing. A profound silence ensued, broken only by the stifled groans of the brave sufferers below. It was soon ascertained that the enemy had shot ahead to repair damages, for she was not so disabled but she could sail without difficulty, while we were so cut up that we lay utterly helpless ...

A council of war was now held among the officers on the quarter deck. Our condition was perilous in the extreme; victory or escape was alike hopeless ... The enemy would without doubt bear down on us in a few moments, and as she could now choose her own position, she would without doubt rake us fore and aft ... it was determined to strike out bunting. This was done by the hands of a brave fellow named Watson, whose saddened brow told how severely it pained his lion heart to do it. To me it was a pleasing sight, for I had seen fighting enough for one Sabbath; more than I wished to see again on a week day. His Britannic Majesty's frigate *Macedonian* was now the prize of the American frigate *United States*.[121]

Leech joined the US Navy but escaped detection when he was subsequently captured by the British. The British finally defeated an American frigate when *Shannon* took on *Chesapeake* in 1813 and captured her after a very short engagement. Meanwhile they fought a war on the Great Lakes for the defence of Canada, raided the half-built city of Washington and burned what became known as the White House, as well as landing as far south as New Orleans. The war was settled by negotiation at the end of 1814, without any of the main issues being addressed.

THE END OF THE FRENCH WARS

By 1813 a new coalition was organised against the French Emperor, and in 1814 it invaded France and succeeded in overthrowing him. The *coup de grâce* was of course administered by the armies of Britain and her allies, but the victory was the result of a long-term naval campaign. After eleven years of war, the demobilisation of the navy began – only to be halted when Napoleon escaped from exile in Elba and began a new war. The issue of peace or war was one of many that divided the lower deck from the quarterdeck. The crew of *Grampus* were sailing home from South Africa with full expectation of being discharged, when they heard from a passing ship that Napoleon had escaped and resumed the war.

> Nothing could exceed the joy of the officers, and the vexation of the crew, at this piece of information. The former dreaded a peace because it would place many of them on half-pay; while the chances of war inspired them with hopes of promotion; hence they ran alongside almost every ship in the fleet shouting, 'Have you heard the news? Bonaparte has got to Paris with sixty thousand men!' Really, some of them seemed crazy with joy at the idea of a protracted war. Not so, however, the seamen; they longed for peace, since war only brought them hard usage, wounds and death. While, therefore, the officers were rejoicing, they were muttering curses and oaths, wishing Bonaparte and his army to perdition.[122]

Napoleon was soon defeated at Waterloo and surrendered to HMS *Bellerophon*, still carrying Landsman Bartholomew Hughes, unpromoted after twelve years. Europe entered a long era of relative peace. The seamen were discharged and went home to face new problems of slump and unemployment. No one knew it at the time, but the press gang would never be needed again.

7

The LONG PEACE
1815 to 1850

AFTER THE WAR

Following their euphoria at being paid off, the seamen soon found themselves in a harsh economic climate. The navy was reduced from 145,000 men in 1814 to 19,000 in 1817. During more than twenty years of war the merchant marine had had the chance to train thousands of men to replace those who had been pressed, and it was not expanding – it consisted of some 20,000 ships (between 2 and 2.5 million tons) until it began to grow in the 1840s, while the level of world trade remained static.[1] A man like Samuel Stokes had great difficulty in finding work.[2] Some seamen perhaps drifted towards the growing body of industrial workers, which was just beginning to take on the title, and perhaps the attitudes, of the 'working class'. Its consciousness was confirmed by events such as the 'Peterloo Massacre' in Manchester in 1819, when eleven people were killed and about 400 wounded by a charge of yeomanry cavalry. But the seaman of the time was still apolitical and was generally distant from such working-class campaigns.

As well as the working-class troubles, the period also saw the accelerated rise of the middle classes, but that was not entirely reflected in the navy. There were far fewer active-service posts for officers, and those that did exist tended to go to the well-connected. New entrants were fewer but came increasingly from the upper classes. Between 1814 and 1849, nearly 18 per cent of new quarterdeck candidates were from titled families; it had been 12 per cent during the war. The proportion from the landed gentry, however, remained almost constant at a little over a quarter, while the professional classes increased their share slightly to 54 per cent. But business and commercial men fell from nearly 4 per cent to almost nothing, while the 6.7 per cent from working-class origins during the wars was eliminated completely. The peacetime navy was more aristocratic, and its officer corps represented only the professional half of the middle classes, not the commercial half. Meanwhile the old route to the quarterdeck via the lower deck was completely closed. John Kingcombe is often cited as the last man to 'come up through the hawse hole' in this way, in 1818, but the facts of his career do not entirely bear it out. He did indeed enter as a second class volunteer', the current term for 'ship's boy' who was not a candidate for midshipman, in 1808, but he was soon promoted by Captain Frederick Maitland and was a lieutenant by 1815. Another source of officers was from young mates pressed from merchant ships in wartime, who already had some knowledge of navigation and could fit in as masters' mates or midshipmen. Men like that were sometimes driven towards the navy by poverty and unemployment in peacetime but got no promotion. John Bechervaise was a well-educated and literate man, who had even commanded a small merchant ship before he joined the navy and was consistently loyal to his officers afterwards. Yet he was never promoted beyond quartermaster.

The status of the warrant officer promoted from the lower deck was declining. Officers of professional origin – surgeons, pursers and chaplains – already enjoyed the comforts of the wardroom, and from 1843 their standing was increased when they were given commissions signed by the Queen. The boatswains, carpenters and gunners gained no such advantages, and these ranks became less attractive. By the 1850s it was often complained that the extra pay did not compensate for the cost of a uniform. All this meant that the lower deck seaman had a shorter career path for the rest of the century – commissioned rank was barred to him, and a warrant was less desirable.

Despite the benefits of Greenwich Hospital, plenty of men in seaman's dress were to be seen begging on the streets of London. The public was warned, 'not, however, to conclude that because a fellow sports a jacket and trowsers, he must have been a seaman; for there are many fresh-water sailors, who never saw a ship, but from London Bridge'.[3] But there were genuine cases. Joseph Johnson was a negro who had only served in merchant ships and was not eligible for Greenwich. He gained fame by touring the streets with a model of the ship *Nelson* on his head, which could 'give the appearance of sea motion' when he nodded his head. Another negro seaman, Charles McGee, born in Jamaica in 1744, haunted Ludgate Hill: 'He has lost an eye, and his woolly hair, which is almost white, is tied up behind in a tail, with a large tuft at the end, horizontally resting on the cape of his coat. Charles is supposed to be worth money.'[4]

John Bechervaise tried desperately to find a ship. 'Again I advertised, save peace was just spreading her silver wings; transports were useless, and shipping in general unemployed; no success attended my second advertisement ...'[5] He tried France, for as a Jersey man he spoke the language fluently; but he had no luck. Back in London,

> A few days alone were sufficient to convince me that I must not long remain at home; I looked round the docks, nothing was stirring; if there was any difference it was even worse than before I left England. In my rambles I saw men who had been to my knowledge masters and chief mates of vessels, who would now gladly have gone before the mast ... the immense number of men discharged from ships of war who had foolishly spent their money and now got into deep distress strolling about the streets, some begging, others worse, was truly painful to those who possessed any feeling. One man I can never forget, a fine, stout athletic man of very seamanlike appearance was not begging, for the law forbade it, he was singing with a fine open manly voice expressive of feeling ... when the song ended the poor creature collected a few half pence from the crowd that had gathered to listen to him; it was a subsistence, but a wretched one ...[6]
>
> In the latter end of April I observed bills posted up for seamen and petty officers for His Majesty's ship R____, of eighty guns; for a moment and only for a moment the bills took my attention, but when I looked round at my real situation, scanned the future, my thoughts seemed to return to those bills. There certainly was in that moment some divine interposition, for ... I have never looked back with regret. Of all the places then dreaded by seamen in the merchant service, a ship of war is the most. I fully had my share of the prejudice, but there was no alternative; I mentioned to my family my idea of seeking in a ship of war, that support I could meet with no where else. Painful indeed was my parting from home. May the 6th, 1820, early in the morning, I passed by the R____, then fitting out, and for the first time in my life saw the monstrous fabric that was to be my residence for several years, with a shudder of grief I cannot describe.[7]

He went on board the ship by hired boat, and on asking to enter he was examined by a lieutenant:

> Never, oh never while I breathe shall I forget the scrutinizing look he gave me, it seemed to search my very soul, and speak volumes; but I stood unawed; like a gamester, it was my last cast, on that game depended my all, perhaps my life. Satisfied with his penetration, Lieutenant S____ asked me a great many questions about seamanship, was satisfied with the answers I gave, and received and victualled me. I commenced duty as a first class petty officer in His Majesty's navy.[8]

Recruiting methods were as primitive as ever, and despite mass unemployment an individual captain might have trouble manning his ship.

In 1818, William Dillon took command of the frigate *Phaeton* at Portsmouth but soon found 'volunteers did not come in freely'. He set up a rendezvous on the Thames under two midshipmen and had his own lodgings at Havant, just outside Portsmouth, while the ship was fitted out:

> It was here that I was accosted almost every morning by a seaman, sometimes two, who expressed a desire to enter for the *Phaeton*, but they could not, they said, find their way to the ship without a little cash. I would then give each of them a shilling with a line to the First lieutenant desiring him to receive them. But those fellows coolly pocketed the money, never in one instance going to Portsmouth. I lost at least £10 in that way, and at last refused giving any more shillings.

If that is literally true, it means he gave the money to 200 seamen and suggests an almost incredible degree of gullibility. In any case, the ship eventually sailed after more than three months and was 40 men short of a complement of 250. Returning to Portsmouth two months later, Dillon managed to recruit more men by paying local watermen to find them. Two or three musicians applied to join as the ship's band, but by this time Dillon was wise enough to turn down their request for money to buy instruments. Then some of his recruits turned out to be deserters from the Royal Irish Regiment. Dillon was humiliated as the army insisted on searching his ship, while the men themselves apparently made their escape by shore boat.[9]

THE ATTACK ON ALGIERS

It was just as difficult to man a squadron for a special operation. In 1816, Lord Exmouth, already famous as a frigate captain, prepared an expedition against the corsairs of Algiers. He had difficulty with his own flagship at Portsmouth and in July reported, 'I have just come on shore after mustering the ship's company of the *Queen Charlotte* which I find about 200 short including sixty who from infirmity, age and wounds are quite unfit for the service.' These included John Smith, a crippled sail-maker, Andrew Stephenson, an AB with poor eyesight, and several boys who had enrolled as landsmen. The depot ships and guard ships were stripped of all but the most essential petty officers. Fifteen volunteers were found in London, but two of them deserted at Godalming on the way south. After two weeks of this, Exmouth set sail for Plymouth where, the Admiralty assured him, he would find more men. He did, but after he sailed from there he had to transfer many of them between one ship and another, which was much more difficult as they sailed along to take advantage of a favourable wind. It was not likely to please those who had exercised their peacetime privilege of joining a particular ship.[10]

Exmouth joined forces with a Dutch squadron also on the way to Algiers, their combined force making a total of 632 cannon. When the Algerians refused Exmouth's demands, he bombarded the city, and the Algerians gave up and agreed to release 1,642 slaves, 18 of whom were British and 28 Dutch. According to Lieutenant James Hall,

> On being put on board the Transport they ascended the rigging and yards and seemed to be in a delirium of joy. The transition from slavery to liberty was so sudden at thing, so unexpected, that it seemed to these poor men as a dream ... They all looked healthy, were very clean and well clothed. Very different from what we expected to see, and infinitely superior to prisoners in England or France.[11]

In art at least, the lower deck contribution to the affair was recognised. A silver-gilt centrepiece presented to Lord Exmouth showed seamen in each corner, two of them in the act of fighting Algerians, the other two liberating grateful captives. A print showed a carronade crew in action, with a well-dressed black seaman helping out, perhaps because another had been killed.[12] It could not have escaped the notice of the anti-slavery campaigners that here was a black man risking his life to free white slaves. Indeed, the navy was already being drawn into a much longer and far-reaching campaign off the coasts of Africa.

SUPPRESSING THE SLAVE TRADE

Britain abolished the slave trade in 1807 and was followed by other countries in this, but slavery was not easy to suppress. Three thousand miles of West African coastline had to be patrolled, and there were rarely more than half a dozen frigates and sloops to do it. There was little international cooperation and a ship could hoist false colours to escape capture. The United States abolished the trade at the same time as Britain, but after the War of 1812 the right of the British to search American ships was a sore point. Until 1835 it was necessary for a ship to be actually carrying slaves for it to be condemned; after that, it could be seized if it was carrying other evidence, such as chains and manacles or unusually extensive cooking arrangements and water.

The patrols often led to exciting chases, especially after faster naval ships were sent to the station in the 1830s. The capture could be a nauseating as well as a satisfactory experience, as with HMS *Tartar* in 1821. The slaves below decks were,

> clinging to the gratings to inhale a mouthful of fresh air, and fighting with each other for a taste of water, showing their parched tongues, and pointing to their reduced stomachs as if overcome by famine, for although the living cargo had only been completed the day before, yet many who had been longer on board were reduced to living skeletons ...[13]

There were many questions about how effective the patrols were, and in fact the number of slaves actually increased during the period, due to extra demand from Brazil and Cuba. An enquiry of 1845 concluded that the squadron should be increased, and by 1846 it comprised 25 vessels, including five steamers.

There is no lower deck account of the operations against the slave trade from this period, perhaps because comparatively few men served in it – about a thousand at any one time in the 1820s and 1830s, about three thousand in the 1840s. But there is plenty of evidence that the service was disliked by officers but popular with the seamen, and Commander C. W. Riley testified in 1849:

> It is the monotony of the service that is felt more than anything else; we are much cut off from correspondence with home, and we have none of the relaxations of more favoured stations. With the seamen it is very popular. You can at any time get 200 or 300 of the best men in the service willing to go there.[14]

The report concluded, 'Seamen volunteer for Her Majesty's vessels on the African station with greater alacrity than for any others; the reason being stated to be, that the station is considered to be one of activity and hope.'[15] It was also felt that it was good training for general naval service:

> some of the witnesses have delivered an opinion, that the service on the west coast of Africa, on account of the climate and other causes, is not favourable for the training of officers and seamen of the Royal Navy, it is palpable, on the other hand, that under the circumstances of the subdivision into small vessels, and the active nature of the service ... the tendency to form officers and seamen is likely to be at least equal to the average in the navy actually afloat, composed as it is to a great extent of heavy ships, lying long in harbours, and not engaged in operations against anything in the nature of an enemy at sea.[16]

On the positive side, anti-slavery operations offered some chance of head money for the numbers of slaves released, useful in an age when prize money was not available. It could be substantial for a successful ship, and the distribution was less inequitable in a vessel with a small crew – the able seamen of *Waterwitch* had £178 each from 1839–43, compared with the captain's £2,628.[17] On the down side, the station was very unhealthy. Between 1825 and 1845 an average of 54.4 men per thousand died, compared with 18.1 in the West Indies and 9.8 at home. Most of this was accounted for by a few major epidemics, in 1828–9 and 1837–8. It could often be hard in individual ships: for example, in 1841, 25 men out of 141 in *Wolverine* died, and a sixth of *Saracen*'s company died in two and a half years.[18] One officer wrote in 1849:

> Among seamen I believe the African Preventive Service to be generally popular. The frequent excitement of chasing; the variety of boat service; the relaxation of the prize-crews; and the prospect of prize-money at the end of the commission, are so many inducements to men to serve on the African coast. Certain it is, that men are found to serve again and again there, frequently volunteering to remain out when their vessels are ordered home. And I believe it to be a fact, that on a small vessel being commissioned for Africa, her crew is generally completed in a few days at farthest.[19]

CHOOSING A SHIP

The years after 1815 were a golden age for seamen who wanted to choose their ship – the press gang was no longer in active use, and the custom of 'turning over' was less common. According to John Bechervaise,

> A seaman on entering the Navy has every opportunity of choosing his ship, so that he can find no excuse for returning [running?] from it. If he finds his ship different to his expectation, the time is limited; he knows that the end is fast approaching, when he will be free to seek another. It is not now as it was in the days gone by when perhaps, just returned from a long and arduous voyage, he is seated at the fireside with his prattling child on his knees, or worse by far, torn from the very bed of his wife to share the perils of the ocean, and brave the battle.[20]

Naval recruitment was spread very unevenly round the country, and there was no rendezvous in Scotland – Queen Victoria herself later became aware of this and wrote to the First Lord of the Admiralty to suggest that the setting up of a naval establishment at Leith would be 'very popular in Scotland, and by making the Queen's Navy known there, which it hardly is at present, would open a new field for recruiting our marine'.[21] Because of the lack of such a recruiting station in 1826, Charles McPherson had to go south by steamship. Though brought up inland, he had acquired seaman's clothes and a sea chest.

My mind was so taken up with building castles in the air, that I scarcely cast a thought on the friends and relations I had left behind, till after I had got into the steam-boat for Liverpool, and was a number of miles down the Firth of Clyde ... I almost began to repent of the step I had taken, when one of the men who had noticed me a little active in assisting to work the vessel, called, 'Ho, there! *Sailor!* Lend a hand here to coil down this hawser, will ye?' I sprang to the spot; and there, in coiling down the rope, I forgot the time that I had any person belonging to me on the face of the earth. Indeed the term '*Sailor*,' ... had almost an electric effect on me ... and really I thought myself, 'Ay, every inch a *sailor*.'[22]

He found a mixed group in the rendezvous at Liverpool:

At about one o'clock, I came to a house facing the wharf, decorated over the door with the royal arms, and having underneath in large letters the words 'NAVAL RENDEZVOUS.' I made no pause, but bolted in, when I suddenly found myself in the heart of a singular and heterogeneous group, from tradesmen of all descriptions down to tinkers, from worn-out dandies of all sorts down to Johnny Raws from the country, who, with hobnailed shoes, gaping mouths, and staring eyes, laughed out loud at every sally of the quartermaster, whose ridiculous stories were repeatedly interrupted by draughts from some of the mugs that stood near him, prefaced by 'Your health, my lad! I can see in you the making of a true British sailor!' I sat down on the end of a bench near the door, but had not waited long when the quartermaster came up to me, and asked if I wanted a ship. I told him I did. 'Then,' says he, 'you could not choose to enter at a better time: there's the *Java* double bank frigate, as fine a frigate as ever swam the salt sea – ain't she, Harris?'

But Harris claimed that *Java* was 'hell afloat' and the 74-gun *Genoa* was about to sail for Lisbon. 'That's the ship for me,' said McPherson.[23] He went on board the tender *Bittern* to await drafting, but that did not necessarily mean he would go to the ship he had chosen. Word soon spread around *Bittern* that a draft was imminent, the men were summoned on to the quarterdeck and names were read out. McPherson's was sixth on the list. He listened anxiously for his far more experienced friend Riley's name to be called, but it was not. He asked Riley if there was any possibility for an exchange to keep them together, but was told in a sullen manner, 'I did not know the rules of the service so well as him, or I would not be axing him such d—d fool questions.' McPherson was annoyed, until he saw the tear in Riley's eye. Thus he was drafted to *Reynard*.[24]

LIFE ON BOARD

John Bechervaise admitted that in the past, 'The dread of a man of war was next to a French prison', but things had changed by the 1820s:

The wonderful improvements which have taken place render the navy superior beyond compare to any merchant vessel. It is possible the pay may be a little less, that I allow, but taking into consideration the regularity of diet, routine of duty, and comfort of the whole system, it makes up for everything, and pensions for old age.[25]

During his service in the brig *Bittern,* the brig-sloop *Reynard* and *Genoa* in the late 1820s, Seaman Charles McPherson lived a life that was not much different from his predecessors. The country was at peace for most of the time, though McPherson did experience one great battle under sail. His companions were all volunteers rather than pressed men, except for six smugglers who had been sent on board by the courts.[26] But, as in the ships of the Napoleonic Wars a dozen years earlier, there were good and bad officers. Captain Bathurst of *Genoa* was 'greatly beloved by the whole crew, who looked upon him as a father, and who always found in him a ready refuge from injustice and oppression'. His successor, Captain Dickenson, was a fine sailor, who also 'dispensed justice alike on man and messmate'.[27] The captain of *Bittern*, on the other hand, refused to listen to any appeal for justice:

'Hold your mutinous tongue, sir!' cried the commander, in a tone that forbade any more expostulation on the part of the accused. 'I'd take Mr Nightingale's word before your oath, and if I hear any more of this work going on, by G—, I'll see your back bone, you rascal! ... ' I must say that this example of arbitrary power did not add to my good opinion of the service. I plainly saw that a seaman had no chance against an officer, even allowing him to be in the right ...[28]

There were immature midshipmen, including one whose prank seriously injured the gunner's son.[29] There were superstitious seamen, who believed that an old German sailor named De Squaw had 'connexion with the other world, and, in short, was blamed for every good or bad action that was done in the ship'.[30] He saw or took part in fights below deck, drunken orgies and the solidarity of messmates. There were nine women on board, perhaps a throwback to a slightly earlier age.[31]

McPherson was ordered aloft for the first time after only a few days on board to untangle a pennant, much to his horror:

I took my time in going aloft, till I was goaded by the voice of the commander telling me to lift my feet, for that I moved up the rigging like a d—d Russian bear. I mended my pace a little, and at last arrived at the puttock shrouds. Here I made a dead halt, and cast my eyes downwards as if to a place to which I was never again to descend. I saw the whole crew assembled on deck, and had their eyes fixed on me. I was just on the point of turning back, when I was again arrested by the same commanding voice, ordering the boatswain's mate, Sinnet, to go aloft, and *start* me. I did not, at this time, know the meaning of this order, but I suspected it imported no good. I therefore, no sooner saw the *flesh-carpenter* set foot on the lower rattlin than I ... began to make my way (back [facing] downwards) over the toprim. I got into the topmast rigging, and when near the mast-head looked down, and saw my driver standing in the top with a piece of stout rope in his hand, about half a fathom in length, which he no doubt meant to exercise over my back, if I had given him an opportunity. There were no ratlines on the topgallant rigging, and again I was at fault. Sinnet told me to shin up the topgallant shrouds, in a low voice, that I thought was meant to encourage me. I accordingly made my way up, and getting to the royal stay, I got my feet round it, and, grasping it with my hands, slid down till I reached the place where the pennant was foul of it. There was only one turn on the stay; it was easily cleared; but when I looked back to the main-top-gallant-mast-head. I found it would be no easy job to hoist myself, by my hands and feet, back again to the place I left. I therefore now, having gained a little confidence, thought I had better let myself go right down the stay ... which would land me at the fore-top-mast-head. I did this, and, landing at the mast-head I soon arrived in safety on deck. ... This transaction gave so much confidence in myself that I never afterwards hesitated a moment in doing my duty aloft.[32]

Bechervaise describes a week in the life of a ship of the line, 'which in a ship of war may be taken as a sample of three or more years'.[33] On Sunday there were divisions, at which every man was expected to be neatly dressed. 'The clothing of each man must be particularly clean, not a speck to be visible; of late years cropped hair has superseded long tails, and blacking and brushes have found their way into the navy.'[34] Then there was a service. Chaplain Pascoe Grenfell Hill was quite pleased with the behaviour of the crew of the frigate *Winchester* in 1844:

> When the state of the weather is favourable to congregating on the upper deck, the benches used by the men in their messes are brought up and placed in order, under the screen of flags and awnings; and the assemblage of the whole ship's company, on the wide main and under the open sky, raising their united prayer to Him 'who alone spreadeth out the heavens and ruleth the raging sea, who hath compassed the waters with bounds until day and night come to an end,' produces an impressive effect. The outward decorum of deportment in naval congregations may bear little comparison with that which prevails in churches on shore. A liberal supply of bibles and prayer-books is provided by the Admiralty for the use of sailors ...[35]

On Monday, Bechervaise's crew had great-gun practice and exercise with muskets and cutlasses. Every Tuesday there was boat exercise, sometimes with a large group of boats from different ships: 'They certainly form a pretty mosquito fleet; so at least I fancied ... while steering the launch of the beautiful *A*—, in the Tagus, and leading the van of a numerous squadron, I fancied myself a personage of some importance.'[36] The rest of the week also followed a routine:

> Wednesday is the day for sail exercise, at least so it was in the *A*— and she was allowed by all who were competent judges, to be the best regulated ship in commission since the peace. The whole of the forenoon is spent in reefing, furling, and shifting the whole suit of sails, and perhaps the topsail yards may be sent down and up again once or twice. Thursday making and mending clothes occupies the whole day, when Jack has a fair opportunity of repairing damages in his kitt, and preparing for any future examination; also of examining his ditty bag, and having a view of all the presents he had had from his friends or sweetheart ere he left home, and reading over the love letters of Poll and Sue. Friday is general quarters, when every gun in the ship is manned and exercised; sometimes fired with a shot at a target, at others with blank cartridge ... Saturday, is a general cleaning day below, whitewashing the holds, cockpits, &c., evening comes, 'sling clean hammocks,' and thus ends the week ...[37]

Mess-table life continued as before, and Chaplain Hill of *Winchester* reported,

> One peculiar characteristic of society on shipboard is the tone of hilarity often kept up to a pitch which might elsewhere appear inconvenient and overstrained ... It would be, however, a great mistake to conclude, from any apparent levity of disposition, that sailors are a peculiarly thoughtless class. On the contrary, few men are more prone to moods and deep and serious reflection ...[38]

From the inside, McPherson describes some mess-table banter, probably timeless in its content and style:

> 'Well, d'ye see, when I was on board — d—me! what are you laughing at, Smith? Do you think I was coming out with "THE TREMENDOUS" again?' 'I did,' said Smith, 'but get on; I'll promise not to laugh any more.' 'Well, don't then,' said Jack, 'or I'm blessed if I hawl another word out of me this watch. Well, d'ye see, when I was on board the *Barfleur* in the West *Ingees* under old Tommy Harvey, we had a rum time of it; for he was a real Tartar. He was none of your wishy washy old women; for if a man came before him once, he was as sure of his five dozen as he had his biscuit to crack for dinner, and you know that's always sure. (Come, come, Smith; none of your half laughs and purser's grins, for I doesn't like 'em.)'[39]

Sailors still had no right to shore leave, and everything depended on the officers in charge. Admiral Sir George Cockburn believed that they could only want it for two purposes – to get drunk or to desert – while Sir Thomas Hardy had a habit of allowing his men to go on shore, one watch at a time, for up to 48 hours. 'The result was that, at the end of ten days or a fortnight, only about one-half availed themselves of the privilege, for they had spent their money, enjoyed their fun, and experienced no particular amusement in strolling about the streets.' When the ships sailed after a spell of this, there were some murmurs of dissatisfaction among the men raising the anchor. They had heard that two of their number had deserted, and this was seen as a breach of faith with their officers. At last, 'loud cheers were heard, and the two missing men were seen fast approaching in a bumboat'.[40] But after returning home from months abroad and victory in battle, the men of *Genoa* were not allowed to land at Plymouth: 'We had no liberty ashore, notwithstanding the length of time we had been away, and the action in which we had been engaged. Our captain, however, was himself regularly ashore all day ...'[41] When they did get ashore, the men often showed contempt for foreign customs, as when they watched a religious ceremony in Lisbon:

> We kept our hats on, and paid no more respect to the procession as it passed than if we had been a body of Musselmen; some of our men, indeed, indicated their contempt of it by squirting forth unmitigated floods of tobacco juice. The Portuguese cast us many an angry look, and doubtless mingled execrations at us in their prayers ...[42]

DRESS

According to Bechervaise there was some improvement in the seaman's dress in the 1820s:

> During the first six years of my naval career provisions and very rough clothing were all that was issued in a ship of war; blue jackets of the coarsest kind, with black horn buttons, on which was stamped a foul anchor, and 'sailor bold' for a motto; duck frocks and trousers, the trousers cut by a machine and double the size for a moderate man; and the frocks scarcely half long enough with a coarse felt hat, that you might bend into any shape, and easily restore; check shirts with a collar one-and-a-half inches deep, and these very dear, completed the catalogue of clothes which the seaman possessed.[43]

Since 1757 it had been customary for the purser to charge fifteen per cent on top of the cost price of each item, with five per cent going to the purser and the rest covering official expenses. That was reduced to ten per cent by an order of 1820. In 1823 a committee looked at the issue of clothing and found that the amount spent on it was increasing, from just under £17,000 in 1819 to more than twice that in 1822.⁴⁴ Bechervaise, for one, was satisfied with the improvement in quality:

> Now, see the difference; cloth, flannel and duck, all of good quality, silk handkerchiefs, drawers, in fact every article of dress necessary for a man at his entry ... The prices are so moderate, that it would be quite impossible for anyone ashore to get them at the same price.⁴⁵

A new style of seaman's dress was beginning to emerge. Prints of the 1820s often show seamen wearing broad collars on their shirts. Some were white with blue stripes running parallel to the collar, or at right angles to it. A dark blue collar with one or two white stripes round the edges was becoming increasingly common, though it is difficult to tell how far this was what the purser issued, and how far it was the seaman's own taste. The same prints tend to show the seamen in more uniform dress than in the past, suggesting that captains were imposing some order. Captain Charles Austen mustered his crew at divisions in 1828 and noticed, 'the Men in White Frocks the Crown and Anchor worked in Blue on the Petty Officers'.⁴⁶ By the late 1830s the collar seems to have acquired its characteristic v-neck, often worn outside a white shirt or blouse and with a large square shape at the back. By the 1840s, the men in *Excellent* were shown wearing identical white 'frocks' with blue collars.⁴⁷ Trends towards uniformity were reinforced by the crew of the royal yachts, and in 1846 Queen Victoria had a sailor suit made for the Prince of Wales in this style. It was also perhaps taken up by the owners of private yachts and by captains in the navy. By the middle of the century the dark blue, square-backed, v-necked collar with at least one white stripe round it was worn by most naval seamen; an official uniform still lay some way in the future.

NAVAL REMINISCENCES

The 1820s saw a wave of naval publishing about the recent war. There were histories such as William James's monumental work, which saw it through the eyes of the officers. Captain Frederick Marryat's famous series of novels started with *The Naval Officer* in 1829 and generally saw the service as an opportunity for adventure for young men. Marryat did deal with the lower deck to a certain extent in *Poor Jack*, but his favourite characters were young midshipmen, especially in his most famous work,

Mr Midshipman Easy. They appealed to the growing number of middle-class boys and were hugely popular.

A Statement of Certain Immoral Practises, published anonymously in 1822, gave a far less rosy picture:

> It has become an established practice in the British Navy to admit, and even to invite, on board our ships of war, immediately after their arrival in port, as many prostitutes as the men, and, in many cases, the officers may choose to entertain, to the number, in the larger ships, of several hundred at a time; all of whom remain on board, domesticated with the ship's company, men and boys, until they again put to sea. The tendency of this practice is to render a ship of war, while in port, a continual scene of riot and disorder, of obscenity and blasphemy, of drunkenness, lewdness and debauchery. During this time, the married seamen are frequently joined by their wives and families (sometimes comprising daughters from ten to fifteen years of age), who are forced to submit to the alternative of mixing with these abandoned women, whose language and behaviour are usually of the most polluting description; or of foregoing altogether the society of their husbands and parents. They all inhabit the same deck, where, whatever be their age or sex or character, they are huddled promiscuously together, eating, drinking and sleeping, without any adequate means of inspection or privacy, for the most part even without the slightest screen between their births [*sic*]; where, in the sight and hearing of all around them, they live in the unrestrained indulgence of every licentious propensity which may be supposed to actuate inmates of this description.[48]

Much of the concern was about the effect on young midshipman: 'Little do the parents of the poor boys, who go on board as midshipmen, know into what a furnace they plunge their sons, and to what profligacy they expose them, when they send them into the naval service ...'[49]

Lower deck memoirs began with John Nicol's in 1822. He was found destitute in Edinburgh by the publisher John Howell, who wrote his story down and had it published by the well-known firm of Blackwood's. Nicol had had his life ruined by the need to evade the press gang during the Napoleonic War – Howell found him 'walking feebly along, with an old apron tied round his waist, in which he carried a few small pieces of coal he had picked up in wandering through the streets'. Despite this, Nicol was not bitter about naval life: 'Old as I am, my heart is still unchanged and were I young and stout as I have been, again would I sail upon discovery; but, weak and stiff, I can only send my prayers with the tight ship and her merry hearts.'[50] George Watson's *Adventures of a Greenwich Pensioner*, published in 1827, took a positive view of the navy. Very different was *Nautical Economy, or Forecastle Recollection of Events during the last War* by William Robinson. He used the pseudonym 'Jack

Nastyface', as he was 'politely called by the officers' – but in fact it was quite a common nickname, 'a sea term, signifying a common sailor'.[51] In fact a good deal of Robinson's service from 1805 onwards was reasonably happy, and it was only when Captain Sir Charles Paget took command of the ship after Trafalgar that it started to go wrong. He described the ineptitude of his captain and the tyranny of a young midshipman, but it was his final section, 'The different modes of punishment in the British navy' that was most controversial. Most of the punishments such as gagging and starting had already fallen into disuse, but the public was left with the impression of a very cruel and capricious service. And the practice of allowing prostitutes on board was greatly diminished, now that seamen were no longer transferred from ship to ship at the end of a voyage and were allowed more shore leave during the commission. This negative view was partly balanced by the works of James and Marryat. It was against this background that debates took place about the reform of the navy in the 1830s.

Theatre became increasingly popular with the introduction of gas lighting, and the navy was a favourite subject. Douglas Jerrold's 1829 melodrama *Black-Eyed Susan* was about a seaman who rescued his girlfriend from the attentions of his captain and was only saved from hanging in the nick of time. It had a record-breaking run of 300 nights in the Surrey Theatre before moving to Covent Garden and then Drury Lane. The favourite naval actor was T. P. Cooke, who had fought at the Battle of St Vincent and brought the bold, active and romantic spirit of the seaman to his roles. He was particularly noted as Long Tom Coffin in *The Pilot* in 1827, bringing hints of 'thoughtfulness and mystery, of deep-toned passion and pathos' to the part.[52]

THE BATTLE OF NAVARINO

When the Greeks revolted against Turkish rule in 1822 they had the support of many classically educated Britons, including the poet Lord Byron, who died in their cause. The British government stood aloof until 1827, when it combined with France and Russia to send fleets to enforce a compromise peace. As the Turks prevaricated about implementing it, in September the combined squadron found the Turkish-Egyptian Fleet anchored in Navarino Bay. As the naval commanders manoeuvred and negotiated, the crews only heard what was happening by rumour and personal account, the officers making no real attempt to inform them:

I saw ... an old messmate, who informed me that the Allied Admirals had held
a consultation the day before, whether they should blockade the Turks in the
harbor during the winter, or go to force them to agree to the treaty of the 6th
July; and they had resolved in the latter proposition. 'I'm glad of it,' said Tom
Morfiet, who was along with me, 'I should not like to be boxing off this here
place all winter. I'd far rather go in and have a slap at their canisters ...'[53]

But there was some sadness around the mess tables as they sailed into
action on 20 October:

We were now within two miles or less of the entrance to Navarino Bay, all sail
set, stud-sails low and aloft, when the boatswain piped to dinner, and many a
one assembled at the mess-table for the last time. The probability of never
meeting again cast a soberness over the mess, which is generally a scene of
banter and mirth. One or two tried to raise the spirits of their messmates by the
usual sallies of nautical wit, but the effect was only momentary.[54]

McPherson provides one of the longest and most moving lower-deck
accounts of any naval battle. He had a fine view of the preparations for the
action:

The pipe went to bring the ship to anchor, and to furl sails. I was sent to the fore
topsail yard-arm ... I here had a grand bird's eye view of the whole harbour ...
In the Bay, and round about us, were ranged in a triple line the Turco-Egyptian
fleet ... We could see in a moment the situation our ship was placed in – a
situation more perilous than any other ship in the whole three squadrons. Right
abreast of us, and bringing nearly every gun to bear upon us, lay two of the
enemy's line of battle ships: a little further ahead on our starboard bow now lay
another two deck ship, and three double-bank frigates were so placed on our
larboard bow and ahead, that they could gall us severely with their shot, while
a large frigate lay athwart our stern that raked us with success for some time,
till a French ship hove down and relieved us from her fire.[55]

In fact the enemy was far less strong than he appeared. The British, French
and Russians had ten ships of the line, nine frigates and five other vessels,
the Turks had only three of the line, seventeen frigates and nineteen
smaller craft.

As the fight began, McPherson said goodbye to his friend, who was
stationed at a different gun. 'Tom and I were just making our way down
from the fore-top-sail yard, when the enemy's guns opened upon us.
Morfiet grasping my hand, exclaimed, "Don't forget Tom Morfiet, M. –
farewell! – to your gun! to your gun!"'[56] On reaching his station there,
McPherson came under the command of Lieutenant Broke, the son of the

victor over *Chesapeake*, who drew his sword and told his men, 'Point your guns sure men, and make every shot tell – that's the way to show them British play!' The gun captain was 'a young Irish lad, and a capital marksman'.[57] The first broadside was fired on command, then the order was given: 'Fire away, my boys, as hard as you can.' Officers tried to restrain the lower-deck habit of overloading the guns, but to no avail:

> We were ordered to only double-shot the guns, but, in this particular, we ventured to disobey orders; for after the first five or six rounds, I may venture to say that the gun I was at was regularly charged with two 32 lb. shot and a 32 lb. Grape; and sometimes with a canister crammed above all. On being checked by the officer for over-charging, one of the men replied, as he wiped the blood and dirt from his eyes, that he liked to give them a *speciment* of all our *pills*.[58]

This was at the height of the action:

> The battle at this time was raging with the most relentless fury; vessel after vessel was catching fire; and when they blew up they shook our ship to its very keelson. We sustained a most galling fire from the two line-of-battle ships abreast of us, which kept playing upon us till they were totally disabled by having all their masts shot away, and whole planks tore out of their sides, by the enormous discharge of metal from our guns.[59]

Later the gun captain had his weapon 'loaded nearly to the muzzle with grape' as the Turkish admiral's yacht came into range:

> Her figure-head was a red lion bearing a shield, on which were three half-moons or crescents, a broad gold stripe was above her port-holes all the way aft; her stern had large figures of angels, all gilt, supporting a balcony or stern-walk, which was also gilt; and when the sun pierced the dense cloud of smoke, which was only at intervals, the vessel glittered brilliantly. 'Stand clear there,' cried the captain of our gun, 'She's coming! she's coming! d— me, if I don't spoil her gingerbread work! ....' He pointed the gun, and, taking aim, fired; and when the smoke cleared away, I heard him above all the noise that assailed out ears, vociferating, 'I told ye! I told ye! I've done more than I bargained for; I've carried her spanker boom as well as her gingerbread away!'[60]

The men were then ordered to leave their guns to fit springs to the anchor cable so that the ship could be swung round to bring her guns to bear. They were typically reluctant to obey, for as McPherson said, 'during the action, a deep impression lay in my mind that I was safer at my gun than anywhere else'.[61] The captain himself had to come down to persuade them. The battle did however produce a rare example of lower-deck cowardice, when a 'big stout Manxman' on one of the lower deck guns slipped down below and did not reappear. He lay there feigning injury but was spotted by the master-at-arms who ordered him on deck, with blows from his starter. He was later given three dozen lashes, disgraced in front of the crew and had the word 'Coward' sewn on his jacket.[62]

During the battle the women helped the surgeon in the cockpit, though several of them were too distressed to be of any use, while Hannah Buckley and Mrs Clark 'acted with the greatest calmness and self-possession'. Mrs Rooney's husband was killed, while Mrs Buckley was not sure of the fate of hers until after she met McPherson:

> I made the best of my way to the cockpit ladder, where I was met by Mrs B., who said, 'Oh! M., dare I ask for my John? He is, perhaps, dead or dying!' 'Neither one nor t'other, Hannah,' said her husband, a smart little fellow, who came forward and caught her in his arms. Dear was the meeting between them ... and the exclamation of 'Thank God, you're safe' was passed between them.

Going further down into the cockpit, McPherson saw a scene 'more horrible than before':

> The heavy smell of the place, and the stifled groans of my suffering shipmates, brought a cold sweat over me; and I found myself turn so sick, that I was obliged to sit down for a little on one of the steps of the ladder. On recovering, I snatched up a lantern, and proceeded to look at those who were lying stretched on their backs; some of them, on a close examination, I could perceive, still breathed, but that was the only sign they shewed of life.[63]

McPherson and his shipmates were less battle-hardened than their predecessors, or at least were more prepared to show their emotions. He saw a boy traumatised by the death of his friend: 'It was with great difficulty that we could separate little Anderson from the body of his comrade. He implored us not to take his "dear Ned" from him.'[64]

The combined fleet had destroyed more than 50 of the Turkish ships and lost none of its own. McPherson could not relax, as 'Visions of the conflict flitted before my eyes ...' Next morning the crew began to repair the damage to the ship, with burning Turkish vessels still exploding around them, until they were mustered to count the casualties.

> The names had been called for a little, and the answer was, 'Here,' till one didn't answer. 'He's killed, sir,' said one. 'Mark him off, Mr Andrews,' said the Captain. Thus it went on, every two or three names that were called being

answered by the words, 'Killed,' or 'Wounded.' I, having answered my own, listened with anxiety to hear poor Tom's. At last his name was called. 'Thomas Morfiet,' cried the Purser. 'Mortally wounded, but not yet dead,' said a voice on the other side.[65]

As soon as the hands were dismissed, McPherson rushed below to say goodbye to his friend, only to find his body being carried up wrapped in a bread bag. Determined to give him a proper burial, he found Morfiet's hammock and began to sew the body up in it.

> I undid the mouth of the bag, and cut it down with my knife, for I could not bear my fingers about the body, and I had nobody at this time to help me. The wound on the back of his head seemed to be the only one, but the neat white frock that he had on was sticking to his back with clotted blood. He had his knife with the lanyard round his waist, to which was attached the very thimble with which he had mended my jacket, sitting in the streets of Malta. The thimble I took to keep for his sake; and having stretched out the body on the hammock, I proceeded to sew it up, beginning at the feet. While thus engaged I was accosted by someone behind. I did not look up, for I was still crying ...[66]

In the absence of a chaplain, McPherson and his messmates 'buried' Morfiet by dropping the body out of a gunport while reading a service. 'I let go of my hold, and with a gentle push, the body of poor Tom was launched into the water. We looked out, and saw it gradually sinking under the water; and the hands being turned up, we went on deck to do our duty.'[67]

EXPLORERS

The idea of the North-West Passage around the north of Canada was still very attractive, and many expeditions were fitted out to find it after 1815, some supported by the navy, others by commercial interests such as the Hudson's Bay Company, but most were commanded by naval officers. The most prolific in the early days was Edward Parry, who led four expeditions between 1819 and 1827. He was well known for his good relations with his crews, and men often signed up for repeat voyages, despite having already spent months in the Arctic winter. He reciprocated this with high praise for his men and described one of them. Thomas Scott had once been 'a reckless, swearing man' but was converted:

> I have his fine, tall, powerful figure now before me, stalking across the ice, when it was breaking up with violence, almost under his feet, with the end of a six-inch hawser over one shoulder, and an axe for the other, to make a hole

in the ice for an anchor, to secure the ship from danger, often requiring unusual activity and verve.

Scott was promoted to petty officer for the second voyage but died in an anchoring accident on the Thames.[68]

One of the greatest problems was to keep the men amused during the winter, which might consist of nine months with the ship iced in, including three of complete darkness. Religion was an important part of Parry's system, and regular services were held, to which the men responded well, and some were deeply affected, as a purser describes:

> We assembled as usual, and Captain Parry read us an excellent sermon. We then read over three or four times the second lesson for the day, and I expounded it to the best of my ability. After this, we went to prayers, and, having closed, I wished them good night as usual, when my friend John Darke (one of the *Hecla*'s seamen) said he wished to say a few words. He then returned to his knees, and, in a few simple but affecting words, returned thanks for the blessing enjoyed by himself and shipmates in a Christian captain, and a Christian teacher, imploring the blessing of God on behalf of both Captain Parry and myself.[69]

Parry also set up classes for his men during the long winter months: 'In short, what with reading, writing, making and calculating observations, observing the various natural phenomena, and taking the necessary exercise to preserve health, nobody felt any symptoms of ennui, during our imprisonment in winter quarters.'[70] In addition there were entertainments put on by the officers, described rather patronisingly by one of them:

> It must not be supposed that the pleasure afforded by these exhibitions arose from the great merit of the performers and the excellence of the acting. The audience were of a class ready to be amused by any novelty, and, in an especial manner, to be gratified by seeing the officers, to whom they were in the habit of looking up with respect and obedience, voluntarily exerting themselves for their sole amusement. The exertion was not made in vain; the men were amused, and to their heart's content.[71]

On his first voyage Parry took his ships farther north than anyone had gone before and won a parliamentary award, which was shared with the men. He explored many parts of the region, both the coasts and inland, but he never found a navigable passage, and more attempts were necessary.

John Franklin set out on his first expedition in 1819, sponsored by the Hudson's Bay Company in their ship *Prince of Wales*. In 1821 a small party had to travel many miles across the land, and the hero turned out to be Ordinary Seaman John Hepburn, the only one who remained fit enough to gather food and firewood and to hunt for meat. Franklin paid tribute to 'the fidelity, exertion and uniform good conduct in the most trying situations, of John Hepburn, an English seaman, and our only attendant, to whom in the latter part of our journey we owe, under Divine Providence, the preservation of the lives of our party'. But even in these circumstances the class system was still in operation. Four out of the five English-speakers were officers, and Hepburn was not allowed to mess with them. Instead he was 'consigned alone to the society of foreigners, whose language he could not speak ...'[72] Hepburn was rewarded by having an island, a lake and a river named after him – more than Boy Nicholas Young of *Endeavour*, and he was more worthy of the honour.

Franklin began his second, and in many ways his most productive, voyage in 1825. *Blossom* under Captain Beechey was sent out to meet him from the Pacific side, and John Bechervaise joined her reluctantly because, 'Just then, ships of war were scarce, I had no alternative.' The crew of *Blossom* was carefully selected:

> The greatest care was bestowed on her outfit; no pains, no expense was neglected to render her safe and comfortable to officers and men. Men were easily to be got, but none were entered but such as produced good characters as thorough seamen, or well recommended.[73]

Even so, Bechervaise left with great trepidation, very unlike those who had sailed with Parry: 'May 14th. Anchored at Spithead; here I had again the melancholy pleasure of seeing my family; melancholy it was, for considering the nature of the voyage we were about to commence, there seemed little prospect of again meeting.'[74]

Fourteen of the crew deserted in Rio de Janeiro, including four who stole the jolly-boat and one who fled from a boat collecting beef from the shore. Beechey could not afford to lose them as 'men were not to be got easily', so he adopted a ruse. The ship pretended to sail, while a well-armed and manned boat waited behind for the deserters to come out of hiding. All were caught except 'two lads who were of little use'.[75] After rounding the Horn, the ship called at Pitcairn Island, where there was an echo of a past age – John Adams, the last of the *Bounty* mutineers, now 'a venerable old man, fair as possible, locks short and thin, white as the driven snow and a countenance a perfect model of benevolence'. He hesitated as he climbed up the side of his first warship since *Bounty* but was quickly reassured by Captain Beechey's reception of him. Bechervaise and his messmates listened to his tales with rapt attention: 'From Adams' own lips, as we sat at the table in his home I got the whole account of the fatal mutiny which forever blasted the prospects of Mr. Christian and his companions ...' He also saw what was left of the ship, 'laying on her broadside in six fathoms of water'.[76]

Discipline on *Blossom* was far less formal than Bechervaise had been used to in big ships, lacking 'that strict line of distance ... which is kept in regular commissioned ships'. He had a great deal of respect for Captain Beechey. When the ship was in difficulties, 'in this critical moment every eye was fixed upon the Captain and Master, all depending (I mean the men) on their superior courage and judgement ...'

Many parts of the Pacific coast were surveyed, and Bechervaise was sent ashore to help, having to face down a bear and her cubs at one point. He also helped to make signals to Franklin in Kotzebue Sound in Alaska:

> As the time of Captain Franklin's visit was uncertain, if ever it took place, the Captain ordered a cask of flour to be buried as deep as possible on the top of the Uric Rocks, and something else was buried at the east end of Chamisso ... with a bottle containing directions. I was sent to the top of the Uric Rock to paint in large black letters upon the stone the bearing and distance of the articles buried.[77]

On one occasion he was caught ashore during a heavy snowstorm:

> I never during my life suffered so much as I did that night and the next day; my mental anxiety was almost beyond bearing ... During the night we felt a powerful desire to sleep, but all succeeded in combating it, for we knew well that to go to sleep was a certainty of waking no more ... During the day it cleared up and gave us a sight of the dear old *Blossom* in the offing. Oh, the joys of this moment; we very soon walked down to the beach and having a boat sent for us, soon got to the ship with my mind made up never to volunteer for any land expedition.[78]

During a voyage of three and a half years, *Blossom* spent some time in warmer climates, and in the winter of 1828/6 they went to Macao, where Bechervaise was chosen to go to Canton with the Captain in an East India Company yacht. Becharvaise was impressed on the passage up the river:

> The river is very fine; large batteries erected on either side at the narrowest parts, are capable, if well worked, of preventing ships of any strength from

passing; but under present circumstances, a few of our well laid sixty-eights would silence them very soon; the scenery is grand and pleasing. As you ascend the river innumerable boats of all kinds and sizes are moored on each side for the purpose of conveying passengers and goods from one side to the other ... from such a vast number of boats, the river would be impassable without danger of life, were not the rules adhered to with the greatest rigour ...[79]

In September the following year *Blossom* was in her greatest danger:

On the 6th, a few minutes after eight o'clock, while the ship was on stays, she struck on the keel first, and paying off rested on her broadside against a bank of some kind ... At this time it required no whistle to send the men on deck, all were ready to hand, the tide was ebbing; one of the ship's lower anchors and two kedges were immediately got out, and every man exerted himself to the utmost ... our anchors were of no service in getting her off. Several bidairs of natives came off, who appeared sensible that something was amiss, but they were not aware of the extent of our calamity. Towards noon the wind rose high, and the swell increasing the ship heeled over a great deal ...

About three in the afternoon the wind still increasing and sea rising fast, as a last effort, sail was made in the ship, and in a short time during which she bent heavily, she gave one sudden spring, nearly ran over all the boats, natives and all, and in a few moments was in 8 fathoms, and increased it till she got to 22; our people cheered, the Esquimaux clapped their hands, and for a moment all was confusion; order was soon restored, the ship was again afloat.[80]

The plan to meet Franklin was finally called off.

A newspaper sent off shore gave us news that Captain Franklin after experiencing great suffering had returned to England; by this all hands were relieved from an oppressive weight; the dread of another visit to Bering's Straits. The news communicated to all hands caused such an uproar in the ship, that it was long before anything like order was returned, and though at a vast distance, home rose before our eyes with redoubled charms.[81]

But it took many months to get home and anchor at Spithead:

I never in my life recollect having experienced such anxious feelings as I felt that day; I was then in sight of home, without knowing what might be the news I should get; however my anxiety was soon relieved, for about a quarter of an hour after the anchor was down, a respectable waterman came alongside with a letter to the Captain, which having delivered he came to me and said 'pray is your name not Bechervaise?' 'Yes', said I, 'well then, two hours since I saw your family in good health.'[82]

Though conditions were far harder than on Captain Bligh's voyage, there was no sign of mutiny during the Arctic explorations. Possibly this was because a higher standard of man was selected, and certainly there are signs of far better leadership from the officers.

In the 1830s the Admiralty's interest in exploration was turned in different directions. During his famous voyage of 1831–6, Charles Darwin was fully absorbed with his scientific observations and relations with the officers among whom he lived. He said very little about the crew except to note early on that the commander, Robert Fitzroy, must be a good captain as two thirds of his previous crew offered to sign on again. Only once did he take an interest in the sailing, on the entrance to Rio de Janeiro when Fitzroy wanted to make 'a display of smartness'. Darwin helped to take in sail by holding 'a main-royal-sheet in each hand and a top-mast studding-tack in his teeth. At the order "shorten sail" he was to let go and clap on to any rope he saw was short-handed. This he did and enjoyed the fun of it often afterwards remarking "the feat could not have been performed without him."' He also took a servant from among the crew, Syms Covington, who was originally enrolled as 'Fiddler and Boy to the Poop cabin'. Darwin found him 'an odd sort of person. I do not very much like him; but he is, perhaps, from his very oddity, very well adapted to all my purposes'. Nevertheless, Covington accompanied Darwin on his trips ashore and stayed on with him after the voyage.[83]

HMS *EXCELLENT*

The frigate actions of the American War had given the British something of a shock, not least in the matter of gunnery. High rate of fire at close range was good enough against less skilled navies, but Americans could manoeuvre more confidently, and a much higher standard of aiming was required. Operations against the shore also required more accuracy; when Sir Howard Douglas watched Home Popham's ships firing off the north coast of Spain in 1812, he was appalled by their poor aiming. Another problem was that there was no standard gunnery drill in use. One petty officer was reprimanded for getting the procedure wrong and replied, 'I beg pardon, sir, but this is the thirteenth gunnery drill I have been taught, and when I have had my dinner and a glass of grog, somehow or other, at times, the whole thirteen drills comes up at once, and my head gets bothered.'[84]

The idea for a gunnery school was drawn up by several officers including Commander George Smith in 1829. He proposed,

> to place the ship at Portsmouth, off the North end of the Dockyard, for the purpose of firing at Targets, representing Ships' sides. Masts, Yards, etc, made

of old hammock cloths, stretched on Spars, and placed in the direction of the Collegians fire: thus affording the means of trying Men's skill and various experiments in Gunnery.[85]

HMS *Excellent* was an old 74-gun ship, which had fought at St Vincent. She became a receiving ship in Portsmouth Harbour until she was fitted out as the home of the navy's first gunnery school. According to the prospectus of 1832, the main purpose of *Excellent* was, 'establishing a permanent corps of seamen to act as Captains of Guns, as well as a Depot for the instruction of the officers and seamen of His Majesty's Navy in the theory and practice of Naval Gunnery, at which a uniform system shall be observed and communicated throughout the navy.' It was to be populated by 'intelligent, young and active seamen' who would be 'engaged for five or seven years, renewable at their expiration, with an increase of pay attached to each consecutive re-engagement, from which the important situation of Master Gunner, Gunner's Mate and Yeoman of the Powder Room shall hereafter be selected to instruct the officers and seamen on board such ships as they may be appointed to the various duties at the guns'. Each qualified man was allowed two shillings extra pay per month.[86]

This introduced several new principles to the navy – harbour-based training, the adoption of standard principles throughout the fleet, a certain amount of permanence to ratings, who would sign on for five or seven years and return to a fixed depot, and the idea of extra pay for longer service and greater skills. Trainees were to learn about the dispart – the difference in thickness of metal between the breech and the muzzle, which was essential for aiming; the importance of windage, the gap between the shot and the inside of the barrel, which was necessary in a breech-loading gun; the names of all the different parts of a gun and carriage; and 'the importance of preserving shot from rust, the theory of the most material effects of different charges of powder applied to practice with a single shot, also with a plurality of balls, showing how these affect accuracy, penetration and splinters, to judge the condition of gunpowder by inspection, to ascertain its quality by the ordinary tests and trials, as well as by actual proof'.[87]

In 1836, Seaman John Burnett wrote to his father that he was 'comfortable and happy here and quite well; what time I have to spare is fully taken up in learning my cards of instruction.' He described the daily routine:

They pipe 'Up hammocks' at 6 o'clock in the morning. We then clean ourselves and the mess tables till 7 o'clock. We are then piped to breakfast, which consists of cocoa; at half past 7 o'clock I go the rigging loft in the dockyard till 12 o'clock; which is very good of Captain Hastings of the ship to put me there, being the only one in the ship that goes there. At 12 o'clock on board again and piped to dinner. At 1 o'clock the drum beats to quarters where we are instructed in the great gun exercise; after that the sword and musket exercises, the boats are hoisted up and our day's work is nearly done. At half past four o'clock, tea, and liberty men are piped away.

The illusion of being in a ship at sea was kept up by means of station bills allocating them to duties as if they were at sea, but trainees had to pay for much of their equipment:

I am a mizzentop man, No. 86 at instructions. I shall have to buy a set of instruments before long, as soon as ever I get out of the second instructions, because I shall be put in the schoolroom and not be able to do without them. I pay 2/- per month for washing, subscribe twopence per month to the library and 1/- entrance money. I shall have to buy a fresh monkey jacket as mine is is very shabby and you must be clean and neat and if you are always so, you are sure to be taken notice of.[88]

Gunnery practice was carried out across the open spaces of Portsmouth Harbour. Firing only took place at low water, when the mudflats were uncovered and there was no small-boat activity. A red flag was hoisted from the ship, and ten beacons were sited along the line of fire to give an instant measurement of the fall of shot. Men known as mudlarks, mainly from the Grub family, strapped boards to their feet to recover the shot, which they could sell back to *Excellent*.

Samuel Bechervaise found his time on board very enjoyable and useful:

Of all the places presented by Her Majesty's naval service for the good of seamen, I deem the *Excellent* the very best; those who wish to obtain a better education may have a good opportunity of doing so ... I know one petty officer who had joined the ship *Asia* but a few weeks before me, and on joining did not know his own name when placed before him; but before he left he had gone through decimals. Here I passed 16 months in comfort, learned the art of naval gunnery in all its various branches, and on leaving her to join the *Melville* obtained a certificate class No. 1, well endorsed as to conduct etc.[89]

The first captain, Sir Thomas Hastings, worked hard against the seaman's well known tendency to overload his gun:

As Sir Thomas expected, when left to themselves they rammed in as many shot as they thought the gun would safely hold, fired it off, and looked with intense anxiety to see the effect of their performance. The shot, of course, fell short, as the charge of powder was inadequate. He said, 'Try again, my men! How is this?' They fired as before with the same result.

Sir Thomas then said. 'We will now try what we can do.' Only one shot was put into the gun and fired; the target was struck and knocked to pieces. He then proposed to the seamen that they should try what they could do if they inserted only one shot; this they did, and were surprised to find that they had hit the target, and much damage was occasioned.[90]

When the fleet bombarded Acre during the Syrian Campaign of 1840 there were many favourable comments on the gunnery: 'three guns were ordered to be pointed at a hole in a castle, not more than four feet in diameter, through which three fellows were looking out, to fire upon our boats inshore; the whole went off as one gun, and every shot went slap into the hole.'[91]

FIVE-YEAR ENTRY

The Second Viscount Melville, son of William Pitt's great political manager, had a long term as First Lord of the Admiralty from 1812 to 1827. He was not as ultra-conservative as his successors painted him, but with a reduced naval budget he had little scope for innovation. In 1827 he was succeeded by the King's brother, the Duke of Clarence, who had served under Nelson in the West Indies in the 1780s and commanded the 74-gun *Valiant*. He was given the ancient title of Lord High Admiral, as befitted a member of the royal family, but soon got into difficulties over plans to reform naval gunnery. He even took his fleet to sea for a short time, and was in favour of Codrington's action at Navarino.

In 1830 his brother George IV died – the last of the King Georges, whose interests all leaned towards the army rather than the navy. Clarence was now William IV, the 'sailor king'. By this time Britain was changing faster than ever. The railway age had already begun with the opening of the Stockton and Darlington line in 1825 and the Rainhill trials four years later. A Whig government came to power and was largely supported by the new king. Reform was now high on the agenda and large elements of the rising middle classes were given the vote with the Reform Act of 1832. Conditions in factories and mines were regulated, slavery was abolished in the colonies, and many other social reforms were carried out. It would be surprising if the navy had not come under scrutiny at this stage, especially since the First Lord of the Admiralty from 1830 to 1834, Sir James Graham, was one of the reforming Whigs and was motivated largely by a desire for efficiency. The Admiralty was merged with the Navy Board, which meant that it became too absorbed in detail for the rest of the century, but the actual power of the Admiralty did not necessarily reach down to the decks of the individual ships, and the means of recruiting men for them, so little was done for the lower deck.

Meanwhile Parliament was demanding that something be done about the seaman's conditions, and especially about the press gang. It was James Buckingham, author, former sailor and Member for Sheffield, who expressed these feelings eloquently in the House of Commons:

> Let the House ask itself what were the principal features that characterized the Slave Trade, and Slavery, and what were its chief wrongs and sufferings that roused up the indignation of the whole British people. The answer would be this. Slavery was first characterized by the brutal and inhuman act of dragging a man from his own home and family by force, and compelling him, against his will, to enter a service of which he had a rooted abhorrence. Secondly, by compelling the slave thus dragged from his home, to labour for inadequate wages, for an indefinite length of time, and subject to the lash of the whip, if he offended the regulations imposed on him by his tyrant, or even if he expressed dissatisfaction with his hard lot. Thirdly, by subjecting the severest torture of flogging, or sometimes even the punishment of death, any attempt to desert from the state of suffering to which an act of tyranny and cruelty alone had consigned him. These were the characteristics of Slavery: and to abolish this, the united voices of all classes of people in the British empire had been lifted up and heard. He contended, then, that the impressment of seamen for His Majesty's fleet was characterized by every one of these revolting features.[92]

He moved an enquiry into the navy, to find 'some plan by which His Majesty's navy may be manned in time of war without recourse to the practice of forcible impressments'. As First Lord of the Admiralty, Graham had to react to this:

> In resisting the motion I announced on the part of the Government two measures; one, a measure with respect to the merchant service, and the other the measure ... for giving greater encouragement to the voluntary enlistment of seamen, and to make regulations for the more effectual manning of His Majesty's navy. After full consultation with my colleagues in Lord Grey's cabinet, I strenuously resisted any legislative enactment which should in the slightest impair the prerogative of impressment ... With reference to the royal navy, I intimated that encouragement would be given by increase of pay, and that rewards proportioned to length of service should be introduced – that there should be a limit to the service – that leave of absence at the expiration of the

service, and even during the service, should be given to the seamen – that the checks on the infliction of corporal punishment which then existed should be strengthened, and that every effort should be made to make the service in the Queen's [sic] ships preferable to service in merchant ships.[93]

A bill was drawn up, to provide,

> that no Person shall be liable to be detained in the Navy against his consent for a longer period than five years, unless he shall have volunteered for a longer term ... At the expiration of the five years' continuous service, the Seaman, upon his application, is to be entitled to his discharge.[94]

He could be kept on for up to six months more in an emergency but would be entitled to 25 per cent extra pay. After his discharge he was to be protected from the press gang for two years. Using the carrot as well as the stick, it was decreed that any man offering himself for service within six days of a royal proclamation was entitled to double bounty; and in an attempt to make this fair, men already in the service were to be paid the bounty as well – that would cause trouble in the future. It was an ambiguous act, which put impressment on a stronger statuary basis than ever before, while claiming to limit its effects. And the five years of 'continuous service' was taken to apply to peacetime volunteers as well as pressed men, so that the navy took a rather small step towards a more permanent force.

But the five-year engagement was not a success, for it did not fit the needs of either side. The navy usually commissioned a ship for three years or a little longer, by which time it was ready for a major repair in the dockyard, and its men were paid off. It might have been possible to enforce the letter of the law and keep the men on for the remaining two years or so, but there would be the inconvenience of paying a man off in the middle of a commission, probably in foreign parts with the difficulty of getting him home. The seamen tended to ignore the five-year term when they signed up. After fourteen years' naval experience, Frederick Price testified, 'They enter for a ship's supposed period of commission. The term of five years is never mentioned.' After twenty years' service, Petty Officer Watkins claimed, 'I know I enter for five years, but think I am only bound for the ship; if sent to another, I know 'tis the law, but I should not like it.'[95] Officers deplored the influence that short service had on efficiency:

> We are in error in paying off our ships after a period of three years commission, when the crews are generally in the best state of discipline, which is entirely

destroyed after they are paid off, and become free agents ... It is well known that it takes months to bring into good discipline and fighting order the crew of a newly-commissioned ship, and this state of comparative disorder is caused by a number of undisciplined and half sailors being mingled with a few men-of-war's men; the latter, finding these new-raised men ignorant of their duties on board a man-of-war, and that in consequence they have a greater amount of labour than their share, become careless; and not until these new men gain knowledge of their duties sufficient to excite a spirit of emulation amongst the crew, does discipline progress. [96]

However, the Admiralty did offer some practical improvement in seamen's conditions by an order-in-council of September 1846:

> Their Lordships desire it may be distinctly explained to the Men that, if they choose to continue in the Service, they may have a month or six weeks' leave of absence, during which their Time and Pay will go on, and they will be at liberty to join any of Her Majesty's ships fitting out at any of the Ports upon their return from such leave; and that every facility may be given to the Men to deposit their hammocks, clothes, etc. at the dockyards during their stay on shore.[97]

This was a small but useful step towards continuous service, making it advantageous to the seaman to consider himself part of a permanent navy even on leave while still allowing him to choose his ship on his return. But again it was largely ruined by the mistrust of the men. Frederick Price though that 'on their return to the flag-ship, they believe they are likely to be sent where it may be disagreeable for them to go'. According to Petty Officer Watkins, few men took advantage of it because, 'men like to choose their own ships, and not to be drafted into a ship they would not like'.[98]

THE REGISTRY OF SEAMEN

Britain moved towards free trade from the 1820s onward, and the Navigation Acts were finally abolished in 1849. Generally the merchant service was efficient enough to cope with foreign competition, though America offered attractive wages, and the gold rushes to Australia and California also lured many seamen away at the end of the 1840s. The merchant marine was becoming gradually less reliable as a source for naval seamen in the event of war, and parliament passed legislation that it hoped would make it easier to mobilise men. According to Sir John Barrow, Secretary to the Admiralty,

> The other Act of Sir James Graham ... for forming and maintaining a register of all merchant seamen of the United Kingdom, and for amending and

consolidating the laws relating to them, is of the greatest importance to the commercial interests, and of mutual benefit to the owners and masters of merchant ships and to the seamen ... An office is established at the Custom-house, in London; a registrar, with the proper number of clerks appointed, who corresponds with the Customs at the outports, and makes periodical returns to the Admiralty of the number of seamen registered ... [99]

Barrow was over-optimistic. The office was indeed established, and Lieutenant Charles Brown, the Registrar, applied great energy to collecting names and producing statistics, but the methods were flawed. The onus was on the masters of ships leaving British ports to send in lists, but their men were suspicious of this and there were no effective means of enforcing it. There was no provision for checking ships that returned from foreign voyages, so there was much duplication. Even names that were collected were not always accurate:

When sailors are unable to write from ignorance or temporary disablement, their names are often written phonetically and variations on spelling the same name are constant. The same confusion arises when the men are not required to sign Agreements and the Master has to prepare a list of the crew. Even when there is no intention to deceive, sailors make variations in both Christian and Surnames and unreliable statements as regards their ages, while they not infrequently have motives for concealing their identity. Their signatures also are occasionally undecipherable. [100]

Brown himself was well aware of the faults, and in 1838 he suggested a more thorough register, 'taking minute individual description of each as to age, capacity, etc.'. But in an age before photographs, fingerprints or birth certificates, even that would not have been enough. Furthermore, from a naval point of view, it was never quite clear whether the act was intended to replace impressment or to make it easier for the authorities to implement it. Replacement, perhaps by some form of ballot, was 'implied if not directly declared' when the act was passed, but no mechanism was set up. For the moment, Brown concluded the act would 'accomplish nothing towards manning the Fleet'. He recommended a naval reserve made up of volunteers who would be paid a retainer. [101]

There was another provision in the 1835 act:

But, perhaps, the most important part of the bill is that which relates to parish boys and others being put apprentices to the sea service, and the number of apprentices which every ship is compelled to take, according to her tonnage. All former Acts on this subject were evaded; but the regulations now in force, and the penalties attached to any deficiency in the numbers, bid fair to introduce into the merchant service a very considerable number of seafaring men.[102]

This too was unsuccessful and was dropped in 1850, so there was no longer any legal requirement for a British merchant ship to carry apprentices.

GREENWICH

With tens of thousands of former naval seaman after the wars, the resources of Greenwich Hospital were naturally in demand. There had been several important changes in the system in the preceding few years. The ancient Chatham Chest with its sixpences was transformed into the Greenwich Chest in 1803. In 1814 it was absorbed into Greenwich Hospital, which now had to pay huge sums in out-pensions, with considerable strain on its funds.

In 1821 the Royal Asylum, the school for 700 boys and girls from naval families founded by George III, was merged with the British Endeavour School, which had been founded in 1798 at Paddington. In 1825 this organisation was re-named the Royal Hospital School, with 200 boys, the sons of officers in the Upper School, alongside 600 sons and 200 daughters of seamen and marines in the Lower School. Edward Hawke Locker, now secretary of Greenwich Hospital, wrote to his former protégé Robert Hay offering his son a place; but Hay had deserted from the navy and had to turn it down.[103] John Bechervaise did get his son in and was pleased with the result:

> We called at Greenwich to see our dear boy; it is really gratifying to the eye of a parent to see the cleanliness and comfort that pervades the place, they all looked cheerful and healthy; as for mine, who was but just ten years of age, a sweet chubby boy, had the glow of health and happiness on his cheek; how happy I felt while pressing him to my bosom and blessed the hand of those who had placed him in that happy institution.[104]

In 1843 a sloop of war called *Fame* was built at Chatham Dockyard, dismantled and then reassembled in front of the Queen's House at Greenwich. Fully rigged, it was used to train the boys in sail-handling, gunnery and boarding. It would be replaced by two other ships over the next thirty years, and a ship of this type dominated the Greenwich landscape until the 1920s, though it gradually fell into disuse. Boys were admitted to the school between the ages of nine and eleven, but the average age on entry was about ten-and-a-half. Lieutenant Rouse, the

Superintendent of the Upper and Lower Schools after 1841, describes the daily routine around 1850:

> To have them paraded for the class-room studies by the drill-masters (one to each 100 boys) at the minute of 9 and 2 o'clock, when they are marched in military order into their respective class-rooms for instruction, by the schoolmasters, till 12 o'clock at noon; and the same from 2 to 5 o'clock. After breakfast every day, a division loose sails, and after dinner furl sails. A division from noon till dinner time are at the gun drill of the six-pounders on board the ship, another division at the sword drill (wooden swords), another at gymnastic exercises, or marching drill; this last, chiefly the juniors; others in the rigging-room or sail-room in the ship.[105]

Throughout the nineteenth century the Royal Hospital School was seen as an important source of recruits for the navy, though the numbers were quite small – 53 boys in 1847, 57 in 1848 and a peak of 75 in 1849.[106] Boys were discharged at the age of fifteen and were allowed to state their preference for a ship in the fleet, being equipped with, 'the best suit of clothes in wear, and the sum of £3 10s sent to the captain for the boy's outfit'. Some captains suggested that the Greenwich boys were weak and undersized compared with others, while Captain Chads of *Excellent* thought that they were 'clever, well-taught at their books, well conducted, but slow in their movements; they want life – and some are not well grown for their ages.'[107] Lieutenant Rouse explained:

> These boys at 15 years of age, when they are discharged into the navy, are, in my very decided opinion, generally very superior in strength in comparison with other institutions of the same nature – their very extraordinary gymnastic feats are proofs of it; and if in appearance they are deficient at that precise age of discharge,15, it must be borne in mind, that the officers who are entrusted with the selection for our men-of-war, will only take boys of very decidedly strong appearance – they have a choice – where we are bound to take those who are sent to us, chosen from the service-claims of the father.[108]

Once on board they were sometimes employed as servants, but this tended to reduce them to an equal footing with less well-trained boys, and undermined the scheme. Captain Arthur Lowe believed that 'it would retard their progress in other essential points' and that '*school* boys imbibe loftier notions than could arise from emptying a bucket of slops'.[109]

PUNISHMENT

After Queen Victoria came to the throne in 1837, she and her husband Albert set an example of family life that was very different from the loveless marriages, the mistresses and the family feuds of the Georges. She too took interest in the navy, partly through her use of steam-powered royal yachts to take her to her favourite home at Osborne on the Isle of Wight and for voyages round the country. Her sons wore sailor-suits as children, and some of them entered the navy in their teens. She launched many warships, and it was probably this which originated the tradition that a ship should be launched by a woman.

Yet in many ways the navy was out of step with the rest of the community. It did nothing to encourage family life. It was increasingly aristocratic when the power of lords was being challenged in parliament. In the very moral Victorian Age, sailors were still associated with drunkenness and promiscuity. And the public view of the navy was largely based on an increasingly remote past during the wars with France. Ashore, the prisons were reformed after the efforts of Elizabeth Fry, and the death penalty was gradually restricted, so that by 1838 it was virtually confined to murder and attempted murder, while corporal punishment for adults was gradually reduced – philosophers believed that punishment should encourage the victim towards reform and hard work.

Admiral Sir Thomas Byam Martin represented the conservative face of the navy in many matters, and it is not surprising that he was convinced that 'the power of corporal punishment *must be preserved*', even though it had gained a bad reputation from over-use during the wars with France.[110] There was no point in a captain being too lenient –

> The reverse of the picture is to be found in ships where a relaxed system prevails; there the service is disgraced and the well-disposed men disgusted; in such ships every one is uncomfortable; the willing seamen there do all the duty, while the vicious and lazy indulge their propensities with impunity; and when good men desert from the king's service, it is mostly from ships of this description ...[111]

Phillip Colomb, who first went to sea in 1846, was also in favour of flogging as he looked back in later life:

> The offences for which men were flogged, and so finished within ten minutes, are the same which are now met with more prolonged but not less severe punishment of from three to fourteen days' confinement in a cell on board, or the prolonged, and wearying, if less severe, confinement in a prison on shore ... but where severe punishment is necessary, it must ever remain a question whether, apart from the sentiment which has made it impossible, the ten minutes severe bodily pain, applied outwardly, has not much to recommend it as an alternative to a system of pain applied inwardly by means of partial starvation and incarceration.[112]

John Knowles, who served in four ships between 1833 and 1856 and rose to petty officer for a time, had a very different view. He was apparently doing quite well until he was subjected to 'the vile and degrading punishment of the lash' for going ashore without leave to visit his dying father. After this he 'felt degraded and became listless and indifferent and subsequently suffered similar punishment' so that he took a total of nine dozen lashes over the years. He still had the marks on his back 30 years later and claimed that it had made him unable to do manual labour, so he was forced to work as a peddler. He asserted that abolishing the cat would 'induce a better class than the average recruits to join the navy, but who are now deterred from joining solely from fear of the cat'.[113]

In many ships it was the marines who were flogged most often, despite the belief that they were a force for discipline:

> 'Spare the cat and spoil the seaman or marine – but especially the marine'
> Might have been run round the *Russell's* wheel after the manner of a ship's motto ... it was the custom of the Service, and no-one minded it much. There was a certain art in being flogged, which was taught on the Lower Deck; and a fine marine, in good practice, would take four dozen with a calmness of demeanour which disassociated the operation of the lash from the idea of inflicting pain by way of punishment and warning, and connected it up in people's mind with ordinary and routine ...[114]

Despite the efforts of radical MPs led by Joseph Hume, Parliament was not able to abolish flogging, but it began to place restrictions on it: from 1846 returns of floggings on individual ships had to be laid before the House of Commons. This had a strong moral effect – more than two thousand men were flogged in 1839; 860 in 1847. In 1848 there was a total of 719 floggings, involving 19,340 lashes or an average of 27 per flogging. The highest number inflicted was 48; the lowest was one. There was great variation between ships. *Caledonia* only flogged one marine, with 36 lashes for 'drunkenness, theft, and using mutinous language'. *Bellerophon* flogged 21 seamen with a total of 414 lashes, for 'incapacity, drunkenness, leave-breaking, uncleanliness, skulking, theft, disobedience of orders, insolence, using mutinous language, and stabbing'. Fourteen marines were punished, along with four boys.[115]

THE REDUCTION OF GROG

The offence of drunkenness remained prominent on the punishment lists, and there were many who attributed most of the problems of the navy to it, in the wardroom as well on the mess-deck. James Dundas showed that in 1846–8 half of offences that merited formal punishment were due to alcohol – 527 for drunkenness and 526 for other offences in 1848, for example.[116] It also contributed to accidents, and Bechervaise gives a tragic example:

> On Sunday evening ... I observed a man named Tooey, captain of the foretop, standing under the half-deck, ready to spring upwards at the first flourish of the boatswain's whistle. One glance convinced me that Peter Tooey had been cook that day; or in other words that he was by far too much intoxicated to go to the earing in safety. A few words with him confirmed my suspicions, I begged him not to go aloft; and promised that the second captain of the top should take his place. But, alas, my words went unheeded. Poor fellow! at the 'Pipe hands shorten sail,' he about flew up the fore rigging; it seemed to me that his feet scarcely touched the rat lines. Before the order 'Lower away topsails,' was given, he was ready to spring off the yard. Indeed he was standing on it before it was secured, and walking outward towards the yard-arm, but he walked too far; in his blind haste to be first he walked clear over the yard-arm, struck the fore chains, and passed aft as a corpse.[117]

It was generally agreed that the quantities of beer and wine issued were not excessive, but rum was far stronger, and it was being established as the standard naval drink, especially after beer was replaced in 1832. In 1825 it was decided to reduce the rum ration by half to a quarter of a pint a day. This does not seem to have inspired any serious protest, and John Bechervaise was happy with the results:

> I would not advocate the cause of total abstinence in the Navy, but this I feel assured of, that the less spirits are issued the better. The proof is easily obtained. If it were possible to examine the logs of two different ships of the same class, the one at the time when the half a pint of rum was issued to each man daily, and the other ... when the allowance was reduced to half that quantity, then carefully compare the punishment returns of both periods, I feel convinced that it would be found that the number of lashes inflicted in the first period would be far more than double the latter period.[118]

Of course it did not solve all the problems, and in 1841 Captain Alexander Milne wrote, 'all the precautions in the world won't check the inclination Jack has for his grog, and then follows all sorts of punishments – by no means a pleasant duty.'[119] The Admiralty did its best to find substitutes for alcohol. By 1847 it had received applications 'on the part of the Crews of Her Majesty's Ships, to be allowed the indulgence of taking up an additional quantity of Tea and Sugar, in lieu of the daily ration of Spirits ...' It was agreed that half an ounce of tea and two ounces of sugar could be issued to men who gave up their grog, with half the amount of tea and sugar for those who gave up half their drink allowance. The circular was 'to be read to the different Ships' Companies, and fully explained, that the proposed change [was] entirely voluntary on their part.'[120]

In 1850 a committee of naval officers met to consider the spirits issue, for it was clear that the reforms of the 1820s had not removed the problem of alcoholism. It was generally agreed that an experienced man could not get drunk on his allowance alone, but there was some concern about younger men, who were not used to it. Moreover, all sorts of ways were found to get around the regulations. In many ships it was common for the cook of the mess to be given a share of each man's ration; in some he was given the whole of it, with power to decide how it was distributed. Some men drank tea but still took their allowance of grog, to sell it on to others. It was usually possible for at least one man in each mess to get drunk every night. African seamen known as 'kroomen' were issued with neat rum but expected to drink it on the spot to prevent hoarding or selling on. According to reports, a man might keep it in 'his capacious mouth' and then spit it into a receptacle, to be sold on to seamen who were 'willing to pay large prices for this highly rectified spirit'.[121] Then there was the perpetual problem of liquor smuggled on board from shore boats and men on leave. Some seamen were clearly chronic alcoholics: 'A good many of the men would almost put their victuals aside for the sake of their allowance of grog, particularly at sea, when on salt provisions.' Grog was blamed for much indiscipline, and seaman-gunner Henry Mason claimed that nine out of ten cases of punishment were still due to excessive drinking. Much was blamed on the evening issue, which was when most drunkenness occurred.

One solution, tried over two years in HMS *Constance*, was to make the men drink their grog at the tub in the presence of an officer. This was not popular, as it wasted a good deal of the men's precious mealtime. In other ships it was only used as a punishment for excessive drunkenness. Another was to reduce the allowance yet again which was done by an order of March 1850.[122]

THE SEARCH FOR FRANKLIN

Sir John Franklin set off on his final voyage to find the North-West Passage in May 1845. He had two steam-powered converted bomb vessels, *Erebus* and *Terror*, and the best-equipped British expedition so far. The combined crews totalled 129 officers and men, including a large proportion of petty officers. But after two years nothing had been heard of them, and there was serious concern. The fate of the expedition was not known for some years, and in the meantime more than thirty expeditions set out to find Franklin, some of them sponsored by the Admiralty. *Plover* left in January 1848, under Captain Thomas Moore; William Simpson, a sergeant of marines, served as her master at arms and sometimes the purser's steward. He was impressed with the aurora borealis – 'the prettiest thing I ever saw without exception' – but in general he was focussed on events on board ship and among the crew, as befitted his position. As they crossed the equator there was the long-standing ceremony: 'Received a visit from Old Father Neptune and his tribe and proceeded with the usual ceremony of shaving etc. and spliced the main brace.' On calling at the Falkland Islands, the crew were allowed ashore to shoot wild fowl, 'but there were few who troubled themselves sporting, there being a grog store, they (most of them) just popped in to have one glass which brought another and another until they became careless as to any other amusement.' Some lemon juice went missing, and Simpson was publicly accused of stealing it, which made his position intolerable.

> Captain Moore, you have accused me of theft. I trust you will investigate this charge, and should I be deemed guilty of course must abide the consequences but if on the contrary such is not the case I have to request on our arrival at Baha you will send me out of the ship.[123]

Instead, Moore threatened to flog him, but the matter was cleared up a month later when the missing articles were found in the spirit room. After rounding the Horn, the ship headed north and the crew began to prepare for the cold and ice:

> The carpenters are very busy doubling over the Pinace and otherwise preparing the Boats to encounter ice – Ship's company making Fearnought Sleeping Bags – stockings, gloves, caps etc from sea skins each man being provided with skin for that purpose, also large sealskin cloaks for travelling parties.[124]

Simpson himself was ordered to skin birds and preserve them for the official collection, as 'the captain says this is no place for idle people'. They were too late to enter the Bering Strait that year, so they wintered off the Siberian coast, where they were, 'very comfortable, at least as far as circumstances will admit, the weather is extremely cold, the temperature being 21 degrees below zero'. They went ashore to play football and made contact with the natives, though they came across the old problem of dealing with a society in which concepts of property-owning were very different: 'We have found cases of theft amongst them which on being made known to the chiefs are restored.' The temperature dropped even further. 'We find the cold very severe, although we have a fire (stove) in the main hold and pipes leading from it round the lower deck, yet in the morning when we turn out of our hammocks there are icicles 4 or 5 inches long hanging from the deck and beams overhead.' Christmas Day was celebrated in some style, and Simpson devoted more than 1200 words to his description. He was grateful for the 'kind and handsome manner' in which the officers treated them, with the doctor and purser acting as waiters. 'Old Riggs the armourer' rose to make a speech on behalf of the lower deck, proposing the toast: 'Sir John Franklin, the officers and men composing his expedition; may we find them, in health and safety, and not in the lamentable condition to which it is feared they may have been reduced.' They sang songs such as *See the conquering hero comes* and *The girls we left behind us*, and the captain came on deck to be greeted by four petty officers, placed in a chair and cheered. 'Nothing was to be seen but our cheerful and contented faces, there we sat enjoying our Pipes and our grog.'[125] But over the months Simpson became increasingly bored and troubled with his legs. He was sent home in 1851, while the search continued.

In fact all the members of the Franklin expedition were already dead by the middle of 1847, having abandoned their ships and attempted to trek south, apparently indulging in cannibalism on the way. The preserved bodies of three of the men were recovered and analysed in the 1980s. Leading Stoker John Torrington of *Terror* was twenty years old, of rather frail appearance and racked with diseases including tuberculosis, emphysema and anthracosis, which he may have picked up in the conditions of the engine room. It seems likely that he got his petty officer rate for his skill with the engines rather than his strength as a stoker, which was not unusual at the time. Able Seaman John Hartnell of *Erebus* was older and more experienced, and his face showed his death agonies. He was buried in a striped shirt bearing the initials of his brother, who was also on the voyage. William Braine was a marine of *Erebus*. All three showed signs of lead poisoning, which must have come from the canned food used in the expedition, and this probably played a large part in its demise.[126] Franklin's body was never found, despite his wife's persistence in sending out expeditions to look for him.

THE FIRST STEAMERS

Steam engines were first used in mines and in the Royal Dockyards in the 1790s to pump out docks rather than power ships. Sir Marc Isambard Brunel, the father of the great Victorian engineer, used them for his highly innovative block-making machinery in Portsmouth Dockyard. The first commercially successful steamship in Europe, *Comet*, sailed on the Clyde in 1812, but steam engines were still only suitable for short, inshore voyages. In 1815 the navy acquired its first paddle-tugs for hauling ships in and out of harbour in light or unfavourable winds.

As First Lord of the Admiralty from 1812, Lord Melville is often accused of stating, 'Their Lordships feel it is their bounden duty to discourage to the utmost of their ability the employment of steam vessels, as they consider the introduction of Steam is calculated to strike a fatal blow at the supremacy of the Empire.'[127] In fact, he did much to encourage steam power and in 1823 wrote, 'There is every reason to believe from the purposes to which Steam Vessels are now applied that they would be found very useful in the protection of our trade in the Channel ... It will be proper now to provide Steam Engines for at least six vessels ... and I therefore desire that you will take the necessary steps for that purpose.'[128] The first iron steamship, *Aaron Manby*, made a voyage from London to Paris in 1822. But it was the development of the screw propeller in the 1830s and 1840s that gave the first boost to naval steam, for the old paddle wheels had interrupted the ships' broadsides too much.

The status of the early engineers was highly ambiguous, though in some senses they might be counted as members of the lower deck. Early steamships were usually naval auxiliaries, so the engineers were clearly civilians. By the time the first truly naval steamships were commissioned in 1827 and appeared on the Navy List, it was not clear whether the chief engineer was a petty officer or a warrant officer. He was certainly junior to the old standing officers, and during that year 36 carpenters of Portsmouth complained that it was 'derogatory to the positions of Warrant Officers in His Majesty's Dockyards to have the charge of the enginemen and their stores'.[129] The issue was no clearer by 1832, when the two engineers of the paddle-steamer *Alban* were living in the fore cockpit along with the boatswain's mate and two stewards. Captain Hugh Pigot of HMS *Barham* ordered Thomas Harris, Chief Engineer, of *Alban*, to be flogged. Her commanding officer, Lieutenant Henry Walker, complained, and Pigot was tried for 'arbitrary and oppressive conduct at variance with the custom of the Service ...' When the flogging order was given, Walker had pointed out that Harris was a petty officer and could not be flogged according to recent orders. Pigot then ordered Walker to disrate him, but Walker replied that he did not think it possible to disrate a man appointed by order of the Navy Board. However, the actual order from the Navy Board could not be found, and Pigot said that Harris 'could not be recognised as a warrant or petty officer' and could therefore be flogged. When the court found Pigot not guilty, the essential issue remained unresolved.[130] Ultimately, in 1837, engineers were appointed to warrant rank by Order-in-Council, ranking 'with but after' carpenters.

Meanwhile a class of stokers was beginning to emerge under the engineers, and they were definitely of the lower deck. According to John Dinnen, the Inspector of Steam Machinery, they were 'really the prime movers of the ships, almost as much as the men who rowed the galleys of the ancients ...'[131] In the early days they were recruited casually or chosen from among the seamen, but in 1828 Captain John Ross advised differently:

> The Engineer and his Assistant should have no duty to perform but their own; neither should the stokers be employed on anything but the care of the fire ... The stokers should be regularly bred to the calling. It is a mistaken notion that an ordinary seaman is able to attend the fire; a regular stoker will not only keep a better fire, and a more steady heat on the boiler, which is of great importance, but will save in fuel, what would soon pay the wages of the whole crew.[132]

Captain Sir John Ross agreed: 'The stokers to be men brought up to that calling; they may be landsmen.'[133]

Stokers were quite few in number, due to the small power of the engines and their infrequent use. According to Captain Otway, 'The engine room is attended by six men, in addition to the engineers and their apprentices; four as stokers, and two as coal-trimmers: the four stokers relieve each other in succession, at the end of every two hours, making two hours on, and six hours off duty; the coal trimmers are at watch, and watch for four hours each.'[134] They were generally given good conditions and pay, and were not difficult to recruit. Dinnen, wrote in 1838,

> There is a wide difference both in the selection and the treatment of the fire-men in the Government and in the merchant service; and the reason which is usually assigned for the superior attention paid to the stokers n the Royal Navy is, that unless the comfort and conveniences of the men were in some measure attended to, the interests of the service would suffer considerably by the difficulty of replacing them, when wanted, in vessels remaining a long time on

foreign stations ... Hence the preference generally given by intelligent fire-men to the Government service.[135]

There was a growing feeling that more control should be exercised over the stokers for the sake of fuel efficiency. As one authority put it,

> Many instances of steamers are to be found at the present day in which the same quantity of coal is burnt per hour, whether the engines are going fast or slow; whether forty cylinders full of steam are used per minute, or only thirty. In such cases, one quarter of the fuel is thrown away through ignorance of the despised art of stoking; for the firemen may have either allowed the surplus steam generated to blow off at the waste-pipe steam; or they may have thrown open the fire doors, by which means the steam is only prevented from being generated by the rush of cold air which takes place through the flues, while the same quantity of coal is being burnt as before.[136]

Dinnen agreed that 'stokers consult their own convenience; and as long as they keep plenty of steam flying off to waste, they are seldom called to account...'[137] Ross advised double rations of beer for stokers while the engines were at work and that they should be relieved every two hours.[138]

Promotion was not impossible for the early stoker. In 1830 it was complained that poor conditions drove the best engineers out of the service, which led to 'the advancement of the second and third assistants, and even the stokers to the office of 1st Engineer, thus putting the most valuable machinery and the safety of the vessel into the hands of men who, but for such a train of circumstances, would never have been deemed worthy of such a trust'.[139] In 1840 the rating of 'leading stoker' was introduced to supervise in the boiler room, and in 1842 the first official complement lists for steamships were drawn up. A sixth rate with 200 men would have five engineers, five engineer boys under training, five leading stokers and 21 stokers and coaltrimmers; it was added, 'Should the power of the engines be increased in vessels of any given class, the establishment of Engineers, Engineers' boys and stokers will be increased in proportion, without an addition to their total complements.'[140]

The heavy labour of coaling ship was normally done by convicts in the home ports, though Captain Otway complained that 'their whole day's duty' was 'not worth an hour's purchase'. Otherwise it was done by the crew, 'every man in the ship except the permanently excused idlers', and Williams advised captains to have 'a couple of fiddlers going' and to 'serve out the extra allowance of grog authorized by the Admiralty, and let the ship's cook have hot fresh water ready for the men to wash themselves in at diner and supper'. Demand for coal at this time was still moderate, for engines were small and rarely used. Williams was satisfied that by these means, 'you may thus hoist in at the rate of a hundred tons a day, which soon finishes the matter'.[141]

THE PETTY OFFICER

By the 1840s, the authorities were increasingly looking to use the carrot rather than the stick to improve the conduct and quality of seamen. There was some attempt to improve the status of petty officers in 1827, when they were awarded badges to be worn on the sleeve – an anchor for second class petty officers, with a crown above for first class. John Bechervaise was grateful for promotion:

> One afternoon as I stood on the gangway, it being my watch, the Captain came up and taking a turn or two on deck came towards me, and having pulled a paper out of his pocket presented it to me, saying, 'Here, read this and follow the instructions it contains; your exertions and good conduct merit my esteem.' To a man who has a family however trifling the addition of pay may be, it is welcome; but the addition was given to me in a manner so kind, so gentlemanly, that it was doubly pleasing.[142]

Captains were not always happy with the behaviour of the petty officers. Though *Plover* had a hand-picked crew in 1848, the captain complained,

> The commander called the whole of the petty officers on deck this day and reprimanded them, not only for the manner in which they did their duty, but also for the example shown by them to the men who performed their duties in a very careless manner. Indeed it was about time something was done as some of them appeared to think they could do as they liked not being in what is termed a regular Man of War.[143]

There were plenty of bullying petty officers, such as boatswain's mate Sinnet, whom McPherson had to fight during his first day on board but who turned out to be a friend before choking on a plug of tobacco and dying.[144] Bechervaise offered some advice on conduct:

> Suppose you are now a petty officer, and captain of the top, these rules are invaluable ... To gain respect and ensure comfort, keep the men that are placed under you at a proper distance. ... I do not mean that you are to top the officer over them, but simply that whenever anything requires to be done, never do it yourself – a working petty officer is only encouraging the lazy – but give your orders in such a way that all may know they must be obeyed, and that without demur. Have no favourites at board or in the top; let every man bear his own

share of the general burthen; or in other words, let every man do his own work. You may occasionally have young men placed under your care for instruction; do all you can to teach them, and be assured that a day will arrive when they will be grateful for your kindness.[145]

In January 1849 the Admiralty decided that, 'the undermentioned marks of distinction shall, for the future, be worn by the Petty Officers of the Fleet, in lieu of those at present in use.' A first class petty officer was now to have two crossed anchors with a crown above; a second class PO was to have a single anchor with a crown. In addition, a new rating of 'chief boatswain's mate' was established in all seagoing ships of the line, with the pay of £2 12s per month. He had to have passed the examination for boatswain. The captain of the afterguard was promoted to first class petty officer, while new ratings of second class petty officer were established for second captains of the masts and afterguard, and the coxswains of the barge and cutter. Their Lordships decided to 'mark their approbation of the services of the Petty Officers of the Fleet, and the high sense they entertain of the same' by awarding selected men gratuities of £7 and £5 when the ship paid off.[146]

GOOD CONDUCT

In January 1849 the Admiralty recognised the value of long service when, 'with the view of encouraging good conduct in the Seamen of the Fleet', it decreed, 'Every Seaman who shall have served seven years in the Navy, including Boys time, and who shall have maintained good character throughout, shall be entitled, when authorized by the Captain or Commanding Officer, to wear an anchor on the upper part of the left Sleeve of his Jacket, and shall not be liable to Corporal punishment, except for Mutiny, without having been, in the first instance, deprived of the above distinctive mark.'[147]

That year Parliament voted an extra £30,000 'for the encouragement of the petty officers and seamen of the fleet', and the naval administration debated how best to spend this. Four separate proposals emerged. One was to increase the pay of all petty officers (except leading stokers, who had recently had a rise), and their number was estimated at 6,800. The second was to give a more limited increase to all petty officers and to promote certain grades, such as second captains of stations and coxswains of cutters, to petty officer. At the Admiralty it was considered that both of these would be 'doing too much for one class without considering the others'. A third was to give an increase to all petty officers and men on a sliding scale, by length of service, which would involve 'a long series of calculations, and even then the chief terms [would be] uncertain ...' The fourth was to award good conduct badges and pay to the seamen, 'on the principle of the good conduct warrant of the army'. Captain Milne was in favour of the fourth on the grounds that it would be 'highly advantageous to the men of good character for in the present system of the service there is nothing to excite emulation or to distinguish the seamen of exemplary character from those of indifferent character'. He wanted to 'give every man who conducts himself well a good conduct badge with 1d additional pay and on being paid off to receive a certificate stating his being entitled to the privileges (viz. being free from corporal punishment) so long as he was entitled by good conduct to wear the badge.'[148] This was approved, and orders were issued on January 1849.

Boys' Training

The navy had used boys at sea since time immemorial, but by the 1830s admirals were beginning to look at them again as a possible solution to problems of recruiting, training and retention. In the naval vote for 1834–5, a thousand boys were allowed for in place of 500 men. At first they were distributed throughout the fleet as supernumeraries, but by an order of October 1834 they were to be 'blended with complements'. The number was increased to 2,000 in the following year 'with the view to forming a nursery for seamen'. That figure of 2,000 remained in the navy estimates for many years, but there was nothing to prevent their Lordships from exceeding it, and they did so as they became increasingly keen on training boys. And by 1846, as the failure of the five-year term and the register became increasingly clear, they began to think about apprenticeships, with the conventional civilian term of seven years, to keep the services of boys after their training. This was legalised by an act of 1847, which decreed that,

> every boy who, when under the age of sixteen years, shall enter the service of Her Majesty's Navy shall be liable to be detained in the said service, either with or against his consent, for any period not exceeding seven years, to be computed from the day of his being entered into the same; and at the expiration of such seven years he shall, upon his application for that purpose, be entitled to be discharged, unless the Admiral or Commanding Officer of the fleet, division or squadron under whose command he be shall, in consequence of any special emergency, deem it advisable not to discharge him ...[149]

More thought was given to the 'systematic education of such boys', rather than leaving it to individual captains as in the past. Static training ships were planned for each of the main mercantile and naval ports so that the boys would spend about a year before going to sea – though some officers were of the opinion that 'there is no school – as to seaman ship – like a cruiser or sea going ship'. One scheme suggested ships at Portsmouth, Plymouth, Cork and Chatham producing 200 boys each a year, and a hundred more trained at Leith. With a hundred or so from Greenwich, that would give a thousand boys a year, while a thousand more were at sea for the second part of their training.

In practice the training would be concentrated at Cork and on the south coast of England, particularly in *Impregnable* at Plymouth, commanded by Captain Arthur Lowe, which had entered 360 boys by August 1849 and sent all but seven of them to the fleet. They learned gunnery and musket drill during the week, alternating with school work that included reading, writing, arithmetic, geography, geometry, trigonometry and religious studies. Sail drill and bathing were carried out when the weather permitted. Every Saturday they cleaned ship and set up church for the service the following day. After four months of that they went on board the tender *Nautilus* to be instructed in 'seamanship in all its branches, including the use of lead and line'. At Portsmouth the boys trained on board Nelson's old flagship *Victory*, which was serving as a depot ship and used for other purposes as well.

Attitudes to the teaching of swimming were beginning to change now that desertion was much less of a problem. Basil Hall found:

> It is surely very odd that there should ever be such a thing as a sailor who cannot swim. And it is still more marvellous that there should be found people who actually maintain that a sailor who cannot swim has a better chance than one who can ... This strange doctrine, as may well be supposed, deprives but slender support from any well-established facts. It is merely asserted that, on some occasions of shipwreck, the boldest swimmers have been lost in trying to reach the shore, when they might have been saved had they staid by the ship. This may be true enough in particular cases, and yet the general position grounded upon it is utterly absurd. The most skilful horsemen sometimes break their necks, but this is hardly adduced as an argument against learning to ride.[150]

By 1837, Lieutenant Alexander Fordyce believed that, 'Learning to swim is so necessary for a sailor, that it should be much encouraged.'[151] As well as saving life, swimming had other practical uses. At Navarino, *Genoa's* captain of the maintop swam out to retrieve a hawser from *Asia* so that the ship could be hauled out of difficulties.[152] Swimming was considered important in the new training ships

Among the first boys to be trained was James Gorman, the son of a nurseryman born in Islington in 1834. He joined *Victory* in March 1848 at the age of thirteen, and after six months he was transferred to the tender *Rolla*. He was good enough to be kept on as an instructor to the next intake of apprentices and eventually joined the 90-gun *Albion* as a boy 1st class in 1850. He was short at 5 feet 3½ inches, had blue eyes and light brown hair and had been vaccinated against smallpox. He was promoted to ordinary seaman in May 1852 at the age of seventeen, and able seaman two months later.[153] The entry and training of boys was a small start in solving the navy's manning problems, but it was to be very important for the future.

CONCLUSION

Over the three hundred years between the loss of *Mary Rose* in 1545 and the middle of the nineteenth century, the lower deck seaman changed both his country and the world. He fought off the Spanish Armada, battled against the Dutch, and defeated the French both as monarchists and revolutionaries. He did not do these things just on the orders of his officers but brought his own bravery, skill and enthusiasm into the equation. He explored the world under Cook and Franklin, he landed in hundreds of shore expeditions and defended the British Empire both afloat and ashore. He died in his hundreds from disease far more than in battle. He changed the course of history with his support of Parliament in 1642 and with the Spithead mutiny in 1797. He was almost always badly treated by the authorities and rarely got what he deserved from the state or the public.

How much did the seaman change over these centuries? Clearly not as much as society. Henry VIII's reign was a period of religious intolerance, with regular burnings of heretics. Victoria's reign was also noted for its religiosity, but it was a much more open society in which even Roman Catholics, once considered enemies of the state, were tolerated and often flourished. The British Empire only really began in Elizabeth's reign; by Victoria's it dominated the world. Britain was no longer a pair of states on the fringes of Europe, subject to frequent internal conflict and civil war, but a unified force. Aristocratic rule was no longer unchallenged: the middle classes were almost equal to them in power and influence, while the new working classes were demanding their share of it. Historians are divided about whether there really was an 'industrial revolution' between about 1760 and 1820, but no one questions the vast changes in technology and organisation between 1545 and 1850. In addition, the electric telegraph and steam power were revolutionising communications both by land and sea.

The seaman had changed in some respects. For one thing, he was far less political. In 1642 he had deliberately intervened to maintain the British constitution. In 1797 he had threatened the British state, though with far less obvious political motive. The seaman always kept his sense of fair play and his loyalty, while much longer periods at sea and on foreign service had isolated him from events on shore. The seamen of Queen Victoria's time would probably have agreed with their counterparts of Charles I's time when they stated of the constitution, 'We, who are always abroad, can best tell no government upon earth is comparable to it.'

The 'common seaman' of the mid-nineteenth century also had far less promotion prospects than in the past, as a definite class of commissioned officers had emerged. This had led to some subtle changes in the ranks of the petty officers – a term which had once included the midshipmen but was now reserved for lower deck seamen. The midshipman was now clearly a potential commissioned officer, while the quartermaster, who had lived aft with the officers early in the seventeenth century, was now clearly of the lower deck. As early as the 1670s, Pepys had observed that, 'the whole race of seamen ... find themselves reserved only for the toil and hazard of the trade, while they shall observe themselves excluded from the best rewards of it.' But the greatest change was quite recent. Largely due to the laws of supply and demand rather than any written policy, from 1815 it was practically impossible for a seaman to rise to commissioned rank.

In some ways it was the navy and society that had changed rather than the seaman himself. Pepys had believed that 'seamen, love their bellies above everything else', and this is reflected in James Morrison's obsession with food during the *Bounty* voyage. It was also mentioned by the Spithead mutineers, and one can forgive them for being suspicious that they were being short-changed by the authorities. The Victorian seaman was probably no less greedy, but the supply system was generally more efficient, and he rarely went hungry except in such extreme cases as the Franklin expedition. Seaman still needed good leaders and suffered from bad ones, but the extremes of Hugh Pigot of *Hermione* and Robert Corbett of *Africaine* were not likely to be tolerated. They despised cowards, as when they chanted, 'A man of war ahead, a man of war ahead', to Captain John Best in 1656, but men like that were far less likely to be appointed as officers in the mid-nineteenth century. Edward Barlow wrote, 'a poor man is abused with proud and ambitious masters, finding no recompense, having no money to try the law...' By Victorian times, a seaman was unlikely to be cheated of his wages in the Royal Navy, though it might still happen among the more dubious merchant shipping companies. And if the seaman was less likely to desert, it was only because he had entered the navy voluntarily in the first place, rather than being pressed.

But in many other ways the seamen had not changed very much. As in 1700, most people still believed, 'Our ships of war are indisputably the best in the world, and so might the sailors be too; for all depends on the merit of the commander ...' The seaman was still theoretically subject to the press gang and liable to be flogged, though these were far less likely than in the past. He still lived in a wooden ship with tall masts, even if it now had a steam engine to help it along. He still slept in a hammock, and it was still true to say that he would 'lie a whole night as dormant as Mahomet hanging betwixt two lode-stones'. He ate his meals in his mess, and Richard Braithwaite's comment of 1631 was still apt: 'Stars cannot be more faithful in their society than these Hans-kins in their fraternity. They will brave it valiantly when they are ranked together, and relate their adventures with wonderful terror.' Despite the coming of steam power, he still had his supreme skills with the rigging, as Braithwaite had observed, 'he can spin up a rope like a spider and down again like lightning. The rope is his road, and the topmast his beacon.' He was generally unambitious, as witness a cook around 1700: 'My niggard stars never designed me a loftier mansion than a cook-room; so ... I conformed my ambition to my supposed destiny.' Despite pockets of evangelism and many attempts at reform, the sailor was still largely indifferent to religion, though few would go as far as the Elizabethans who considered that to put him on oath was 'lost labour and offence to God'. He swore as much as he had done in the days of Sir Richard Hawkins, when the practice of cursing 'amongst the common sort of Mariners, and Sea-faring men, [was] too ordinarily abused'. The seaman was likely to get drunk on board ship despite cuts in the rum ration. He was even more likely to misbehave during his short and infrequent periods of leave, and the puritans of the nineteenth century would have agreed with William Canton in the 1650s: 'And being permitted to go a shore, either about your business or to see your friends, or to refresh your bodies, or the like, even at such times do you most shamefully abuse your selves, by drinking excessively till you make your selves more like beasts than men ...' In the days of Queen Victoria, as in the time of Queen Anne, 'No music-house but had his presence.' The seaman still tended to disregard his future, as in the 1630s: 'They sleep without fear of losing what they enjoy; and in enjoying little, they share in the less burden of cares.'

The seaman still wore no established uniform despite the attempts of individual captains to force him into one. He mostly signed on for a single voyage or commission despite legislation that he should stay for five years. He was just as likely to have been recruited from the merchant navy as to be trained within the Royal Navy itself. All these things would change in the decade after 1850, with profound effects on the character of the seaman himself.

APPENDIX
TRACING NAVAL RATINGS

Naval seamen of the age of sail are among the most interesting of ancestors – they travelled the world when most people rarely went beyond their own towns and villages, they braved all kind of hardship, and sometimes they witnessed the great events of history. The vast majority of seamen and other naval personnel were not officers: they were of the lower deck. There is a huge amount of material for tracing an officer's career in the navy, including biographies of most captains and passing certificates, which give details of every ship the officer served in. The position is far more difficult for members of the lower deck.

It should be remembered that a rating did not 'join the navy' as such during the age of sail – he was 'entered' for a particular ship. Even if he was transferred to one after another, perhaps against his will in wartime, the Admiralty kept no centralised record of his movements. This means that, despite meticulous record keeping, it is difficult to trace the career of an individual rating unless the name of at least one of his ships is known. As with most forms of research, the task becomes easier the closer one is to the present day. There are few sources for ratings before the late seventeenth century except the occasional muster book; after that, muster and pay books become common. Lists and indexes of individual men and their services become available in limited form by the time of the great French wars from 1793.

Certainly, research has become much easier over the years, with the publication of various lists and access to many series of records through the internet. That is likely to increase rapidly in the next few years, and this appendix can only report on the situation as it is in the middle of 2010, but almost certainly research into an individual will involve a visit to the National Archives at Kew. As always when looking into public records, it must be remembered that they were not created for the convenience of modern researchers but for the use of the people at the time, who understood what they were for and the background in which they were created. It is always useful to understand something of the system of naval administration. Useful guides are to be found in N. A. M. Rodger's pioneering *Naval Records for Genealogists* (several editions since 1984) and Bruno Pappalardo's *Tracing Your Naval Ancestors* (2003). Both of them deal with officers as much as ratings, and because of the nature of the sources they are much stronger on the period after 1850.

WAYS OF FINDING INDIVIDUALS

There is no universal way of starting research into an individual rating whose ships are not known, though there are some sources that may give leads for particular men. One of the most obvious is the Trafalgar Database at the National Archives. This lists the 18,000 men present at the battle, about 15 per cent of the fleet at the time. It is searchable by the name of an individual and will give his rating and the name of the ship he served in, with reference to the muster or pay book his name was found in, and his number within the book – all this is very useful for continuing the search.

Another useful source is Adm 29 at the National Archives. This includes the service records of ratings who applied for a pension. It can be searched on the National Archives website (www.nationalarchives.gov.uk/catalogue) by entering the man's name in the 'Word or phrase' field, and 'Adm 29' in the Department or Series code. For example, it can be found that John Bechervaise served between 1820 and 1838, though his age is not given in this document. The series only starts with applications from 1802 onwards, but that might include actual service up to 40 years earlier. Success in this procedure would lead on to Adm 73, the actual application for admission to Greenwich Hospital, which began about 1790, and often record much earlier service. Sometimes they give details of individual ships served in, which is a great advantage and cuts out much of the need to search muster books.

Another source is the Naval General Service Medal (originally known as the Naval War Medal), which was issued retrospectively in 1848 for actions stretching back many years to the French wars. Unlike earlier medals, it was issued to ratings as well as to officers, though they had to have survived until the time of the issue, and to go to the trouble of applying for it. Men were awarded clasps for particular actions, from such great battles as Trafalgar down to single-ship and boat actions. All of these are listed in K. Douglas-Morris's *The Naval General Service Roll,* 1793–1840 (London, 1982), but it is indexed by action and not by the name of individual men. The list includes the name of the ship the man was serving in at the time and his rating, with cross-references to other actions for which he was awarded clasps.

Far more clasps were awarded for Trafalgar than for any other action of the French Revolutionary and Napoleonic Wars – 1,613 – closely followed by the other post-war actions at Algiers in 1816 and Navarino in 1827. For the later action of the bombardment of Syria in 1840 by far the most clasps of all were awarded – nearly 7000.

Another medal of Victorian times is the Naval General Service Medal, awarded from 1830 and also catalogued by Douglas-Morris in *Naval Long Service Medals,* 1830–1990 (London, 1991): 1,430 seamen are known to have been issued with it, from 1830 onwards but often for service long before that.

If a rating subsequently became a warrant officer, probably as a cook, master at arms, carpenter, boatswain or gunner, then various papers will probably be found in different Admiralty series, such as passing certificates giving a list of his service in particular ships up to the time of his warrant. Some men, such as coopers, armourers, and sailmakers, were also warranted by the Navy Board, and their records are easier to trace.

HOW TO READ A MUSTER OR PAY BOOK

The key to finding out about individual men is to be found among the quarter of a million muster and pay books held in the National Archives. The purser of each ship had to keep a record of the men on board, including their date of entry to the ship, their rating, the amount paid or to them, clothing and tobacco issued and even in some periods treatment for venereal diseases. These are to be found, from 1688 onwards, in Admiralty classes 36, 37, 38, 39 and 41 in the National Archives. The Navy Board also kept more or less the same information in the ships' pay books, Adm 31–35. These have the advantage of being slightly neater and better organised, and usually having an 'alphabet' or index of the men's names, which is not always present in the muster books before about 1765. A muster book was produced every quarter.

Each muster or pay book contains several lists. The first and by far the largest is the general one of the officers and crew. There are separate lists for boys of different classes, for marines and for supernumeraries of different types, according to whether they were borne for victuals only, for reduced victuals, or for wages and victuals. The first, more general, section is the most important part for tracing a rating, but the supernumeraries section also has to be looked at as the individual might be entered there on first joining a ship, or if he is being transferred to another station. The general section usually starts with the first officers appointed to the ship, and also the 'widows' men', fictitious seaman who were borne at the rate of one per hundred men, with their wages going to relief funds for naval widows. Seamen gradually begin to appear in greater numbers, often drafted in from receiving ships or other vessels. After that, every officer and man is recorded from the time of joining the ship.

The book consists of a series of double-page spreads divided into columns. The first one has the man's number from the date of entry – he would keep this for his whole time on board, apart from any time he might have served as a supernumerary or boy. The next column contains the date of entry, and 'appearance' means the date on which he actually appeared on board. This was often left blank as being identical to the previous column. Then comes the man's name, usually forename followed by surname. The next column was to indicate whether he was 'prest or not' or a similar form of words – the actual information given here varied in nature and quality and is not always reliable. The next column, from 1764 onwards, gives the man's age on joining the ship, followed by the date and place of birth. The column on 'quality' refers to his rating and might record changes, either up or down, during the period of that muster. The column on discharges usually includes 'D' if discharged to another ship; 'Ds' if sent to sick quarters; 'R' if he was believed to have deserted; and the callous 'DD' for discharged dead. The date of discharge is in the next column, and the reason is given. It could be promotion, 'unserviceable' on medical survey, or turning over to another, named, ship. The opposite page of the muster book includes details of various deductions from the man's wages including slop clothes, trusses for ruptures, buying of dead men's clothes, hammocks and wages remitted to family ashore.

There are various problems with searching muster and pay books. In the first place they are usually very heavy, and it may be necessary to search several volumes to find the full extent of a man's service in a particular ship. Sometimes men were mustered under false names, either because they had already deserted from another ship or intended to desert in the future. Not all seamen were fully literate, and often the spelling of a name varies from one ship to another. If the muster book from one ship is missing, the chain will be broken, and it will be difficult to trace which ship the man transferred to next. Even at best, it may be necessary to look at several volumes to find out when a man joined and left a ship, and then to repeat the process with another ship.

FINDING MORE DETAIL

In exceptional cases, more details may be found out about individuals and their activities. Perhaps the most dramatic are the 'Description Books' kept by captains to record the personal details of men in case of desertion. The most complete known ones are those of *Bellerophon* just after the Battle of Trafalgar and the 74-gun *Blake* under Captain Codrington from 1808 onwards (National Maritime Museum LBK/38). These give descriptions that are often frank and unflattering: for example, Samuel Lindley of *Bellerophon* was 24 years old, from Lenham in Suffolk, and had three years' experience in the merchant service. He had a pale, thin face but was considered 'well looking'. Isaac Harrison of Norwich had spent 32 of his 45 years at sea. He is describes as 'bald, a little deaf, thick set and strong made' and was a quarter gunner. John Hillock from Dundee had first gone to sea in 1787 at the age of 11, and his time had been divided between the merchant and royal navies.[1]

In *Blake*, William Kinchett was a 24-year old landsman from Storrington in Sussex, 5 feet 4½ inches tall, with brown short hair and brown eyes. He was single and been a husbandman before joining the navy and could not take the helm, take the lead or sew a seam with the sailmaker.

The surgeon's journals of particular ships, in Adm 101, are also quite frank in their details of individuals, but only selected ones have been preserved, and, of course, the man would have had to come to the attention of the surgeon to feature in them. Hospital admissions papers are rather more general and based around particular hospitals in the naval bases at home and abroad.

One useful source of family detail is the allotments of wages that men made to their next of kin from 1795 onwards. These give the name, address and relationship of the recipient and are mostly to be found in Adm 27. Seaman's wills, usually in a standard from, can be found in Adm 48.

THE STORY OF THE SHIPS

Once it is known which ships a man served in, it is possible to trace the movements and actions of each. Ship's log books, kept by the captain, master and lieutenants, are available in great numbers in the National Archives and National Maritime Museum, but they are not very useful in tracing seamen – in general, their names only appear of they were flogged or died. Log books are more useful in tracing the story of a ship in which a man served, though they do not provide all the answers. They are filled with technical navigational detail, which is difficult for the layman to understand, and they say nothing about the purpose of a particular voyage.

To follow a man's career on board a particular ship, it is best to start with the short histories available in Rif Winfield's volumes – *British Warships in the Age of Sail, 1603–1714* (London, 2009), *1714–1792* (London, 2007) and *1793–1817* (London, 2005). More generally, a potted history of practically every naval ship is to be found on microfiche in the National Museum. The biography of the captain and other officers can also be useful here. Those appointed up to 1760 can be found in John Charnock's *Biographia Navalis* (6 volumes, London, 1794–8), which records every officer who reached the rank of captain from 1660 to 1760. John Marshall's *Royal Naval Biography* (12 volumes, London, 1823–35) carries a biography of every living admiral, captain and commander in the early 1820s, which gives a great deal of detail of the French Revolutionary and Napoleonic Wars. William O'Byrne published his *Naval Biographical Dictionary* in 1849 with details of every living sea officer, including lieutenants. For more information, the replies to O'Byrne's questionnaires, and much other detail, are contained in Additional Manuscripts 38039–38054 in the British Library; though by that stage one is probably moving away from the story of the ship and into the details of the career and prejudices of the officer concerned. Finally, the detailed events surrounding an individual ship can often be traced in the Adm 1, Admiralty in-letters, series in the National Archives. Captains rarely wrote directly to the Admiralty giving accounts of operations, but if they did their letters are filed under the year and the initial letter of the name. More likely they would write to the admiral in charge of the fleet, who would then send a copy on to the Admiralty. These letters are also filed in Adm 1, under the station concerned. Such letters often contain details of the crew, such as transfers and desertions, and they are usually worth a look.

GLOSSARY

Main Sources: *Oxford English Dictionary*; W. Burney, *Universal Dictionary of the Marine*, 1815; and H. L. Blackmore, *The Armouries of the Tower of London*, 1976. Note that the meaning given is the one in use at the time, which is not necessarily the same as the modern meaning.

Able Seaman. A highly skilled seamen with several years of experience
Admiralty. The government body that administered the navy by means of the Board of Admiralty
Aft. Towards the stern in a ship; by association, the seamen who lived there
Apron. A lead plate placed over the touch-hole of gun to prevent accidental ignition
Armament. A mobilisation on the threat of war
Armourer. Appointed by Navy Board Warrant. As well as repairing muskets, cutlasses, etc., he was the principal metalworker in a ship
Athwart, Athwartships. Across the ship, from one side to the other
Balinger. A kind of warship based on a whaling-boat
Ballast. Weights, usually gravel or iron, placed in the hold to give a ship stability.
Bar Shot. Similar to double-headed shot
Barge. Originally a small sailing vessel; later, a ship's boat mainly used by the captain, or a sailing vessel used in estuaries, etc.
Barque, Bark. A general name for a small ship, or a broad-sterned ship without a figurehead
Before the Mast. The state of being a common seaman rather than an officer
Berth, Birth. The position of a ship at anchor, or a man's sleeping accommodation, or the space for a mess between two guns
Bilboes. Iron stocks used to restrain a prisoner's feet
Biscuit. Dried bread, main item of naval diet
Boat. A small craft usually with open decks; a ship's boat is one that belongs to a ship and can be hoisted on board or towed behind
Boatswain. One of the standing officers of a ship, in charge of boats and rigging as well as the organisation and discipline of the crew
Bohea. Black tea of the cheapest sort
Boom. A pole used to extend the bottoms of a sail or for other purposes
Bounty. Money paid to seamen on volunteering for the navy
Bower. A large anchor, placed in the bow
Bowse, To haul on a gun tackle
Bowsprit. A mast-like structure extending diagonally forward from the bow, used to support square sails below it or triangular sails above
Bridewell. A prison, after the House of Correction in London
Brig. A small to medium-sized vessel with two masts, both square rigged
Broadside. The guns on one side of a ship, not counting those firing forward or aft, or the shot produced by firing them all at once
Bungs. A slang term for a cooper
Burthen or Burden. A measure of the capacity of a merchant ship, in tons
Cable. The very thick rope attached to an anchor
Calibre. The size of a piece of ordnance, usually measured by the internal diameter of the barrel, or by the weight of a solid iron ball

Canister Shot. Small balls inside a cylinder, used against personnel

Cannon. A general term for a large gun, or more specifically one firing a 42-pound shot

Capstan. A device for allowing large numbers of men to operate on a particular rope, especially an anchor cable

Captain. A naval rank, equal to a colonel or lieutenant-colonel in the army according to seniority. Also a courtesy title for the commanding officer of any ship, especially naval

Captain of Gun. A seaman appointed to a particular gun. He was unpaid, though he might also hold the rating of quarter gunner, etc.

Captain of Mast, etc. The leader of a group of seaman in a part of the ship, e.g., foremast, forecastle, waist, etc. Unpaid until 1806

Carpenter. One of the standing officers, appointed to maintain the hull, masts, etc. of a ship

Carrack. A large, heavy sailing ship of Portuguese origin

Carvel Building. Building a ship with the planks laid side by side, rather than overlapping

Cask. The generic term for a wooden container; strictly, the term 'barrel' should only be used for a specific size

Castle. Originally a structure in the bow or stern of a merchant ship converted to a warship; developed into the 'forecastle', which was a permanent part of the ship

Cat-of-Nine-Tails. A kind of whip with nine strands of rope, used for flogging

Caulker. A skilled man who used oakum and tar to seal the gaps between the planks, etc. of a ship

Chain and Hammer Shot. Two balls linked together by a chain, used against rigging

Chase. The bow or stern guns of a ship

Clerk of the Acts. An official of the Navy Board, in effect its secretary

Clinker Building. Building a boat with the edges of the planks overlapping

Coal Trimmer. A man who shovels coal from the bunkers towards the stokers.

Cockpit. A compartment aft on the orlop deck, used by the midshipmen and by the surgeon in battle

Cog. A medieval ship with straight bow and stern

Collier. A ship designed for carrying coal, mostly from the north-east of England

Commander (*Master and Commander* until 1795). The officer in charge of a small warship, a sloop or smaller; after 1827, the second-in-command of a large warship

Commissioner. A Navy Board official, often one in a particular dockyard

Common Sailor or Seaman. This term is often used to distinguish the non-officers; 'common' as 'ordinary' would imply a more specific rating

Con. Conn, Cond, Cunn, etc. To supervise the steering of a ship

Conduct money. A sum paid to seamen as expenses for joining a ship

Convoy. At this time this usually meant warships appointed to escort merchant ships, rather than the merchant ships themselves

Corporal. In the navy, an assistant to the master at arms.

Corsair. A sea raider, with more legal authority than a pirate

Coxswain. A petty officer who steers a ship's boat and leads its crew, often under the charge of a midshipman

Crab. A small, portable capstan

Crew. As well as the ratings of an individual ship, this can mean a particular group, e.g., carpenter's crew, gunner's crew.

Cruiser. A ship that puts to sea, as distinct from a guardship, etc. Also one carrying out raids on enemy shipping.

Culverin. A gun firing an 18-pound ball, originally with a very long barrel

Demi-Cannon. An older term for a 32-pounder

Demi-Culverin. A gun firing a 9-pound shot, also with a long barrel

Disrated. Reduced in rate

Division. A group of the crew under a lieutenant for disciplinary, health and welfare purposes

Double-Headed Shot. A ball cut in half with a bar of iron between them, for use against rigging

Double Shot. To put extra balls in a gun

Earring, Ear-ring, etc. loops of rope attached to the upper corners of a sail

Falcon. A light, long-barrelled gun firing a ball of about 2½ to 3 pounds

Falconet. Similar to the above, firing a ball of about 1½ pounds

Fathom. Six feet, mainly used in the measurement of depth of water

Fearnought. Stout, thick woollen cloth

Fireship. A ship loaded with combustible materials to be set in the direction of the enemy

Flagship. A ship carrying an admiral and therefore flying his flag

Fleet. Either the navy as a whole, or a large body of major warships, including several squadrons

Flesh Carpenter. Apparently a slang term for a boatswain's mate, presumably because of his role in flogging

Fore and Aft Rig. Cutters, schooners, etc., in which the sails run fore and aft in their neutral position

Forward. The fore part of the ship, or moving towards it

Fowling Piece. A breech-loading gun firing small shot or stones

Gasket. A rope used to lash a sail to the yard during furling

Grape Shot. Musket balls inside a canvas bag, used against personnel

Grapnel. A device shaped like a small anchor with four or five hooks and used to anchor a boat or to hold one ship to another, especially in battle

Grass-Comber. A sailor's term for a farm labourer

Great Guns. The artillery of a ship, mounted on carriages rather than fired by an individual

Gromet. A novice at sea

Guarda Costa. A Spanish coastguard or customs vessel

Guardship. A ship partly fitted out, manned and kept in readiness in harbour, at a higher state than ship in ordinary

Gundeck. A deck bearing guns, especially the lower gundeck in a ship of the line

Gunner. A warrant officer in charge of the maintenance of the guns, carriages, ammunition, etc.

Gunport. A square hole in the side of the ship to allow a gun to fire through it, usually closed by a lid when not in use

Gunroom. Space aft on the lower deck, used by midshipmen, etc., in a ship of the line, and the equivalent of wardroom for officers in a frigate

Galleon. An ocean-going sailing ship of Spanish origin, taken up and adapted by the English

Galley. A rowing warship, usually long, narrow and flimsy in construction compared with a sailing warship

Galley. The cooking facility in a ship

Gentleman Officer. An officer appointed through royal favouritism without much practical knowledge

Grog. Originally rum diluted with two parts of water; later any alcoholic drink issued to the crew

Halyard. Originally 'haul-yard', a rope used to haul up a sail

Handspike. A wooden lever used by gun crews to traverse the rear part of the gun for aiming

Hawse. The fore part of a ship's bow, where the anchor cables come out through the hawse holes; also refers to the situation of a ship at anchor; for example, 'a clear hawse' means the cables are not fouled.

Hawser. A thick rope, but smaller than a cable, often used for anchoring

Heel. The lean of a ship to one side or the other, usually caused by the wind. Unlike a list, it is considered normal and is not a subject of concern

Helmsman. The man who actually steers the ship, as distinct from the officer of the watch or quartermaster who supervises him

Hoy. A small, single-masted vessel mostly used in an estuary

Idler. A member of the lower deck who does not keep watches and is normally allowed to sleep the night through

Impressment. The practice of pressing seamen into the Royal Navy

Inferior Officer. An early term for petty officer, though less specific

Irons. The bilboes; also 'in irons', of a ship that has failed to tack and is stuck in position

Jews. Shore-based tradesmen and dealers, not necessarily of the Jewish faith or race

Kedge. A small anchor that can be slung under a boat and placed ahead of the ship

Keel. The straight, square-section timber that is the lowest part of a ship and forms its backbone; also a small cargo vessel, mostly employed on the River Tyne

Keelman. A crew member of a keel (see above)

Kersey. A coarse woollen cloth, usually ribbed.

Ketch. A two-masted vessel with the forward mast larger than the after one; usually square rigged in the seventeenth century, fore and aft rigged by the nineteenth

Kittisol. A sunshade or parasol of Chinese origin

Landsman. An unskilled adult who helps with the sailing of the ship

Larboard. The left-hand side when facing the bows of the ship; also one of the watches in a two-watch system

Lead. A lead weight attached to a long line, used to measure the depth of water

Leeward. The side of a ship, etc., away from the wind

Lieutenant. The most junior grade of commissioned officer. Originally the captain's deputy, later an officer who took charge of a watch and a division of the ship's company

Lock. A device fitted to the rear of a gun to produce a spark to fire it

Lodesman or Lodeman. originally a leader or guide, later a pilot

Longship. A clinker-bult rowing and sailing boat as used by the Vikings

Long Boat. The largest of the ship's boats until the middle of the eighteenth century, used for heavy work such as moving kedge anchors and carrying stores. Replaced by the launch

Lord High Admiral. The government official in charge of the navy. From the late seventeenth century onwards he was usually replaced by the Board of Admiralty

Manger. A space just aft of the hawse holes on the lower deck intended to prevent water getting to the rest of the deck, but also a place for keeping live animals

Marine. A soldier recruited with a view to service at sea

Master at Arms. The most senior petty officer in a ship, originally to train the men at small arms but later the chief of the ship's police

Mate. A petty officer and assistant to a warrant officer, e.g., master's mate, gunner's mate

Merchantman. A merchant ship

Mess. A group of seaman who get together for meals and recreation, and the table at which they eat

Midships. The centre part of a ship, either in the fore and aft direction, or athwarsthips; also to put the helm amidships, to have the rudder in the neutral position

Midshipman. By the eighteenth century, a trainee officer

Minion. A small, long-barrelled gun firing a ball of about 4 pounds

Monkey Jacket. A close-fitting, short jacket worn by sailors

Murderer. A small cannon used to clear the decks during boarding

Muster Book. An official document listing the crew of the ship, with certain details of age, joining the ship, payment, etc.

Mutiny. Deliberate disobedience of orders, either by a small group or as a mass movement

Nablette. Obscure, presumably a type of gun

Navy Board. A board under the Admiralty that supervised the Royal Dockyards, shipbuilding, naval finance and administration

Navy List. A publication that listed all the ships in the fleet and officers in order of seniority

Navy Office. The London headquarters of the Navy Board

Ordinary. The state of a ship laid up, without most of her guns and equipment on board, and looked after by her standing officers

Ordinary Seaman. A man with approximately two to seven years at sea, less skilled than an able seaman

Orlop. In the early seventeenth century, a deck; later the lowest deck in a ship, below the waterline and carrying no guns

Outport. A port in the United Kingdom other than London, or a small one that does not have a customs house

Partridge Shot. A number of missiles fired together from a cannon

Paterero. Originally 'pedero', a type of gun used for firing stone shot

Pendant. A long, narrow banner flying from the masthead and indicating that a ship is in commission

Penny. A unit of currency, a twelfth of a shilling and equivalent to 0.4 of a decimal penny.

Pensioner. A retired or disabled seaman in receipt of a pension from Greenwich Hospital, or living there

Petty Officer. An officer without a commission, the equivalent of a non-commissioned officer in the army. Originally the term included midshipmen. Some petty officers, mostly skilled tradesmen, had warrants from the Navy Board; others were appointed by the captain of the ship

Pilot. A mariner with local knowledge to guide a ship into or out of a specific port, or through a particular area

Pinnace. A ship's boat, mainly used for rowing officers

Placard. Used in the sense of a document with a seal attached, giving formal authority

Point. A division of the compass, 1/32 of the full circle, or 11¼ degrees

Poop. A short deck above the quarterdeck in a ship of the line or other large ship, covering the captain's cabin

Pound. The basic unit of British currency, consisting of 20 shillings or 240 pence. Also a measure of weight, especially of the ball fired by a gun, equal to 0.454 kilograms

Press. To force seamen to serve in the Royal Navy

Pressing Tender. A vessel used by the press gang to take seamen from merchant ships, and to keep men afloat and transport them to naval ships

Press Gang. A group of men under a commissioned officer to press men into the navy, either afloat or ashore

Press Warrant. The document, signed by the Lords of the Admiralty, that gave an officer authority to press men into the navy

Press of Sail. Carrying an unusual amount of sail in a chase, possibly endangering the sails or the masts

Prest. Originally ready money paid as an advance on enlistment

Prestmaster. An official appointed locally to impress seamen for the navy

Prize Money. The money raised by selling a captured enemy merchant ship or warship and dividing the proceeds between officers and crew

Privateer. A private man of wear, making its living by captures from the enemy

Pug. In 1611 this term was used to describe bargemen, and possibly it was extended to sailors generally

Purser. The supply officer of a ship; he made a part of his living by selling goods to the crew, by whom he was always held in suspicion

Q for 'Query'. Put against a man's name in the muster book if he failed to appear on board ship and it was not clear whether he had deserted

Quadrant. An instrument for measuring the angle of a celestial body, the forerunner of the sextant

Quarter bill. The list of the crew and their positions for fighting or battle practice

Quarterdeck. The deck above the upper gundeck, running about half the length at the same level as the forecastle, and used mainly by the officers; hence also, the officers of a ship

Quarter gunner. A petty officer, part of the gunner's crew under the gunner's mate.

Quartermaster. A petty officer who supervises the helmsmen

Quarters. The men's positions in action, hence 'beat to quarters'

Quota, Quota Acts. Acts of Parliament of 1797 that obliged each local authority to find a specified number of men for the navy.

R for 'Run'. The mark put against a man's name in the ship's muster book when he was believed to have deserted

Rammer. A wooden pole with a cylinder attached, for ramming home the cartridge, wads and shot into a gun

Race-Built. A comparatively low-built galleon

Rate, Rating. As applied to a seaman, his rating in a particular level of skill as a seaman. For a ship, the rate was based on the number of guns and was used to assess the pay of the captain and heads of departments, such as the standing officers. By about 1700 it had also come to mean a man holding a rating, i.e., a member of the lower deck

Ratlines. Ropes attached across the shrouds to provide a kind of ladder for seamen to climb the rigging

Rattan. A stick carried by warrant and petty officers to enforce discipline

Rear. The rearmost part of a squadron in line of battle, hence 'Rear Admiral'

Reeve. To pass the end of a rope through a hole

Regulating Officers. Appointed to supervise press gangs in particular areas

Rendezvous. A public house or other building hired for use as a headquarters of the press gang

Roband, etc. Originally 'rope-band', a rope used to bind the outer edge of a square sail to the yard

Rode, Rid, etc. To stay in position by means of an anchor

Rope's End. Used by a petty officer to 'start' the men, an alternative to the rattan

Round Ship. In medieval times, a sailing ship as distinct from a galley, which was much longer and narrower.

Rove. Past tense of 'reeve'

Saker. A long-barrelled gun firing a ball of about 5 to 6 pounds

Scuttle. A small aperture in a ship's deck or side

Servant. An apprentice, a domestic servant, or simply an employee

Shilling. A twentieth of a pound, consisting of twelve pennies

Ship of the Line. A ship that was large enough to stand in the line of battle, with at least two complete decks of guns

Shrouds. Thick ropes attached to the channel off the side of a ship, or the edge of a top, to support a mast from behind and laterally

Slops. Clothing sold to the seamen by the purser

Small Arms. Firearms that could be used by a single man – muskets and pistols

Sommer Castle, Summercastle. A castle built above another one on the bow or stern

Sponge. Attached to a wooden staff and used to clean out the barrel of a gun after firing

Spring. A rope attached to an anchor cable to allow the ship to be manoeuvred

Spritsail. A sail hung from a yard under or above the bowsprit

Squadron. A group of warships smaller than a fleet, usually ten or less

Square Rig. A rig in which the sails are hung from yards and are at right angles to the direction of movement of the ship when in their neutral position

Starting. Using a rattan or rope's end to stimulate the men at their work, or to punish a minor misdemeanour

Standing Officers. The carpenter, boatswain and gunner of a ship, so called because they stayed with their ship even when she was out of commission

Station. The position of an individual man for various activities, e.g., in battle, tacking, raising anchor, etc.

Station Bill. The list of each man's position during various manoeuvres

Stave. The curved pieces that form part of a cask. As a verb, to dismantle a cask to save space

Stays. A ship is 'in stays' when she fails to tack; similar to 'in irons'

Steering Oar. An oar hung near the stern of an early or medieval ship, before the invention of the rudder

Stern. The rear part of a ship

Steward. A servant in the wardroom or captain's cabin, or the purser's assistant

Stoker. A man employed to shovel coal into a furnace and to tend the water in a boiler

Straggler. A man missing from his ship, not necessarily because of desertion

Suit. A ship's complete outfit of sails

Supernumerary. A man borne in a ship who is not part of the crew but is fed and possibly paid

Tacking. Turning the ship to bring the wind on the other side, by pointing her bow towards the wind

Tarpaulin. Canvas covered with tar to make it waterproof; also an officer who has attained command through the merchant service

Tender. A small vessel, larger than a boat, attached to a man-of-war for pressing men and carrying stores

Ticket. A certificate given to a seaman to claim his wages, to allow him to go on leave or for another purpose

Three-Decker. A ship with three complete decks of guns

Tier. A deck of guns

Tompion, Tampion. A wooden plug inserted to protect the muzzle of a gun

Tons. In a merchant ship, the measurement of the capacity of a ship. In a warship, the result of a standard calculation that gives an approximate comparison between one ship and another, but not the same as her actual displacement

Top. A structure at the head of a lower mast, used to spread the shrouds as a base for the men working there.

Top Castle. A castle at the top of a mast in medieval times

Topgallant mast. The mast above the topmast, the highest mast in most ships

Topmast. A mast above the lower mast and overlapping with it in the area of the join

Topman. Skilled seaman, fit enough to work aloft in the rigging

Toprim. The rim of a top

Transport. Usually a merchant vessel hired to carry troops and naval and military supplies

Tricing Line. A light rope used to haul an object clear of an area where work is going on

Trinity House. The body charged with aiding navigation in English waters, by mean of buoys, lighthouses, etc.

Turning Over. Moving men from one ship to another, often against their will

Starboard. The right-hand side of a ship, looking forward; also one of the watches in a two-watch system.

Two-Decker. A warship with at least two complete decks of guns, independent of those mounted in the forecastle, quarterdeck, etc.

Van. The leading part of a squadron, theoretically commanded by a Vice Admiral

Virginia. Tobacco

Wad. A plug, usually of straw or rope, used to keep the powder and shot in position when loading a gun

Waist. The lower part of the ship, between the quarterdeck and the forecastle; hence waisters, the men who worked there.

Wardroom. The dining and recreation room for commissioned and certain warrant officers

Warrant Officer. An officer appointed by the Navy Board, at any level from physician of the fleet to ship's cook

Watch. A period of two or four hours during which particular seamen are on duty; or a group of seaman who are on watch together

Watch Bill. A list of the men in watches on a particular ship

Waterline. The line on a ship's hull level with the water in which the ship floats; or a horizontal line used to assess the streamlining of the underwater hull

Waterman. A man employed on boats and barges in rivers, especially the Thames

Weather. The side of a ship, etc., closest to the wind; identical to 'windward'; opposite of 'leeward'

Weigh. To raise an anchor

Whipstaff. A piece of wood attached vertically by a pivot to the end of the tiller to give extra leverage and raise the steering position by one deck.

Windward. The side of a ship, etc., nearest to the wind.

Yare. To move quickly

Yeoman. A trusted men of junior petty officer status, e.g., yeoman of the sheets, or of the powder room

Younker. A young man or unskilled seaman

NOTES

Introduction

1 For example: Anthony Carew, *The Lower Deck of the Royal Navy, 1900–1939*, Manchester, 1981; B. Lavery, *Shipboard Life and Organisation*, 1998; Christopher Lloyd, *The British Seaman*, London, 1968; Christopher McKee, *Sober Men and True*, Cambridge, Massachusetts, 2002; M. Oppenheim, *A History of the Administration of the Royal Navy*, London, 1896; N. A. M. Rodger, *The Safeguard of the Seas*, London, 1997, and *The Command of the Ocean*, London, 2004

1. The Early Seaman, before 1642

1 W. S. Laird Clowes, *The Royal Navy: A History from the Earliest Times to the Present*, vol 1, London, 1987, p 13
2 Carl Stephenson and F. G. Marcham, *Sources of English Constitutional History*, New York, 1937, pp 162–3
3 Laird Clowes, op cit, vol 1, pp 188–9
4 Navy Records Society, vol 131, *British Naval Documents, 1204–1960*, ed John B. Hattendorf et al, 1993, pp 23–4
5 *Sources of English Consitutional History*, p 137
6 F. W. Brooks, *The English Naval Forces*, London, 1932, p 171
7 Dorothy Burwash, *English Merchant Shipping 1460–1540*, Toronto, 1947, p 67
8 *Black Book of the Admiralty*, vol II, p 225
9 Laird Clowes, op cit, vol 1, pp 104–5
10 *English Merchant Shipping 1460–1540*, p 35
11 Navy Records Society, vol 43, *Monson*, Vol III, p 192
12 Laird Clowes, op cit, vol 1, p 137
13 Ibid

14 Sir Harry Nicolas, *The History of the Royal Navy*, London, 1847, vol I, p 467
15 N. A. M. Rodger, *The Safeguard of the Seas*, London, 1997, p 140
16 Navy Records Society, vol 123, *The Navy of the Lancastrian Kings*, ed Susan Rose, 1982, pp 42–3
17 Ibid, p 47
18 Nicholas, *The History of the Royal Navy*, vol I, p 465
19 *Black Book of the Admiralty*, vol I, p 13
20 Ibid
21 H. J. Hewitt, *The Organisation of War under Edward III*, Manchester, 1966, p 83
22 2 Richard II, stat 1, cap. 4
23 *Mariners Mirror*, vol 63, no 1, Feb 1977
24 *The Navy of the Lancastrian Kings*, op cit, pp 247–52
25 Navy Records Society, vol 8, *Naval Accounts and Inventories in the Reign of Henry VII*, ed M. Oppenheim, 1896, pp 194–5
26 *The Safeguard of the Seas*, pp 160–1
27 M. Oppenheim, *A History of the Administration of the Royal Navy*, London, 1896, p 56
28 H. L. Blackmore, *The Armouries of the Tower of London*, vol I, *Ordnance*, London, 1976, p 393
29 Navy Records Society, *The Anthony Roll*, ed C Knighton and D. M. Loades, 2000, p 13
30 Navy Records Society, vol 29, *Fighting Instructions 1530–1816*, ed Sir Julian Corbett, 1905; reprinted 1971, p 15
31 *Materials for a History of the Reign of Henry VII*, ed W. Campbell, London, 1877, vol 2, p 403*ff*
32 *Letters and Papers of Henry VIII, 1544*, vol 19, part l, ed James Gairdner and R. H. Brodie, 1903, p 89
33 Ibid, p 398

34 Pepys Library, Magdalene College, Cambridge, ms no 2872
35 *State Papers During the Reign of Hnery VIII*, vol 1, London, 1831, p 792
36 *Letters and Papers of Henry VIII, 1544*, vol 20, part 2, ed James Gairdner and R. H. Brodie, London, 1907, p 84
37 Ibid, p 98
38 Ibid, part 1, pp 36–7
39 Ibid, vol 19, part 2, 1544, p 397
40 Calendar of State Papers, Venetian, 1534–54, vol 5, ed R. Brown, London, 1873, p 351
41 Ibid, pp 548–9
42 Peter Marsden, *Sealed by Time*, Portsmouth, 2003, p 20
43 Julie Gardiner, ed, *Before the Mast*, Portsmouth, 2005, *passim*
44 Pepys Library, Magdalene College, Cambridge, ms no 1266
45 5 Elizabeth cap. 27
46 Navy Records Society, vol 11, *Papers Relating to the Spanish War, 1585–87*, ed J. S. Corbett, 1897, p 281
47 Ibid, p 265
48 Ibid, p 153
49 *A History of the Administration of the Royal Navy*, p 388
50 Ibid, p 384
51 Papers Relating to the Spanish War, p 165
52 Acts of the Privy Council, new series, vol XV, edited by John Roche Dasert, 1587–8, p 254
53 Ibid, p. 200
54 Pepys Library, Magdalene College, Cambridge, ms no 1774
55 Navy Records Society, vol 1, *Papers Relating to the Defeat of the Spanish Armada*, 1895, ed J. K. Laughton, reprinted 1981, vol 1, p 190
56 Ibid, p 273
57 Ibid, p 323
58 Ibid, p 190
59 Ibid, vol 2, pp 96–7
60 Sir Walter Raleigh, *Works*,

vol 8, ed Oldys and Birch, London, 1829, p 344

61 Ibid, p 346

62 Sir Julian S. Corbett, *The Successors of Drake*, London, 1900, p 173

63 Ibid, p 172

64 Navy Records Society, vol 23, *The Naval Tracts of Sir William Monson*, ed M. Oppenheim, vol 2, 1902, p 383

65 Historical Manuscripts Commission, *Foljambe Manuscripts*, ed Kirk and Cartwright, London, 1897, p 69

66 Navy Records Society, vol 45, *Sir William Monson's Naval Tracts*, vol 4, ed Oppenheim, 1913, p 199

67 H. W. Hodges and E. A. Hughes, *Select Naval Documents*, Cambridge, 1922, p 22

68 Historical Manuscripts Commission, *Cecil Manuscripts at Hatfield*, ed Scargill-Bird, vol 4, 1883, pp 120–3

69 *A History of the Administration of the Royal Navy*, p 134

70 *The Observations of Sir Richard Hawkins*, 1622, reprinted Amsterdam and New York, 1968, p 12

71 Ibid, p 20

72 Ibid, p 41

73 Ibid, p 32

74 Ibid, p 44

75 Ibid, p 45

76 Navy Records Society, vol 22, *The Naval Tracts of Sir William Monson*, ed Oppenheim, vol 1, 1902, p 293

77 Pepys Library, Magdalene College, Cambridge, ms no 2911, f. 31

78 Calendar of State Papers, Domestic, James I, 1611–8, ed M. A. E. Green, 1858, p 177

79 Navy Records Society, vol 116, *The Jacobean Commissions of Enquiry, 1608 and 1618*, ed A. P. McGowan, 1971, p 280

80 Navy Records Society, vol 65, *Boteler's Dialogues*, ed W. G. Perrin, 1929

81 Navy Records Society, vol 56, *The Life and Works of Sir Henry Mainwaring*, vol 2, ed G. E. Mainwaring and W. E. Perrin, 1921, pp 86–7

82 Navy Records Society, vol 45, *Sir William Monson's Naval Tracts*, vol 4, ed Oppenheim, 1913, p 60

83 Ibid, p 16

84 Ibid, p 199

85 Ibid, p 32

86 Ibid, p 33

87 *Boteler's Dialogues*, p 16

88 Navy Records Society, vol 43, *The Naval Tracts of Sir William Monson*, vol 3, ed Oppenheim, 1912, p 185

89 *Boteler's Dialogues*, p 51

90 *The Naval Tracts of Sir William Monson*, vol 4, p 228

91 Ibid, p 228

92 *The Life and Works of Sir Henry Mainwaring*, vol 2, p 183

93 *The Naval Tracts of Sir William Monson*, vol 4, p 58

94 Richard Braithwait, *Whimzies*, London, 1631

95 Captain John Smith, *A Sea Grammar*, ed Kermit Goell, London, 1970, p 49

96 *The Life and Works of Sir Henry Mainwaring*, vol 2, p 253

97 Ibid, p 130

98 *Boteler's Dialogues*, p 13

99 *The Naval Tracts of Sir William Monson*, vol 4, p 198

100 *Boteler's Dialogues*, p 15

101 *The Naval Tracts of Sir William Monson*, vol 4, p 56

102 *Boteler's Dialogues*, pp 257–8

103 *A Sea Grammar*, p 49

104 *The Naval Tracts of Sir William Monson*, vol 4, p 8

105 *Boteler's Dialogues*, pp 42–3

106 *The Naval Tracts of Sir William Monson*, vol 3, pp 386–7

107 George Kendal, *The Clerk of the Surveigh Surveighed*, London, 1656, pp 2–8

108 *The Naval Tracts of Sir William Monson*, vol 3, p 434

109 *The Naval Tracts of Sir William Monson*, vol 4, p 21

110 *Boteler's Dialogues*, pp 17–18

111 Ibid, pp 296–7

112 London Record Society,

Trinity House Transactions, 1609–35, ed G. G. Harris, London, 1983, p 92

113 *The Life and Works of Sir Henry Mainwaring*, vol 2, pp 107–8

114 *A History of the Administration of the Royal Navy*, p 214

115 *Trinity House Transactions*, p 116

116 Pepys Library, Magdalene College, Cambridge, ms no 2122

117 Christopher Lloyd, *The British Seaman*, London, 1968, p 60

118 Calendar of State Papers, Domestic, James I, 1623–5, ed M. A. E. Green, 1859, p 504

119 Ibid, p 503

120 National Maritime Museum manuscripts, ADL/J/3

121 *A History of the Administration of the Royal Navy*, p 219*n*

122 Ibid, pp 223–4

123 C. D. Yonge, *The History of the British Navy*, London, 1863, p 101

124 *A History of the Administration of the Royal Navy*, p 231

125 Yonge, op cit, 112

126 *Three Sea Journals of Stuart Times*, ed Bruce S. Ingram, London, 1936, p 12

127 Ibid, p 17

128 *The Constitutional Documents of the Puritan Revolution*, ed S. R. Gardiner, Oxford, 1906, pp 106–7

129 British Library, *Harleian manuscripts*, 6843 f 141

130 Calendar of State Papers, Domestic, Charles I, 1635, ed J. Bruce, 1865, p 363

131 Ibid, p 332

132 Navy Records Society, vol 7, *Holland's Discourses on the Navy*, ed J. R. Tanner, 1896, pp 380 and *passim*

133 Calendar of State Papers, Domestic, Charles I, 1637–8, ed John Bruce, 1869, p 236

134 Ibid, p 337

135 Raleigh, op cit, vol 8, p 344

136 *Holland's Discourses*, pp 370–4

137 Calendar of State Papers, Domestic, Charles I, 1635–6, ed John Bruce, 1866, p. 388, 393

138 Ibid, 404, 325
139 Ibid, 1636–7, 533
140 Ibid, p 500
141 Ibid, 1635–6, 554
142 *Boteler's Dialogues*, p 7
143 Ibid, 53
144 British Library, *Harleian manuscripts*, 163*ff*
145 l7 Charles 1 cap. 23
146 Ibid, Cap 26

2. Civil War and Dutch Wars, 1642 to 1689
1 Edward Hyde, Earl of Clarendon, *The History of the Rebellion and Civil Wars in England*, Oxford, 1849, vol 1, p 537
2 Granville Penn, *Memorials of Sir William Penn*, London, 1833, vol 1, pp 15–19
3 Navy Records Society, vol 105, *Documents Relating to the Civil War*, ed J. R. Powell and E. K. Timings, 1963, p 18
4 Clarendon, op cit, vol 2, p 263
5 British Library, *Thomasson Tracts*, E95 (8)
6 Calendar of State Papers, Domestic, Commonwealth, 1644–5, ed W. D. Hamilton, 1890, p 631
7 *Thomasson Tracts*, E 340 (31)
8 *Documents Relating to the Civil War*, pp 89–90
9 Ibid, p 207
10 Ibid, p 39
11 Ibid, p 75
12 Ibid, p 145
13 Penn, op cit, vol 1, p 203
14 *Documents Relating to the Civil War*, p 291
15 Ibid, p 355
16 Ibid, p 334
17 Ibid, p 355
18 Ibid, p 332
19 Ibid, p 369
20 Ibid, p 380
21 Ibid, p 379
22 Ibid, p 377
23 Clarendon, op cit, vol 4, pp 469–70
24 Bernard Capp, *Cromwell's Navy*, Oxford, 1992, p 116; and J. R. Powell, *Robert Blake*, London, 1972, p 80
25 Navy Records Society, vol 76, *The Letters of Robert Blake*, ed J. R. Powell, 1937, p 39
26 Navy Records Society, vol 30, *The First Dutch War*, ed S. R. Gardiner and C. T.

Atkinson, vol 3, 1905, p 298
27 British Library, *Stowe manuscripts*, 428; and Oppenheimer, *History of the Administration of the Royal Navy*, p 314
28 Calendar of State Papers, Domestic, 1659–60, 549
29 *Cromwell's Navy*, p 220
30 Ibid, p 222
31 Ibid, p 226
32 Ibid, pp 229
33 Ibid, pp 243–4
34 Ibid, pp 256–7
35 William Caton, *The Seamens Invitation*, London, 1659, pp 7, 8
36 *Constitutional Documents of the Puritan Revolution*, p 468
37 Edward Coxere, *Adventures by Sea*, ed E. H. W. Meyerstein, Oxford, 1945, pp 4–5
38 Ibid, pp 5–6
39 Calendar of State Papers, Domestic, Commonwealth, 1650 ed. M. A. E. Green, 1876, pp 113–14
40 Navy Records Society, vol 13, *The First Dutch War*, vol 1, ed S. R. Gardiner, 1898, pp 9, 240, 371, 374
41 Ibid, p 362
42 Ibid, pp 352–4
43 Ibid, vol 3, p 325
44 Ibid, p 159
45 Ibid, p 307
46 Navy Records Society vol 37, *The First Dutch War*, vol 4, ed C. T. Atkinson, p 43
47 Ibid, p 54
48 Coxere, op cit, p 22
49 Ibid, pp 24–5
50 Ibid, p 25
51 *The First Dutch War*, vol 4, p 357
52 Ibid, p 201
53 Ibid, p 352
54 Ibid, p 346
55 Ibid, p 253
56 *The First Dutch War*, vol 1, p 109
57 Reproduced in Charles Vipont, *Blow the Man Down*, Oxford, nd, pp 208–13
58 Calendar of State Papers, Domestic, Commonwealth, 1658–9, ed M. A. E. Green, 1885, pp 277–8
59 British Library, *Thomasson Tracts*, E 1074(7)
60 Edward Barlow, *Barlow's Journal*, ed Basil Lubbock,

London, 1934, vol 1, p 43
61 Ibid, p 44
62 Pepys's *Diary*, 25 May 1660
63 Barlow, op cit, vol 1, p 23
64 Ibid, pp 31–2
65 Ibid, p 60
66 Ibid, p 164
67 Ibid, p 162
68 Barlow, op cit, vol 2, p 358
69 Navy Records Society, vol 26, *Catalogue of the Pepysian Manuscripts*, vol 1, ed J. R. Tanner, 1903, p 245
70 *Hollond's Discourses*, p 351
71 *Blow the Man Down*, pp 228–31
72 *British Naval Documents*, pp 285–6
73 Calendar of State Papers, Domestic, Charles II, 1663–4, ed M. A. E. Green, p 597
74 Ibid, pp 608, 674
75 Pepys's *Diary*, 4/6/64
76 Barlow, op cit, vol 1, pp 93, 123
77 Calendar of State Papers, Domestic, Charles II, 1664–5, ed M. A. E. Green, 1863, p 40
78 Ibid, p 44
79 Calendar of State Papers, Domestic, 1664–5, p 108
80 Ibid, pp 243–4
81 L. Edye, *The Historical Records of the Royal Marines*, London, 1893, p 6
82 Pepys's *Diary*, 10/5/65
83 *The Historical Records of the Royal Marines*, p 39
84 Navy Records Society, vol 133, *Samuel Pepys and the Second Dutch War*, ed Robert Latham, 1995, p 209
85 Ibid, p 209
86 Navy Records Society, vol 73, *The Tangier Papers of Samuel Pepys*, ed Edwin Chapell, 1935, p 221
87 Barlow, op cit, vol 1, p 102
88 Ibid, p 119
89 Calendar of State Papers, Domestic, Charles II, 1665–6, ed M. A. E. Green, 1864, p 469
90 Pepys's Diary 6/7/66
91 Ibid, 30/6/66
92 Ibid, 1/7/66
93 Calendar of State Papers, Domestic, Charles II, 1666–7, ed M. A. E. Green, 1864, pp 333–4

94   Ibid, pp 509
95   *Three Sea Journals of Stuart Times*, pp 48–9
96   Ibid, pp 48, 49
97   *British Naval Documents*, p 290
98   Barlow, op cit, vol l, p 118–9
99   Ibid, p 122
100 *Three Sea Journals of Stuart Times*, p 54
101 Barlow, op cit, vol 1 pp 125–6
102 Navy Records Society, vol 79, *The Journals of Sir Thomas Allin*, ed R. C. Anderson, vol 1, 1939, pp 291–2
103 Barlow, op cit, vol 1, p 138
104 Ibid, pp 145–6
105 *Samuel Pepys and the Second Dutch War*, p 215
106 Ibid, p 253
107 National Maritime Manuscripts, SER/78, p 121
108 Ibid, f 300
109 Ibid, f 361
110 Ibid, ff 222, 548
111 Ibid, f 249
112 Ibid, f 320
113 Ibid, f 452
114 Ibid, f 136
115 Ibid, f 424
116 Ibid, f 281
117 Ibid, f 155
118 Ibid, f 141
119 National Maritime Manuscripts, SER/78 123
120 National Maritime Manuscripts, ADL/J/1
121 Navy Records Society, vol 27, *Catalogue of the Pepysian Manuscripts*, vol 2, ed J. R. Tanner, 104, p 42–3
122 Navy Records Society, vol 37, *Catalogue of the Pepysian Manuscripts*, vol 4, ed J. R. Tanner, 1923, p 412
123 Pepys Library, Magdalene College, Cambridge, ms no 2853, f 20
124 Ibid, f 53
125 William Derrick, *Memoirs of the Rise and Progress of the Royal Navy*, London, 1806, pp 92–3
126 B. Lavery, *Ship of the Line*, vol 1, London, 1983, p 43
127 Nicolas, *The History of the Royal Navy*, vol 1, p 4
128 *Samuel Pepys and the Second Dutch War*, p 266
129 Based mainly on *Deane's Doctrine of Naval Architecture*, ed B. Lavery, London, 1981, especially pp 74–9, 124–5
130 See B. Lavery, *The Arming and Fitting of British Ships of War*, London, 1987, p 157 etc; and J. D. Davies *Gentlemen and Tarpaulins*, Oxford, 1991, p 88
131 *Three Sea Journals of Stuart Times*, p 42
132 *Catalogue of the Pepysian Manuscripts*, vol 1, pp 157–60
133 James Yonge, *Journal*, ed F. N. L. Poynter, London, 1963, p 41
134 Calendar of State Papers, Domestic, Charles II, 1665–6, pp 130–2
135 Yonge, op cit, p 33
136 *The Arming and Fitting of British Ships of War*, London, p 202
137 Henry Teonge, *Diary*, ed E. D. Ross and E. Power, London, 1927, pp 92–3
138 *Catalogue of the Pepysian Manuscripts*, vol 1, pp 233–40
139 *Samuel Pepys and the Second Dutch War*, p 207
140 *The Tangier Papers of Samuel Pepys*, p 122
141 *Samuel Pepys and the Second Dutch War*, p 207
142 Ibid, p 224
143 *Gentlemen and Tarpaulins*, p 40
144 Teonge, op cit, pp 29, 37
145 Ibid, pp 32–3
146 Ibid, p 49
147 Ibid, pp 252, 255
148 Ibid, pp 39, 79
149 Ibid, p 31
150 *Samuel Pepys and the Second Dutch War*, p 261
151 *Catalogue of the Pepysian Manuscripts*, vol 1, p 60
152 Pepys Library, Magdalene College, Cambridge, ms no 2862, f 10
153 Ibid
154 Ibid, f 40
155 Ibid, ff 244–5
156 John Ehrman, *The Navy in the War of William III*, Cambridge, 1953, p 232

3. European War 1689 to 1739

1   *Sources of English Constitutional History*, p 599
2   John Locke, *Two Treatises of Government*, Cambridge, 1689; reprinted 1963, p 441
3   Derrick, op cit, pp 290–9
4   National Archives, Adm 106/389
5   National Archives, Adm 106/387
6   George St Lo, *England's Safety, or a Bridle to the French King*, London, 1693 np
7   National Archives, Adm 106/401
8   Ibid
9   Admiralty Library, *Corbett manuscripts*, vol x, ff 59, 61, 63, 65
10   Ibid, ff 1–2
11   Edye, op cit, p 332
12   Ibid, pp 564–5
13   Ibid, p 567
14   Ibid, p 568
15   Ibid, p 573
16   Ehrman, op cit, pp 110–1
17   Richard Allyn, *Narrative of the Victory obtained by the English and Dutch Fleet …*, London, 1744, pp 25–7
18   Ibid, p 30–1
19   Phillip Aubrey, *The Defeat of James Stuart's Armada 1692*, Leicester, 1979, p 121
20   Ehrman, op cit, pp 526, 544–6
21   Navy Records Society, vol 89, *The Sergison Papers*, ed R. D. Merriman, 1949, p 173
22   National Archives, Adm 1/3567
23   Historical Manuscripts Commission, House of Lords Manuscripts vol 1, 1693–5, London, 1900, pp 147–50
24   Ibid, pp 150–1
25   William Hodges, *Humble proposals for the Relief, Encouragement, Security and Happiness of the Seamen of England*, London, 1695, p 53–5
26   *The Sergison Papers*, p 169
27   Ibid, p 199
28   Ibid, pp 197–8
29   John Moyle, *Chirugus Marinus, or the Sea Chirugion*, London, 1693, p 3
30   Ibid, p 38
31   Edward Ward, *The Wooden World Dissected*, reprinted London, 1929, p 64

32 Moyle, op cit, pp 59, 77, 80, 90, 97–8, 123

33 Ibid, pp 139, 142

34 *The Sergison Papers*, pp 229–32

35 Ibid, p 210

36 Phillip Newell, *Greenwich Hospital, a Royal Foundation*, Greenwich,1984, p 8

37 Bridget Cherry and Nikolaus Pevsner, *The Buildings of England*, London 2, South, London, 1990, p 262

38 National Archives, Adm 2/20, f 285

39 Ibid

40 7 and 8 William III, cap 21

41 National Archives, Adm 1/3997

42 St Lo, England's Safety, p 39

43 Allyn, Narrative, pp 2–4

44 Barnaby Slush, *The Navy Royal; or a Sea-Cook turn'd Projector*, London, 1709, p A2

45 *The Wooden World Dissected*, p 92

46 Ibid, p 57, 79

47 Ibid, p 14

48 Ibid, p 12

49 Ibid, p 91

50 Ibid, pp 21, 99

51 Ibid, p 76

52 Ibid, p 66

53 Ibid, p 78

54 Ibid, p 78

55 Ibid, p 79

56 Ibid, p 86

57 Historical Manuscripts Commission, *Du Cane Manuscripts*, ed Sir J. K. Laughton, London, 1905, p 23

58 Ibid, pp 28–9

59 *The Wooden World Dissected*, p 90

60 Ibid, p 26

61 Ibid, p 83

62 Ibid, p 82

63 Slush, op cit, p 17.

64 *The Wooden World Dissected*, p 98

65 Robert Crosfield, *England's Glory Reviv'd*, London, 1692, p 18

66 Slush, op cit, p 17

67 John Atkins, *The Navy-Surgeon, or a Practical System of Surgery*, London, 1734, pp 3–4

68 Slush, op cit, p p 35

69 *The Wooden World Dissected*, p 93

70 Francis Grose, *Dictionary of the Vulgar Tongue*, 1811, reprinted Stroud, 2008, p 80

71 *The Wooden World Dissected*, p 98

72 Navy Records Society, vol 103, *Queen Anne's Navy*, ed R. D. Merriman, 1961, p 179

73 *Corbett manuscripts*, vol X, f 33

74 National Archives, Adm 2/28, 28/1/1701/2

75 *Corbett manuscripts*, vol X, f 29

76 *Queen Anne's Navy*, p 201

77 *Corbett manuscripts*, vol X, f 29

78 Matthew Bishop, *Life and Adventures*, London, 1744, p 55

79 Ibid, pp 64–5

80 *Corbett manuscripts*, vol X, f 56

81 Ibid f 23

82 Ibid f 41

83 *England's Glory Reviv'd*, pp 18, 2

84 *The Sergison Papers*, p 192

85 Navy Records Society, vol 119, *Manning Pamphlets 1693–1873*, ed J. S. Bromley, 1974, pp 74n, 78

86 Navy Records Society, vol 125, *The Naval Miscellany*, vol V, ed J. B. Hattendorf, p 150

87 Ibid, pp 157–8

88 Ibid, p 173

89 *New Oxford Dictionary of National Biography* entry

90 *Queen Anne's Navy*, p 186

91 R. Pares, 'The Manning of the Navy in the West Indies, 1702–63' in *Transactions of the Royal Historical Society*, 4th series XX, 31ff

92 Bishop, op cit, p 21

93 J. H. Owen, *War at Sea under Queen Anne 1702–1708*, Cambridge, 1938, pp 284–5

94 *Queen Anne's Navy*, p 185–6

95 Navy Records Society, vol 44, *The Old Scots Navy*, ed James Grant, 1914, p 367

96 *Corbett manuscripts*, vol X

97 *The Old Scots Navy*, pp 371ff

98 B. Lavery, *Shield of Empire: The Royal Navy and Scotland*, Edinburgh, 2007, pp 35, 37, 43

99 *Corbett manuscripts*, vol x, f 9

100 Ibid, pp 30, 29

101 National Archives, Adm 2/55, 27/7/1738

102 *Greenwich Hospital*, p 61

103 *Chirugus Marinus*, pp 304–5

104 John Moyle, *Chyrurgic Memoirs; being an Account of Many Extraordinary Cures ...*, London, 1708, pp 18, 11

105 Ibid, pp, 22, 34

106 Atkins, op cit, pp 120–1

107 Ibid, p 9

108 J. J. Keevil, *Medicine and the Navy*, vol 3, 1714–1815, Livingstone, 1961, pp 99–100

4. Imperial War, 1739 to 1783

1 Daniel A Baugh, *British Naval Adminstration in the Age of Walpole*, Princeton, 1965, p 163

2 W. H. Long, *Naval Yarns*, reprinted London, 1973, p 20

3 Baugh, op cit, pp 164–5

4 Long, op cit, p 20

5 Navy Records Society, vol 99, *The Vernon Papers*, ed B. McL. Ranft, 1958, p 163

6 Baugh, op cit, p 217

7 Ibid, p 186

8 Ibid, p 190

9 Ibid, p 168

10 National Archives, Adm 1/160

11 *Shield of Empire*, p 133

12 Phillip Saumarez, *Log of the Centurion*, ed Leo Heaps, New York 1973, pp 34–5

13 Navy Records Society, vol 109, *Documents Relating to Anson's Voyage Round the World*, ed Glyndwr Williams, 1967, p 49

14 Ibid, p 101

15 Ibid, p 102

16 Chaplain Richard Walter, *Anson's Voyage Round the World*, ed Percy G. Adams, New York, 1974, p 96

17 *Documents Relating to Anson's Voyage Round the World*, p 127

18 Ibid, p 129

19 Ibid, p 131

20 Ibid, p 132

21 Ibid, p 134

22 Ibid, p 237

23 Ibid, p 236

24 Ibid, p 240

25 Ibid, pp 239, 248, 249

26   J. Byron, *Narrative of the Loss of the Wager*, 1822, Aberdeen, p 2
27   John Bulkeley and John Cummins, *A Voyage to the South-Seas, by His Majesty's Ship Wager*, London, 1743, reprinted London, 1927, p 32
28   S. W. C. Pack, *The Wager Mutiny*, London, 1964, p 45
29   Byron, op cit, p 13
30   Ibid, p 15
31   Ibid, p 16
32   Pack, op cit, p 72
33   Ibid, p 82
34   Ibid, p 66
35   Bulkeley and Cummins, op cit, pp 49–50
36   Pack, op cit, p 100
37   Ibid, p 111
38   Ibid, p 127
39   Ibid, p 165
40   National Archives, Adm 2/59, 5/5/43
41   National Archives, Adm 1/3663
42   Long, op cit, pp 23–4
43   Lloyd, *British Seaman*, pp 286, 289
44   *Parliamentary History of England*, Vol 14, 1747–53, London, 1813, Col 860
45   William Spavens, *Narrative*, Louth, 1796, reprinted Chatham, *c*.1998, p 74
46   *Parliamentary Debates*, vol XIV, 1747–53, cols 829–30, 835–6
47   B. Lavery, *The Royal Navy's First Invincible*, Portsmouth, 1988, pp 61–2
48   National Archives, Adm 2/75, 23/1/55
49   William Falconer, *Dictionary of the Marine*, London, 1769, reprinted Newton Abbott, 1970, p 137
50   Matthew Bishop, op cit, p 55
51   Tobias Smollett, *Roderick Random*, first published 1748, Chapter XXIV
52   *Shield of Empire*, pp 133–4
53   Spavens, *Narrative*, p 4
54   Dudley Pope, *At 12 Mr Byng was Shot*, London, 1962, p 59
55   Augustus Hervey, *Journal*, ed David Erskine, London, 1953, p 203
56   Ibid, pp 208, 213
57   Mary Lacy, *The Female Shipwright*, 1773,

reprinted Greenwich, 2008, p 26
58   Ibid, p 50
59   Long, op cit, p 116
60   *The Female Shipwright*, pp 48–9
61   Ibid, p 47
62   Spavens, *Narrative*, p 23
63   Ibid, pp 23–4
64   Ibid, p 27
65   B. Lavery, *Ship of the Line*, vol 2, London, 1984, p 106
66   Navy Records Society, vol 148, *The Rodney Papers*, vol 1, ed David Syrett, 2005, p 440
67   Long, op cit, pp 106–7
68   Charles Derrick, *Memoirs of the Rise and Progress of the Royal Navy*, London, 1806, pp 132, 148, 219
69   Spavens, *Narrative*, p 10
70   John Nicol, *Life and Adventures*, 1822, reprinted London, 1937, p 60
71   *The Wooden World Dissected*, p 34
72   Spavens, *Narrative*, p 35
73   R. F. Johnson, *The Royal George*, London, 1971, pp 82, 102
74   *Dictionary of the Marine*, pp 194–5
75   Long, op cit, p 118
76   *The Wager Mutiny*, pp 84–5
77   Geoffrey Marcus, *Quiberon Bay*, London, 1960, p 189
78   Navy Records Society, vol 138, *Shipboard Life and Organisation 1731–1815*, ed B. Lavery, 1998, p 73
79   Ibid, p 74
80   Ibid, p 64
81   Ibid, p 83
82   *Dictionary of the Marine*, p 110
83   *Shipboard Life and Organisation*, pp 90–1
84   *Dictionary of the Marine*, pp 116–20
85   Peter Padfield, *Guns at Sea*, London, 1973, p 114
86   Hakluyt Society, extra series, no 34, *The Journals of Captain James Cook*, vol 1, *The Voyage of the Endeavour*, ed J. C. Beaglehole, 1999, p 4
87   Ibid, p 592
88   Ibid, p 593
89   Ibid, p 594
90   Ibid, p 217 and *n*
91   Ibid, p cxxviii
92   Ibid, pp 169n, 25n
93   Ibid, p 27

94   Ibid, p 590
95   Ibid, p ccxxxv
96   Ibid, p 16
97   Richard Hough, *Captain James Cook*, London, 1994, p 81
98   James Mario Matra, *A Journal of a Voyage Round the World*, London, 1771, reprinted 1975, p 46
99   *The Voyage of the Endeavour*, p 99
100   Ibid, p 98 and *n*
101   Ibid, p 99
102   Ibid, p 125n
103   Matra, op cit, p 107
104   *The Voyage of the Endeavour*, p 618
105   Ibid, p 633
106   Ibid, p 158
107   Ibid, p 39
108   Ibid, p 346
109   Ibid, 448
110   Ibid, p 459
111   Ibid, p 595
112   Hakluyt Society, extra series, no 35, *The Journals of Captain James Cook*, vol 2, *The Voyage of the Resolution and Discovery*, ed J. C. Beaglehole, 1999, pp 880, 882
113   Ibid, pp 403–4
114   John Marra, *Journal of the Resolution's Voyage*, London, 1775
115   Ibid, pp 7–8
116   Ibid, p 114
117   Ibid, p 128
118   Ibid, pp 134–5
119   Ibid, pp 235–6
120   Hough, *Captain James Cook*, op cit, pp 279–80
121   Ibid, p 332
122   Quoted in Linda Colley, *Britons*, London, 1994, p 99
123   *American Neptune*, vol 23, pp 174–185
124   *Naval Documents of the American Revolution*, ed William Bell Clark, vol 1, Washington, 1964, p 91–4
125   Ibid, p 501
126   Ibid, p 628
127   Ibid, p 1141
128   Ibid, p 717
129   Navy Records Society, vol 78, *The Private Papers of John, Earl of Sandwich*, ed G. R. Barnes and J. H. Owen, vol 1, 1932, p 213
130   M. J. Williams, *The Naval Administration of the Fourth Earl of Sandwich*, thesis, Oxford University,

1962, National Maritime Museum THS/1

131 Spavens, *Narrative*, p 67

132 Nicol, op cit, p 63

133 *The Naval Administration of the Fourth Earl of Sandwich*

134 Jonathan R. Dull, *The French Navy and American Independence*, Princeton, 1975, pp 359–60

135 *The Naval Administration of the Fourth Earl of Sandwich*

136 Nicol, op cit, pp 39–40, 49

137 Navy Records Society, vol 78, *The Private Papers of John, Earl of Sandwich*, vol 4, 1938, p 157

138 Ibid, p 430

139 Long, op cit, pp 126–7

140 Nicol, op cit, p 50

141 Navy Records Society, vol 107, *The Health of Seamen*, ed Christopher Lloyd, 1965, p 145

142 Ibid, p 146

143 Ibid, p 211

144 Ibid, p 147

145 Ibid, p 210

146 *The Royal George*, pp 103–4

147 *Samuel Kelly: an Eighteenth Century Seaman*, ed Crosbie Garstin, London, 1925, p 81–2

148 Long, op cit, pp 14–5

5. The Crisis 1783 to 1803

1 Navy Records Society, vol 38, *The Barham Papers*, ed Sir J. K. Laughton, vol 2, 1910, p 184

2 Report and Appendix of the 1852 Committee on Manning the Navy, House of Commons, 1859, p 16

3 William Richardson, *A Mariner of England*, ed Spencer Childers, 1908; reprinted London, 1970, pp 65–9

4 James Morrison, *After the Bounty: A Sailor's Account of the Mutiny and Life in the South Seas*, Washington DC, *c*.2010, p 12

5 Gavin Kennedy, *Captain Bligh*, London, 1989, p 28

6 Morrison, op cit, pp 16–17

7 Ibid, pp 114–15

8 Ibid, p 119

9 Kennedy, op cit, p 136

10 Long, op cit, p 165

11 Ibid, p 167

12 Ibid, pp 170–1

13 Oliver Warner, *The Glorious First of June*, London, 1961, pp 79, 84, 164

14 Ibid, p 79

15 Nicol, op cit, pp 188–9

16 Ibid, p 189

17 Lloyd, op cit, p 289

18 National Archives, ADM 11/579

19 Lewis, op cit, p 105

20 National Maritime Museum Manuscripts, UPC/3

21 W. Mark, *At Sea with Nelson*, London, 1929, p. 67

22 Samuel Leech, *A Voice from the Main Deck*, 1857; reprinted Chatham, 1999, pp 45–6

23 G. V. Jackson, *The Perilous Adventures and Vicissitudes of a Naval Officer*, London, 1927, p 29

24 Thomas Cochrane, Earl of Dundonald, *Autobiography of a Seaman*, London, nd, p 92

25 J. J. Sheahan, *General and Concise History and Description of the Town and Port of Kingston-upon-Hull*, London, 1864, p 150

26 Navy Records Society, vol 97, *Dillon's Narrative*, ed Michael Lewis, vol II, 1956, p. 9

27 Ibid

28 Rodger, *The Wooden World*, p 166

29 National Archives, ADM 11/579

30 *Dillon's Narrative*, vol 2, p 10

31 National Maritime manuscripts, MEL/2

32 Thomas Trotter, *A Practicable Plan for Manning the Royal Navy*, Newcastle, 1819, pp 34–5

33 National Archives, ADM 7/361

34 National Archives, ADM 30/63/8

35 John Ehrman, *The Younger Pitt*, vol 2, *The Reluctant Transition*, London, 1986, pp 497, 642–3

36 *The Health of Seamen*, p 268

37 Glascock, *Tales of a Tar*, London, 1830, p 329

38 *The Health of Seamen*, p 239 note

39 G. E. Mainwaring and Bonamy Dobrée, *The Floating Republic*, London, 1935, p 266

40 *Shipboard Life and Organisation*, p 425

41 Ibid, p 424

42 Ibid, p 423

43 Ibid, p 355

44 B. R. Mitchell, *Abstract of British Historical Statistics*, Cambridge, 1962, pp 468–9, 488

45 *The Health of Seamen*, p 238n

46 *The Floating Republic*, pp 20–1

47 Ibid, pp 26–7

48 Ibid, p 28

49 Ibid, pp 30–1

50 Henry Baynham, *From the Lower Deck*, London, 1969, p 10

51 Ibid, pp 10–11

52 Quoted in *New Oxford Dictionary of National Biography* article

53 *The Floating Republic*, pp 262–3

54 *The Health of Seamen*, p 238–9n

55 *The Floating Republic*, pp 265–6

56 *From the Lower Deck*, p 10

57 *The Floating Republic*, p 78

58 *From the Lower Deck*, p 12

59 *The Floating Republic*, p 86

60 Ibid, p 90

61 Ibid, p 93

62 Ibid, p 123

63 Ibid, p 230

64 Ibid, p 274

65 Ibid, p 275

66 National Archives, ADM 1/5486

67 Navy Records Society, vol 90, *The Keith Papers*, ed Christopher Lloyd, vol 2, 1950, p 28

68 *The Floating Republic*, pp 141–3

69 Edward Brenton, *The Naval History of Great Britain*, vol 1, London, 1837, pp 283–4

70 Dugan, op cit, London, 1966, p 475

71 Brenton, op cit, p 285

72 *The Keith Papers*, vol 2, p 18

73 Ibid, p 17

74 Dugan, op cit, p 479

75 *The Floating Republic*, p 277

76 Ibid, p 105
77 *The Health of Seamen*, p 239
78 Conrad Gill, *The Naval Mutinies of 1797*, Manchester, 1913, p 327
79 *The Floating Republic*, p 251
80 *Shipboard Life and Organisation*, p 355
81 *The Floating Republic*, pp 198–9
82 Quoted in Gill, *Naval Mutinies*, p 337
83 National Archives, Adm 1/5346
84 *An Account of the Bravery and Happy Death of James Covey*, Chelsea, 1817, p 3
85 National Archives, Adm 101/85/7
86 *The Adventures of John Wetherell*, ed C. S. Forester, London, 1954, *passim*
87 National Archives, Adm 1/5343
88 National Archives, Adm 11/5340
89 Nicol, op cit, p 4–5
90 *Shipboard Life and Organisation*, pp 100–13
91 Sir Nicholas Harris Nicolas, *The Dispatches and Letters of Lord Nelson*; reprinted Chatham, 1997, vol 2, p 397
92 G. S. Parsons, *Nelsonian Reminiscences*, 1843; reprinted Maidstone, 1973, p 241
93 See B. Lavery, *Nelson and the Nile*, Chatham, 1997, p 132
94 Long, op cit, p 201
95 Ibid, pp 1932–3
96 *Nelson and the Nile*, p 189
97 Nicol, op cit, p 193
98 Ibid, p 197

6. A Large Fleet in a Long War 1803 to 1815
1 *Parliamentary History of England*, Vol 36, 1801–3, London, 1820, col 1162*ff*
2 *The Adventures of John Wetherell*, pp 31–4
3 Ibid, p 102
4 Navy Records Society, vol 14, *The Blockade of Brest*, ed John Leyland, vol I, 1898, p 8
5 National Maritime Museum manuscripts, MS93/037
6 National Maritime Museum manuscripts, BGY/T/1

7 *The Adventures of John Wetherell*, p 56
8 National Maritime Museum manuscripts, WEL/30
9 Ibid
10 Peter Warwick, ed, *Voices from the Battle of Trafalgar*, Newton Abbott, 2005, p 71
11 Ibid, p 87
12 Ibid, p 109
13 Ibid, p 128
14 Frederick Hoffman, *A Sailor of King George*, 1901; reprinted Chatham, 1999, p 114
15 *The Nelson Dispatch*, vol 6, part 6, April 1998, p 242
16 William Robinson, *Jack Nastyface*, 1836; reissued Annapolis, 1973, p 44
17 *Macmillan's Magazine*, vol 81, p 419
18 *The Nelson Dispatch*, vol 6, part 9, January 1999, p 384
19 Warwick, op cit, pp 171–2
20 Ibid, p 153
21 Long, op cit, p 235
22 Robinson, op cit, pp 61–2
23 Ibid, p 51
24 Lloyd, The British Seaman, op cit, p 296
25 Sir Nicholas Harris Nicolas, The Dispatches and Letters of Lord Nelson, reprinted Chatham, 1997, vol 7 p 417
26 Quoted in B. Lavery, *Ship of the Line*, vol 1, p 133
27 Lloyd, *The British Seaman*, p 206
28 *Manning Pamphlets 1693–1873*, p 352
29 Ibid, p 66
30 M. D. Hay, ed, *Landsman Hay*, London, 1953, pp 76–7
31 Ibid, pp 75–6
32 Ibid, p 128
33 *The Adventures of John Wetherell*, p 38
34 Ibid, p 66
35 *Shipboard Life and Organisation*, pp 401–2
36 Ibid, p 405
37 *Five Naval Journals*, p 374
38 Basil Hall, *Fragments of Voyages and Travels*, London, 1860, p 168
39 *Landsman Hay*, p 64
40 Jeffrey de Raigersfield, *The Life of a Sea Officer*, London, 1929, pp 70–1
41 *The Adventures of John Wetherell*, p 36
42 B. Lavery, *Nelson's Fleet at*

Trafalgar, pp 19–20
43 Hall, op cit, p 233
44 *Shipboard Life and Organisation*, p 632
45 Manning Pamphlets 1693–1873, p 348n
46 *Landsman Hay*, p 121
47 *Shipboard Life and Organisation*, p 264
48 *Shipboard Life and Organisation*, p 133
49 William Burney, *New Universal Dictionary of the Marine*, 1815; reprinted New York, 1970, p 376
50 *Shipboard Life and Organisation*, p 264
51 Ibid, p 265
52 *The Adventures of John Wetherell*, p 74
53 *Shipboard Life and Organisation*, p 133
54 *The Adventures of John Wetherell*, p 42
55 *The Health of Seamen*, pp 265–7
56 Anon, *The Adventures of a Ship-Boy*, Edinburgh, 1823, pp 118–19
57 Ibid, p 137
58 *Shipboard Life and Organisation*, p 627
59 John Delafons, *A Treatise on Naval Courts Martial*, London, 1805, pp 271–2
60 *Shipboard Life and Organisation*, p 354
61 *Five Naval Journals*, p 243
62 *Shipboard Life and Organisation*, p 266
63 Ibid, p 265
64 Ibid, p 451
65 *A Voice from the Main Deck*, pp 43, 48
66 *Shipboard Life and Organisation*, p 439
67 Ibid, p 443
68 Ibid, p 441
69 B. Lavery, *Jack Aubrey Commands*, London, 2003, p 96
70 *Shipboard Life and Organisation*, p 219
71 Ibid, p 218
72 Ibid, p 231
73 Ibid, pp 633–4
74 Nicol, op cit, pp 195–6
75 *Dillon's Narrative*, vol 1 p 96
76 *Shipboard Life and Organisation*, pp 210–1
77 Nicol, op cit, pp 193–4
78 *Nelson and the Nile*, pp 116, 218
79 B. Lavery, *Nelson's Fleet at Trafalgar*, Greenwich, 2004, p 182

80 Ibid, p 87
81 *Jack Nastyface*, pp 87–8
82 Quoted in Lewis, *The British Seaman*, p 247
83 Grose, *Dictionary of the Vulgar Tongue*, p 31
84 *Shipboard Life and Organisation*, p 382
85 Navy Records Society, vol 155, *Naval Courts Martial, 1793–1815*, ed John D Byrn, 2009, pp 328–9
86 Ibid, pp 337–43
87 *Five Naval Journals*, pp 10, 9
88 *Jack Nastyface*, pp 32–3
89 Ibid, p 33
90 *Shipboard Life and Organisation*, p 355–6
91 *The Adventures of John Wetherell*, p 46
92 *Landsman Hay*, p 67
93 *Five Naval Journals*, p 256
94 *Jack Nastyface*, p 34
95 National Maritime Museum manuscripts, WEL/8
96 *From the Lower Deck*, p 116
97 *The Adventures of John Wetherell*, p 61
98 Ibid, p 61
99 *Shipboard Life and Organisation*, p 151
100 *Five Naval Journals*, pp 257–8
101 *A Voice from the Main Deck*, p 42
102 *Shipboard Life and Organisation*, p 124
103 Ibid, pp 271–2
104 Ibid, p 628
105 B. Lavery, *Nelson's Navy*, London, 1989, p 143
106 *Landsman Hay*, pp 225–30
107 *Jack Nastyface*, p 81
108 Ibid, pp 102–3
109 Long, op cit, pp 250–2
110 A. L. F. Schaumann, *On the Road with Wellington*, ed Ludovici, London, 1924, pp 1–2
111 Ibid, pp 144–5
112 Navy Records Society, vol 96, *The Keith Papers*, vol 3, ed Christopher Lloyd, p 269
113 *From the Lower Deck*, pp 131–2
114 Ibid
115 Benjamin Silliman, *Journal of Travels in England, Holland and Scotland*, Boston, 1812, vol 1, pp 284–5
116 *A Voice from the Main Deck*, pp 45–6 and *n*
117 *The Naval War of 1812: A Documentary History*, ed W. S. Dudley, vol 1, Washington, 1985, p 28
118 Ibid, pp 62–3
119 Ibid, p 172
120 *A Voice from the Main Deck*, p 76
121 Ibid, pp 76–7
122 Ibid, p 124

7. The Long Peace 1815 to 1850

1 *Abstract of British Historical Statistics*, pp 217–8
2 *From the Lower Deck*, p 139
3 *Vagabondiana*, ed John Thomas Smith, London, 1874, p 19
4 Ibid, pp 23–4
5 John Bechervaise, *Thirty-Six Years of a Seafaring Life, by an Old Quarter Master*, Portsea, 1839, p 94
6 Ibid, pp 107–8
7 Ibid, p 10
8 Ibid, p 109
9 *Dillon's Narrative*, vol 2, pp 433–9
10 National Archives, Adm 1/434
11 *Sea Saga, being the Diaries of Four Generations of the King-Hall Family*, ed Louise King-Hall, London, 1936, p 62
12 *Nelson's Navy*, p 176; and Gloria Clifton and Nigel Rigby, eds, *Treasures of the National Maritime Museum*, Greenwich, 2004, p 153
13 Christopher Lloyd, *The Navy and the Slave Trade*, London, 1949, p 70
14 Parliamentary Papers, *First Report from the Select Committee on the Slave Trade*, 1849, pp 26, 3, 49
15 Ibid, p 12
16 Ibid, pp 13
17 *The Navy and the Slave Trade*, p 83
18 Ibid, pp 132–5, 288
19 *United Service Magazine*, 1849, vol 1, pp 578–9
20 Henry Baynham, *Before the Mast*, London, 1972, p 69
21 *Letters of Queen Victoria*, ed Arthur Christopher Benson and Viscount Esher, London, 1908, Vol III, p 151
22 Charles McPherson, *Life on Board a Man-of-War by a British Seaman*, Glasgow, 1829, p 2
23 Ibid, pp 14–15
24 Ibid, pp 52–3
25 *Before the Mast*, p 59
26 *Life on Board a Man-of-War*, p 157
27 Ibid, pp 68, 82
28 Ibid, p 33
29 Ibid, p 110
30 Ibid, p 107
31 Ibid, pp 151, 158
32 Ibid, pp 34–6
33 Ibid, p 121
34 Ibid, p 113
35 Pascoe Grenfell Hill, *A Voyage to the Slave Coasts*, London, 1849, p 7–8
36 *Thirty-Six Years of a Seafaring Life*, op cit, p 121
37 Ibid, p 121
38 Ibid, p 19
39 Ibid, p 84
40 J. H. Briggs, *Naval Administrations 1827 to 1892*, London, 1897, pp 13, 18
41 *Life on Board a Man-of-War*, p 189
42 Ibid, p 77
43 *Before the Mast*, p 68
44 National Maritime Museum microfilm, *Papers Relating to Seamen's Clothing*, passim
45 *Before the Mast*, p 69
46 Amy Miller, *Dressed to Kill*, Greenwich, c.2007, p 84
47 Reproduced in B. Lavery, *Empire of the Seas*, London, 2009, p 216
48 *A Statement of Certain Immoral Practises*, London, 1822, pp 1–2
49 Ibid, p 5
50 Nicol, op cit, pp 21, 31
51 Grose, *Dictionary of the Vulgar Tongue*, p 113
52 *Jack Nastyface*, pp 240–4
53 *Life on Board a Man-of-War*, p 117
54 Ibid, p 131
55 *From the Lower Deck*, p 150
56 *Life on Board a Man-of-War*, p 136
57 Ibid, p 140
58 Ibid, p 139
59 Ibid, p 138–9
60 Ibid, p 140
61 Ibid, p 144
62 Ibid, pp 142–4
63 Ibid, p 158

64 Ibid, p 138
65 Ibid, p 171
66 Ibid, p 173
67 Ibid, p 174
68 Edward Parry, *Memoirs of Rear-Admiral Sir W. E. Parry*, London, 1857, pp 140–2
69 Ibid, pp 189–90
70 Ibid, 155–6
71 Ibid, 153
72 Hood, *To the Arctic by Canoe*, Montreal, 1974, pp 195, 125
73 *Before the Mast*, p 44
74 Ibid, p 45
75 Ibid, p 45
76 Ibid, p 46
77 Ibid, p 50
78 Ibid, p 51–2
79 Bechervaise, op cit, p 225–6
80 Ibid, pp 53–4
81 Ibid, p 56
82 Ibid, p 57
83 *The Correspondence of Charles Darwin*, ed Burkhardt and Smith, Cambridge, 1985, pp 315*n*, 392 and *passim*
84 *Naval Administrations*, p 28
85 John G. Wells, *Whaley, the Story of HMS Excellent*, Portsmouth, 1980, p 202
86 Ibid, p 6
87 Ibid, pp 6–7
88 Ibid, p 11
89 *Thirty-Six Years of a Seafaring Life*, p 6
90 *Naval Administrations*, pp 27–8
91 John Winton, *Hurrah for the Life of a Sailor*, London, 1977, p 73
92 *Hansard*, Vol 21, 1834, cols 1064–5
93 *Royal Commission Report of 1859*, p 51, para 672
94 5 and 6 William IV, cap 24
95 *Report and Appendix of the 1852 Committee on Manning the Navy*, House of Commons, 1859, p 50, para 15, p 52, para 15
96 Ibid, p 34
97 Order in Council, 1846
98 *1852 Committee on Manning the Navy*, p 50 para 16, p 52, para 16
99 *Manning Pamphlets 1693–1873*, pp 359–60
100 BT 167/23
101 Ibid
102 *Manning Pamphlets 1693–1873*, pp 359–60
103 *Landsman Hay*, pp 246–8
104 *Before the Mast*, p 60
105 *1852 Committee on Manning the Navy*, p 10, para 2
106 Ibid, p 11, para 16
107 Ibid, p 29, para 30
108 Ibid, p 10 para 4
109 Ibid, p 9, para 5
110 *Manning Pamphlets 1693–1873*, p 188
111 Ibid, p 186
112 Ibid, p 169
113 National Archives, Adm 1/6495
114 Michael Lewis, *The Navy in Transition 1814–1864*, London, 1965, p 168
115 National Archives, Adm 1/5598
116 Navy Records Society, vol 147, *The Milne Papers*, vol 1, ed John Beeler, 2004, p 273
117 *Before the Mast*, pp 65–6
118 Ibid, p 66
119 *The Milne Papers*, p 153
120 Parliamentary Papers, *Report of the Commissioners Appointed to Inquire into the Best Means of Manning the Navy, 1859*, p 423
121 *United Service Magazine*, June 1850, p 213
122 Parliamentary Papers, 1850, *Report on the Expediency of Reducing the Present Quantity of Spirits in the Royal Navy*, *passim*
123 *Before the Mast*, p 81
124 Ibid, p 75
125 Ibid, pp 77–80
126 Owen Beattie and John Geiger, *Frozen in Time*, London, 1987, *passim*
127 Quoted in *The Navy in Transition*, p 195
128 See Peter Hore, 'Lord Melville, the Admiralty and the Coming of Steam Navigation', in *Mariners Mirror*, vol 86, May 2000, pp 157–172
129 Geoffrey Penn, *Up Funnel, Down Screw*, London, 1955, p 22
130 Ibid, p 24
131 J. Dinnen, *An Essay on Steam Boilers for Marine Engineers*, 1838, p 25
132 P. M. Rippon, *The Evolution of Engineering in the Royal Navy*, vol 1, Tunbridge Wells, 1988, p 40
133 Sir John Ross, *A Treatise on Navigation by Steam*, London, 1828, p 138
134 Robert Otway, *Treatise on Steam Navigation*, London, 1832, p 51–2
135 *Essay on Steam Boilers*, p 25
136 Robert Murray, *Rudimentary Treatise on Marine Engines and Steam Vessels*, London, 1852, p 44
137 Ibid, p 25
138 *The Evolution of Engineering in the Royal Navy*, p 40
139 *Up Funnel, Down Screw*, p 31
140 Ibid, pp 40–1
141 Ibid, p 46
142 *Before the Mast*, p 48
143 Ibid, p 73
144 *Life on Board a Man-of-War*, pp 23–5
145 Bechervaise, op cit, pp 62–3
146 National Archives, Adm 1/5590
147 Ibid
148 *The Milne Papers*, pp 237–45
149 10 Victoria cap 30
150 *Voyages and Travels*, p 215
151 Alexander Fordyce, *Outlines of Naval Routine*, London, 1837, p 180
152 *Life on Board a Man-of-War*, p 147–8
153 Victoria Cross Society website

Appendix: Tracing Naval Ratings
1 NMM LBK/38.

BIBLIOGRAPHY

Anyone studying British naval history is well advised to pay attention to the many volumes published by the Navy Records Society since its inception in 1893. The same is true of *Mariner's Mirror*, the journal of the Society for Nautical Research, since 1911.

General History

Calendar of State Papers, Domestic, for most of the seventeenth century; they contain many important naval papers, especially before 1673. Occasionally it is necessary to consult the originals in the State Papers series in the National Archives.

Calendar of State Papers, Venetian, 1534–54, ed. R. Brown, London, 1873

Carswell, John, *The Descent on England*, London, 1969

Clark, G. Kitson., *The Making of Victorian England*, London, 1965

Colley, Linda, *Britons, Forging the Nation, 1707–1837*, London, 1992

Ehrman, John, *The Younger Pitt*, vol. 2, *The Reluctant Transition*, London, 1986

— *The Younger Pitt*, vol. 3, *The Consuming Struggle*, London, 1996

Gairdner, James, and R. H. Brodie, eds., *Letters and Papers of Henry VIII*, vol. 20, *1544*, part 2, London, 1907

Gardiner, S. R., ed., *The Constitutional Documents of the Puritan Revolution*, Oxford, 1906

Hewitt, H. J., *The Organisation of War under Edward III*, Manchester, 1966

Hyde, Edward, Earl of Clarendon, *The History of the Rebellion and Civil Wars in England*, Oxford, 1849 (first published 1702)

Mackesey, Piers, *The War for America*, London, 1964

Mitchell, B. R., *Abstract of British Historical Statistics*, Cambridge, 1962

Morillo, Stephen, *The Battle of Hastings*, Woodbridge, 1999

Ogg, David, *England in the Reign of Charles II*, Oxford, 1967

— *England in the Reigns of James II and William III*, Oxford, 1969

Sheahan, J. J., *General and Concise History and Description of the Town and Port of Kingston-upon-Hull*, London, 1864

Silliman, Benjamin, *Journal of Travels in England, Holland and Scotland*, Boston, 1812

Stephenson, Carl, and F. G. Marcham, *Sources of English Constitutional History*, New York, 1937

Wedgwood, C. V., *The King's War 1641–1647*, London, 1958

Wilson, Ben, *Decency and Disorder*, London, 2007

Parliamentary and Official Papers

Acts of the Privy Council, new series, edited by John Roche Dasert

Parliamentary History of England, vol. 14, 1747–53, London, 1813

Parliamentary History of England, vol. 36, 1801–3, London, 1820

Parliamentary Papers, *First Report from the Select Committee on the Slave Trade*, 1849

Parliamentary Papers, *Report on the Expediency of Reducing the Present Quantity of Spirits in the Royal Navy*, House of Commons, 1850

Parliamentary Papers, *Report and Appendix of the 1852 Committee on Manning the Navy*, House of Commons, 1859

Parliamentary Papers, *Report of the Commissioners Appointed to Inquire into the Best Means of Manning the Navy*, House of Commons, 1859

Naval History

Aubrey, Phillip, *The Defeat of James Stuart's Armada, 1692*, Leicester, 1979

Baugh, Daniel A., *British Naval Administration in the Age of Walpole*, Princeton, 1965

Beattie, Owen, and John Geiger, *Frozen in Time*, London, 1987

Brenton, Edward, *The Naval History of Great Britain*, 2 vols., London, 1837. Generally considered unreliable, except for events were Brenton was present

Briggs, J. H., *Naval Administrations, 1827 to 1892*, London, 1897

Brooks F. W., *The English Naval Forces*, London, 1932

Brown, D. K., *Paddle Frigates*, London, 1993

Burney, William, *New Universal Dictionary of the Marine*, 1815; reprinted New York, 1970

Burwash, Dorothy, *English Merchant Shipping 1460–1540*, Toronto, 1947,

Capp, Bernard, *Cromwell's Navy*, Oxford, 1992

Clowes, W. S. Laird., *The Royal Navy: A History from the Earliest Times to the Present*, vol. 1, London, 1897

Crowhurst, Patrick, *The Defence of British Trade 1689–1815*, Folkestone, 1977

Davies J. D., *Gentlemen and Tarpaulins*, Oxford, 1991

Derrick, William, *Memoirs of the Rise and Progress of the Royal Navy*, London, 1806

Dugan, James, *The Great Mutiny*, London, 1966

Ehrman, John, *The Navy in the War of William III*, Cambridge, 1953

Fox, Frank, *Great Ships*, London, 1980

Gardiner, Julie, ed., *Before the Mast*, Portsmouth, 2005

Gardiner, Robert, *The First Frigates*, London, 1992

Gill, Conrad, *The Naval Mutinies of 1797*, Manchester, 1913

Goodwin, Peter, *Nelson's Ships*, London, 2002

Gradish, Stephen, *The Manning of the British Navy During the Seven Years' War*, London, 1980

James, William, *The Naval History of Great Britain*, various editions, 6 vols., 1822–4

Johnson, R. F., *The Royal George*, London, 1971

Hill, Richard, *The Prizes of War*, Stroud, 1998

Hutchinson, Gillian, *Medieval Ships and Shipping*, Leicester, 1994

Hutchison, J. R., *The Press Gang Afloat and Ashore*, London, 1913

Keevil, J. J., *Medicine and the Navy*, vol. 3, 1714–1815, Livingstone, 1961

B Lavery, ed, *Deane's Doctrine of Naval Architecture*, London, 1981

— *Ship of the Line*, 2 vols., London, 1983–4

— *The Arming and Fitting of British Ships of War, London*, 1987

— *The Royal Navy's First Invincible*, Portsmouth, 1988

— *Nelson and the Nile*, Chatham, 1997

— *Nelson's Fleet at Trafalgar*, Greenwich, 2004

Lewis, Michael, *A Social History of the Navy, 1793–1815*, London, 1960

— *The Navy in Transition 1814–1864*, London, 1965

Lloyd, Christopher, *The Navy and the Slave Trade*, London, 1949

— *The British Seaman*, London, 1968

Mainwaring, G. E., and Bonamy Dobrée, *The Floating Republic*, London, 1935
Geoffrey Marcus, *Quiberon Bay*, London, 1960
Marsden, Peter, *Sealed by Time*, Portsmouth, 2003
Martin, Colin, and Geoffrey Parker, *The Spanish Armada*, London, 1988
National Maritime Museum, *Armada: the Official Catalogue*, London, 1988
Nicolas, Sir Harry, *The History of the Royal Navy*, London, 1847
Oppenheim, M., *A History of the Administration of the Royal Navy*, London, 1896
Owen, J. H., *War at Sea under Queen Anne 1702–1708*, Cambridge, 1938
Pack, S. W. C., *The Wager Mutiny*, London, 1964
Padfield, Peter, *Guns at Sea*, London, 1973
Penn, Geoffrey, *Up Funnel, Down Screw*, London, 1955
Pope, Dudley, *At 12 Mr Byng was Shot*, London, 1962
Powley, E. B., Th*e English Navy in the Revolution of 1688*, Cambridge, 1928
Rippon, P. M., *The Evolution of Engineering in the Royal Navy*, vol. 1, Tunbridge Wells, 1988
Rodger, N. A. M., *The Wooden World*, London, 1986
— *The Safeguard of the Seas*, London, 1997
— *The Command of the Ocean*, London, 2004
Tedder, A. W., *The Navy of the Restoration*, Cambridge, 1916
Warner, Oliver, *The Glorious First of June*, *London*, 1961
Wells, John G., *Whaley, the Story of HMS Excellent*, Portsmouth, 1980
Winton, John, *Hurrah for the Life of a Sailor*, London, 1977
Yonge, C. D., *The History of the British Navy*, London, 1863

Navy Records Society Volumes

Vol. 7, *Hollond's Discourses on the Navy*, ed. J. R. Tanner, 1896
Vol. 8, *Naval Accounts and Inventories in the Reign of Henry VII*, ed. M. Oppenheim, 1896
Vol. 11, *Papers Relating to the Spanish War, 1585–87*, ed. J. S. Corbett, 1897
Vol. 13, *The First Dutch War*, vol. 1, ed. S. R. Gardiner, 1898
Vol. 14, *The Blockade of Brest*, ed. John Leyland, vol. I, 1898
Vol. 22, *The Naval Tracts of Sir William Monson*, ed. Oppenheim, vol. 1, 1902
Vol. 23, *The Naval Tracts of Sir William Monson*, ed. M. Oppenheim, vol. 2, 1902
Vol. 26, *Catalogue of the Pepysian Manuscripts*, vol. 1, ed. J. R. Tanner, 1903
Vol. 27, *Catalogue of the Pepysian Manuscripts*, vol. 2, ed. J. R. Tanner, 1904
Vol. 29, *Fighting Instructions 1530–1816*, ed. Sir Julian Corbett, 1905
Vol. 30, *The First Dutch War*, ed. S. R. Gardiner and C. T. Atkinson, vol. 3, 1905
Vol. 37, *The First Dutch War*, vol. 4, ed. C. T. Atkinson, 1909
Vol. 37, *Catalogue of the Pepysian Manuscripts*, vol. 4, ed. J. R. Tanner, 1923
Vol. 38, *The Barham Papers*, ed. Sir J. K. Laughton, vol. 2, 1910
Vol. 43, *The Naval Tracts of Sir William Monson*, vol. 3, ed. M. Oppenheim, 1912
Vol. 44, *The Old Scots Navy*, ed. James Grant, 1914
Vol. 45, *Sir William Monson's Naval Tracts*, vol. 4, ed. M. Oppenheim, 1913
Vol. 65, *Boteler's Dialogues*, ed. W. G. Perrin, 1929
Vol. 76, *The Letters of Robert Blake*, ed. J. R. Powell, 1937,
Vol. 79, *The Journals of Sir Thomas Allin*, ed. R. C. Anderson, vol. 1, 1939
Vol. 89, *The Sergison Papers*, ed. R. D. Merriman, 1949
Vol. 90, *The Keith Papers*, ed. Christopher Lloyd, vol. 2, 1950

Vol. 97, *Dillon's Narrative*, ed. Michael Lewis, vol. II, 1956

Vol. 99, *The Vernon Papers*, ed. B. McL. Ranft, 1958

Vol. 105, *Documents Relating to the Civil War*, ed. J. R. Powell and E. K. Timings, 1963

Vol. 103, *Queen Anne's Navy*, ed. R. D. Merriman, 1961

Vol. 107, *The Health of Seamen*, ed. Christopher Lloyd, 1965

Vol. 109, *Documents Relating to Anson's Voyage Round the World*, ed. Glyndwr Williams, 1967

Vol. 119, *Manning Pamphlets 1693–1873*, ed. J. S. Bromley, 1974

Vol. 123, *The Navy of the Lancastrian Kings*, ed. Susan Rose, 1982

Vol. 125, *The Naval Miscellany*, vol. V, ed. J. B. Hattendorf

Vol. 131, *British Naval Documents, 1204–1960*, ed. John B. Hattendorf et al, 1993

Vol. 138, *Shipboard Life and Organisation, 1731–1815*, ed. B. Lavery, 1998

Vol. 147, *The Milne Papers*, vol. 1, ed. John Beeler, 2004

Vol. 148, *The Rodney Papers*, vol. 1, ed. David Syrett, 2005

Vol. 155, *Naval Courts Martial, 1793–1815*, ed. John D. Byrn, 2009

The Anthony Roll, ed. C. Knighton and D. M. Loades, 2000

Seamen's Biographies
(arranged by men's names)

Anon, *The Adventures of a Ship-Boy*, Edinburgh, 1823

Barlow, Edward, *Barlow's Journal*, ed. Basil Lubbock, London, 1934

Bechervaise, John, *Thirty-Six Years of a Seafaring Life, by an Old Quarter Master*, Portsea, 1839

— *A Farewell to my Old Shipmates and Messmates*, Portsea, 1847

Bishop, Matthew, *Life and Adventures*, London, 1744

Bulkeley, John, and John Cummins, *A Voyage to the South-Seas, by His Majesty's Ship Wager*, London, 1743; reprinted London, 1927

Coxere, Edward, *Adventures by Sea*, ed. E. H. W. Meyerstein, Oxford, 1945

Hay, M. D., ed, *Landsman Hay*, London, 1953

Samuel Kelly: An Eighteenth Century Seaman, ed. Crosbie Garstin, London, 1925

Mary Lacy, *The Female Shipwright*, 1773; reprinted Greenwich, 2008

Leech, Samuel, *A Voice from the Main Deck*, 1857; reprinted Chatham, 1999

Lurting, Thomas, 'The Fighting Sailor Turn'd Peaceble Christian', reproduced in Charles Vipont, *Blow the Man Down*, Oxford, nd

McPherson, Charles, *Life on Board a Man-of-War by a British Seaman*, Glasgow, 1829

Marra, John, *Journal of the Resolution's Voyage*, London, 1775

Matra, James Mario, A *Journal of a Voyage Round the World*, London, 1771; reprinted 1975

Morrison, James, *After the Bounty: A Sailor's Account of the Mutiny and Life in the South Seas*, Washington, DC, c.2010

Nicol, John, *Life and Adventures*, 1822; reprinted London, 1937

Richardson, William, *A Mariner of England*, ed. Spencer Childers, 1908; reprinted London, 1970

Robinson, William, *Jack Nastyface*, 1836; reissued Annapolis, 1973

Spavens, William, *Narrative*, Louth, 1796; reprinted Chatham, c.1998

The Adventures of John Wetherell, ed. C. S. Forester, London, 1954

Officers' Biographies, Journals and Collections of Letters

(arranged by officers' names)

Allyn, Richard, *Narrative of the Victory Obtained by the English and Dutch Fleet ...*, London, 1744

Kennedy, Gavin, *Captain Bligh*, London, 1989

Byron, J., *Narrative of the Loss of the Wager*, Aberdeen, 1822

Cochrane, Thomas, Earl of Dundonald, *Autobiography of a Seaman*, London, nd

Hough, Richard, *Captain James Cook*, London, 1994

Hakluyt Society, Extra Series, No. 34, *The Journals of Captain James Cook*, vol. 1, *The Voyage of the Endeavour*, ed. J. C. Beaglehole, Woodbridge, 1999

Hakluyt Society, Extra Series, No. 35, *The Journals of Captain James Cook*, vol 2, *The Voyage of the Resolution and Discovery*, ed. J. C. Beaglehole, Woodbridge, 1999

Hall, Basil, *Fragments of Voyages and Travels*, London, 1860

The Observations of Sir Richard Hawkins, 1622; reprinted Amsterdam and New York, 1968,

Hervey, Augustus, *Journal*, ed. David Erskine, London, 1953

Hill, Pascoe Grenfell, *A voyage to the Slave Coasts*, London, 1849

Hoffman, Frederick, *A Sailor of King George*, 1901, reprinted Chatham, 1999

Hood, Robert, *To the Arctic by Canoe,* Montreal, 1974

Jackson, G. V., *The Perilous Adventures and Vicissitudes of a Naval Officer*, London, 1927

Sea Saga, Being the Diaries of Four Generations of the King-Hall Family, ed. Louise King-Hall, London, 1936

Mark, W., *At Sea with Nelson*, London, 1929

Nicolas, Sir Nicholas Harris, *The Dispatches and Letters of Lord Nelson*, 1844–6; reprinted Chatham, 1997

Parry, Edward, *Memoirs of Rear-Admiral Sir W. E. Parry*, London, 1857

Parsons, G. S., *Nelsonian Reminiscences*, 1843; reprinted Maidstone, 1973

Penn, Granville, *Memorials of Sir William Penn*, London, 1833

Raleigh, Sir Walter, *Works*, vol. 8, ed. Oldys and Birch, London, 1829

Saumarez, Phillip, *Log of the Centurion*, ed. Leo Heaps, New York, 1973

Teonge, Henry, *Diary*, ed. E. D. Ross and E. Power, London, 1927

Walter, Chaplain Richard, *Anson's Voyage Round the World*, ed. Percy G. Adams, New York, 1974

Yonge, James, *Journal*, ed. F. N. L. Poynter, London, 1963

Other Collections of Documents

Baynham, Henry, *From the Lower Deck*, London, 1969. This and the volume below are both essential sources for lower deck history

— *Before the Mast*, London, 1972

Clark, William Bell, ed., *Naval Documents of the American Revolution*, vol. 1, Washington, 1964

Dudley, W. S. ed., *The Naval War of 1812, a Documentary History*, vol. 1, Washington, 1985

Harris, G. G., ed., London Record Society, *Trinity House Transactions, 1609–35*, London, 1983

Hodges, H. W., and E. A. Hughes, *Select Naval Documents*, Cambridge, 1922

Ingram, Bruce S., ed., *Three Sea Journals of Stuart Times*, London, 1936

Kirk and Cartwright, eds., Historical Manuscripts Commission, *Foljambe Manuscripts*, London, 1897

Laughton, Sir J. K., ed., Historical Manuscripts Commission, *Du Cane Manuscripts*, London, 1905

Long, W. H., *Naval Yarns*, reprinted London, 1973

Warwick, Peter, ed., *Voices from the Battle of Trafalgar*, Newton Abbott, 2005

Dictionaries

Burney, William, *New Universal Dictionary of the Marine*, 1815; reprinted New York, 1970

Falconer, William, *Dictionary of the Marine*, London, 1769; reprinted Newton Abbott, 1970

Grose, Francis, *Dictionary of the Vulgar Tongue*, 1811; reprinted Stroud, 2008

Smith, Captain John, *A Sea Grammar*, ed. Kermit Goell, London, 1970

Contemporary Pamphlets, etc.

Anon, *A Statement of Certain Immoral Practises*, London, 1822

An Account of the Bravery and Happy Death of James Covey, Chelsea, 1817

Braithwait, Richard, *Whimzies*, London, 1631

Caton, William, *The Sea-mens Invitation*, London, 1659

Crosfield, Robert, *England's Glory Reviv'd*, London, 1692

St Lo, George, *England's Safety or a Bridle to the French King*, London, 1693

Slush, Barnaby, *The Navy Royal; or a Sea-Cook turn'd Projector*, London, 1709

Trotter, Thomas, *A Practicable Plan for Manning the Royal Navy*, Newcastle, 1819

Ward, Edward, *The Wooden World dissected*, reprinted London, 1929

Technical and Specialist Subjects

Atkins, John, *The Navy-Surgeon, or a Practical System of Surgery*, London, 1734

Dinnen, J. *An Essay on Steam Boilers for Marine Engineers*, bound in Tredgold, Steam Engine, np, 1838

Fordyce, Alexander, *Outlines of Naval Routine*, London, 1837

Moyle, John, *Chirugus Marinus; or the Sea Chirugion*, London, 1693

Moyle, John, *Chyrurgic Memoirs; being an Account of Many Extraordinary Cures ...*, London, 1708

Murray, Robert, *Rudimentary Treatise on Marine Engines and Steam Vessels*, London, 1852,

Otway, Robert, *Treatise on Steam Navigation*, London, 1832

Ross, Sir John, *A Treatise on Navigation by Steam*, London, 1828

Other Works

Blackmore, H. L., *The Armouries of the Tower of London*, vol. I, *Ordnance*, London, 1976

Delafons, John, *A Treatise on Naval Courts Martial*, London, 1805

Edye, L. *The Historical Records of the Royal Marines*, London, 1893

Locke, John, *Two Treatises of Government*, Cambridge, 1689; reprinted 1963

Miller, Amy, *Dressed to Kill*, Greenwich, *c.*2007

Newell, Phillip, *Greenwich Hospital: A Royal Foundation*, Greenwich, 1984

Robinson, C. N., *The British Tar in Fact and Fiction*, London, 1911

Styles, John, *The Dress of the People*, Yale, 2007

INDEX